THE PENGUIN BOOK OF

INFIDELITIES

EDITED BY
Stephen Brook

VIKING

VIKING

Published by the Penguin Group
Penguin Books Ltd, 27 Wrights Lane, London W8 5TZ, England
Penguin Books USA Inc., 375 Hudson Street, New York, New York 10014, USA
Penguin Books Australia Ltd, Ringwood, Victoria, Australia
Penguin Books Canada Ltd, 10 Alcorn Avenue, Toronto, Ontario, Canada M4V 3B2
Penguin Book (NZ) Ltd, 182–190 Wairau Road, Auckland 10, New Zealand

Penguin Books Ltd, Registered Offices: Harmondsworth, Middlesex, England

First published 1994
1 3 5 7 9 10 8 6 4 2
First edition

Introduction and selection copyright © Stephen Brook, 1994

The acknowledgements on pp. 368–72 constitute an extension of this copyright page

Filmset by Datix International Limited, Bungay, Suffolk
Printed in England by Clays Ltd, St Ives plc
Set in 11.5/14.5 pt Monophoto Garamond

A CIP catalogue record for this book is available from the British Library
ISBN 0–670–84717–8

For Maria

Contents

Introduction   ix

PART ONE

Passion, Fashion and Morals   3
An Interlude of Gossip   35
Celebrated Infidelities I:
    The Caesars to Byron   46
Celebrated Infidelities II:
    Lord Melbourne to Cecil Parkinson   84

PART TWO

Cravings   123
Deception   142
Seduction   158
The Spouse's Shadow   188
Sex: Real and Imagined   198
Love   232
Learning the Truth   247
The Sense of Betrayal   288
After the Affair   319
'Indelible Constancy'   359

Acknowledgements   368
Index   373

Introduction

Infidelity is a negation. It reverses an ideal rather than a norm, for fidelity is more often an aspiration than a reality. Fidelity is static. By its very nature it is unalterable. Infidelity lobs a rock into that placid pool, whipping up waves and cross-currents in waters previously unruffled. It disturbs us not only because it nearly always brings pain to those involved, but because it is by definition an unpredictable element that shatters the uneasy truce of marital sexuality. Once the infidelity card has been played, it usually turns in on itself, until its dizzy rapture either self-destructs or comes to resemble the more tranquil arrangement that characterized the fidelity initially ruptured. In marital terms, divorce brings an honourable conclusion to the shattered relationship, and allows frayed emotions to settle into a fresh approximation of fidelity. Until, perhaps, the next time.

Thus infidelity is dangerous, for it confounds the stable order, and introduces notes of deception and betrayal into relationships intended to be harmonious. An infidelity unavoidably breaches trust, alarming those who witness it from the safer shores of their own supposedly stable relationships. There, we often sigh as our married friends split up and go their bitter separate ways, there, but for a tremendous amount of luck, go we.

Yet infidelity is also exhilarating – at least to the parties perpetrating it. When stability has turned into staleness, when security has become indistinguishable from emotional paralysis, when the pleasant routines of matrimonial life have become stultifying and confining, then infidelity breezes in, bringing freshness, new hope, vitality. It alters, it invigorates, it reshapes. Destroying one relationship, it at the same time creates a new one. Strong second marriages often build on the wreckage of badly structured first ones. Annette Lawson formulates the positive aspects of adultery in this way: 'Far from *always* being something chaotic, experienced as a loss of control over one's own life, adultery is often a way in which the world is actually *reordered* according to strongly held beliefs about the proper relationship between women and men. The marriage comes to be seen as where the chaos is; the alternative relationship one where sense and meaning are rediscovered or perhaps discovered for the first time.'[1]

For many people infidelity offers a means of escape. No one reading *Anna Karenina* would want to consign that heroine to a lifetime with the man to whom she is married. Her lover Vronsky is a liberating force. Yet the progress of their adulterous relationship illustrates as exquisitely as anything in modern literature how the constraints imposed by such a relationship can lead to its dissolution from within. For Anna Karenina that seed of dissolution is largely social; for Emma Bovary it is the growing weariness and subsequent indifference of sexual partners who cannot accommodate her great emotional need that spells doom. Infidelity can break an unsatisfactory mould but it cannot create happiness or stability for those whose emotional lives are blighted by circumstances, psychological or social, that remain untouchable by novelty or dislocation.

Infidelity fascinates us because our attitude to it is necessarily relative. The best friend of a deserted wife will be aghast, whereas the devotees of the blissful girl who has captured the strong eager heart of her lover will celebrate her good fortune. We tend to avoid judgement, both because our view is coloured by our own relationship to the parties committing the infidelity and because we never know when the smiling faithless intruder will break in on our own stable lives.

After all, it usually does. A study of American marriage published in 1987[2] estimated that half of all Americans have been

1. Annette Lawson, *Adultery*, Blackwell, 1989, p. 276.
2. P.E. Lampe, *Adultery in the United States*, Prometheus, 1987.

adulterous at some time or other. In the same year a journal called *Marriage and Divorce Today* put the percentage at seventy rather than fifty. It is impossible to know how much credence to give to such estimates, but they strike me as entirely plausible.

Americans and Europeans function within Judaeo–Christian moral networks that lay down clear guidelines about how marriages are to be conducted. Other societies operate according to entirely different rules. Helen Fisher has observed: 'Of 139 societies surveyed in the 1940s, 39% permitted men and women to have extramarital affairs either during certain holidays or festivals, with particular kinfolk, such as one's wife's sister or husband's brother, or under other special circumstances.'[3]

Anthropologists have happily identified entire cultures that make assumptions that would make any bishop flinch. The Kuikuru, an Indian tribe within the jungles of Brazil, assume that married couples will take lovers, up to twelve at a time. There is no prohibition against it, though a certain amount of discretion is considered appropriate. Within this context, such behaviour hardly constitutes infidelity. The Todas tribe of southern India have no objection to their wives circulating among the neighbours, and the Marquesans of the equatorial Pacific can't fathom the notion of sexual jealousy. Inuit males generously offer their wives on temporary loan to men with whom they feel a need to cement closer ties. Fisher interprets this practice thus: 'Inuit women see these extramarital couplings as precious offerings of everlasting kinship, not as social indiscretions.'[4]

Even within the more familiar codes of Jewish law as it evolved 2,500 years ago, male infidelity with an unmarried partner was permissible, and prostitutes and maids were among those who provided such services. Leviticus 20:10 makes it clear that adultery is only committed by a male if his partner is also married: 'The man that committeth adultery with another man's wife, even

3. Helen Fisher, *Anatomy of Love*, Simon & Schuster, 1992, p. 321.
4. ibid., p. 78.

he that committeth adultery with his neighbour's wife, the adulterer and the adulteress shall surely be put to death.' The ancient
Greeks also enjoyed prostitutes and courtesans, and in addition
they could avail themselves of homosexual diversions that the
Jews prohibited. Both the Chinese and the Turks were more than
familiar with the practice of keeping concubines, but the Chinese
male would be liable to execution if he slept with another man's
wife. Extramarital sex on the part of a Chinese or Indian wife was
also regarded as a capital offence. In the *Mahabharata* (Book XII),
the offence is aggravated by cross-caste liaisons: 'Whenever a
woman commits adultery with a man of a caste inferior to her
husband's she shall be torn to pieces by dogs, and in some public
place.'

The Roman system was more complicated. 'Under the Justinian
6th-century code,' explains Annette Lawson, 'the adulterous wife
was subject to exile or death; and her lover could be decapitated if
he was a free man or burned if a slave; yet a slave could obtain a
pardon if he denounced his mistress. Before this period . . . neither
the infidelity of a fiancée nor that of a female slave was punished
but a concubine could, if she had the status of matron, be accused
of adultery. If she changed her status to that of prostitute, she
could avoid the accusation. It was thus both gender and social
status that marked the boundary to the offence: the nearer a
woman was to being a full wife, the nearer she came to being
able to commit the crime of adultery: a prostitute might be "possessed" by a man and paid for by a man, but she could not
commit adultery.'[5] Ovid's *Amores*, on the other hand, laid down
the rules by which illicit liaisons were to be conducted.

In medieval Europe adultery was a common theme among
troubadours and others who entertained courtly circles with ribald
tales, but legal penalties for adultery were draconian. When in the
early fourteenth century Marguerite of Burgundy was accused of
the offence, she was imprisoned and her lover castrated and then

5. Annette Lawson, *Adultery*, p. 42.

flayed alive.[6] In noble circles, where marriage had nothing to do with love, such punishments probably had as much to do with power struggles as with morality and the dictates of the Church; and among the lower orders in medieval Europe penalties were applied more judiciously, with specific circumstances taken into account. There is little to suggest that the European peasantry and middle classes were any more strict in their sexual mores than their bawdy Elizabethan descendants, while the nobility's adherence to the principles of courtly love encouraged the expression of romantic and sexual impulses that had no place within medieval marriage. As C.S. Lewis pointed out, 'Any idealization of sexual love, in a society where marriage is purely utilitarian, must begin by being an idealization of adultery.'[7]

The situation had hardly improved for married women by the time the Renaissance flourished in Italy. Wives were restricted to their domestic roles, while public life was the preserve of their husbands, who considered themselves at liberty to frequent the courtesans, who if successful enjoyed great wealth and status, a role emulated by their Parisian counterparts in the nineteenth century. Nikkie Roberts writes that 'the talents of these ladies were by no means limited to the art of love-making; many were artists in their own right: Tullia d'Aragona (a cardinal's daughter) was a renowned poet who won the patronage of one of the most powerful political figures of the period, the great Cosimo de' Medici. Veronica Franco was another prominent intellectual and courtesan, fluent in several languages and a talented musician. She was a close friend of the painter Tintoretto, and numbered King Henri III of France among her more illustrious clients.'[8]

It is hard to know whether to brand men who patronized Florentine courtesans – or, centuries later, sophisticated French mistresses – as adulterers. From a legalistic viewpoint there is no

6. Nina Epton, *Love and the French*, Cassell, 1959, p. 25.
7. C.S. Lewis, *The Allegory of Love*, OUP, 1936, p. 13.
8. Nikkie Roberts, *Whores in History*, HarperCollins, 1992, pp. 101–2.

doubt about it, but in a society in which such behaviour was universally tolerated, at least among the males who perpetrated it, it is pressing the point to include such regular dissipations as examples of infidelity. For the purposes of this book, I have not taken a dogmatic approach. The nonchalance of the male no doubt had its wretched counterpart in the misery and anxiety of many a wife well aware that her husband's nocturnal hours were spent in the arms of women who were giving him sexual delights she could not or would not provide and who possibly, for good measure, were giving him a dose of the clap.

In England the Puritan reaction sought to overturn the licentiousness of the preceding decades, when, as Lawrence Stone has pointed out, 'husbands felt free to take lower-class mistresses and to beget bastards without any sense of shame and any attempt at concealment'.[9] Under Commonwealth legislation adultery was punishable by the death penalty, with a few technical exemptions. It was not only the irreligious who posed a threat to public morals; there were radical preachers who argued, and lived, a libertarian philosophy. Thomas Webbe, rector of Langley Burnhill, was put on trial for adultery and was reported as having proclaimed that 'there's no heaven but women, nor no hell save marriage'. 'Another witness asserted that Webbe claimed to "live above ordinances, and that it was lawful for him to lie with any woman". He enjoyed music and mixed dancing, wore long shaggy hair, and thought Moses was a conjuror.'[10] Webbe was acquitted.

During the same period in New England, an eighteen-year-old woman married to an elderly husband was sentenced to be hanged after her conviction for adultery with twelve men.[11] The New England colonists maintained their sexual monitoring for decades, as Hawthorne's *The Scarlet Letter* so memorably records. One of its

9. Lawrence Stone, *Family, Sex and Marriage*, Weidenfeld & Nicolson, 1977, pp. 502–3.
10. Christopher Hill, *The World Turned Upside Down*, Viking, 1972, p. 182.
11. John D'Emilio and Estelle B. Freedman, *Intimate Matters: A History of Sexuality in America*, Harper & Row, 1988, pp. 11–12.

least savoury aspects was that it turned entire communities into nests of espionage: 'In Maryland, for example, several people witnessed John Nevill having sexual relations with Susan Attcheson, a married woman; they testified that they had seen her hand in his breeches and his "in Susan's placket" (a slit in her skirt). The court fined Nevill and ordered Attcheson whipped. When Susanna Kennett and John Tully of Virginia heard snoring in the next room, they stood on a hogshead of tobacco and peered over the wall to see that "Richard Jones laye snoring in her placket and Mary West put her hand in his Codpis". Kennett then pried loose a board to observe Mary West "with her Coates upp above her middle and Richard Jones with his Breeches down Lying upon her".'[12]

Meanwhile, the British had gratefully submitted to the cynical embrace of the Restoration and its double-dealers. Across the Channel in France, the court, to an even greater extent than its British counterpart, empowered the royal mistresses, ensuring a high status for the costly courtesan that persisted well into the present century. While the French continued in the eighteenth century to tolerate, even encourage, duplicity, as the memoirs of Madame d'Epinay and the novel *Dangerous Acquaintances* by Choderlos de Laclos make clear, the British turned to a sterner moralizing such as we encounter in the pronouncements of Samuel Johnson. Of course the British hesitate to practise what they preach, and so the path opened up to the sublime hypocrisies of the Victorian era, when prostitution was rampant but social disaster awaited anyone detected in an illicit liaison. In the United States, especially in the South, Puritan restraints were forgotten as gentlemen found new uses for their female slaves.

In all these cultures and social contexts, the double standard was applied with a vengeance, although in the western literary tradition cuckolding a husband is not regarded as more heinous than a husband taking a mistress. For Europeans and Americans, the insistence on wifely fidelity even by men who routinely stopped in

12. ibid., p. 29.

at the brothel on their way home from the club seems bloody-minded male pride. For other societies the justification for the double standard was more reasoned. As Helen Fisher writes: 'A woman's sexual rights in traditional India, China, and Japan were an entirely different matter. A woman's worth was measured in two ways: her ability to increase her husband's property and prestige with the dowry she brought into the marriage and her womb's capacity to nurture her husband's seed. Because a woman's responsibility in life was to produce descendants for her mate, she had to be chaste at marriage and sexually faithful to her husband all her life – paternity had to be secure so as not to jeopardize her husband's family line. As a result, a respectable girl was often married off by age fourteen, before she succumbed to clandestine suitors. Then she was tethered to her husband's home under lifelong surveillance by his kin.'[13]

It is clear that with some colourful exceptions, most cultures take a dim view of adultery, though punishments are not handed out equally to the players. Most societies are more severe in punishing female lapses than male ones. Church law makes a clear distinction between adultery – sexual intercourse between a spouse and a third party – and fornication, in which an unmarried person has sexual intercourse with someone who is married. For the purposes of this anthology, this distinction is blurred, since I am more interested in the fact that the relationship is illicit than in the precise marital status of each participant. Many spouses, sociologists' studies suggest,[14] do not take too censorious a view of a rare one-night stand so long as it poses no threat to the stability of the marriage. This book attempts no judgements, but chronicles, in documentary and imaginative form, the vagaries of the sexual impulse and its capacity to cause pain as well as confer pleasure.

Of course there is more to infidelity than sex. Promises broken and secrets revealed are also forms of infidelity. This book, for

13. Helen Fisher, *Anatomy of Love*, pp. 79–80.
14. Annette Lawson, *Adultery*, pp. 35–6.

eminently practical reasons, does not concern itself with such examples. Judas does not appear within these covers. As infidelities go, treason is no doubt far more serious than many of the sexual and emotional adventures reproduced in the pages that follow. But for the purposes of this anthology, infidelity is the breaching of an existing emotional relationship between individuals, which need not be marital. Infidelity often encompasses a seduction, as a result of which the new relationship is formed, but seduction alone is not embraced by this book.

Don Juan is a libertine, but his relationships with women are too short-lived and frenetic for fidelity to be established, let alone broken. Donna Elvira may believe that she and the Don are a duo of sorts, but he takes a very different view. (Byron's account of Juan's initiation into the delights of illicit sex is, however, too delicious to omit.) Casanova is a rake, but his memoirs are oddly colourless for all their surface vivacity. His numerous sexual encounters with a succession of countesses, nuns, and servant girls are studded with 'the ardour of our mutual kisses', 'burning desires', 'delicious enjoyment' and 'amorous transports'. Lucky old Casanova, but it makes for dreary reading.

Infidelity, as portrayed in fiction from the nineteenth century onwards, is seen as destructive of relationships between individuals, and there is still a tendency to view such breaches of faith as more than a personal matter. When the former Chief Rabbi Immanuel Jakobowitz told me that he believed adultery should be a criminal offence,[15] he was reflecting his conviction that actions that threatened society as a whole should be subject to legal sanctions. For him, as a religious leader, adultery was damaging not only to individuals but to the social fabric. That is not a belief that would find much support even in religious circles, but the underlying view of the social gravity of adultery was certainly shared in times past. In at least two epic works, Homer's *Iliad* and Malory's *Morte D'Arthur*, the adultery of some leading characters is directly

15. Stephen Brook, *The Club: The Jews of Modern Britain*, Pan, 1990, p. 203.

responsible for the disaster that befalls the social structures which the poems portray.

It has long been taken for granted by the rich and noble that they should marry for money or dynastic security, and find sexual pleasure elsewhere. It is hard to know whether to categorize such extramarital relationships as instances of infidelity. King Charles II had a queen, of course, but he preferred other bedmates such as Nell Gwynn. The king was being technically unfaithful, but few would have expected him to behave otherwise. As for Nell, she was not ashamed to admit that she was a whore, and if she remained faithful to Charles for a decade or more, it was because the position of royal mistress was the highest status which an ambitious whore could attain.

I have taken a pragmatic view. Charles and Nell play a minor part in the pages that follow, but the more richly documented goings-on at the French court are included, partly because the material available is more entertaining than the scabrous verse squibs with which English observers used to chronicle licentiousness at court.

Although royal mistresses seem to be an institution that is not yet defunct, the role of compulsive womanizing has been taken over by public figures, notably politicians, who have not failed to divert the public by lapsing from the marital straight-and-narrow in spectacular fashion. John F. Kennedy established precedents that even his most ardent followers have found hard to equal, let alone surpass. In the heydays of the goatish Lloyd George and of John F. Kennedy, knowledge of their philandering was confined to the political equivalent of court circles. Those journalists who knew about it did not write about it. Such protection is no longer available, and contemporary newspapers vie with each other to break the latest scandal. As readers invited to witness the mess politicians make of their private lives, we find it hard to avoid *Schadenfreude*. The sight of David Mellor, still a Cabinet minister, airily organizing a happy family photograph at the garden gate just days after his adventures with the willowy Miss Antonia de Sancha had been exposed in the press was one of the more hilariously sickening photo opportunities of the early 1990s. One Monday in October 1993 a British minister, Steven Norris, was disclosed as being in possession of a mistress. By Friday it was known that he had no fewer than five (one of whom used to break bread, though not bed, with this author). If we relish the frailties of our politicians, it is because they pose as pillars of family life while dashing off – like the rest of us, of course – to the arms of the moll of the moment.

The leader of the Israeli Likud Party, Binyamin Netanyahu, brashly told his electorate that he had been unfaithful to his wife; he came clean rather than give in to threats of blackmail. He got away with it, since Israelis, like the French, are less sanctimonious than, say, the upright church-going millions of the United States. The British public found Mellor's hypocrisy hard to stomach, but rewarded the leader of the Liberal Democrats, Mr Paddy Ashdown, with a slight boost in the opinion polls when an extinct affair with his secretary became public knowledge. Senator Edward Kennedy has long been in danger of being remembered more for his philandering than for his vigorous promotion of liberal legislation.

The unmasking of their adulteries makes for interesting reading at the time, but after the passage of months or years one politician's romp with an actress becomes hard to distinguish from any other politician's romp with another actress. So although the sexual lapses of public figures will feature in this book, they have been relegated to a secondary role. This is above all a literary anthology, and public figures, if they have any sense, don't put their indiscretions down on paper. (Indeed, when in 1994 it became known that a British M.P. had penned amorous verses to his research assistant, this quaint lapse cost him his junior ministerial position.) Just as pornography wearies through repetition of a limited permutation of sexual acts, so an anthology of this kind would soon become tedious if it were primarily a chronicle of celebrated adulteries.

Prominence has been given to infidelities that have been well expressed, either in letters or diaries or memoirs. This excludes, sadly, the irresistible adulteries of born-again preachers. The television screen, not the printed page, is the eloquent archive in which one can recall the exquisite pleasure of seeing the likes of Jim Bakker and Jimmy Swaggart begging their duped congregants for forgiveness. Not surprisingly, some of the most persuasive infidelities are entirely fictional. Reiteration of the simple facts of infidelity are elevated by style and imagination. The French have been more creative in this respect than most: not only Flaubert in *Madame Bovary* but Choderlos de Laclos and Stendhal before him. The development of the novel made possible the richest psychological explorations of these themes, which had previously been portrayed most vividly in Jacobean and Restoration drama.

It was not of course the Renaissance that invented the literary depiction of infidelity. It was one of the paramount themes of medieval storytellers. Entire collections, such as Boccaccio's *Decameron* and the anonymous French *fabliaux*, as well as parallel compilations from the Middle East such as the *Arabian Nights*, were composed of chronicles of cuckoldry. They presuppose that infidelity is a universal condition, that any woman given half the chance will exercise considerable ingenuity to get between the sheets with any man younger and more virile than her husband, and that there is no finer entertainment than being regaled with tale after tale on this theme.

This medieval tradition is under-represented in the collection that follows, chiefly for practical reasons. Existing translations of these texts tend to be archaic, and the same is true of later gatherings of tales such as Marguerite of Navarre's *Heptameron* of the sixteenth century. A blend of coyness and floweriness soon becomes unreadable. Some of Chaucer's *Canterbury Tales* are spirited reworkings of Boccaccio that would have been quoted at even greater length had space permitted.

No anthology can afford to ignore the quality of the writing included, and this is my justification for omissions that connoisseurs of infidelity will surely notice. Both Henry Miller and Anaïs Nin, for example, are absent, for the simple reason that I cannot bear their prose styles and am therefore exercising editorial prerogative by protecting the reader from their work. Other more admirable writing resists the anthologist. Drama is a conspicuous example. Harold Pinter's *Betrayal* ought to appear in this book in its entirety, but since that is not feasible, it is wiser to omit it altogether rather than butcher the text. Similar reasons have led to the exclusion of extracts from Jacobean plays by Middleton and others and of modern plays such as Tom Stoppard's *The Real Thing* and Peter Nichols's *Passion Play*.

Other texts have been offered piecemeal. It does little service, I admit, to the narrative skill of Andre Dubus to wrench paragraphs from some of his short stories, but it would have been perverse to omit a writer who, like the very different John Updike, examines the anguish of infidelity with such open-heartedness.

I have deliberately sought examples from the realm of fiction as well as from biography. It is one thing to experience, either actively or passively, infidelity; it is quite another to express that experience in words. Grief and shock on the one hand, and lust and triumphalism on the other, are not necessarily articulate states of being. Reading a letter is a private experience; but a Vermeer painting of a young woman reading a letter makes that experience public, suggesting a multiplicity of resonances. Similarly, good fiction or drama can convey with great complexity the maze of conflicting feelings that accompanies any infidelity. The classic texts include Shakespeare's *Troilus and Cressida*, Tolstoy's *Anna Karenina*, Flaubert's *Madame Bovary* and the novels of Colette, so I believe it is appropriate that they appear in substantial excerpts in this book.

It has been difficult to order material. Sometimes, especially in the sections that deal primarily with actual infidelities, I have opted for a chronological approach, which seems marginally preferable to a random organization. In sections dealing with the emotional ramifications of the experience – and this makes up the bulk of the book – I have attempted a more thematic structure. Inevitably there are links that are perhaps less strong than I would hope and some transitions where you can hear the gears crunch. None the less this structuring by mood seemed the least perverse of the possibilities available.

What follows is entertainment, I hope, rather than a treatise. I wish to preach no sermons, draw no conclusions. The theme is endlessly fascinating because we are all implicated. Even those whose conscience is as unblemished as a Carmelite's wimple never know when the thunderbolt might fall. The prim and self-righteous, one suspects, are in particular danger because they are least equipped to cope with the trauma that will follow, and will thus inflict maximum pain on all the parties involved. So I urge the reader to suspend judgement, keep fingers crossed and take a sympathetic enjoyment in the frailties of mankind.

Most of the friends whose brains I attempted to pick as I sought help in finding unfamiliar material failed to offer more than Emma Bovary, which made my research more arduous than I expected. Nevertheless I do want to thank for their fruitful suggestions: Hugh Black-Hawkins, Steven Haskell, Giles MacDonogh, Christopher Middleton, Zachary Leader, and the staff of the London Library, who did their best to explain the Byzantine system of cataloguing with which they confuse and divert borrowers such as myself.

Stephen Brook
London, 1994

PART ONE

Passion, Fashion and Morals

Do not adultery commit;
Advantage rarely comes of it.

A.C. Clough, 'The Latest Decalogue'

North European travellers were often surprised by the casual way in which institutionalized adultery was condoned in other parts of Europe. Infidelity, instead of being an aberration, was a way of life. The adventurous Lady Mary Wortley Montagu wrote to Lady Rich on 20 September 1716 about Viennese mores:

That perplexing word Reputation has quite another meaning here than what you give it at London, and getting a Lover is so far from loseing, that 'tis properly geting reputation, Ladys being much more respected in regard to the rank of their Lovers than that of their Husbands. But what you'l think very odd, the 2 sects that divide our whole nation of Petticoats are utterly unknown. Here are neither Coquets nor Prudes. No woman dares appear coquet enough to encourrage 2 lovers at a time, and I have not seen any such Prudes as to pretend fidelity to their Husbands, who are certainly the best-natur'd set of people in the World, and they look upon their Wives' Galants as favourably as Men do upon their Deputys that take the troublesome part of their busynesse off of their hands, tho they have not the less to do, for they are gennerally deputys in another place themselves. In one word, 'tis the establish'd custom for every Lady to have 2 Husbands, one that bears the Name, and another that performs the Dutys; and these engagements are so well known, that it would be a down right affront and publickly resented if you invited a Woman of Quality to dinner without at the same time inviteing her 2 attendants of Lover and Husband, between whom she allways sits in state with great Gravity. These sub-marriages gennerally last 20 years together, and the Lady often commands the poor Lover's estate even to the utter ruin of his family, tho they are as seldom begun by any passion as other matches. But a Man makes but an ill figure that is not in some commerce of this Nature, and a Woman looks out for a Lover as soon as she's marry'd as part of her Equipage, without which she could not be gentile; and the first article of the Treaty is establishing the pension, which remains to the Lady tho the Galant should prove inconstant, and this chargable point of honnour I look upon as the real foundation of so many wonderfull instances of Constancy.

And to her sister Lady Mar she reported on the mores of Turkish ladies:

As to their Morality or good Conduct, I can say like Arlequin, 'tis just as 'tis with you, and the Turkish Ladys don't commit one Sin the less for not being Christians. Now I am a little acquainted with their ways, I cannot forbear admiring either the exemplary discretion or extreme Stupidity of all the writers that have given accounts of 'em. 'Tis very easy to see they have more Liberty than we have, no Woman of what rank so ever being permitted to go in the streets without 2 muslins, one that covers her face all but her Eyes and another that hides the whole dress of her head and hangs halfe way down her back; and their Shapes are wholly conceal'd by a thing they call a Ferigée, which no woman of any sort appears without. This has strait sleeves that reaches to their fingers ends and it laps all round 'em, not unlike a rideing hood. In Winter 'tis of Cloth, and in Summer, plain stuff or silk. You may guess how effectually this disguises them, that there is no distinguishing the great Lady from her Slave, and 'tis impossible for the most jealous

Husband to know his Wife when he meets her, and no Man dare either touch or follow a Woman in the Street.

This perpetual Masquerade gives them entire Liberty of following their Inclinations without danger of Discovery. The most usual method of Intrigue is to send an Appointment to the Lover to meet the Lady at a Jew's shop, which are as notoriously convenient as our Indian Houses, and yet even those that don't make that use of 'em do not scruple to go to buy Pennorths and tumble over rich Goods, which are cheiffly to be found amongst that sort of people. The Great Ladys seldom let their Gallants know who they are, and 'tis so difficult to find it out that they can very seldom guess at her name they have corresponded with above halfe a year together. You may easily imagine the number of faithfull Wives very small in a country where they have nothing to fear from their Lovers' Indiscretion, since we see so many that have the courrage to expose them selves to that in this World and all the threaten'd Punishment of the next, which is never preach'd to the Turkish Damsels. Neither have they much to apprehend from the resentment of their Husbands, those Ladys that are rich having all their money in their own hands, which they take with 'em upon a divorce with an addition which he is oblig'd to give 'em. Upon the Whole, I look upon the Turkish Women as the only free people in the Empire.

Mary Wortley Montagu, *Complete Letters*, Clarendon Press, 1965, Vol. 1, pp. 327–9.

Montesquieu adopted the literary device of inventing fictitious Persian travellers whose letters reported back on the strange ways of the Europeans, notably the Parisians:

Here, husbands accept their lot with a good grace, and the infidelities of their wives seem to them as inevitable as fate. A husband, who would wish to monopolise his wife, would be looked upon as a disturber of the pleasure of the public, as a lunatic who wanted to enjoy the light of the sun to the exclusion of everybody else.

Here, a husband who loves his wife is a man who has not enough merit to engage the affections of some other woman; who makes a bad use of the power given him by the law to supply those pleasures which he can obtain in no other way; who claims all his rights to the prejudice of the whole community; who appropriates to his own use that which he only holds in pawn; and who tries, as far as he can, to overturn the tacit agreement, in which the happiness of both sexes consists. The fame, so little desired in Asia, of being married to a beautiful woman, is here the source of no uneasiness. No one has ever to seek far for entertainment. A prince consoles himself for the loss of one place by taking another: when Bagdad fell to the Turks, were we not taking from the Mogul the fortress of Candahar?

Generally speaking, a man who winks at his wife's infidelities, does not lose respect; on the contrary, he is praised for his prudence: dishonour only attaches to special cases.

Not that there are no virtuous women; there are, and they may be said to be distinguished too. My conductor always took care to point them out; but they were all so ugly that one would require to be a saint not to hate virtue.

After what I have told you of the morals and manners of this country, you will easily imagine that the French do not altogether plume themselves upon their constancy. They believe that it is as ridiculous to swear eternal love to a woman, as to insist that one will always be in the best of health, or always as happy as the day is long. When they promise a woman to love her all their lives, they suppose that she on her side undertakes to be always lovable; and if she breaks her word, they think that they are no longer bound by theirs.

Charles Louis de Montesquieu, *Persian Letters*, Routledge, 1923, Letter LV (translated by John Davidson).

The memoirist Grammont took a dim view of the draconian measures adopted by some cultures to preserve their women from straying:

Every man who believes that his honour depends upon that of his wife is a fool who torments himself, and drives her to despair; but he who, being naturally jealous, has the additional misfortune of loving his wife, and who expects that she should only live for him, is a perfect madman, whom the torments of hell have actually taken hold of in this world, and whom nobody pities. All reasoning and observation on these unfortunate circumstances attending wedlock concur in this, that precaution is vain and useless before the evil, and revenge odious afterwards.

The Spaniards, who tyrannize over their wives, more by custom than from jealousy, content themselves with preserving the niceness of their honour by duennas, grates, and locks. The Italians, who are wary in their suspicions, and vindictive in their resentments, pursue a different line of conduct: some satisfy themselves with keeping their wives under locks which they think secure; others by ingenious precautions exceed whatever the Spaniards can invent for confining the fair sex; but the generality are of opinion, that in either unavoidable danger or in manifest transgression, the surest way is to assassinate.

But, ye courteous and indulgent nations, who, far from admitting these savage and barbarous customs, give full liberty to your dear ribs, and commit the care of their virtue to their own discretion, you pass without alarms or strife your peaceful days, in all the enjoyments of domestic indolence!

Anthony Hamilton, *Memoirs of the Count de Grammont*, John Lane, 1928, pp. 130–31.

But Lord Byron, some decades later, clearly had more success than Grammont with Spanish women. He wrote to his mother from Gibraltar on 11 August 1809:

. . . I beg leave to observe that Intrigue here is the business of life, when a woman marries she throws off all restraint, but I believe their conduct is chaste enough before. – If you make a proposal which in England would bring a box on the ear from the meekest of virgins, to a Spanish girl, she thanks you for the honour you intend her, and replies 'wait till I am married, & I shall be too happy.' – This is literally & strictly true.

Lord Byron, *Letters & Journals*, Murray, 1973, Vol. 1, p. 220.

Stendhal, travelling around Italy, gave a graphic account of the marital system prevailing in aristocratic circles:

28th October, 1816 . . . In Italy, it is the height of absurdity for a pretty woman to have no object for the affections of her heart. There is nothing ephemeral about these *liaisons*; they may last eight or ten years, perhaps as long as life itself. All this was told to me, with as little circumlocution as I am using in the writing of it, by signora M***. If, after a year of marriage, when a woman may be assumed to be no longer in love with her husband, she shows no sign of interest elsewhere, the young men merely shrug their shoulders, saying: '*E una sciocca*' ('She is a goose'); and henceforward, at dances, the *beaux* are wont to relegate her to the shameful status of wallflower. In the course of this evening, I observed (or thought I observed) every shade and *nuance* of attachment. For instance, the handsome features of young Count Botta, as his gaze strayed towards signora R***, were a perfect study in the dawning phases of love, before the crisis of declaration.

[19th November, 1816] . . . In Milan, if a woman be both pretty and pious, public opinion will respect in her the victim of an overmastering passion: *the Fear of Hell*. Signora Annoni, one of the loveliest women in all the city, is in this case. By contrast, a silly creature who has no lover of her own, or none but others' cast-offs (*spiantati*), is greeted on every hand with undisguised contempt. For the rest, any woman may pick her lover where she will; no invitation will exclude her recognised admirer. On more than one occasion, at a Friday *soirée*, I have observed a woman arrive as a guest with a lover upon her arm as yet unknown to the mistress of the house; nevertheless, the normal practice is for the women to drop word privately in a note, giving the name of her *cavaliere servente*, who later leaves his card in a formal visit, and thereafter will be invited by name.

As soon as a woman gives reason to suspect that her choice of lover is in the minutest degree influenced by financial considerations, there is no limit to the contempt to which she will be exposed. If there are grounds for believing that she entertains several lovers at once, she will cease to be invited. Even so, such severities are new, and date only from the days of Napoleon, who, in his passion for law and order, and in the interests of his own despotic authority, restored to Italy a glimpse of moral conscience.

And in Rome . . .

[1st October, 1817] . . . When a man finds favour in a woman's eyes, she will seldom seek to conceal her pleasure. *Dite a *** che mi piace* is a phrase which, in Rome, a woman may readily employ, with neither shame nor scruple. If the man who is fortunate enough to inspire such tender feelings should chance to reciprocate them, he may enquire:

'*Mi volete bene?*'

'*Si.*'

'*Quando ci vedremo?*'

Such are the simple beginnings of a *liaison* which will normally endure for a considerable span of time, no less, perhaps, than eight or ten years. An attachment which is broken after a year or two brings little honour to the lady concerned; she will find herself spoken of as a 'sorry creature', one that is unsure, incapable of knowing her own mind. The perfect reciprocity of obligation which exists between the lover and his mistress plays no little part in strengthening the bonds of constancy. Another curious phenomenon, in this land of super-subtle political machinations, is that, in love, the art of dissimulation is steadfastly rejected. Only recently I had occasion to observe, at the sumptuous ball given by the banker Torlonia, Duke of Bracciano, that a woman will dance only with such partners as her lover may deem acceptable. Should you find in your heart sufficient impudence to enquire of some pretty woman the reason *why* she has refused your request, she will reply in all simplicity:

'*Il mio amico non lo vuole. Domandate al mio amico.*'

And each year you may expect to find one or two worthy Teutons blessed with sufficient *naïveté* to seek out the *amico* in question, and to sue for gracious permission to dance with his mistress.

Stendhal, *Rome, Naples and Florence*, Calder, 1959, pp. 44, 85, 468–9.

Lord Byron ponders the Venetian attitude to infidelity, from a predictably subjective viewpoint, in a letter to John Murray of 18 May 1819:

The fair one is eighteen – her name Angelina – the family name of course I don't tell you. She proposed to me to divorce my mathematical wife – and I told her that in England we can't divorce except for *female* infidelity – 'and pray, (said she), how do you know what she may have been doing these last three years?' – I answered *that* I could not tell – but that the status of Cuckoldom was not quite so flourishing in Great Britain as with us here. – But – She said – 'can't you get rid of her?' – 'not more than is done already' (I answered) 'you would not have me *poison her*?' – would you believe it? She made me *no answer* – is not that a true and odd national trait? – it spoke more than a thousand words – and yet this is a little – pretty – sweet-tempered, – quiet, feminine being as ever you saw – but the Passions of a Sunny Soil are paramount to all other considerations; – an unmarried Girl naturally wishes to be married – if she can marry & love at the same time it is well – but at any rate She must love.

In another letter to John Murray (21 February 1820) he set out the rules of the game:

Their system has it's rules – and it's fitnesses – and decorums – so as to be reduced to a kind of discipline – or game at hearts – which admits few deviations unless you wish to lose it. – They are extremely tenacious – and jealous as furies – not permitting their Lovers even to marry if they can help it – and keeping them always close to them in public as in private whenever they can. – In short they transfer marriage to adultery – and strike the *not* out of that commandment. – The reason is that they marry for their parents and love for themselves. – They exact fidelity from a lover as a debt of honour – while they pay the husband as a tradesman – that is not at all. – You hear a person's character – male or female – canvassed – not as depending on their conduct to their husbands or wives – but to their mistress or lover. – And – and – that's all. – If I wrote a quarto – I don't know that I could do more than amplify what I have here noted.

It is to be observed that while they do all this – the greatest outward respect is to be paid to the husbands – and not only by the ladies but by their Serventi – particularly if the husband serves no one himself – (which is not often the case however) so that you would often suppose them relations – the Servente making the figure of one adopted into the family. – Sometimes the ladies run a little restive – and elope – or divide – or make a scene – but this is at starting generally – when they know no better – or when they fall in love with a foreigner – or some such anomaly – and is always reckoned unnecessary and extravagant.

Lord Byron, *Letters & Journals*, Murray, 1976, Vol. 6, pp. 133–4; 1977, Vol. 7, pp. 43–4.

For those more plagued by conscience than the likes of Stendhal or Byron, the only way to deal with the conflicts provoked by their own priapism was to rationalize like mad. Boswell proves a master at it. For a start his wife was a relative, and thus . . .

[29 March 1772] Having received a kind invitation to breakfast with the Honourable Mrs. Stuart, an old and intimate friend of my wife's, I accepted it with pleasure. She lived in Queen's Street, Mayfair . . . She candidly declared that from what she had seen of life in this great town she would not be uneasy at an occasional infidelity in her husband, as she did not think it at all connected with affection. That if he kept a particular woman, it would be a sure sign that he had no affection for his wife; or if his infidelities were very frequent, it would also be a sign. But that a transient fancy for a girl, or being led by one's companions after drinking to an improper place, was not to be considered as inconsistent with true affection. I wish this doctrine may not have been only consolatory and adapted to facts. I told her I was very happy; that I had never known I was married, having taken for my wife my cousin and intimate friend and companion; so that I had nothing at all like restraint.

Alternatively:

[8 June 1784] In Westminster Abbey I said I was perpetually falling in love, though I was as fond of my wife as any man. She could not complain. I was always willing to prefer her when she was fond of me; and when she was indifferent, it was better I should be fond of others than allow my fondness to grow cold and perhaps irrecoverable.

James Boswell, *Boswell for the Defence*, Heinemann, 1960, pp. 78–9; *The Applause of the Jury*, Heinemann, 1982, p. 229.

Boswell's smugness has the virtue of simplicity. Fictional rationalizers can justify their frailty with greater elaboration, as in the case of Brian, an academic married to Erica, who contemplates an affair with his infatuated student Wendy . . .

Wendy was suffering (he told himself), and had been suffering for perhaps a year, from unconsummated love. It was the worse for her because, in her world, such feeling was so rare as to be almost unknown. Among her friends even the most transitory physical attraction was consummated as a matter of course, and at once. But romantic passion, as De Rougemont has pointed out, is a plant which thrives best in stony soil. Like the geraniums in Erica's kitchen, the less it was watered, the better it flowered. That was why Wendy loved him; while for the boys she casually slept with she felt little.

Therefore, Brian argued with himself as the soapy waves of false logic sloshed toward the shore, what he really ought to do was to sleep with Wendy himself, as soon as possible. She would see then that he was only a man like other men; her disease would be cured. He owed it to her to provide this cure, even at the cost of deflating his value in her eyes and ruining his moral record. He didn't *want* to commit adultery, he told himself, but it was his duty. It was a choice between his vanity, his selfish wish for moral consistency, and Wendy's release from a painful obsession.

Looking back now, Brian finds it hard to understand how he had entertained such self-righteous nonsense; how he, a serious political scientist, had been able to fool himself with the old means–end argument. For he had applied this argument to himself as well as to Wendy; he had hoped to cure his obsession as well as her passion by sating it. He had been intermittently aware, he recalls now, that outsiders might not appreciate the extent of his altruism in screwing Wendy Gahaghan, if they heard of it – but he had counted that almost one more thorn in his martyr's crown.

He did not realize then that he was already becoming addicted to Wendy, and that he was planning to increase the dose partly because he needed to quiet the anxiety that he was in every sense, including the most private, a small man. In a shady part of his mind which he did not usually visit he wished to learn her opinion on this matter. Erica could not judge it, any more than she could judge his professional competence, since, having known no other men, she had no means of comparison. It was true that earlier in his life several women had assured Brian that he was of average size. But what if they had been politely lying? Or what if he had shrunk, in fifteen years? Brian recognized the childish, neurotic stupidity of these ideas, but he could not suppress them entirely. 'Just once; just one shot, that's all, to cure you both,' his addiction whispered; and at last he promised it what it wanted.

When Wendy appeared in Brian's office after Christmas vacation he was momentarily embarrassed. He had denied her for so long that changing direction was awkward. Fortunately, almost miraculously, she provided him with an opening.

'How are you?' he asked, falling into the traditional starting gambit.

'Just the same,' Wendy grinned. 'Or worse, maybe.'

'I'm sorry.' Uncharacteristically, Brian had risen when she knocked, ostensibly to shelve some books, but in fact to get out from behind his desk – that old defensive fortification which had now become a military impediment.

'Nothing helps any more. Being away from you hurts. And being here hurts worse, some ways.'

'I don't like to see you unhappy.' Having replaced his books, Brian was now standing next to Wendy. He thought that he hadn't realized before how small she was, how childlike. He towered over her not only intellectually and chronologically, but physically. A pleasant sensation.

'I know.' She gave a little apologetic smile and shrug. 'If you would kiss me, just once, I'd feel better.'

'You know, I've been thinking about that,' Brian said, smiling down. 'I think just possibly you might be right.' He had imagined that he would explain his analysis of Wendy's problem and outline the solution he proposed, before putting it into practice. But events moved too fast for him. It was not until the next day that he was able to present his theory – which, by then, was already being proved incorrect.

Alison Lurie, *The War Between the Tates*, Heinemann, 1974, pp. 50–52, 57–8.

Easier by far just to write off the whole business of fidelity. The Earl of Rochester, a notorious Restoration rake and scurrilous poet, expressed such a view with characteristic robustness:

> Tell me no more of constancy,
>> The frivolous pretence
> Of cold age, narrow jealousy,
>> Disease, and want of sense.
>
> Let duller fools, on whom kind chance
>> Some easy heart has thrown,
> Despairing higher to advance,
>> Be kind to one alone.
>
> Old men and weak, whose idle flame
>> Their own defects discovers,
> Since changing can but spread their shame,
>> Ought to be constant lovers.
>
> But we, whose hearts do justly swell
>> With no vainglorious pride,
> Who know how we in love excel,
>> Long to be often tried.
>
> Then bring my bath, and strew my bed,
>> As each kind night returns;
> I'll change a mistress till I'm dead –
>> And fate change me to worms.

Lord Rochester, 'Against Constancy' (1676?),
Complete Poems, Yale U.P. 1968.

Joseph Heller's hero Bob Slocum in *Something Happened* knows that once outside the home, in office circles, infidelity is fine, but he finds it hard to follow the line with the insouciance of a Rochester:

The company has a policy about getting laid. It's okay.

And everybody seems to know that (although it's not spelled out in any of the personnel manuals). Talking about getting laid is even more okay than doing it, but doing it is okay too, although talking about getting laid with your own wife is never okay. (Imagine: 'Boy, what a crazy bang I got from my wife last night!' That wouldn't be nice, not with gentlemen you associate with in business who might know her.) But getting laid with somebody else's wife is very okay, and so is talking about it, provided the husband is not with the company or somebody anybody knows and likes. The company is in favor of getting laid if it is done with a dash of élan, humor, vulgarity, and skill, without emotion, with girls who are young and pretty or women who are older and foreign or glamorous in some other way, without too much noise and with at least some token gesture toward discretion, and without scandal, notoriety, or any of the other serious complications of romance. Falling in love, for example, is *not* usually okay, although marrying someone else right after a divorce is, and neither is 'having an affair', at least not for a man.

Getting laid (or talking about getting laid) is an important component of each of the company conventions and a decisive consideration in the selection of a convention site; and the salesmen who succeed in getting laid there soonest are likely to turn out to be the social heroes of the convention, though not necessarily the envy. (That will depend on the quality of whom they find to get laid with.) Getting laid at conventions is usually done in groups of three or four (two decide to go out and try and take along one or two others). Just about everybody in the company gets laid (or seems to), or at least talks as though he does (or did). In fact, it has become virtually *comme il faut* at company conventions for even the very top and very old, impotent men in the company – in fact, *especially* those – to allude slyly and boastfully to their own and each other's sexual misconduct in their welcoming addresses, acknowledgments, introductions, and informal preambles to speeches on graver subjects. Getting laid is a joking matter on all levels of the company.

Joseph Heller, *Something Happened*, Knopf, 1974, pp. 65–6.

It's a short step from scorning fidelity to condoning infidelity. James Boswell found all the reasons in the world to justify his lax behaviour:

8 March 1775. I was quite in love with her [his wife] tonight. She was sensible, amiable, and all that I could wish, except being averse to hymeneal rites. I told her I must have a concubine. She said I might go to whom I pleased. She has often said so. I have not insisted on my conjugal privilege since this month began, and were I sure that she was in earnest to allow me to go to other women without risk either of hurting my health or diminishing my affection for her, I would go. Thus I thought; but I was not clear, for though our Saviour did not prohibit concubinage, yet the strain of the New Testament seems to be against it, and the Church has understood it so. My passion, or appetite rather, was so strong that I was inclined to a laxity of interpretation, and as the Christian religion was not express upon the subject, thought that I might be like a patriarch; or rather, I thought that I might enjoy some of my former female acquaintances in London. I was not satisfied while in this loose state of speculation. I thought this was not unlike Izaak Walton or Dr. Donne. But then the patriarchs, and even the Old Testament men who went to *harlots*, were devout. I considered indulgence with women to be like any other indulgence of nature . . .

5 April 1776. After I had written to my wife, I went and paid a visit to a lady, who argued with me that marriage was certainly no more but a political institution, as we see it has subsisted in so many different forms in different parts of the world. 'Therefore,' said she, 'it is merely a mutual contract which if one party breaks, the other is free. Now,' said she, 'my husband I know has been unfaithful to me a thousand times. I should therefore have no scruple of conscience, I do declare, to have an intrigue, and I am restrained only by my pride, because I would not do what is thought dishonourable in this country, and would not put myself in the power of a gallant.' I argued that the chastity of women was of much more consequence than that of men, as the property and

rights of families depend upon it. 'Surely,' said she, 'that is easily answered, for the objection is removed if a woman does not intrigue but when she is with child.' I really could not answer her. Yet I thought she was wrong, and I was uneasy, partly from my own weakness as a reasoner, partly from the pain which one feels on perceiving established principles sapped.

James Boswell, *The Ominous Years*, Heinemann, 1963, pp. 74, 320.

The French, however, experienced far less anguish about such lapses, as Madame d'Epinay made clear in her memoirs. Here Mlle d'Ette advises Mme d'Epinay, who is married to an unfaithful husband, to take a lover:

'Oh, I shall never have a lover,' I told her.

'And why not?' said she. 'Religious scruples?'

'No,' I answered. 'But I don't think a husband's misconduct authorises a wife to misbehave herself.'

'What do you call misbehaviour?' said she. 'I don't suggest that you should advertise the fact that you have a lover, nor that you should have him always around: on the contrary he must be the man with whom you are least seen in public. I don't suggest meetings, whisperings, letters, notes, or any stuff of that sort, which afford but a passing pleasure, and lay one open to a thousand and one unpleasantnesses.'

'How nice!' said I. 'You propose a lover whom one never sees and with whom one has nothing to do.'

'Not at all,' said she, 'I suggest a lover of whom people can say nothing one way or another.'

'Ah, you agree then,' I told her, 'that in spite of all precautions, people would talk, and there I should be with my reputation gone!'

'What makes you think so? First and foremost where is the woman who is not talked about? What have you gained by not having a lover? Haven't people coupled your name with that of the Chevalier de Canaples?'

'Goodness!' I cried, 'the Chevalier de Canaples! They think that!'

'Poor child,' she returned, 'you get surprised and shocked over everything. But in this world folk say just what comes into their heads and believe every word, or not a word, of all they happen to hear. Who bothers to verify a yarn that's floating round? Besides it's only by chopping and changing one's lovers, or making an unfortunate choice, or, as I have already said, by advertising the fact that one has a lover, that a woman loses her good name. The essential thing is to make a right choice: people may talk about it for a week or indeed may not talk about it at all, and then they will say no more about you, except to say well of you.'

'I don't take to these morals,' I said. 'There are three points here which beat me. The first is, how to have a lover, unashamed, since the liaison entails a perpetual traffic in deceit: the second, how to have a lover and keep him in the dark: and the third, how to endure the looks of those who know or guess.'

Mme d'Epinay, *Memoirs* (1746), Routledge, 1930, pp. 49–50.

In fiction too, infidelity can be justified on the grounds that everybody does it, as in Andre Dubus's novella 'We Don't Live Here Anymore'. Jack is talking to his close friend Hank, who is unaware that Jack, although married to Terry, is having an affair with his wife Edith.

'Did you ever want to leave with her?' I said.

'Why?'

'You said you loved her.'

'I still do. You're nineteenth century, Jack.'

'That's what you keep telling me.'

'It's why you've been faithful so long. Your conscience is made for whores but you're too good for that, so you end up worse: monogamous.'

'What's this made for whores shit.'

'The way it used to be. Man had his wife and kids. That was one lie. And he had his whore. He knew which was which, see; he

didn't get them confused. But now it's not that way: a man has a
wife and a girlfriend and they get blurred, you see, he doesn't
know where his emotional deposits are supposed to be. He's in
love, for Christ sake. It's incongruous. He can't live with it, it's
against everything he's supposed to feel, so naturally he takes
some sort of action to get himself back to where he believes he's
supposed to be. Devoted to one woman or some such shit. He
does something stupid: either he breaks with the girl and tries to
love only his wife, or he leaves the wife and marries the girl. If he
does that, he'll be in the same shit in a few years, so he'll just have
to keep marrying —'

'Or stay monogamous.'

'Aye. Both of which are utter bullshit.'

'And you think that's me.'

'I think so. You're a good enough man not to fuck without
feeling love, but if you're lucky enough for that to happen, then
you feel confused and guilty because you think it means you don't
love Terry.'

I looked him in the eyes and said: 'Have you been talking to my
mistress?'

'Mistress pistress. I've been talking to *you* for three years. I've
been watching you watching women.'

I believed him. If he knew about Edith and me, it was because
he'd guessed: they had not been talking.

'Am I right?' he said.

'I worry about Terry, that's true. Just getting caught, I mean. I
worry about love affairs too: the commitment, you know.'

'What's commitment got to do with a love affair? A love affair
is abandon. Put the joy back in fucking. It's got to be with a good
woman, though ... Commitment. That's with Terry. It doesn't
even matter if you love Terry. You're married. What matters is
not to hate each other, and to keep peace. The old Munich of
marriage. You live with a wife, around a wife, not through her.
She doesn't run with you and come drink beer with you, for Christ
sake. Love, shit. Love the kids. Love the horny wives and the girls

in short skirts. Love everyone, my son, and keep peace with your wife. Who, by the way, is not invulnerable to love either. What'll you do if that happens?'

'That's her business.'

'All right. I believe you.'

Andre Dubus, 'We Don't Live Here Anymore', *Separate Flights*, Godine (Boston), 1975, pp. 25–7.

For sociologists, adultery can be value-free, or, at the very least, it can have its positive aspects:

Adultery, because it is secret, permits people endless variation. In adultery, each partner can make the lover represent anyone or anything – mother, father, sibling, superordinates or subordinates, angel or devil – with very little risk because, unlike marriage, adultery does not, at the outset, include permanence. Truth need never be revealed; the inadequacies of the reality of the self need never be demonstrated to the other. So long as the adultery is brief, the fantasy can endure. In this sense, adultery is far from dangerous; it is safe. Partners can switch gender roles, play with sex and fantasy, satisfy particular desires, *be* all the things for which marriage has no room.

Annette Lawson, *Adultery*, Blackwell, 1989, p. 310.

Des Grieux in Rousseau's *La Nouvelle Héloïse* would probably have concurred with that approach, as he urges the married Julie to become his lover by stressing its social neutrality and by employing arguments which Laclos's protagonists (see pp. 161–6) would have accepted:

Listen to one who loves you. Why should we alone be more prudent than the rest of mankind and chase with childish simplicity these chimerical virtues which everybody talks about and nobody practises? Are we really better moralists than the crowds of philosophers with which London and Paris are populated, who poke fun at marital fidelity and think of adultery as just a game? I can give you examples that aren't at all shocking: all sensible people would roar with laughter at someone who ignores the yearnings of his heart out of respect for his marriage vows. Actually, they're saying, isn't a wrong which exists only in people's opinions no wrong at all as long as it's kept secret? What injury is sustained by a husband when it's inflicted by an infidelity he knows nothing about? Can't a woman make up for her faults by being especially obliging? Can't she employ her charms to prevent or disarm any suspicions? Deprived of an imaginary good, his life is in fact made even happier, and this supposed crime which provokes such indignation is no more than one more thing that binds society together.

Jean-Jacques Rousseau, *Julie, or La Nouvelle Héloïse*, pp. 247–8 (translated by Stephen Brook).

A similar view is put more coarsely in an anonymous poem of the seventeenth century:

> Thou dost deny me 'cause thou art a wife.
> Know, she that's married lives a single life
> That loves but one. Abhor the nuptial curse,
> Tied thee to him, for better and for worse.
> Variety delights the active blood,
> And women the more common, the more good,
> As all goods are. There's no adultery,
> And marriage is the worst monopoly.
> The learned Roman clergy admits none
> Of theirs to marry; they love all, not one.
> And every nun can teach you, 'tis as meet
> To change your bedfellows, as smock or sheet.
> Say, would you be content only to eat
> Mutton or beef, and taste no other meat?

It would grow loathsome to you, and I know
You have two palates, and the best below.

Anon., quoted in *Making Love* (ed. Alan Bold),
Picador, 1978.

John Updike, characteristically, imagines Rev. Tom Marshfield, his clerical hero of *A Month of Sundays*, finding theological and other justifications for his taste for adultery:

Jesus preached, scholarship tells us, in a time of cosmopolitan laxity in sexual morals. The Jew, indeed, ever had this fault – in contrast to the rigorous fetishist – of a certain humanistic tolerance. Though Leviticus and Deuteronomy excellently specify death for those who break the Seventh Commandment, the great Hebraic scholar John Lightfoot, in his masterwork, *Horae Hebraicae et Talmudicae*, was unable to locate a single instance of the punishment being carried out ... Bathsheba, though she betrayed Uriah in adultery with David, became the Queen of Israel and the mother of Solomon. Eve, seduced by the serpent, yet was the mother of mankind. Gomer, the whorish wife of Hosea, is given to him to be loved, in paradigm of the Lord's continuing love of faithless Israel. And in the new dispensation: Joseph, confronted with swelling evidence of Mary's infidelity, found himself not even willing to make her a public example, and mildly was 'minded to put her away privily.' ...

Adultery, my friends, is our inherent condition: 'Ye have heard that it was said by them of old time, Thou shalt not commit adultery: But I say unto you, That whosoever looketh on a woman to lust after her hath committed adultery with her already in his heart.'

But who that has eyes to see cannot so lust? Was not the First Divine Commandment received by human ears, 'Be fruitful, and multiply'? Adultery is not a choice to be avoided; it is a circumstance to be embraced. Thus I construe these texts.

But if, dearly beloved, we find our Master abrasively liberal upon the matter of adultery, we find Him even less comfortably stringent upon the matter of divorce. The Pharisaical law of His time was well advanced toward the accommodation of the institution of marriage to the plastic human reality which is never far, I fear, from the heart of Judaism. Bills of divorcement, as described in Deuteronomy 24, might be written when the wife had ceased to find favor in the husband's eyes, 'because of some uncleanness in her.' Nor did it stop there. A contemporary of the living Jesus, one Rabbi Hillel, propounded that a man might divorce his wife if 'she cook her husband's food too much'; and a follower of Hillel, one Rabbi Akiba, offered, with a purity by whose lights our present divorce laws are seen as the hypocritic shambles they are, that he might properly divorce her 'if he sees a woman fairer than she.'

What does Jesus say to such precepts? That they have been composed in 'hardness of heart.' That what 'God hath joined together, let not man put asunder.' That 'Whosoever shall put away his wife, and marry another, committeth adultery against her.' I quote, from memory, from Mark, the primal Gospel, where the words of our Saviour are least diluted by later incursions of Semitic reasonableness and Greek sophistry. Paul, in Ephesians 5, manfully attempted to mysticize this admittedly 'great mystery,' claiming of the married couple that 'they two shall be one flesh,' and substituting, as cosmological analogy, for the covenant between the Lord and Israel the union of Christ and the Church. He writes, 'So ought men to love their wives as their own bodies.' But most men dislike their own bodies, and correctly. For what is the body but a swamp in which the spirit drowns? And what is marriage, that supposedly seamless circle, but a deep well up out of which the man and woman stare at the impossible sun, the distant bright disc, of freedom?

Let us turn from Holy Writ to the world that surrounds us. Wherein does the modern American man recover his sense of worth, not as dogged breadwinner and economic integer, but as romantic minister and phallic knight, as personage, embodiment, and hero? In adultery. And wherein does the American woman, coded into mindlessness by household slavery and the stupefying companionship of greedy infants, recover her powers of decision, of daring, of discrimination – her dignity, in short? In adultery. The adulterous man and woman arrive at the place of their tryst stripped of all the false uniforms society has assigned them; they come on no recommendation but their own, possess no credentials but those God has bestowed, that is, insatiable egos and work-able genitals. They meet in love, for love, with love; they tremble in a glory that is unpolluted by the wisdom of this world; they are, truly, children of light. Those of you – you whose faces stare mutely up at me as I writhe within this imaginary pulpit – those of you who have shaken off your sleep and committed adultery, will in your hearts acknowledge the truth of my characterization.

The Word is ever a scandal. Do not, I beg you, reflexively spurn the interpretation which my meditation upon these portions of Scripture has urged to my understanding.

Verily, the sacrament of marriage, as instituted in its adamant impossibility by our Saviour, exists but as a precondition for the sacrament of adultery. To the one we bring token reverence, and wooden vows; to the other a vivid reverence bred upon the carnal presence of the forbidden, and vows that rend our hearts as we stammer them. The sheets of the marriage bed are interwoven with the leaden threads of eternity; the cloth of the adulterous couch with the glowing, living filaments of transience, of time itself, our element, our only element, which Christ consecrated by entering history, rather than escaping it, as did Buddha.

Why else, I ask you, did Jesus institute marriage as an eternal hell but to spawn, for each sublimely defiant couple, a galaxy of little paradises? Why so conspicuously forgive the adulterous but to lend the force of covert blessing to the apparent imprecation of 'adulterous generation.' We *are* an adulterous generation; let us rejoice . . .

What else did I learn in this unfallow summer of my ministry? That adultery is not one but several species. The adultery of the freshly married is a gaudy-winged disaster, a phoenix with hot ashes, the revelation that one has mischosen, a life-swallowing mistake has been made. Help, help, it is not too late, the babies scarcely know their father, the wedding presents are still unscarred, the mistake can be unmade, another mate can be chosen and the universe as dragon can be slain. Murders, abductions, and other fantasies flit into newspaper print from the hectic habitat of this species. The adultery of the hopelessly married, the couples in their thirties with slowly growing children and slowly dwindling mortgages, is a more stolid and more domestic creature, a beast of burden truly, for this adultery serves the purpose of rendering tolerable the unalterable. The flirtation at the benefit dance, the lunch invitation stammered from a company phone, the clock-conscious tryst in the noontime motel, the smuggled letters, the pained and sensible break-up – these are rites of marriage, holidays to the harried, yet, touchingly, not often understood as such by the participants, who flog themselves with blame while they haul each other's bodies into place as sandbags against the swamping of their homes. The adultery of those in their forties recovers a certain lightness, a greyhound skittishness and peacock sheen. Children leave; parents die; money descends; nothing is as difficult as it once seemed. Separation arrives by whim (the last dessert dish broken, the final intolerable cigar-burn on the armchair) or marriages are extended by surrender. The race between freedom and exhaustion is decided. And then, in a religious sense, there is no more adultery, as there is none among schoolchildren, or slaves, or the beyond-all-reckoning rich.

John Updike, *A Month of Sundays*, Knopf, 1975, Chs. 6 and 17, pp. 43–7, 137–8.

D.H. Lawrence, in unexpected contrast, perceives fidelity, not its opposite, as the deeper instinct:

All the literature of the world shows the prostitute's ultimate impotence in sex, her inability to keep a man, her rage against the profound instinct of fidelity in a man, which is, as shown by world history, just a little deeper and more powerful than his instinct of faithless sexual promiscuity. All the literature of the world also shows how profound is the instinct of fidelity in both man and woman, how men and women both hanker restlessly after the satisfaction of this instinct, and fret at their own inability to find the real mode of fidelity. The instinct of fidelity is perhaps the deepest instinct in the great complex we call sex. Where there is real sex there is the underlying passion for fidelity. And the prostitute knows this, because she is up against it. She can only keep men who have no real sex, the counterfeits: and these she despises. The men with real sex leave her inevitably, as unable to satisfy their real desire.

D.H. Lawrence, *Apropos of Lady Chatterley*, Heinemann, 1961, pp. 24–5.

Samuel Johnson was a lifelong believer in fidelity, and when Boswell, a chronic womanizer, attempted to soften Johnson's stance, he got nowhere. Johnson's espousal of strict fidelity did, of course, allow for the occasional lapse on the part of the husband:

He [Johnson] talked of the heinousness of the crime of adultery, by which the peace of families was destroyed. He said, 'Confusion of progeny constitutes the essence of the crime; and therefore a woman who breaks her marriage vows is much more criminal than a man who does it. A man, to be sure, is criminal in the sight of God; but he does not do his wife a very material injury, if he does not insult her; if, for instance, from mere wantonness of appetite, he steals privately to her chambermaid. Sir, a wife ought not greatly to resent this. I would not receive home a daughter who had run away from her husband on that account. A wife should study to reclaim her husband by more attention to please him. Sir, a man will not, once in a hundred instances, leave his wife and go to a harlot, if his wife has not been negligent of pleasing.'

Here he discovered that acute discrimination, that solid judgement, and that knowledge of human nature, for which he was upon all occasions remarkable. Taking care to keep in view the moral and religious duty, as understood in our nation, he shewed clearly from reason and good sense, the greater degree of culpability in the one sex deviating from it than the other; and, at the same time, inculcated a very useful lesson as to *the way to keep him*.

I asked him if it was not hard that one deviation from chastity should so absolutely ruin a young woman. JOHNSON: 'Why no, Sir; it is the great principle which she is taught. When she has given up that principle, she has given up every notion of female honour and virtue, which are all included in chastity.'

Eight years later, when Johnson was sixty-seven, the great man's views had not altered:

I repeated to him an argument of a lady of my acquaintance, who maintained, that her husband's having been guilty of numberless infidelities, released her from conjugal obligations, because they were reciprocal. JOHNSON: 'This is miserable stuff, Sir. To the contract of marriage, besides the man and wife, there is a third party – Society; and if it be considered as a vow – God: and, therefore, it cannot be dissolved by their consent alone. Laws are not made for particular cases, but for men in general. A woman may be unhappy with her husband; but she cannot be freed from him without the approbation of the civil and ecclesiastical power. A man may be unhappy, because he is not so rich as another; but he is not to seize upon another's property with his own hand.' BOSWELL: 'But, Sir, this lady does not want that the contract should be dissolved; she only argues that she may indulge herself in gallantries with equal freedom as her husband does, provided she takes care not to introduce a spurious issue into his family . . .' JOHNSON: 'This lady of yours, Sir, I think, is very fit for a brothel.'

James Boswell, *The Life of Samuel Johnson*, (1768), Vol. 1, pp. 347–8, (1776), Vol. II, p. 19.

The Catholic novelist Alexander Theroux is even more uncompromising. In his aptly titled novel *An Adultery*, the narrator steps aside to deliver a moralistic exploration of his own condition . . .

Adultery is the vice of equivocation.

It is not marriage but a mockery of it, a merging that mixes love and dread together like jackstraws. There is no understanding of contentment in adultery. The nature of it is its divided aim. It prevents the bond it nevertheless always leaves an anticipation for, dooming you to the agitated vigil of expecting to see what at the same time you are forced to conceal. You are left where in fact you must always remain, not formally committed yet forever engaged in supreme futility to a policy of separation sworn on the very covenant by which you've come together. You belong to each other in what together you've made of a third identity that almost immediately cancels your own. There is a law in art that proves it. Two colors are proven complementary only when forming that most desolate of all colors – neutral gray.

All acts of adultery are acts of thievery. It is a world of intolerable inversion where everything operates from the premise of deceit. What you steal, in fact, alone testifies to your honesty.

There is no union in its condition. It is only a pairing of two cohabitating solitudes, a mimicry of love as it seeks to approximate it, a parody of love appropriating its terms which upon use, however, are instantly found to vouch it false, your words becoming a continual reminder as you speak of exactly what you don't mean. It is impure and like all alloys a bad conductor. It invents affection in its wickedness diametrically opposed to the ways of one's belief. Assertions are annulled. Adultery, in fact, forces you to use a language as uncustomary and outmoded as the word itself has become. In what is spoken of love there is always *simultaneously* something else never being said of doubt and disapproval, something yet audible, a shadow of accusation cast below every statement of affection . . .

Adultery is the crime that always requires an accomplice – an accessory, not an associate. There is no confidence transmitted, so there can be no trust. How can there be? Who is a thief, then a policeman? It leads to the suspension, not the function, of personality. You have to pretend to be not only what you aren't, but in the strategy of accommodation by which, because you must compromise and relinquish your desires as often as you act on them, you must relinquish part of yourself to the same degree. You are soon lost to a category where you become only a type – archetypal goons out of popular French theater, whether lover, cuckolded buffoon, or misunderstood wife, acting out a farce of synchronized evasion in a corridor of comic doors that open and shut in ludicrous sequence. Adultery is, beyond all else, *undignified*. It wears a nose cone, bells, great flapping feet.

It is not transaction but transgression, a two-way cancellation in a continuous circuit of misexchange. It is the wrong combination, an unstable alliance, an extracontractual snare. Adulterers trust nothing. Nothing in adultery is additive or cumulative. No one wins, all the time. And nothing can stem the torment of what is by what could be, for the memory of what has been contaminates your bed and makes even the very act of renunciation promiscuous. You become but two cold copulars lapping frost off each other's rectitude. Memories, passed on like a body from hand to hand, preempt the present with warnings of further corruption and whisper enough of the sluttish past to make even the most robust promises a joke, which only leads to more promises. And soon you are forced into the vanity of consistently having to justify yourself. Adulterers are notorious egomaniacs and, like them, maladaptive and sadly insufficient. Narcissism doesn't replenish the self, it empties it. It seems like power, but proves only low esteem and a desperate need for attention.

A paradox is that almost to the degree that you come to despise your lover you also come to depend on her for such self-respect as you can scrape together. One has to look for moral support somewhere, and where is one to find it if not in the person whose standards you have substituted for your own? But the trouble is only compounded by another of adultery's legacies, for you soon realize you have become critically disconnected from your former self without any definition of a newer. The despair at the heart of adultery is that it cannot be rescued from the contingency of its origins, and any attempt at total stability is consistently undermined by the lack of commitment taught by the very means it came your way. Every rule therefore becomes an infraction, every luxury a privation, and every privilege a forfeiture.

Adultery is so unheroic, so small, so hopelessly a pantomime of pretended ease and insouciant losing, while being yet paralyzed by sterile emotions built upon the ridiculous inability to assert any claim of recognition, that the crime itself is its own punishment. Its gifts make slaves just as whips make dogs. The sexual acts of adultery, a coarse gluttony, are curiously uninhibited only because they are noncommittal. But in the process of feigning indifference and seeming offhand with the tentativeness of the relationship – bewildered at having to loathe morally what emotionally you need to approve and coldly planning to leave or be forsaken by what at the same time you also feel the need to be loyal to – you soon find yourself ludicrously on the watch for the least sign of unfaithfulness, which is, ironically enough, the very vice in adultery that has *engendered* it . . .

Adultery is finally a fraud. It is envious, proud, gluttonizing, slothful, and angry all at once, and while lustful, oddly impotent, braying with power only until the frightened note underlying it can be heard of its inevitable defeat by the standards its every act contravenes. It is a lie, and the lie creates a myth, and the myth only for a time the pathetic belief in its own conventions. To its way of life society gives no sanction or assurance, leaving its victims unassimilated and quarantined and desperately alone, outcast mortals desperately alone, hurrying away like Adam and Eve in Masaccio's *The Expulsion from Paradise*, stripped to the skin and exposed to the world in the shivering humiliation of their sin, for there is, ultimately, no sense of community in it that ever can be had. You go unmocked only where you go unrecognized, leaving you to brandish the empty arms you can fit to no conclusion and forcing you to create a world out of your own desertion and solitude and uncomprehending rejection.

And it is there, with ominous intimation, that adultery best recognizes itself, skulking and keeping to corners and drawing in until, sick of division and dimmed with dismay, it seeks the only sepulcher it knows, slouching back to its bed of precarious and fatal forgetfulness, where once again in the tired and face-aching grimace of pretense it must assume lust and love – as far apart as hell is from the arch above – fall down.

Alexander Theroux, *An Adultery*, Hamish Hamilton, 1988, pp. 196–200.

Perhaps it is best to acknowledge, as Emilia does in *Othello*, that frailty is a human vice, not restricted to one sex or the other, and that men carry the ultimate responsibility for lapses of fidelity:

> But I do think it is their husbands' faults
> If wives do fall: say, that they slack their duties,
> And pour our treasures into foreign laps;
> Or else break out in peevish jealousies,
> Throwing restraint upon us: or say they strike us,
> Or scant our former having in despite,
> Why, we have galls: and though we have some grace,
> Yet have we some revenge. Let husbands know,
> Their wives have sense like them: they see, and smell,
> And have their palates both for sweet, and sour,
> As husbands have. What is it that they do,

When they change us for others? Is it sport?
I think it is: and doth affection breed it?
I think it doth. Is 't frailty that thus errs?
It is so too. And have not we affections?
Desires for sport? and frailty, as men have?
Then let them use us well: else let them know,
The ills we do, their ills instruct us so.

William Shakespeare, *Othello*, Act IV:iii.

Since Christianity has not, in recent centuries, been known for a relaxed attitude to marital straying, let us end this chapter with a strikingly non-judgemental passage from the Gospels:

Jesus went unto the mount of Olives.

And early in the morning he came again into the temple, and all the people came unto him; and he sat down, and taught them.

And the scribes and Pharisees brought unto him a woman taken in adultery; and when they had set her in the midst,

They say into him, Master, this woman was taken in adultery, in the very act.

Now Moses in the law commanded us, that such should be stoned: but what sayest thou?

This they said, tempting him, that they might have to accuse him. But Jesus stooped down, and with his finger wrote on the ground, as though he heard them not.

So when they continued asking him, he lifted up himself, and said unto them, He that is without sin among you, let him first cast a stone at her.

And again he stooped down, and wrote on the ground.

And they which heard it, being convicted by their own conscience, went out one by one, beginning at the eldest, even unto the last: and Jesus was left alone, and the woman standing in the midst.

When Jesus had lifted up himself, and saw none but the woman, he said unto her, Woman, where are those thine accusers? Hath no man condemned thee?

She said, No man, Lord. And Jesus said unto her, Neither do I condemn thee: go, and sin no more.

John 8:1–11.

An Interlude of Gossip

There's nothing in the world like the devotion of a married woman. It's a thing no married man knows anything about.

Oscar Wilde, *Lady Windermere's Fan*

The wife of the Lieutenant Civil du Châtelet . . . absconded one day [in 1521] at four a.m. with a Monsieur Aignan de Saint-Mesmin and his brother (who slept with her chambermaid while she slept with the elder brother), taking with her most of her jewellery and the household silver. This double romance lasted for three months at the end of which the lady brazenly returned to Paris where a trial awaited her. She was condemned to beg her husband's pardon before two witnesses, and be transported to the Convent of the Cordelières to be beaten, have her head shaved and don the religious habit for a period of three years (during which time her husband could, if he wished, visit her and enjoy conjugal relations). The abbess of the convent was to 'administer discipline', i.e., beat her, three times a month. As for the two brothers St-Mesmin, they went scot-free! The lady appealed to François I, and that gallant, broad-minded monarch ordered her release.

Nina Epton, *Love and the French*, Cassell, 1959, p. 104.

[Mary Herbert, Countess of Pembroke] was sister to Sir Philip Sydney: maried to Henry, the eldest son of William Earle of Pembroke; but this subtile old Earle did see that his faire and witty daughter-in-lawe would horne his sonne, and told him so, and advised him to keepe her in the Countrey and not to let her frequent the Court.

She was a beautifull Ladie and had an excellent witt, and had the best breeding that that age could afford. Shee had a pritty sharpe-ovall face. Her haire was of a reddish yellowe.

She was very salacious, and she had a Contrivance that in the Spring of the yeare, when the Stallions were to leape the Mares, they were to be brought before such a part of the house, where she had a *vidette* (a hole to peepe out at) to looke on them and please herselfe with their Sport; and then she would act the like sport herselfe with *her* stallions. One of her great Gallants was Crooke-back't Cecill, Earl of Salisbury.

His father found out a rich Wife for him [Henry Martin, a leading anti-royalist who signed the death warrant for the execution of Charles I], whom he maried something unwillingly. He was a great lover of pretty girles, to whom he was so liberall that he spent the greatest part of his estate. When he had found out a maried woman that he liked (and he had his Emissaries, male and female, to looke out) he would contrive such or such a good bargain, 20 or 30 pounds per annum under rent, to have her neer him. He lived from his wife a long time. If I am not mistaken, shee was sometime distempered by his unkindnesse to her.

[John Selden, a scholar and Member of Parliament] was quickly taken notice of for his learning, and was Sollicitor and Steward to the Earle of Kent, whose Countesse, being an ingeniose woman and loving men, would let him lye with her, and her husband knew it. After the Earle's death he maried her. He did lye with Mris. Williamson (one of my Lady's woemen) a lusty bouncing woman, who robbed him on his death-bed. I remember in 1646, or 1647, they did talk also of my Lady's Shee Blackamore.

I remember my Sadler (who wrought many years to that Family) told me that Mr. Selden had got more by his Prick then he had done by his practise. He was no eminent practiser at Barre.

John Aubrey, *Brief Lives*, Secker & Warburg, 1950, pp. 138, 193, 271.

Jan. 26 1664: Mr R. B: a chapleyn of Xt Ch. [Christ Church], one much given to the flesh and a great lover of Eliz. the wife of Funker and daughter of Woods of Bullock's lane, having mind one night in the month of Jan. about the 26, 1664, to vent or coole his passion sent his servitor (a little boy) to Carfax where shee sold apples to come to his chamber and 12d in apples. The boy forgetting her name went to another huckster and told her that she (who it seems told her that she knew Mr. Berry) must come downe to his chamber and bring apples. Well, she comes at a little past 6 at night up to his chamber; who against her comming (supposing her to be Eliz . . .) shut the shuttings of his window and put out his candle. And when shee was come in, he said 'Oh Betty art come? I am glad with all my hart; I have not seene thee a great while': and kissed and groped her and felt her brests. 'Come, what wilt have to supper? what joynt of meat wilt have?' and the like. 'Come, I have not layd with thee a great while,' and soe put his hands under her coates. But shee bid him 'forbear' and told him 'he was mistaken: if he would pay her for her apples, well and good; she would not play such vile actions with him.' 'Who' quoth he 'are you not Eliz . . .' 'Noe, marry, I am not.' With that he thrust her downe stairs and kikt her. After this she goeth up to Carfax; and their goes in full rage and open mouth to Eliz . . . with whome she sorely fell out the day before; and twitted her in the teeth of it, and called her 'whore' before all the street and brought up Mr. Berry's name in publick divers times. And after this scolding had lasted till 8 or 9 of the clock, it was then concluded till the next day. The next day he kiked the servitor for mistaking.

Anthony à Wood, *Life and Times*, OUP, 1961, pp. 141–2.

24 June 1667: . . . [Mr Povy, the Treasurer of the Duke of York's Household] says that to this day the King doth fallow the women as much as ever he did. That the Duke of York hath not got Mrs Middleton, as I was told the other day; but says that he wants not her, for he hath others and hath alway had; and that he hath known them brought through the Matted Gallery at White-hall into his closet. Nay, he hath come out of his wife's bed and gone to others laid in bed for him . . .

29 July 1667: . . . The bottom of the quarrel is this: she [Lady Castlemaine] is fallen in love with young Jermin [Henry Jermyn, Master of the Horse to the Duke of York], who hath of late lain with her oftener then the King and is now going to marry my Lady Falmouth. The King he is mad at her entertaining Jermin and she is mad at Jermin's going to marry from her, so they are all mad; and thus the kingdom is governed . . .

30 July 1667: . . . Mr. Cooling, my Lord Chamberlaines secretary . . . stopped to speak to us; and he proved very drunk and did talk and would have talked all night with us, I not being able to break loose from him, he holding me so by the hand. But Lord, to see his present humour; how he swears at every word and talks of the King and my Lady Castleman in the plainest words in the world. And from him I gather that the story I learned yesterday is true – that the King hath declared that he did not get the child of which she is conceived at this time, he having not as he says lain with her this half year; but she told him – 'God damn me! but you shall own it.' It seems he is jealous of Jermin and she loves him, so that the thoughts of his marrying of my Lady Falmouth puts her into fits of the mother. And he, it seems, hath lain with her from time to time continually, for a good while; and once, as this Cooling says, the King had like to have taken him a-bed with her, but that he was fain to creep under the bed into her closet. He says that for a good while the King's greatest pleasure hath been with his fingers, being able to do no more.

Samuel Pepys, *Diary*, Bell, 1970, Vol. 8, pp. 286, 366, 368.

Anthony Hamilton, a member of the Scottish and Irish nobility, began in 1704 collecting the memoirs of his brother-in-law, the Count de Grammont, who died three years later. The memoirs were a joint work, with Hamilton himself incorporating his reminiscences of the court of Charles II.

The Duke of York, having quieted his conscience by the declaration of his marriage, thought that he was entitled, by this generous effort, to give way a little to his inconstancy: he therefore immediately seized upon whatever he could first lay his hands upon: this was Lady Carnegy, who had been in several other hands. She was still tolerably handsome, and her disposition, naturally inclined to tenderness, did not oblige her new lover long to languish. Everything coincided with their wishes for some time: Lord Carnegy, her husband, was in Scotland; but his father dying suddenly, he as suddenly returned with the title of Southesk, which his wife detested; but which she took more patiently than she received the news of his return. Some private intimation had been given him of the honour that was done him in his absence: nevertheless, he did not show his jealousy at first; but, as he was desirous to be satisfied of the reality of the fact, he kept a strict watch over his wife's actions. The Duke of York and her ladyship had for some time been upon such terms of intimacy as not to pass their time in frivolous amusements; however, the husband's return obliged them to maintain some decorum: he therefore never went to her house, but in form, that is to say, always accompanied by some friend or other, to give his amours at least the appearance of a visit.

A few months after the celebration of the Duke of Monmouth's nuptials, Killegrew, having nothing better to do, fell in love with Lady Shrewsbury; and, as Lady Shrewsbury, by a very extraordinary chance, had no engagement at that time, their amour was soon established. No one thought of interrupting an intimacy which did not concern any one; but Killegrew thought proper to disturb it himself. Not that his happiness fell short of his expectation, nor did possession put him out of love with a situation so enviable; but he was amazed that he was not envied, and offended that his good fortune raised him no rivals.

He possessed a great deal of wit, and still more eloquence, which most particularly displayed itself when he was a little elevated with the juice of the grape: he then indulged himself in giving luxurious descriptions of Lady Shrewsbury's most secret charms and beauties, which above half the court were as well acquainted with as himself.

The Duke of Buckingham was one of those who could only judge from outward appearances: and appearances, in his opinion, did not seem to promise anything so exquisite as the extravagant praises of Killegrew would infer. As this indiscreet lover was a frequent guest at the Duke of Buckingham's table, he was continually employing his rhetoric on this subject, and he had full opportunity for his harangues; for they generally sat down to dinner at four o'clock, and only rose just in time for the play in the evening.

The Duke of Buckingham, whose ears were continually deafened with descriptions of Lady Shrewsbury's merits, resolved at last to examine into the truth of the matter himself. As soon as he had made the experiment, he was satisfied; and, though he fancied that fame did not exceed the truth, yet this intrigue began in such a manner that it was generally believed its duration would be short, considering the fickleness of both parties, and the vivacity with which they had engaged in it: nevertheless, no amour in England ever continued so long.

The imprudent Killegrew, who could not be satisfied without rivals, was obliged, in the end, to be satisfied without a mistress. This he bore very impatiently; but so far was Lady Shrewsbury from hearkening to, or affording any redress for the grievances at first complained of, that she pretended even not to know him. His spirit could not brook such treatment; and, without ever considering that he was the author of his own disgrace, he let loose all his abusive eloquence against her ladyship; he attacked her with the most bitter invectives from head to foot: he drew a frightful picture of her conduct; and turned all her personal charms, which he used to extol, into defects. He was privately warned of the inconveniences to which these declamations might subject him, but despised the advice, and, persisting, he soon had reason to repent it.

As he was returning one evening from the Duke of York's apartments at St. James's, three passes with a sword were made at him through his chair, one of which went entirely through his arm. Upon this, he was sensible of the danger to which his intemperate tongue had exposed him, over and above the loss of his mistress. The assassins made their escape across the Park, not doubting but they had dispatched him.

Killegrew thought that all complaints would be useless; for what redress from justice could he expect for an attempt of which his wounds were his only evidence? And, besides, he was convinced that if he began a prosecution founded upon appearances and conjectures, the parties concerned would take the shortest and most effectual means to put a stop to all inquiries upon the subject, and that their second attempt would not prove ineffectual. Being desirous, therefore, of deserving mercy from those who had endeavoured to assassinate him, he no longer continued his satires, and said not a word of the adventure. The Duke of Buckingham and Lady Shrewsbury remained for a long period both happy and contented. Never before had her constancy been of so long a duration; nor had he ever been so submissive and respectful a lover.

This continued until Lord Shrewsbury, who never before had shown the least uneasiness at his lady's misconduct, thought proper to resent this: it was public enough, indeed, but less dishonourable to her than any of her former intrigues. Poor Lord Shrewsbury, too polite a man to make any reproaches to his wife, was resolved to have redress for his injured honour: he accordingly challenged the Duke of Buckingham; and the Duke of Buckingham, as a reparation for his honour, having killed him upon the spot, remained a peaceable possessor of this famous Helen. The public was at first shocked at the transaction; but the public grows familiar with everything by habit, and by degrees both decency and even virtue itself are rendered tame and overcome. The queen was at the head of those who exclaimed against so public and scandalous a crime, and against the impunity of such a wicked act. As the Duchess of Buckingham was a short, fat body, like her majesty, who never had had any children, and whom her husband had abandoned for another; this sort of parallel in their situations interested the queen in her favour; but it was all in vain: no person paid any attention to them; the licentiousness of the age went on uncontrolled, though the queen endeavoured to raise up the serious part of the nation, the politicians and devotees, as enemies against it.

Anthony Hamilton, *Memoirs of the Count of Grammont*, John Lane, 1928, pp. 114–15, 212–14.

[27 March 1700] The Duke of Norfolk divorc'd from his Wife by the Parliament: for Adultery with one Sir J. Germain a Dutch gamster of meane extraction, who had gotten much by Gaming (She was the onely daughter to the Earle of Peterboro Mordaunt:) after long debates in Parliament, & undenyable proofe: The Duke having also leave to marry againe, by which (if he have Children) the Dukedome, will go from my late Lord Thomass Children, Papists indeede, but very hopefull & vertuous Gent: as was their father. The now Duke & Unkle, a dissolute protestant.

John Evelyn, *Diary*.

At about this time [1706] old [Marquis de] Bellegarde, who had a long and distinguished record of service, died at the age of 80. He was a general and a commander of the Order of Saint-Louis. In his day he had had an extremely good figure and was a great gallant. He was for many years the lover of the wife of one of the chief magistrates of the Parlement, who suspected as much, to say the least of it, but had his own reasons for not objecting – they said that he was impotent. One fine day the wife, who was amorous by nature, brought to her husband's study a little boy in a peasant's smock. 'Eh! wife,' said he, 'who may this child be?' 'This is your son,' said she firmly. 'I come to present him to you; is he not handsome?' 'What do you mean, son?' he exclaimed. 'You know perfectly well that we have no children.' 'I know perfectly well that I have had this one, and that he is yours also,' she retorted. The poor fellow, seeing her so determined, scratched his head, but did not hesitate long. 'Very well, wife, no scandal! I shall put up with this one, but you must promise to make me no others.' She did so promise, and she kept her word, but Bellegarde still continued to haunt their house. The little boy thus became one of the family. His mother loved him well, his father not at all, but he was prudent.

Duc de Saint-Simon, *Memoirs*, Hamish Hamilton, 1967, Vol. I, p. 287 (translated by Lucy Norton).

Your acquaintance, D. Rodrigue, has had a small accident befallen him. Mr Annesley found him in bed with his wife, prosecuted, and brought a bill of divorce into Parliament. Those things grow more fashionable every day, and in a little time won't be at all scandalous. The best expedient for the public, and to prevent the expense of private families, would be a general act of divorcing all the people of England. You know those that pleased might marry again; and it would save the reputations of several ladies that are now in peril of being exposed every day.

Lady Mary Wortley Montagu, letter to the Countess of Mar, 1725.

In a letter to Sir David Dalrymple, written on 11 December 1780, Walpole recalls Lancelot Blackbourne, archbishop of York, who died in 1743:

He lived within two doors of my father in Downing Street, and took much notice of me when I was near man . . . In point of decorum he was not quite so exact as you have been told, Sir. I often dined with him: his mistress Mrs Cruwys sat at the head of the table, and Hayter, his natural son by another woman, and very like him, at the bottom, as chaplain; he was afterwards Bishop of London. I have heard, but do not affirm it, that Mrs Blackbourne, before she died, complained of Mrs Cruwys being brought under the same roof.

Horace Walpole, *Correspondence*, OUP, 1951, Vol. 15, pp. 142–3.

A squib from the Goncourt brothers from 5 March 1858:

Overheard at the next table at Broggi's:
  'I've met his mistress.'
  'But that's his wife!'
  'He introduced her to me as his mistress, to rehabilitate her . . .'

And many years later, a tribute, dated 20 January 1886, to a man of passion:

The only sincere lover, the only real lover of our times, is probably Octave Mirbeau – a sort of Othello in miniature! One evening when he arrived to spend the night with the woman for the love of whom he had become a stockbroker and found that she was sleeping out, he went into her dressing-room and tore into shreds, with his murderous hands, his mistress's little dog, the only creature on earth that she really loved.

Edmond and Jules Goncourt, *Pages from the Goncourt Journals*, OUP, 1962, pp. 33, 312 (translated by Robert Baldick).

Earl Beauchamp was married to Bend'Or's sister, Lettice. The marriage seemed successful: they produced a number of attractive children and Beauchamp held many public offices. Bend'Or had maintained amicable, but not close, relations with his brother-in-law. They had few tastes in common, Beauchamp being no sportsman or warrior, but family relationships were maintained, especially since Bend'Or had always been very fond of his sister. As he grew older Beauchamp's behaviour seems to have become more lurid, and became impossible to ignore in one who was to other appearances a pillar of the Church of England and the House of Lords. When the scandal threatened to break Bend'Or was furious at the thought of what it might do to his sister. Beauchamp would certainly have gone to prison and the thought of the Grosvenors being subjected, even by marriage, to such disgrace, was intolerable. Bend'Or had a strong sense of personal honour . . . and regarded homosexuality with abhorrence. He certainly used his influence to ensure that Beauchamp went abroad and stayed there, in order that Lettice might be spared the consequences of a public exposure.

George Ridley, *Bend'Or Duke of Westminster*, Robin Clark, 1985, pp. 172–3.

Celebrated Infidelities I:
The Caesars to Byron

The first step of error none ever could recall
And the woman once fallen forever must fall,
Pursue to the last the career she begun,
And be *false* unto *many*, as *faithless* to *one*.

Byron, Letter to Lady Melbourne, 18 September 1812

The Roman historian Suetonius gave a brightly detailed account of the imperial careers and personal misadventures of the Caesars:

When members of his family died Augustus bore his loss with far more resignation than when they disgraced themselves. The deaths of Gaius and Lucius did not break his spirit; but after discovering his daughter Julia's adulteries, he refused to see visitors for some time. He wrote a letter about her case to the Senate, staying at home while a quaestor read it to them. He may even have considered her execution; at any rate, hearing that one Phoebe, a freedwoman in Julia's confidence, had hanged herself, he cried: 'I should have preferred to be Phoebe's father!' Julia was forbidden to drink wine or enjoy any other luxury during her exile; and denied all male company, whether free or servile, except by Augustus's special permission and after he had been given full particulars of the applicant's age, height, complexion, and of any distinguishing marks on his body – such as moles or scars. He kept Julia for five years on the prison island of Pandataria before moving her to Reggio in Calabria, where she received somewhat milder treatment. Yet nothing would persuade him to forgive his daughter; and when the Roman people interceded several times on her behalf, earnestly pleading for her recall, he stormed at a popular assembly: 'If you ever bring up this matter again, may the gods curse you with daughters as lecherous as mine, and with wives as adulterous!' While in exile Julia the Younger gave birth to a child, which Augustus refused to let the father acknowledge; it was exposed at his orders . . .

Not even his friends could deny that he often committed adultery, though of course they said, in justification, that he did so for reasons of state, not simple passion – he wanted to discover what his enemies were at by getting intimate with their wives or daughters. Mark Antony accused him not only of indecent haste in marrying Livia, but of hauling an ex-consul's wife from her husband's dining-room into the bedroom – before his eyes, too! He brought the woman back, says Antony, blushing to the ears and with her hair in disorder . . .

As an elderly man he is said to have still harboured a passion for deflowering girls – who were collected for him from every quarter, even by his wife!

Suetonius, *The Twelve Caesars*, Penguin, 1957, pp. 86, 88, 90 (translated by Robert Graves).

Caligula, on the other hand, was more experimental in his sexual behaviour:

It was [Caligula's] habit to commit incest with each of his three sisters in turn and, at large banquets, when his wife reclined above him, placed them all in turn below him. They say that he ravished his sister Drusilla before he came of age: their grandmother Antonia, at whose house they were both staying, caught them in bed together. Later, he took Drusilla from her husband, the ex-Consul Lucius Cassius Longinus, quite unashamedly treating her as his wife; and when he fell dangerously ill left Drusilla all his property, and the Empire too . . .

It would be hard to say whether the way he got married, the way he dissolved his marriages, or the way he behaved as a husband was the most disgraceful. He attended the wedding ceremony of Gaius Piso and Livia Orestilla, but had the bride carried off to his own home. After a few days, however, he sent her away, and two years later banished her, suspecting that she had returned to Piso in the interval. According to one account he told Piso, who was reclining opposite him at the wedding feast: 'Hands off my wife!' and took her home with him at once; and announced the next day that he had taken a wife in the style of Romulus and Augustus. Then he suddenly sent to Greece for Lollia Paulina, wife of Gaius Memmius, the consular Governor, because somebody had remarked that her grandmother was once a famous beauty; but he soon discarded Lollia, forbidding her ever again to sleep with another man . . .

Besides incest with his sisters, and a notorious passion for the prostitute Pyrallis, he made advances to almost every well-known married woman in Rome; after inviting a selection of them to dinner with their husbands he would slowly and carefully examine each in turn while they passed his couch, as a purchaser might assess the value of a slave, and even stretch out his hand and lift up the chin of any woman who kept her eyes modestly cast down. Then, whenever he felt so inclined, he would send for whoever pleased him best, and leave the banquet in her company. A little later he would return, showing obvious signs of what he had been about, and openly discuss his bed-fellow in detail, dwelling on her good and bad physical points and criticizing her sexual perform-ance. To some of those unfortunates he issued, and publicly registered, divorces in the name of their absent husbands.

Suetonius, *The Twelve Caesars*, Penguin, 1957, pp. 161, 161–2, 167–8 (translated by Robert Graves).

Edward Gibbon, a great historian and meticulous stylist, examines the later rulers of imperial Rome:

Faustina, the daughter of Pius and the wife of Marcus [Aurelius], has been as much celebrated for her gallantries as for her beauty. The grave simplicity of the philosopher was ill calculated to engage her wanton levity, or to fix that unbounded passion for variety which often discovered personal merit in the meanest of mankind. The Cupid of the ancients was, in general, a very sensual deity; and the amours of an empress, as they exact on her side the plainest advances, are seldom susceptible of much sentimental delicacy. Marcus was the only man in the empire who seemed ignorant or insensible of the irregularities of Faustina; which, according to the prejudices of every age, reflected some disgrace on the injured husband. He promoted several of her lovers to posts of honour and profit, and, during a connexion of thirty years, invariably gave her proofs of the most tender confidence, and of a respect which ended not with her life. In his Meditations he thanks the gods, who had bestowed on him a wife so faithful, so gentle, and of such a wonderful simplicity of manners. The obsequious senate, at his earnest request, declared her a goddess.

Edward Gibbon, *The Decline and Fall of the Roman Empire*, Ch. IV.

Gibbon also cast his eye over other cultures:

The heat of the climate inflames the blood of the Arabs; and their libidinous complexion has been noticed by the writers of antiquity. Their incontinence was regulated by the civil and religious laws of the Koran; their incestuous alliances were blamed; the boundless licence of polygamy was reduced to four legitimate wives or concubines; their rights both of bed and of dowry were equitably determined; the freedom of divorce was discouraged, adultery was condemned as a capital offence, and fornication, in either sex, was punished with an hundred stripes. Such were the calm and rational precepts of the legislator; but in his private conduct Mahomet indulged the appetites of a man and abused the claims of a prophet. A special revelation dispensed him from the laws which he had imposed on his nation; the female sex, without reserve, was abandoned to his desires; and this singular prerogative excited the envy, rather than the scandal, the veneration, rather than the envy, of the devout Musulmans . . . The temper of Mahomet was inclined to jealousy; but a divine revelation assured him of her [Ayesha, one of his wives] innocence; he chastised her accusers, and published a law of domestic peace that no woman should be condemned unless four male witnesses had seen her in the act of adultery. In his adventures with Zeineb, the wife of Zeid, and with Mary, an Egyptian captive, the amorous prophet forgot the interest of his reputation. At the house of Zeid, his freedman and adopted son, he beheld, in a loose undress, the beauty of Zeineb, and burst forth into an ejaculation of devotion and desire. The servile or grateful freedman understood the hint, and yielded, without hesitation, to the love of his benefactor. But, as the filial relation had excited some doubt and scandal, the angel Gabriel descended from heaven to ratify the deed, to annul the adoption, and gently to reprove the apostle for distrusting the indulgence of his God. One of his wives, Hafsa, the daughter of Omar, surprised him on her own bed in the embraces of his Egyptian captive; she promised secrecy and forgiveness; he swore that he would renounce the possession of Mary. Both parties forgot their engagements; and Gabriel again descended with a chapter of the Koran, to absolve him from his oath, and to exhort him freely to enjoy his captives and concubines without listening to the clamours of his wives. In a solitary retreat of thirty days, he laboured, alone with Mary, to fulfil the commands of the angel. When his love and revenge were satiated, he summoned to his presence his eleven wives, reproached their disobedience and indiscretion, and threatened them with a sentence of divorce both in this world and in the next: a dreadful sentence, since those who had ascended the bed of the prophet were for ever excluded from the hope of a second marriage. Perhaps the incontinence of Mahomet may be palliated by the tradition of his natural or preternatural gifts: he united the manly virtue of thirty of the children of Adam; and the apostle might rival the thirteen labours of the Grecian Hercules.

Edward Gibbon, *The Decline and Fall of the Roman Empire*, Ch. LV.

Italian Renaissance rulers, like their Roman precursors, led tempestuous lives of violence and depravity. Muzio Attendolo (1369–1424), the founder of the Sforza dynasty, was typical in his contradictions:

His advice to his promising son Francesco is interesting. 'I wish you to be assiduous in your observance of justice to everybody. When hereafter you come to rule over people, it will not only recommend you to the favor of Heaven, but it will make you especially popular among men. Take particular care not to offend any of your subjects by the commission of adultery. This is an injury which both the wrath of God and the bitter anger of men punish with the greatest severity.'

Was this an old soldier speaking? In the Renaissance when a man's part in adultery was not even regarded as a peccadillo, much less a sin? Muzio himself had thirteen children (six of them illegitimate, including Francesco). Needless to say, Francesco paid no attention to this good advice and continued to commit adultery throughout his life, including the last night before his death at the age of sixty-five.

In Ferrara a few years later, the marquis Niccolò III (1383–1441) was equally inconsistent:

Niccolò was fat and jolly, but he also was cruel, vengeful and absolutely convinced of his right to rule others despotically. He was equally convinced that it was his privilege to enjoy as many women as he wished but that his wife should be above reproach. His young wife, Parisina Malatesta, who had married Niccolò when she was fifteen and he thirty-six, did not agree with him.

In 1424 Parisina fell in love with a handsome young man her own age, her stepson Ugo d'Este. Ugo was Niccolò's favorite son and his heir. On a journey to some neighboring town the young couple became lovers. The following year in Ferrara one of Parisina's maids who had been beaten by her mistress betrayed the guilty couple to a courtier, who in turn informed Niccolò. A doubtful but imperishable legend has it that by means of an artfully arranged mirror Niccolò looked across the courtyard of the Este castle ʿand into the chamber where the lovers were embracing.

Parisina and Ugo were arrested at once, to be confined in a dungeon for one day and beheaded the next. Niccolò refused to speak to them or look at them. All through the night before the executions Niccolò in a frenzy of grief and rage roamed through the corridors of the palace, gnawing on his sceptre, calling for his beloved son Ugo and crying out for his own death. In his great emotional turmoil the Marquis issued a decree that henceforth any woman in his domains who committed the same offense as Parisina's would be beheaded. As far as it is known, only one woman, the wife of a judge, was executed under the new law.

Orville Prescott, *Princes of the Renaissance*, Allen & Unwin, 1970, pp. 90–91, 188–9.

French rulers were a touch more civilized:

One of François I's most famous mistresses was Françoise de Châteaubriant, who was married to Jean Laval at the age of eleven and gave birth to a child a year later. Ten years afterwards François heard about this beauty who lived with her husband in a château in Brittany, and he resolved to invite them both to Blois ... The king's fame as a lover being all too well known, Jean Laval was suspicious ...

Françoise arrived at Blois in a whirlwind of excitement, and the courtiers were highly amused by Jean's ill-disguised fury. As soon as the easily inflammable king looked into Françoise's violet eyes he fell deeply in love with her. The lady was not so shy as she had been made out to be, but she was shrewd and had no intention of giving in to the royal caprice so easily. It took the king three years to persuade Françoise to share his bed. This may seem surprising to us in our age of impatient love, but François was a true lover who agreed with Guillaume Lorris that 'who wins the prize must pay the toll, for game hath ever sweeter taste which wary foot hath hotly chased'. François did not approve of virtuous people – he called them hypocrites – but it was not his custom to force a woman, for he believed that the greatest pleasure in life is to persuade a woman to capitulate voluntarily.

Nina Epton, *Love and the French*, Cassell, 1959, pp. 91–2.

Pietro Aretino of Arezzo (1492–1556) was a charismatic Renaissance intriguer, blackmailer, connoisseur and pornographer known for his capacious bisexual appetites:

It is certain that [Aretino] kept at least a dozen girls, who all appear to have been quite contented with their lot, for a reasonable time at least, at the Casa Aretino . . .

Pietro also greatly relished the company of the excitable and choleric wives of gondoliers and 'servant-girls of twenty-five carats', who were to be found in the streets. From these, and from pseudo-respectable spouses of tradesmen and merchants, from famous and wealthy courtesans and, on occasion, from the aristocracy, he recruited housekeepers and housemaids, cooks and cup-bearers, who all became his mistresses sooner or later, as well as those, now and again, of his male servants and friends.

Children were born, stayed on or disappeared. Pietro could not have cared less who might have been their real father. Shrill feminine disputes broke out which he was never at a loss to settle. The Casa was more like an aviary of tropical parakeets than a writer's mansion . . .

He kept all these resident women well supplied with gold ornaments, silk gowns, red stockings and sweetmeats. They had to be a credit to him when important visitors came, as they did every day. But he rarely paid the recipients of his momentary favours in cash, even the prostitutes. They all knew who he was and felt themselves sufficiently remunerated just by being seen with such an almighty scoundrel as gossip reported Pietro Aretino to be ...

There is evidence, however, that this apparently indiscriminate debauchee experienced a true and deep passion for at least three of his mistresses not named in the above catalogue. In the first place the auburn-haired Caterina Sandella, endowed with a figure which neither Titian nor Tintoretto could resist, acted for ten years as queen of his seraglio. She had married a gay young nobleman named Polo Bartolo, who had a highly developed taste for courtesans. Her complaints on this score to Pietro caused him first to lecture the errant husband and then to counsel Christian resignation to the hitherto faithful wife. The third step he took, naturally, was into Caterina's bed – that is, the one he fixed up for her at the Casa.

Bartolo made a fuss to begin with and talked of taking legal action. But he had really lost interest in his consort by this time and was weak enough to allow Pietro's long tongue to persuade him that all was for the best, especially as Caterina's imposing lover not only always treated her with great respect, as befitted her rank, but also introduced her delinquent spouse to lots of other pretty girls not required for the moment by the master of the Casa Aretino ...

His second serious love-affair, which had less happy issue, concerned a certain Perina Riccia ... Perina had been married at fourteen, an age regarded as unquestionably nubile in sixteenth-century Italy. Her husband dealt, like many Venetians, in cotton and pepper ... He, like Caterina's spouse, was also called Polo and, by an even stranger coincidence, surnamed Bartolini. He also resembled Polo Bartolo in his vain, frivolous character ...

As Perina's [poor] health improved and Bartolini was more and more often away 'on business', she began, naturally enough, to flirt with younger, simpler and slenderer Don Juans than her

weighty and sophisticated admirer, whose funds of wit and experience were quite beyond her powers of appreciation. Pietro understood the danger only too well. He redoubled his efforts at a
complete physical conquest of the girl, no doubt hoping that his
renowned amorous prowess might save her from inferior junior
practitioners. To his surprise Perina, with her newly awakened
erotic proclivities – Bartolini, it seems, had never been much use
to her in bed – yielded almost at once . . .

But on a certain morning in July 1541 he awoke to be faced
with an example of one of the oldest dramas in the world. Perina
was gone. So was one Marco, a handsome, muscular young
gondolier he had often employed. Youth must be served and
Pietro's beard, despite the dye, was more silver than black now . . .

The third young woman he loved at this depth, but at an earlier
date, for she died suddenly in 1540, after he had lost interest in
her, differed considerably in character from both Caterina Sandella
and Perina Riccia. Angela Serena lived up to her name by a calm,
ethereal presence. Yet significantly enough Pietro often refers to
her as 'the Siren' rather than 'the Serene One'. She must have
physically attracted him in some way; but he appears rather to
have idealised her mentally.

Like Caterina she came of a noble family, Sienese in her case . . .
Unlike both Caterina and Perina she was dark, with a great deal of
splendid black hair – turned 'golden' by her eyes, wrote Pietro –
and an alabaster complexion which glowed as though illuminated
from within. Yet like the other two women she was already
married when Pietro first met her. Once again the young husband
had certain bad habits, largely homosexual . . . Intellectual intimacy
with the long-suffering wife duly followed. The pair read each
other their literary compositions. They discussed philosophy, love,
virtue and religion in passionate abstractions . . .

But this idyll could not last. It would have culminated in a
bodily show-down, Pietro being the man he was, if Giovanni
Antonio Serena had not intervened. The Sienese nobility were
more straitlaced about their women than the Venetians. Angela

was summoned to a family conclave and told bluntly to stop associating with a notoriously loose-living and plebeian blackmailer. Thereafter she was 'not at home' to the visits of her 'Platonic' adorer. She returned his letters unopened. She cut him dead in a narrow street.

James Cleugh, *The Divine Aretino*, Blond, 1965, pp. 158, 159–61, 164, 166–7, 167–8, 171–2, 172, 173.

As an adulterer, Secretary to the Admiralty Samuel Pepys is particularly endearing, as he is willing to confess to his failures as well as brag of his successes. His use of cod Spanish to disguise his activities is fortunately transparent:

[1.8.1662] ... And so at the office all afternoon, till evening to my chamber; where, God forgive me, I was sorry to hear that Sir W Pens maid Betty was gone away yesterday, for I was in hopes to have had a bout with her before she had gone, she being very pretty. I have also a mind to my own wench, but I dare not, for fear she should prove honest and refuse and then tell my wife.

[18.7.1663] ... By and by Mrs. Lane comes ... She and I parted and met at the Crowne in the palace-yard, where we eat (a chicken I sent for) and drank and were mighty merry, and I had my full liberty of towsing her and doing what I would but the last thing of all; for I felt as much as I would and made her feel my thing also, and put the end of it to her breast and by and by to her very belly – of which I am heartily ashamed. But I do resolve never to do more so.

[23.7.1664] ... Walked toward Westminster; and being in an idle and wanton humour, walked through Fleet-alley, and there stood a most pretty wench at one of the doors. So I took a turn or two; but what by sense of honour and conscience, I would not go in. But much against my will, took coach and away to Westminster-hall, and there light of Mrs. Lane and plotted with her to go over the water; so met at Whites stairs in Channel-row, and over to the old house at Lambeth-marsh and there eat and drank and had my pleasure of her twice – she being the strangest woman in talk, of love to her husband sometimes, and sometimes again she doth not care for him – and yet willing enough to allow me a liberty of doing what I would with her. So spending 5 or 6s upon her, I could do what I would; and after an hour's stay or more, back again and set her ashore there again, and I forward to Fleetstreete and called at Fleet-alley, not knowing how to command myself; and went in and there saw what formerly I have been acquainted with, the wickedness of those houses and the forcing a man to present expense. The woman, endeed, is a most lovely woman; but I had no courage to meddle with her, for fear of her not being wholesome, and so counterfeited that I had not money enough. It was pretty to see how cunning that Jade was; would not suffer me to have to do in any manner with her after she saw I had no money; but told me then I would not come again, but she now was sure I would come again – though I hope in God I shall not, for though she be one of the prettiest women I ever saw, yet I fear her abusing me.

[6.5.1668] . . . Then I did see our Nell, Payne's daughter, and her yo did desear venga after migo, and so ella did seque me to Tower-hill to our back entry there that comes upon the degres entrant into nostra garden; and there, ponendo the key in the door, yo tocar sus mamelles con mi mano and su cosa with mi cosa et yo did dar-la a shilling; and so parted, and yo home to put up things against tomorrow's carrier for my wife.

Samuel Pepys, *Diary*.

The court of Charles II was devoted to the sensual pleasures, swiftly summarized as follows:

Mistress [of Charles II] followed mistress, and the guilt of a troop of profligate women was blazoned to the world by the gift of titles and estates. The royal bastards were set among English nobles.

The ducal house of Grafton springs from the King's adultery with
Barbara Palmer, whom he created Duchess of Cleveland. The
Dukes of St Albans owe their origin to his intrigue with Nell
Gwynn, a player and courtesan. Louise de Quérouaille, a mistress
sent by France to win him its interests, became Duchess of
Portsmouth and ancestress of the house of Richmond. An earlier
mistress, Lucy Walters, was mother of a boy he raised to the
Dukedom of Monmouth and to whom the Dukes of Buccleuch
trace their line.

J.R. Green, *A Short History of the English People*, 1874.

A far greater formality reigned at the French court, where taking a
royal mistress was not a matter of whim and lust alone.

When Louis [XIV] became king, the greatest ambition of all the
court beauties, married or unmarried, was to become his mistress.
'Many of them have told me,' wrote Visconti, the Italian ambas-
sador, 'that it was no offence to their husband, to their father, or
to God, to be loved by their king.' Relatives, including husbands,
were flattered by such a prospect and readily boasted about it
when it had become a fact.

As is well known, Louis's chief favourites were the blonde
Louise de la Vallière, modest, slightly lame, 'a little violet', as
Mme de Sévigné called her, who loved the king sincerely, her
scheming rival, Mme de Montespan, who unwittingly introduced
her own successor at court, and austere Mme de Maintenon, who
ultimately became the king's morganatic wife and filled Versailles
with repentant gloom.

La Vallière was frankly ashamed of her role. Twice she escaped
to a convent and each time the king brought her back – the first
time (from St-Cloud) after having threatened to have the convent
set on fire by his troops, and the second time from the Convent of
the Visitation at Chaillot, where he went to fetch her in person.
Seven years later, when the king had tired of her, and La

Montespan was in the ascendant, Louise obtained royal permission to retire to the Carmel, where she spent the next thirty-five years – the greatest part of her life. No less a preacher than Bossuet was in the pulpit on the day she received the veil and no less a person than the forgiving queen sat by her side during the ceremony.

The simultaneous reign of Louis's two mistresses shocked many of his contemporaries. 'The king lives with his favourites,' wrote Visconti, 'as in the midst of a legitimate family. The queen receives their visits and those of their natural children as if it were her bounden duty. When they hear Mass at St-Germain, they sit under the eyes of the king: Madame de Montespan with her children on the left, in front of everybody, and the other one [La Vallière] on the right. They pray devoutly, holding a rosary and a prayerbook in their hands, their eyes raised in ecstasy – like saints. In brief, this court is the greatest farce in the world.'

It was a costly farce. A duchy and lands were given to La Vallière, the châteaux and lands of Clagny and Glatigny to La Montespan, châteaux to Françoise Scarron (later Madame de Maintenon), nearly seventeen millions to the Princesse de Soubise, 200,000 crowns pension and a duchy to Mademoiselle de Fontanges – not to mention extravagant fêtes and masquerades which marked the advent of each new mistress.

Nina Epton, *Love and the French*, Cassell, 1959, pp. 130–31.

The Duc de Saint-Simon was a peer of France and courtier, and the indefatigable chronicler of the courts of Louis XIV and Louis XV. Here he describes the Duc d'Orléans, the nephew of Louis XIV, who was about to become Regent of France:

He was very young, full of health, vigour, the joys of freedom from the schoolroom, and the embarrassments of his marriage and his timidity. The ensuing boredom, a love-affair of the kind that so often proves fatal in early youth, blind admiration for people of fashion and the desire to emulate and surpass them, the allurements of passion, the young men whose pride and tool he had become, some of whom had persuaded him to live like them and with them, all served to accustom him to loose-living, and, worse still, to the scandal which it created, until the time came when he could no longer exist without it, and found relaxation only in the midst of noise, confusion, and excess.

That is what led him to commit such terrible, such shocking improprieties and, as though wishing to exceed the worst rakes, to mingle blasphemies with his ordinary conversation, and to engage deliberately in scandalous debauches on saints' days. Thus during the Regency, even, he several times indulged in amorous escapades by choice on Good Friday, and on other holy days too. The more persistently experienced, the more steeped in sin a man's reputation made him appear, the more M. le Duc d'Orléans respected him; I myself can bear witness to his blind admiration – his reverence almost – for the Grand Prieur, merely because he had not been to bed sober for the past forty years, and publicly and continuously kept mistresses, never ceasing to utter impious, nay, blasphemous remarks. It is scarcely to be wondered at that, having such principles, and acting in accordance with them, he was openly unfaithful, even boasting of it, and priding himself on being the most sophisticated, the cleverest of deceivers. He and Mme la Duchesse de Berry would sometimes argue to prove which of them took the palm in that line, and this kind of discussion would take place while she dressed, in the presence of Mme de Saint-Simon and those who entered before the general public, with M. le Duc de Berry, who was extremely proper, listening in horror and disgust, and Mme de Saint-Simon quite unable to quell them by turning their tone to jesting, or by indicating the door to show their lack of discretion. M. le Duc d'Orléans was incredibly indiscreet about himself in all that concerned his daily life.

Duc de Saint-Simon, *Memoirs*, Hamish Hamilton, 1968, Vol. II, p. 436 (translated by Lucy Norton).

James Boswell, best known for his adulatory biography of Samuel

Johnson, fancied himself as a womanizer, and was usually able to justify to himself every lapse from virtue:

[11 September 1764] I was quite drunk with brisk spirits, and about eight, in came a woman with a basket of chocolate to sell. I toyed with her and found she was with child. Oho! a safe piece. Into my closet. 'Habs er ein Man?' 'Ja, in den Gards bei Potsdam.' To bed directly. In a minute – over. I rose cool and astonished, half angry, half laughing. I sent her off. Bless me, have I now committed adultery? Stay, a soldier's wife is no wife. Should I now torment myself with speculations on sin, and on losing in one morning the merit of a year's chastity? No: this is womanish. Nay, your elegant mystics would not do so. Madame Guyon was of opinion that sin should be forgotten as soon as possible, as being an idea too gross for the mind of a saint, and disturbing the exercise of sweet devotion. Her notion is ingenious. I am sorry that this accident has happened, I know not how. Let it go. I'll think no more of it. Divine Being! Pardon the errors of a weak mortal. Give me more steadiness. Let me grow more perfect. What a curious thing is it to find a strict philosopher speculating on a recent fault! Well, I shall not be proud. I shall be a mild and humble Christian.

James Boswell, *Boswell on the Grand Tour: Germany and Switzerland*, Heinemann, 1953, pp. 88–9.

The following year Boswell swans into Turin:

Tuesday 8 January 1765 . . . We all went to a public ball at the Théâtre de Carignan. It was very handsome and gay. I danced a minuet with the Spanish Ambassadress. There was here many fine women. The counts and other pretty gentlemen told me whenever I admired a lady, 'Sir, you can have her. It would not be difficult.' I thought at first they were joking and waggishly amusing themselves with a stranger. But I at last discovered that they were really in earnest and that the manners here were so openly debauched that adultery was carried on without the least disguise. I asked them, 'But why then do you marry?' 'Oh, it's the custom; it perpetuates families.' . . .

Saturday 12 January . . . At night I sat a long time in the box of Mme. B., of whom I was now violently enamoured. I made my declarations, and was amazed to find such a proposal received with the most pleasing politeness. She however told me, 'It is impossible. I have a lover' (showing him), 'and I do not wish to deceive him.' Her lover was the Neapolitan Minister, Comte Pignatelli, in whose box she sat. He was a genteel, amiable man. He went away, and then I pursued my purpose. Never did I see such dissimulation, for she talked aloud that I should think no more of my passion, and the *piémontais* around us heard this and said without the least delicacy, 'A traveller expects to accomplish in ten days as much as another will do in a year.' I was quite gone. She then said to me, 'Whisper in my ear,' and told me, 'We must make arrangements,' assuring me that she had talked severely to persuade people that there was nothing between us. She bid me call upon her next day at three . . .

Sunday 13 January. By want of sleep and agitation of mind, I was quite feverish. At seven I received a letter from Mme. — telling me that people talked of us, and forbidding me to come to her or to think more of the 'plus malheureuse de femmes'. This tore my very heart . . .

Monday 14 January. Night before last I plainly proposed matters to Mme. St. Gilles. 'I am young, strong, vigorous. I offer my services as a duty, and I think that the Comtesse de St. Gilles will do very well to accept them.' 'But I am not that kind of woman.' 'Very well, Madame, I shall believe you.' I thought to take her *en passant*. But she was cunning and saw my passion for Mme. B —, so would not hazard with me.

In the autumn he is wooing elsewhere, and tries his epistolary charms on Porzia Sansedoni, the former mistress of his friend Lord Mountstuart and now married with three children:

6 September. Dear, dear Mme. Sansedoni, –

After a night of apprehension, of sorrow, of tears – during which I have not closed my eyes except to think of you, and to be troubled by ideas more keenly melancholy than those which occupy my mind on the day succeeding such a night – dear, dear object of my celestial love, you will permit me to unlock to you, a little more, my afflicted heart.

My situation is indeed *dolorosa*, as you well said. I suffer bitter torments by a cruel fatality. For you are not cruel. No. You are sorry to see me so unhappy. Other women would look on me with triumph. You, with regret. Oh, my dear friend, give a thought on my behalf . . .

. . . It is impossible for me to be wholly satisfied as long as I see that the woman who is the sole object of my desires is not wholly mine. So much I confess to you. But grant me the great proof I seek of your affection for me, and I shall retain all my life a grateful recollection, a sweet felicity mingled with a regret which, however, will be powerless to sadden me. It is not my wish to argue against your resolution of romantic fidelity; but I could desire that some angel should inspire you with another sentiment as romantic as that resolution. I should like to hear you say, 'I have kept for my Lord an inviolate fidelity: I have only bestowed my pity on his worthy friend, who was in the saddest situation and will bless me the rest of his days. In so acting I have done my Lord no offence. Rather, I have proved the real strength of my serious attachment to him in thus contradicting my own fancy to save his friend.'

My dear, dear friend, I am incapable of explaining my sentiments, but you can understand my way of thinking. Never have there been found circumstances more singular than ours. I ought to be content with your friendship, but I cannot be. I am in torment until I have that proof of your goodness towards me – and I swear to you that I desire it only as a proof.

I wish it were over. What a romantic idea! Yes, I could wish it were in the past; for it is not the ecstasy of a moment but the delicious memory of a whole lifetime that I so ardently desire . . .

Permit me to add one word more. To show you the delicacy of my ideas as to the proof which I desire from you, I should like to be with you late at night, and, in a modest darkness, to receive a tender pledge of your favour for an eternal friend. And, Madame, on the word of a man of honour I shall never ask another. There you have the true romantic. I swear by everything that is sacred that after that single proof, no friend will be more respectful than I, or more chaste. I shall regard you with the liveliest gratitude. I shall adore you as my beneficent goddess and you will have in me the noblest of friends.

I entreat you, dear, dear Madame, think seriously of this, for never again will you find yourself in such circumstances as these. Consider well the nature of my passion. Consider well the generosity of my ideas. Your act, which it fills me with transport to picture, will but interrupt for a moment your romantic fidelity to my Lord, to grant a sublime and eternal happiness to his worthy friend.

Adieu, most adorable of women. I am wholly yours,

J. BOSWELL

P.S. If you do not forbid it, I shall wait upon you a moment at five. You ought to see me like that, for a moment, every day.

P.P.S. Read this letter with care. It contains very, very romantic sentiments.

James Boswell, *Boswell on the Grand Tour: Italy, Corsica, and France*, Heinemann, pp. 25–6, 32–3, 33, 35, 131, 132, 133.

Not surprisingly, Boswell's bid to cuckold Lord Mountstuart, as well as Signora Sansedoni's husband, did not succeed.

One evening, after much hard drinking, Boswell, overwhelmed by a 'whoring rage', hits the streets:

31 March 1776: When I got into the street, the whoring rage came upon me. I thought I would devote a night to it. I was weary at the same time that I was tumultuous. I went to Charing Cross Bagnio with a wholesome-looking, bouncing wench, stripped, and went to bed with her. But after my desires were satiated by repeated indulgence, I could not rest; so I parted from her after she had honestly delivered to me my watch and ring and handkerchief, which I should not have missed I was so drunk. I took a hackney-coach and was set down in Berkeley Square, and went home cold and disturbed and dreary and vexed, with remorse rising like a black cloud without any distinct form; for in truth my moral principle as to chastity was absolutely eclipsed for a time. I was in the miserable state of those whom the Apostle represents as working all uncleanness with greediness. I thought of my valuable spouse with the highest regard and warmest affection, but had a confused notion that my corporeal connexion with whores did not interfere with my love for her. Yet I considered that I might injure my health, which there could be no doubt was an injury to her. That is an exact state of my mind at the time. It shocks me to review it.

1 April 1776: . . . I went to Duck Lane, Westminster, and found my last night's harlot by the name of Nanny Cooms, and persuaded myself that she was not infected . . .

28 November 1776: . . . The girl with whom I was last night had told me she lodged in Stevenlaw's Close, and at my desire engaged to be at the head of it generally at eight in the evening, in case I should be coming past. I thought I could not be in more danger of disease by one more enjoyment the very next evening, so went tonight; but she was not there. Had a consultation at home between eight and nine . . . I was shocked that the father of a family should go amongst strumpets; but there was rather an insensibility about me to virtue, I was so sensual . . .

1 December 1776: . . . About eight I got into the street and made Cameron, the chairman, inquire for Peggy Grant at a house in Stevenlaw's Close where she had told me she lived. He brought

her out, and I took her to the New Town, and in a mason's shed in St Andrew's Square lay with her twice. I grew pretty sober by the time I got home, but was in a confused, feverish frame. My dear wife asked me if I had not been about mischief. I at once confessed it. She was very uneasy, and I was ashamed and vexed at my licentiousness. Yet my conscience was not alarmed; so much had I accustomed my mind to think such indulgence permitted . . .

5 February 1777: . . . At night was in a certain degree of intoxication; made Cameron, the chairman, send Peggie Dundas to me to the Castle Hill, where I lay with her without fear because I had been once safe; and such was my state of mind that at the time I felt no check of conscience but enjoyed her with appetite. No sooner was I at home than I was sadly vexed at what I had done, and my dearest wife saw from my countenance what had happened. I at once confessed. She was more seriously affected than I ever saw her . . .

7 April 1777: . . . My wonderful spirits continued. Betty Montgomerie, Lord Eglinton's natural daughter, young Donaldson the printer, and Matthew Dickie dined. My fancy was pleased with Miss Montgomerie having noble blood in her veins. She was not sixteen, and was fresh, plump, and comely. Before dinner she allowed me luscious liberties with kindly frankness. I repeated them so often in my eagerness that my wife saw me and was offended. She agreed to meet me some evening in the Meadow. I at present had free notions as to plurality of women, though without a fixed plan. I drank rather too much after dinner. In the evening I met an old dallying companion, now married. She willingly followed me to a field behind the Register Office. She seemed to wish to have me to press her to let me enjoy her fully, for she was big with child. But I thought it wrong, so only indulged a lesser lascivious sport; struck, however, with the insensibility to the moral doctrines of their country which some women have.

James Boswell, *The Ominous Years 1774–1776*, Heinemann, 1963, pp. 306–7; *Boswell in Extremes*, Heinemann, 1971, pp. 62–3, 84, 107.

Irregularities of conduct were not restricted to the male sex in eighteenth-century Britain:

The notorious Miss Chudleigh began by fascinating the Earl of Bath and nearly married the Duke of Hamilton. She became a maid-of-honour, clandestinely wedded the future Earl of Bristol, had a son by him in secret, went to a ball in a gauze dress, and caught the eye of George II. He overcame his meanness to the extent of presenting her with a watch which cost him thirty-five guineas, 'out of his own privy purse and not charged on the civil list'. She also made a conquest of Frederick II, who admired her ability to swallow two bottles of wine. 'When reproached by her royal mistress,' said Wraxall, 'for the irregularities of her conduct, "Votre Altesse Royale sait," replied she, "que chacun a son But."' (The Altesse Royale was believed to be the mistress of Lord Bute.) Fearing that the Earl of Bristol might die before the marriage could be acknowledged, and that she might lose her secret title, she had taken pains to have the marriage entered by underhand means in the church register. Now, however, she became the whore of the Duke of Kingston, and saw her chance to become a duchess. Complicated *tracasseries* ended in her marriage to the Duke, while the Earl was still alive. When the Duke died, he left her his immense fortune, and she went off to Italy, to vamp Pope Clement XIV. Unfortunately, the story of her bigamous marriage had got about, and it was in the interest of the Duke's other heirs to prove that she was really the Countess of Bristol. It became necessary for her to tamper with the marriage register once again, this time in order to destroy it. The coil was too difficult. She was brought to trial before the House of Lords, found guilty, and barely escaped from being branded in the hand. The Countess–Duchess was now demoted to a countess, but for some reason she was left in possession of the fortune. The Earl of Bristol was unable to divorce her, because there was evidence of his collusion in the bigamy. She retired to Russia, where she got on well with her sister in frailty, Catherine the Great, and thence to France, where she purchased a royal palace for £50,000. She died at sixty-eight, in 1788, after other love affairs, and after receiving an offer of marriage from Prince Radzivil. Her picture as she appeared in the gauze dress still survives, wearing a ravishing smirk. It is a single garment, quite transparent, and probably explains her career. Throughout her life, she had enjoyed two or more of everything that was obtainable, counting the husbands and the bottles of wine. When a two-headed calf was born in Essex, Horace Walpole suggested that it must be hers. Sir Robert Keith said that he would be willing to marry her, if a grenadier might be joined with him in the nuptials.

T.H. White, *The Age of Scandal*, Cape, 1950, pp. 163–4.

The late eighteenth century also saw a revival of the Elizabethan fashion for bastardy:

In 1780 the Earl of Pembroke commented that '*nos dames, douces comme des agneaux, se laissent monter par tout le monde*'. Mrs Armstead, the mistress and later the wife of Charles James Fox, had previously been the well-established mistress successively of Lord George Cavendish, Lord Derby and Lord Cholmondeley. The children of the Countess of Oxford were known as 'the Harleian Miscellany', and in the 1790s there were brought up at Devonshire House and Chatsworth a whole collection of oddly assorted children: three were the children of the fifth Duke of Devonshire and his Duchess, Georgiana; and two were of the Duke and Lady Elizabeth Foster, the Duchess' most intimate friend and life-long companion; while one child of the Duke and Charlotte Spencer and one of the Duchess and Lord Grey were brought up elsewhere . . .

The tenth Earl of Pembroke had children by two mistresses, and his bastard son, who had a successful naval career, was on the best of terms with the legitimate son and heir, Lord Herbert, and also with the Countess. The latter's sole request, which was respected, was that the illegitimate children should not take the family name of Herbert. She also objected when her husband hung prints of his current mistress, the actress La Bacelli, in his bedroom in Wilton House, a protest the Earl rejected, declaring that it could not be taken as an open affront 'between two people who professedly never wish to cohabit together.' In 1812 'the Duke of Manchester was repairing his fortunes abroad as governor of Jamaica; the Duchess had left home years before with one of her footmen.'

Lawrence Stone, *Family, Sex and Marriage*, Weidenfeld & Nicolson, 1977, pp. 533, 533–4.

Emma Hamilton was married to the easygoing antiquarian and diplomat Sir William Hamilton, who was thirty-five years her senior. She met Nelson in 1793 but they did not become lovers until some years later. By 1801 Nelson had become estranged from his wife Fanny, but Emma's marriage accommodated the infidelity and birth of the child Nelson had fathered. Much of their correspondence was destroyed to protect their reputations, but an outpouring from the admiral in March 1801, shortly before sailing with the fleet, has survived:

Now, my own dear wife, for such you are in my eyes and in the face of heaven, I can give full scope to my feelings, for I dare say Oliver will faithfully deliver this letter. You know, my dearest Emma, that there is nothing in this world that I would not do for us to live together, and to have our dear little Child with us. I firmly believe that this Campaign will give us peace, and then we will sett off for Bronte. In twelve hours we shall be across the water and freed from all the nonsense of his friends, or rather pretended ones. Nothing but an event happening to him could prevent my going, and I am sure you will think so, for unless all matters accord it would bring 100 of tongues and slanderous reports if I separated from her (which I would do with pleasure the moment we can be united, I want to see her no more) therefore we must manage till we can quit this country or your uncle dies. I love, I never did love anyone else. I never had a dear pledge of love till you gave me one, and you, thank my God, never gave one to any body else. I think before March is out you will either see us back, or so victorious that we shall insure a glorious issue to our toils. Think what my Emma will feel at seeing return safe, perhaps with a little more fame, her own dear loving Nelson. Never, if I can help it, will I dine out of my Ship, or go on shore except duty calls me. Let Sir Hyde have any glory he can catch – I envy him not. You, my beloved Emma, and my country, are the two dearest objects of my fond heart – *a heart susceptible and true*. Only place confidence in me and you never shall be disappointed. I burn all your dear letters, because it is right for your sake, and I wish you would burn all mine – they can do no good, and will do us both harm if any seizure of them, or the dropping even one of them, would fill the mouth of the world sooner than we intend. My longing for you, both person and conversation, you may readily imagine. What must be my sensations at the idea of sleeping with you, it setts me on fire, even the thought, much more would the reality. I am sure my love and desires are all to you, and if any woman naked were to come to me, even as I am this moment from thinking of you, I hope it might rot off if I would touch her even with my hand. No, my heart, person, and mind is in perfect union of love towards my own dear beloved Emma – the *real bosom* friend of her, all hers, all Emma's . . .

My love, my darling angel, my heaven-given wife, the dearest only true wife of her own till death.

Jack Russell, *Nelson and the Hamiltons*, Blond, 1969, p. 180.

Byron had a weakness for tempestuous women, but he bit off more than he could chew when he succumbed to the charms of Lady Caroline Lamb. In the summer of 1812 he wrote to her just before jilting her:

If tears, which you saw & know I am not apt to shed, if the agitation in which I parted from you, agitation which you must have perceived through the *whole* of this most nervous *nervous* affair, did not commence till the moment of leaving you approached, if all that I have said & done, & am still but too ready to say & do, have not sufficiently proved what my real feelings are & must be ever towards you, my love, I have no other proof to offer; God knows I wish you happy, & when I quit you, or rather when you from a sense of duty to your husband & mother quit me, you shall acknowledge the truth of what I again promise & vow, that no other in word or deed shall ever hold the place in my affection which is & shall be most sacred to you, till I am nothing. I never knew till *that moment*, the *madness* of – my dearest & most beloved friend – I cannot express myself – this is no time for words – but I shall have a pride, a melancholy pleasure, in suffering what you yourself can hardly conceive – for you do not know me. – I am now about to go out with a heavy heart, because – my appearing this Evening will stop any absurd story which the events of today might give rise to – do you think *now* that I am *cold* & *stern*, & *artful* – will even *others* think so, will your *mother* even – that mother to whom we must indeed sacrifice much, much more on my part, than she shall ever know or can imagine . . .

These taunts which have driven you to this – my dearest Caroline – were it not for your mother & the kindness of all your connections, is there anything on earth or heaven would have made me so happy as to have made you mine long ago? & not less *now* than *then*, but *more* than ever at this time – you know I would with pleasure give up all here & all beyond the grave for you – & in refraining from this – must my motives be misunderstood –? I care not who knows this – what use is made of it – it is to *you* & to *you* only that they owe yourself, I was and am *yours*, freely & most entirely, to obey, to honour, love – & fly with you when, where & how you yourself *might* & *may* determine.

In late August she left for Ireland with her husband and mother. Byron wrote to her aunt Lady Melbourne on 10 September . . .

... You will not regret to hear that I wish this to end, & it certainly shall not be renewed on my part. – It is not that I love another, but loving at all is quite out of my way; I am tired of being a fool, & when I look back on the waste of time, & the destruction of all my plans last winter by this last romance, I am – what I ought to have been long ago.

Lord Byron, *Letters & Journals*, Murray, 1973, Vol. 2, pp. 185–6, 192–3.

Byron wrote to Douglas Kinnaird from Venice on 27 November 1816 about his new affair with Marianna Segati:

I have fallen in love – and with a very pretty woman – so much so – as to obtain the approbation of the not easily approving H[obhouse] – who is in general rather tardy in his applause of the fairer part of the creation. – She is married – so our arrangement was formed according to the incontinent continental system – which need not be described to you an experienced voyager – and gifted withal with a modest self-confidence – which my bashful nature is not endowed with – but nonetheless I have got the woman – I do not very well know how – but we do exceedingly well together. – She is not two and twenty – with great black Eastern eyes – and a variety of subsidiary charms &c. &c. and amongst her other accomplishments – is a mighty & admirable singer – as most of the Italians are – (though not a public one) – luckily I can speak the language fluently – & luckily (if I did not) we could employ ourselves a little without talking. – I meant to have given up gallivanting altogether – on leaving your country – where I had been totally sickened of that & every thing else – but I know not how it is – my health growing better – & my spirits not worse – the 'besoin d'aimer' came back upon my heart again – after all there is nothing like it. – So much for that matter ...

On 19 December he writes about her to Augusta Leigh:

... A lady with only *one lover* is not reckoned to have overstepped the modesty of marriage – that being a regular thing; – some have two – three – and so on to twenty beyond which they don't account – but they generally begin by one. – The husbands of course belong to any body's wives – but their own. – My present beloved – is aged two & twenty – with remarkably fine black eyes – and very regular & pretty features ... she is married (of course) & has one child – a girl. – Her temper very good – (as you know it had need to be) and lively – she is a Venetian by birth – & was never further from Venice than Milan in her days – her lord is about five years older than me – an exceeding good kind of a man. – That amatory appendage called by us a lover – is here denominated variously – sometimes an 'Amoroso' (which is the same thing) and sometimes a Cavaliero servente – which I need not tell you – is a serving Cavalier. – I told my fair one – at setting out – that as to the love and the Cavaliership – I was quite of accord – *but as to the servitude* – it would not suit me at all – so I begged to hear no more about it. – You may easily suppose I should not at all shine in the ceremonious department – so little so – that instead of handling the Lady as in duty bound into the Gondola – I as nearly as possible conveyed her into the Canal ...

Lord Byron, *Letters & Journals*, Murray, 1976, Vol. 5, pp. 134–5, 145.

His most famous Venetian pick-up was Margarita Cogni, the baker's wife:

Since you desire the story of Margarita Cogni [la Fornarina] – you shall be told it – though it may be lengthy ... In the summer of 1817, Hobhouse and myself were sauntering on horseback along the Brenta one evening – when amongst a group of peasants we remarked two girls as the prettiest we had seen for some time ... A few evenings after – we met with these two girls again ... and made an appointment with them for the next evening ...

[Margarita] said that she had no objection to make love with me
– as she was married – and all married women did it – but that her
husband (a baker) was somewhat ferocious – and would do her a
mischief. – In short – in a few evenings we arranged our affairs –
and for two years – in the course of which I had more women than
I can count or recount – she was the only one who preserved over
me an ascendancy – which was often disputed & never impaired. –
As she herself used to say publicly – 'It don't matter – he may
have five hundred – but he will always come back to me'. – The
reasons of this were firstly – her person – very dark – tall – the
Venetian face – very fine black eyes – and certain other qualities
which need not be mentioned. – She was two & twenty years old
– and never having had children – had not spoilt her figure – nor
anything else – which is I assure you – a great desideration in a hot
climate where they grow relaxed and doughy and *flumpity* in a
short time after breeding . . . Besides she could neither read nor
write – and could not plague me with letters . . .

She was somewhat fierce and 'prepotente' that is – overbearing
– and used to walk in whenever it suited her – with no very great
regard to time, place, nor persons – and if she found any women
in her way she knocked them down. – When I first knew her I was
in 'relazione' (liaison) with la Signora Segati – who was silly
enough one evening at Dolo – accompanied by some of her female
friends – to threaten her – for the Gossips of the Villeggiatura –
had already found out by the neighing of my horse one evening –
that I used to 'ride late in the night' to meet the Fornarina. –
Margarita threw back her veil (fazziolo) and replied in very explicit
Venetian – '*You* are *not* his *wife*: I am *not* his *wife* – *you* are his
Donna – and I am his *donna* – *your* husband is a cuckold – and mine
is another; – for the rest, what *right* have you to reproach me? – if
he prefers what is mine – to what is yours – is it my fault? if you
wish to secure him – tie him to your petticoat-string – but do not
think to speak to me without a reply because you happen to be
richer than I am.' . . .

At last she quarrelled with her husband – and one evening ran

away to my house. – I told her this would not do – she said she
would lie in the street but not go back to him – that he beat her
(the gentle tigress), spent her money – and scandalously neglected
his Oven. As it was Midnight – I let her stay – and next day there
was no moving her at all. – Her husband came roaring & crying –
entreating her to come back, *not* She! – He then applied to the
Police – and they applied to me – I told them and her husband to
take her – I did not want her – she had come and I could not fling
her out of the window – but they might conduct her through that
or the door if they chose it – She went before the Commissary –
but was obliged to return with that 'becco Ettico' (consumptive
cuckold), as she called the *poor* man who had a Ptisick. – In a few
days she ran away again. – After a precious piece of work she fixed
herself in my house – really & truly without my consent – but
owing to my indolence – and not being able to keep my
countenance – for if I began in a rage she always finished by
making me laugh with some Venetian pantaloonery or other – and
the Gipsy knew this well enough – as well as her other powers of
persuasion – and exerted them with the usual tact and success of
all She-things – high and low . . .

But her reign drew near a close. – She became quite ungovern-
able some months after – and a concurrence of complaints some
true and many false – 'a favourite has no friend' – determined me
to part with her. – I told her quietly that she must return home –
(she had acquired a sufficient provision for herself and mother,
&c. in my service,) and She refused to quit the house. – I was firm
– and she went – threatening knives and revenge. – I told her –
that I had seen knives drawn before her time – and that if she
chose to begin – there was a knife – and fork also at her service on
the table and that intimidation would not do. – The next day while
I was at dinner – she walked in, (having broke open a glass door
that led from the hall below to the staircase by way of prologue)
and advancing strait up to the table snatched the knife from my
hand – cutting me slightly in the thumb in the operation. –
Whether she meant to use this against herself or me I know not –

probably against neither − but Fletcher seized her by the arms − and disarmed her. − I then called my boatmen − and desired them to get the Gondola ready and conduct her to her own house again − seeing carefully that she did herself no mischief by the way. − She seemed quite quiet and walked down stairs. − I resumed my dinner. − We heard a great noise − I went out − and met them on the staircase − carrying her up stairs. − She had thrown herself into the Canal. − That she intended to destroy herself I do not believe − but when we consider the fear women and men who can't swim have of deep or even of shallow water − (and the Venetians in particular though they live on the waves) and that it was also night − and dark − & very cold − it shows that she had a devilish spirit of some sort within her . . .

I had her sent home quietly after her recovery − and never saw her since except twice at the opera − at a distance amongst the audience. − She made many attempts to return − but no more violent ones. − And this is the story of Margarita Cogni − as far as it belongs to me.

Lord Byron, *Letters & Journals*, Murray, 1976, Vol. 6, pp. 192–7 (letter to John Murray, 1.8.1819).

Byron, separated from his wife, embarked on a passionate and protracted affair with the married Countess Teresa Guiccioli, as he wrote to Douglas Kinnaird from Venice on 24 April 1819:

I have fallen in love within the last month with a Romagnuola Countess from Ravenna − the Spouse of a year of Count Guiccioli − who is sixty − the Girl twenty − he has eighty thousand ducats of rent − and has had two wives before − but he is Sixty − he is the first of Ravenna Nobles − but he is sixty − She is fair as Sunrise − and warm as Noon − we had but ten days − to manage all our little matters in beginning middle and end. & we managed them; − and I have done my duty − with the proper consummation . . . They have gone back to Ravenna − some time − but they return in the Winter.

On 16 November Byron wrote to Kinnaird about Teresa's quarrel with her husband:

The Cavalier-Conte Guiccioli came to Venice – where he found his wife considerably improved in health, but hating him so cordially – that they quarrelled *violently*. – He had said nothing before – but at last on finding this to be the case – he gave her the alternative – *him* – or *me* – she decided instantly for *me* – not being allowed to have both – and the lover generally having the preference. – But he had also given her a paper of rules to which he wished her to assent – all of them – establishing *his* authority. – Her friends and relatives of Ravenna were in the meantime in despair – as an *elopement* in Italy is the devil – worse even than with *us* . . . What could I do? – on one hand to sacrifice a woman whom I loved for life – leaving her destitute and divided from all ties in case of my death – on the other hand to give up an 'amicizia' which had been my pleasure my pride and my passion.

The tug between husband and lover continued, as Byron explained to Thomas Moore on 2 January 1820:

I had a sad scene since you went. Count Gu[iccioli] came for his wife . . . There was a great scene, for she would not, at first, go back with him – at least [last?] she *did* go back with him; but he insisted, reasonably enough, that all communication should be broken off between her and me. So, finding Italy very dull, and having a fever tertian, I packed up my valise, and prepared to cross the Alps; but my daughter fell ill, and detained me.

After her arrival at Ravenna, the Guiccioli fell ill again too; and, at last, her father (who had, all along, opposed the liaison most violently till now) wrote to me to say that she was in such a state that *he* begged me to come and see her, – and that her husband had acquiesced, in consequence of her relapse, and that *he* (her father) would guarantee all this, and that there would be no further scenes in consequence between them, and that I should not be compromised in any way. I set out soon after, and have been here ever since.

In May 1820 (?) Byron is perplexed by the Count's behaviour, as he writes to Teresa [translated from Italian]:

He has known – or ought to have known, all these things for many months – there is a mystery here that I do not understand, and prefer not to understand. Is it only now that he knows of your infidelity? What can he have thought – that we are made of stone – or that I am *more* or *less* than a man? I know of one remedy only – what I have already suggested, *my departure. It would be a great sacrifice*, but rather than run into things like this every day it becomes necessary – almost a duty – for me not to remain any longer in these parts.

He says that it is impossible for him to tolerate this relationship any longer – I answer that he *never* should have tolerated it. Assuredly it is not the happiest condition, even for me, to be exposed to his scenes, which come too late, now. But I shall do what a gentleman should do, that is, not cause disturbance in a family . . .

In these circumstances we shall not see each other tonight. Always and *all yours!*

Byron reports to Thomas Moore on 24 May 1820:

There will probably be a separation between them, as her family, which is a principal one, by its connections, are very much against *him,* for the whole of his conduct; – and he is old and obstinate, and she is young and a woman, determined to sacrifice every thing to her affections. I have given her the best advice, viz. to stay with him, – pointing out the state of a separated woman, (for the priests won't let lovers live openly together, unless the husband sanctions it,) and making the most exquisite moral reflections, – but to no purpose. She says, 'I will stay with him, if he will let you remain with me. It is hard that I should be the only woman in Romagna who is not to have her *Amico*; but, if not, I will not live with him; and as for the consequences, love, &c. &c. &c.' – you know how females reason on such occasions.

He says he has let it go on, till he can do so no longer. But he wants her to stay, and dismiss me; for he doesn't like to pay back her dowry and to make an alimony. Her relations are rather for the separation, as they detest him, – indeed, so does every body. The populace and the women are, as usual, all for those who are in the wrong, viz. the lady and her lover . . .

He continues his account in another letter to Thomas Moore on 1 June:

The separation business still continues, and all the world are implicated, including priests and cardinals. The public opinion is furious against *him*, because he ought to have cut the matter short *at first*, and not waited twelve months to begin. He has been trying at evidence, but can get none *sufficient*; for what would make fifty divorces in England won't do here – there must be the *most decided* proofs.

It is the first cause of the kind attempted in Ravenna for these two hundred years; for, though they often separate, they assign a different motive . . .

On 6 July the Pope granted Teresa her separation from Guiccioli. On 13 July Byron wrote to Moore:

She returns to her father's house, and I can only see her under great restrictions – such is the custom of the country. The relations behave very well: – I offered any settlement, but they refused to accept it, and swear she *shan't* live with G. (as he has tried to prove her faithless), but that he shall maintain her; and, in fact, a judgment to this effect came yesterday. I am, of course, in an awkward situation enough.

On 5 October 1821 Byron wrote to his sister Augusta Leigh:

It is nearly three years that this 'liaison' has lasted – I was dreadfully in love – and she blindly so – for she has sacrificed every thing to this headlong passion. – That comes of being romantic – I can say that without being so *furiously* in love as at first – I am more attached to her – than I thought it possible to be to any woman after three years ... If Lady B[yron] would but please to die – and the Countess G's husband – (for Catholics can't marry though divorced) we should probably have to marry – though I would rather *not* – thinking it the way to hate each other.

Lord Byron, *Letters & Journals*, Murray, 1976, Vol. 6, pp. 114–15, 241; 1977, Vol. 7, pp. 17–18, 43–4, 89–90, 105, 112, 126–7; 1978, Vol. 8, p. 234.

George IV, when still Prince Regent, tried to rid himself of his free-wheeling wife Caroline of Brunswick, who soon after their marriage effectively separated herself from her husband. Commissioners were dispatched to gather evidence that could be used to secure a divorce:

One of the earliest witnesses to be examined was Giuseppe Sacchi, a former cavalry captain, for nine months courier to the Princess and for three subsequent months her equerry, who had entered her service at the Villa d'Este in November 1816 and had left it at Pesaro at the end of November 1817. He was later to swear that he had often seen the Princess and Pergami walking about arm in arm and kissing each other, and that the balls which were given at Pergami's villa near Milan – and of which several other witnesses were to speak in similar terms – were 'quite brothels', attended by women of 'very low condition'. Male servants in the Princess's employment would frequently leave the ballroom with these women 'according to their pleasure and will'; and the Princess once jokingly chided Sacchi, 'I know, you rogue, that you have gone to bed with three of them and how many times you have had intercourse with them.' Pergami, 'who was present, began to laugh and to cry aloud, "It is true! It is true! It is true!"'

Sacchi went on to depose that he had seen Pergami more than once enter the Princess's room late at night and that he had heard her call him, 'mon ange', 'mon amour', 'mon coeur'. They travelled by night in the same carriage where 'two or three times' Sacchi found them in the morning 'both asleep and having their respective hands upon one another. Her Royal Highness had her hand upon a particular part of Mr Pergami and Pergami had his own upon that of Her Royal Highness . . . Once Pergami had his breeches loosened and the Princess's hand was upon that part.'

References to the festivities at Pergami's villa near Milan and at the Villa d'Este were also made by numerous other witnesses including Teodoro Majocchi who had entered the Princess's service in December 1817 after having been first postilion to General Pino. Majocchi described in particular the obscene dances performed for the Princess on these occasions by one of her servants, a mulatto from Jaffa named Mahomet. Like Sacchi, Majocchi had seen Pergami enter the Princess's bedroom, and he described how intimate they were; how he held her round the waist when lifting her onto her ass and held her hand while she was riding it; how, when they travelled together, they shared the same carriage in which Pergami kept a bottle 'to make water in'; how they took great care to have rooms as close as possible to each other in all the inns where they stopped for the night, and alternately wore the same blue silk bedgown.

Majocchi, who had accompanied the Princess on her pilgrimage to Jerusalem, gave an account of the sleeping and bathing arrangements on board the polacca which were later to become a subject of heated discussion at dining-tables all over Europe, and were to give rise in London to the much quoted verse about Pergami:

> The Grand Master of St Caroline
> has found promotion's path.

He is made both Night Companion
and Commander of the Bath.

According to Majocchi, the Princess found it so hot on the
polacca that she had a tent fitted up for her on deck, and in this
tent she used to sleep with Pergami. She also had him in her cabin
when she was having a bath for which Majocchi was in the habit
of supplying the water; 'then the door was shut, and Pergami and
the Princess remained alone in the cabin.'

Vincenzo Gargiullo, the captain of the polacca, confirmed that
the Princess and Pergami had slept together under the tent and
that he was present when she had her bath. Indeed, he accompanied
her 'for anything she did, for any other thing she did', even when
she went below to go to the water-closet . . . Both he and his mate,
Gaetano Paturzo, had seen Pergami sitting on a gun on deck,
kissing the Princess who sat on his knee.

Other members of the crew and the Princess's entourage claimed
to have been witnesses of these and worse improprieties; but the
most damning evidence of blatant intimacy came from Louisa
Demont, the Princess's smartly dressed, sly-looking *femme de
chambre* who was also aboard the polacca.

Mlle Demont testified that Pergami was usually present when
the Princess was at her toilet, when she was almost entirely
undressed with her breasts quite bare, and that he would often go
into her room at night scantily clothed, once presenting himself in
nothing but his shirt and slippers. Sometimes in the night Mlle
Demont would hear the Princess's door open and close; and, in the
morning, when she went into her mistress's room to make the bed,
she would find that it had not been slept in. The Princess had
herself painted as a penitent Magdalen with her hair disordered,
her eyes heavenward, naked to the waist. She gave the finished
portrait to Pergami.

So the evidence accumulated and was elaborated . . . Month by
month, as the piles of depositions mounted, the three commissioners felt increasingly confident not only of the Princess's guilt but

of their being able to offer enough unshakable evidence for it to be proved in an English court of law. The Regent could not have felt other than satisfied by the results of their unpleasant work.

Christopher Hibbert, *George IV*, Allen Lane, 1973, pp. 138–40.

Celebrated Infidelities II:
Lord Melbourne to Cecil Parkinson

Ye have heard that it was said by them of old time, Thou shalt not commit adultery. But I say unto you, That whosoever looketh on a woman to lust after her hath committed adultery with her already in his heart.

Matthew 5:27–8

Before succeeding his father as Viscount Melbourne, William Lamb embarked on the first of a number of liaisons with women other than his wife Caroline. In 1827, dispatched to Ireland as Chief Secretary, he met Elizabeth Branden, who was married to an older clergyman who was about to succeed his cousin as Lord Branden:

Branden seems never to have taken his pastoral duties with noticeable seriousness and, after succeeding to the title, abandoned them altogether. Within ten years of his marriage [in 1815] he was crippled by debts and gout, to the first of which disabilities his wife had undoubtedly contributed and which together rendered him unfit to meet her financial and sexual expectations. Though they were never formally separated he passed most of the year taking the waters in Buxton or sunning himself in the south of France, while she led the life of a merry widow in the house in Fitz-William Square which her family had bought her . . . She was without doubt beautiful and educated above the usual level of women of that age. She was intelligent, perceptive and shrewd, and her vivacity served as an acceptable substitute for wit. She had spontaneous gaiety and the gift of communicating it to others; many people in Dublin had better cooks, more numerous servants, grander houses, but no one had created a salon in which it was more agreeable to pass an hour or two.

So much for her virtues. She was also kind and generous on issues which mattered little to her and thereby enjoyed a reputation for amiability which her husband at least would have argued was scarcely deserved. She was, in truth, selfish and egocentric, exigent in matters material and still more emotional, but she was skilled at concealing these weaknesses. Her minimum demand was that she should be the centre of attention, to those who claimed to love her she must be the unique source of light and life. To find pleasure outside her society was treason.

... Within a few weeks of their first meeting [Lamb] was visiting her house every evening, often arriving as late as 11 p.m. He went with her regularly to balls and theatres and those who wished to ingratiate themselves with the Chief Secretary knew that it was wise to invite him to the same parties as Lady Branden. The couple behaved with striking indiscretion, and in her case at least probably got as much pleasure from the excitement which the liaison caused as from the relationship itself. Whether they actually made love is a problem to which there can be no final answer. It was taken for granted by all their friends and acquaintances that they did, yet Lamb, in a letter most emphatically not intended for the public eye, urged her to 'assist and maintain that innocence of which you are conscious' and on other occasions referred to his regret at missed opportunities during their time together . . .

Lamb began to reveal a curious obsession with beating and 'discipline', particularly involving girls or women. The subject arose innocently enough when he urged Lady Branden, half-jokingly, to have greater resort to flogging in dealing with her children. Then he suggested the same treatment for an idle maid, wishing he could order the application of the birch 'upon that large and extensive field of *derrière*, which is so well calculated to receive it'. From that they were soon exchanging anecdotes in which beating was in one way or another involved . . .

In May 1828 Lord Branden brought an action against Lamb, alleging the seduction of his wife. He seems to have laid his hands on some correspondence between the two which he felt conclusively proved their guilt . . . Whether or not he could have proved such allegations it seems Lord Branden had assembled a regiment of witnesses who would show the couple to have been, if not adulterous, at least guilty of the grossest indiscretion. The time came and nothing of the sort occurred; the plaintiff's case was so ludicrously weak that Lord Tenterden dismissed it without even hearing counsel for the defence. Officially, at least, Lamb's honour had been vindicated.

Philip Ziegler, *Melbourne*, Collins, 1976, pp. 101, 102, 106, 108.

Balzac writes to his sister on 12 October 1833 describing the beginning of his affair with Mme Hanska, who would be his mistress for years:

There I found everything calculated to flatter the thousand vanities to which this animal called man is prone, in particular the species called poet, who is most vulnerable of all. But what am I talking about? Vanity! No, it's nothing to do with that. I'm happy, extremely happy in thought and honour. Alas, a cursed husband hasn't left our side for a single second in five days. He scampered between her skirt and my waistcoat. Neuchâtel is a small town where a woman, a distinguished visitor, can't take a single step without being observed. To me it was like being in a furnace. Such constraints don't suit me at all.

The main point is that we are 27 years old, that we are beautiful, with the loveliest black hair ever seen, with silky skin that's deliciously brown, that we have exquisite small hands, a naive heart of 27 years, a real Madame de Lignolle, imprudent enough to be tempted to throw herself on my neck in full view of the world.

That's not even to mention her tremendous wealth. What is that compared to a masterpiece of beauty, someone comparable to the Princess Bellejoyeuse, but infinitely lovelier? A glancing eye, which when met, acquires a voluptuous splendour. In short, I'm intoxicated with love . . .

My God, this Val de Travers is beautiful, and the lake at Bienne quite ravishing. It's there, let yourself imagine, that we dispatched the husband to order lunch. But we remained visible, and so, beneath the shade of a great oak, we exchanged the first furtive kiss of love. Moreover, as the husband is approaching his sixties, I swore to wait, and she promised to reserve for me her hand, her heart.

Wasn't it nice to have uprooted this husband, who resembles a tower, from the Ukraine, and to drag him 600 leagues to place him in front of a lover who had only travelled 150, the monster? . . .

Honoré de Balzac, *Lettres à sa Famille*, Albin Michel (Paris), 1950 (translated by Stephen Brook).

Those assiduous diarists the Goncourt brothers note on 20 July 1868 the habits of Napoleon's brother, King Jerome of Westphalia, father of their friend Princess Mathilde Bonaparte:

The Princess spoke to us today about her father's sensual temperament, his constant need of women. She painted a strange picture of his life at home with his fanatically jealous wife, having leeches applied in her presence by a woman who had formerly been his mistress, and his feet rubbed by another woman who was still his mistress, at the same time taking an interest in a little maid who used to give him assignations in the latrines, while all the while he was living as man and wife with his lawful spouse.

Edmond and Jules Goncourt, *Pages from the Goncourt Journals*, OUP, 1962, p. 139 (translated by Robert Baldick).

At the age of thirty, Victor Hugo, increasingly estranged from his wife

Adèle, begins an affair with the beautiful young actress and courtesan Juliette Drouet. Eight years later he recalled their first night together:

Do you remember it, my best beloved? Our first night was a night of carnival, Shrove Tuesday, 1833. There was, in some theatre or other, I can't remember which, something in the nature of a ball (I can't remember what) at which we were both of us expected. (I break off for a moment to kiss your lovely mouth. Ah! now I can go on.) Nothing, I am sure, not even death, will ever wipe that memory away. In my mind I still go over all the hours of that night, one by one. They are like stars moving before the eyes of my heart. Yes, you were due to go to that ball: but you didn't go, you waited for me! Poor angel! What beauty and what love you lavished on me. Your little room was filled with an adorable silence. Outside, we could hear Paris laughing and singing, and could see masked figures shouting as they passed. In the midst of that general festival, we had set aside, and hidden in the darkness, our own particular celebration. The drunkenness of Paris was a make-believe: ours was true. Never forget, my angel, that hour of mystery which changed the course of all your life. That night of February 17, 1833, was a symbol, the outward and visible sign of the great and solemn thing that was taking place within you. On that night you had left outside, and far from you, the tumult and the noise, the false glitter and the crowds, to enter into mystery, and solitude, and love ... [from Louis Barthou, *Les Amours d'un Poète* (1919), p. 139]

The following year he wrote as she slept:

You will find this little letter when you wake, folded in four upon your bed, and you will smile at me, will you not? I long for a smile from those poor, lovely eyes which have shed so many tears. Sleep, Juliette mine – dream that I love you; dream that I am at your feet; dream that you are mine; dream that I am yours; dream that I cannot live without you; dream that I am thinking of you;

dream that I am writing to you. When you wake you will find that dream is true. I kiss your tiny feet and your great eyes . . . [from Raymond Escholier, *Un Amant de Génie: Victor Hugo* (1953), p. 153]

Hugo persuaded Juliette to give up the stage and she became a virtual recluse, slavishly devoted to her lover but miserable at the marginal role she played in his life. Her fidelity was clearly not reciprocated. On 17 January 1843, she wrote to him:

I have a feeling that the women whose interest in you must be highly flattering to the self-esteem of a poet are rousing in you a good deal of curiosity, and a strong desire to know all about them in considerable detail. I certainly can do nothing to prevent you from acting as you choose, but I do know that your first infidelity will cause my death. That is the long and the short of the matter . . . [from J. Drouet, *Mille et une lettres* (1951), p. 250]

By 1844 Hugo was infatuated with Léonie Biard, who was unhappily married to a mediocre painter. He wrote her ecstatic letters:

The kiss you gave me through your veil at our moment of parting was like love felt through absence, sweet, sad, but quite intoxicating. The obstacle was there, but in spite of it our bodies touched and felt. You are not beside me now, yet I have you here and see you. Your charming eyes are fixed on mine. I speak to you: I say: 'Do you love me?' and I hear your thrilled voice answer me in a low whisper: 'Yes.' It is an illusion, yet it is a reality . . . You are indeed here, my heart can feel your presence. My love has set your loved and charming ghost moving about my chair. But, all the same, I miss you. I cannot long deceive myself. I have but to ask that ghost to kiss me, and it vanishes. Only in dreams can I have you by my side. To dream of you is sweet, but sweeter still to have the feel of you, to talk with you, to take you on my knee, to put my arms about you, to cover you with burning kisses, to see you redden and go pale, to feel you trembling in my arms. That is life – life full, entire and real. That is the light of the sun; that is the glow of paradise . . .

On July 5th [1845] the Commissary of Police of the Vendôme district, acting on representations made by Auguste Biard, demanded access in the name of the Law, and in the early hours of the morning, to a discreet apartment situated in the passage Saint-Roche, and there surprised, *in flagrante delicto*, Victor Hugo and his mistress. Adultery at that time was severely dealt with. The husband showed no mercy. Léonie d'Aunet, 'wife of Biard', was arrested and confined in the Saint-Lazare prison. Victor Hugo claimed immunity as a peer, and the Commissary, after some hesitation, released him. But Biard lodged a complaint with the Chancellor Pasquier. Next day *La Patrie*, *Le National*, and *La Quotidienne* referred in guarded terms to a deplorable scandal, and to the duty which would be laid upon the House of Peers to pass judgment on one of its members for adultery. The king in person had to intervene. He summoned the painter Biard to Saint-Cloud in order to induce him to withdraw his complaint . . . The incident of the passage Saint-Roche did no lasting harm to Victor Hugo's career. The only victim had been Léonie Biard, who remained locked away at Saint-Lazare with prostitutes and adulterous wives. Meanwhile, Madame Hamelin intervened with the husband . . . and tried to prevail with him to take steps for her release, or to insist, as he had a perfect right to do, on her being transferred to the Convent of the Sacred Heart. 'My friend,' she told him gaily, 'only kings and cuckolds have the right to pardon. Why not look on the bright side of this business?' At this he burst out laughing, and forthwith put a stop to the activities of the law.

André Maurois, *Victor Hugo*, Cape, 1956, pp. 192–3, 203, 265, 268, 272–4 (translated by Gerard Hopkins).

Politicians, including prime ministers, are notoriously libidinous:

Gladstone once said that he had known 11 prime ministers and that seven of them had been adulterers. This gives material for a parlour game: who were the seven? The start is easy: Canning (with Queen Caroline when she was Princess of Wales – unlikely, but George IV thought so); Wellington (too many to count); Earl Grey of the Reform Bill (Duchess of Devonshire); Melbourne (Mrs Norton – disputed); Disraeli (mistress traded to Lord Lyndhurst); Palmerston (too many to count). Who was the seventh? Did Gladstone count himself?

A.J.P. Taylor, *An Old Man's Diary*, Hamish Hamilton, 1984, p. 100.

On 15 March 1862 the Goncourts breathlessly recorded the latest sexual titbit:

This morning a doctor gave me this astonishing information about the Emperor's [Napoleon III] amours. Each new woman is brought to the Tuileries in a cab, undressed in an ante-room, and taken naked into the room where the Emperor, likewise naked, is waiting for her, by Bacciochi, who gives her this warning and permission: 'You may kiss His Majesty anywhere except on the face.' In the whole history of deification, I cannot remember another instance of a man's face being made a Holy of holies that would be profaned by a kiss!

Edmond and Jules Goncourt, *Pages from the Goncourt Journals*, OUP, 1962, p. 70 (translated by Robert Baldick).

'Cora Pearl', if her own memoirs are to be believed, also knew a thing or two about Napoleon III. Born in 1837, she was one of the best-known courtesans of the Second Empire, but died in relative obscurity in 1886. Her autobiography, written in old age, is a disappointment. Another volume of memoirs has come to light, but even its editor, William Blatchford, cannot confirm its authenticity. Memoir or forgery, it provides mildly pornographic vignettes of a courtesan's life. Napoleon III's cousin Prince Napoleon was one of her principal lovers.

I never appeared officially at court, though I was once introduced to the Emperor by the Prince, who informed me that his Majesty was eager to tread where his distinguished subjects had trodden, as he somewhat tactlessly put it. The Emperor had slept with various women, among them Marguerite Bellanger and La Castiglione, but, observing protocol, none of them would talk about him, except that he had told them he 'enjoyed a woman as he enjoyed a good cigar'. This did not seem to me to promise a great deal, and in fact our single meeting was soon over; for he strode into the room, late at night after a state dinner to which I was not invited, threw off his breeches (though no other part of his dress) and hurled himself upon me without a word, discharging within a few moments, rolling over, and immediately going to sleep. He was already ill and in pain at the time, which must excuse him.

Two or three years later, I found myself alone with Marguerite, his most constant mistress, who remained faithful to him for many years and is said to have borne his child. I asked whether she had found her duties arduous, and she smiled in such a manner that it was clear he had been no more demanding with her than with me. Such a lover would not suit me; but the explanation is, I think, that Marguerite was of a cooler temperament, who did not need male company and male solace to the extent I did; she was happy in her own style, and an occasional bout with Napoleon in his boots satisfied her without making her wish for any other attention.

Cora Pearl, *Memoirs*, Granada, 1983, pp. 122–3.

Adultery in Victorian Britain was all very well as long as you weren't found out. Discovery usually meant ruin. Charles Stewart Parnell was certainly asking for trouble when he virtually cohabited with Kitty O'Shea, the wife of an M.P. The illicit liaison was well known – except to Captain O'Shea, who, whenever he quizzed his wife, was fobbed off with bland lies, whereas in truth Parnell had fathered two of her children. The following account is by a historian who is more sympathetic to the husband's cause than are most other historians of the affair:

On April 26, 1886, he wrote her, 'With regard to Mr Parnell I believed your assurances, but I have scores of times pointed out to you that however innocent in themselves the frequent visits of a man to a woman during the absence of her husband was an offence against proprieties.'

In the last weeks of May, Captain O'Shea was on the Continent at Carlsbad. One day he was sitting under a tree with a friend, Mrs Pell, who was reading the English papers which had just arrived. 'Oh, Captain O'Shea,' she said, 'here's your name in the *Pall Mall Gazette*.' She started to read the item, but then suddenly realizing the truth, she turned red, stopped and stammered, 'Oh, I can't go on.'

The item was captioned 'Mr Parnell's Suburban Retreat'. It related that on May 21, while Parnell was in a brougham on the way from the railroad station to Eltham after midnight, he had collided with the truck of a market gardener, which led to the disclosure that he was the guest of Captain and Mrs O'Shea at Eltham. It was an elementary deduction that since Captain O'Shea had been sojourning on the Continent, Mr Parnell must have been the guest of Mrs O'Shea after midnight, a rather unusual time for a platonic friend to pay a social call.

Captain O'Shea immediately wired Katherine demanding an explanation, and she was ready with a wire reiterating her usual smooth, brazen denial. She followed the wire with a letter to 'My Boysie, I have not the slightest idea of what it means, unless indeed it is meant to get a rise out of you ... I do not see that it has anything to do with us and I am inclined to agree with Charles, from whom I heard this morning, who says in respect to Healy that it is better to put up with a great deal of abuse rather than retaliate, for it is ill fighting with a chimney-sweep, for right or wrong you'd only get soiled.' As an explanation she enclosed a letter she had received from Parnell saying, 'I had a couple of horses at a place in the neighbourhood of Bexley heath but as I am now unable to be much away from London have turned them to grass for the summer. I am very sorry that you should have had any annoyance about the matter . . .'

They hoped that Captain O'Shea would swallow that.

Now the couple began a flight from home to home to evade the eyes of any detector and the knowledge of Captain O'Shea. In June, Parnell took a house in Eastbourne, and then another one on July 31. Then the Sussex *Daily News* carried an item that Parnell was staying at Eastbourne. In answer to O'Shea's inquiry, Katherine replied that all she knew was that Parnell's brother and family had a house there. She said, 'I am disgusted at your desire and evident attempt to drag my name into a newspaper again when it has not been even mentioned.' . . .

By the end of the year the relation between the O'Sheas was one of complete estrangement . . .

On Christmas Eve, 1889, Parnell was served with papers naming him as co-respondent in a suit for divorce filed by Captain O'Shea.

The wronged husband had waited more than three years in his certain knowledge of the love affair. Even now there were good grounds for hesitation. Almost fifty years old, he had no desire to be free for a second marriage. He was loathe to brand the mother of his three children as an adulteress in public, and the scandal would hurt him professionally in the banking circles where he eked out a living as an agent of a Madrid bank . . .

Though his financial interest pointed in the opposite direction, Captain O'Shea chose to bring the divorce suit . . . He was motivated, of course, by his bitter hatred of Parnell and his lust for revenge. But there is more to the motivation than that. It is very probable that O'Shea was used as a pawn by Parnell's political enemies to accomplish his ruin . . .

Mrs O'Shea entered a defense of connivance on the part of O'Shea, thus admitting her adultery but interposing a bar of condonation; she also entered a counterclaim, a startling one, that her husband had committed adultery with her sister Mrs Steele.

By brandishing these defenses she hoped to deter O'Shea from going through with the suit. These defenses, which were pure bluff, turned out to be very ill advised. O'Shea did not give ground at all, and Mrs O'Shea had to give ground and abandon them . . .

The verdict of Judge Butt was all that might have been expected under the uncontradicted testimony. Summing up the evidence he stigmatized Parnell as a man 'who takes advantage of the hospitality offered him by the husband to debauch the wife' and said, 'If the husband were a conniving and consenting party, why should there have been all the disguises, why should there have been the assumption by Mr Parnell of names which do not belong to him, such as Fox and Preston?' He granted the decree nisi (it would become final in six months) and gave O'Shea the custody of all the children below the age of sixteen, a most serious blow to Parnell since two of them were his children . . .

The impact of the case, with its revelation of furtiveness, trickery and cheap devices for concealment, was a shattering blow for Parnell. He had been the man on a pedestal, not only for the Irish but for the English too, but now the aura of the man of mystery had been dispelled, and the *Times* could gloat that his love life was 'a dreary monotony of middle-class vice over which M. Zola's scalpel so longingly lingers.'

Jules Abels, *The Parnell Tragedy*, Bodley Head, 1966, pp. 247–9, 314, 319, 320–21.

When Florence Vivian, married to another cuckolded M.P., elopes to Paris with the Marquess of Waterford, a friend arranges for Florence to meet the husband she has left.

Husband and wife spent the next hour and a half together, John doing most of the talking. He pointed out that the elopement was still a secret and he implored her to give up Waterford if only for the sake of the children and come back with him, pointing out that otherwise, if he was compelled to divorce her, she would lose the children, and her lover would probably not marry her, owing to the difference in their ages and the pressure the Beresfords [the Waterford family] would certainly bring to bear on him against her. Unfortunately she was so besotted by her passion for the Marquess that the most she would agree to was to think it over and let him have her answer as soon as possible the same day.

She then returned to the Westminster [Hotel] where she saw Waterford, whose enthusiasm for his mistress was not as great as hers was for him. He advised her to go back to London with her husband since he was evidently prepared to forgive her. But she persuaded her lover that she loved him too much to do this, and Waterford, true to the tradition that the Beresfords never let a woman down, amiably consented to continue their liaison.

Towards six the same evening a special messenger arrived at the Grand Hotel and handed Vivian a letter addressed to him in his wife's familiar handwriting. Vivian tore it open and read the following unsigned note: 'Five o'clock. I cannot go. I have tried and tried to give him up, and, against his own urgent advice, I shall stay. For God's sake, don't think too hardly of me or I shall do myself some harm. I am going to my ruin, I know, but it is impossible for me to go back. Try and forgive me in your heart. I could not look at those poor children after what I have done, and do not send for me for Heaven's sake.'

Sadly, Captain John Vivian, M.P., returned to London and filed a petition for divorce, citing John Henry de la Poer Marquess of Waterford as co-respondent.

H. Montgomery Hyde, *A Tangled Web*, Constable, 1986, pp. 91–2.

Edward, Prince of Wales, married to the beautiful Princess Alexandra, had maintained a number of mistresses, but Lillie Langtry was the first who was openly acknowledged. Lillie, a lovely woman from Jersey, had married the dull Edward Langtry in 1874, and three years later was involved with the Prince (Bertie) . . .

[Bertie] made Lillie his first public love, and . . . Alexandra would have to accept the fact, no matter what her feelings might be . . . For the sake of discretion, the prince had messages delivered through the good offices of his tailor, who was also a useful man to arrange for money to be passed from hand to hand when the need was paramount.

Lillie had no rich husband to maintain her, in the hope of some princely favour as a reward for his cooperation. So the prince willingly broke another of his long-standing rules for the treatment of women important to him. In the past he had given brooches and necklaces, but he had a house built for Lillie as a permanent rendezvous whenever he wanted it. The site, bought through an intermediary, could only have delighted her. From the top of sandstone cliffs rising sheer from a sandy beach, the view south stretched unbroken to the sea's horizon.

What led [Bertie] to single her out as the woman he chose to let the world recognize as his partner in adultery? His closest companions thought they had the answer. She refused to be subservient. She stood up to him where few others dared . . . No one could say that Lillie dominated him, but neither did she let him dominate her.

In many respects, they were two of a kind, suited for each other's needs, physically and in the patterns of their thinking. Sentimentality was alien to both of them. He showed more warmth in his general attitudes than she, but he admired her disdainfulness. He was businesslike in all his dealings; so was she. 'Don't let us fuss' became one of her watchwords. She never complained, explained, or gossiped, which was essential in their relationship . . .

They were ready for each other. She was starved of sexual satisfaction, disdainful of men, driven by ambition. He was bored with idleness, and with a wife unsuited for him.

By the summer of '78, most of England suspected that Lillie was the mistress of the prince. The upper classes accepted the fact. No more of them than the stalwarts of Victoria's immediate circle condemned him, though not everybody accepted her. The lower classes envied him. For many of the men, Bertie's was the life they dreamed of leading in their wildest fantasies . . . Only the middle classes as a whole took a distinctly critical view. It was sinful to take a mistress, totally out of keeping with what they imagined the moral standards of the queen to be and accordingly tried to emulate. Sympathy was strong for Alexandra.

Publicity was one of the inventions of the new age. It was fashionable to be famous. For the first time, the personal lives of the swells were hashed over as a permanent commercial commodity that helped to sell newspapers and magazines. Lillie had made herself manna from heaven for editors bent on titillating their readers.

Crowds gathered to goggle at her when she appeared . . . If she entered a ballroom, dowagers would climb on chairs for a better view . . . The prince escorted her to Ascot races . . . The pink dress she wore started the high-class sweatshops in the East End of London producing copies of it . . . She protested that she was more embarrassed than pleased.

With Edward escorting her for appearance's sake, she dined regularly with the prince and Alexandra aboard *Osborne*, where food and wine were served in the same polished style as in Marlborough House. After dinner, if the evenings were fine, the deck served as a dance floor.

Wearing kindness as a badge, Alix treated Lillie with the attentions she showed all her guests. She had long since reconciled herself to Bertie's compulsive appetites, and she gave no signs of resenting the woman he delighted in parading in front of her with all the pretended deference of which he was capable. If her temper was tried, Alexandra kept that a personal secret just as she suppressed any vestige of jealousy.

The prince's life with Lillie at its centre was conducted on a circuit of such houses owned by his friends. They were given no alternative but to welcome her. He imposed his will by the implicit threat that unless she were a guest, he would no longer honour the place with his presence. Bedroom arrangements must be to his liking, too, with due regard for discretion, so that convenient accommodations were provided for Mrs Langtry close to his own.

James Brough, *The Prince and the Lily*, Hodder & Stoughton, 1975, pp. 166, 172–3, 183–4, 192–3, 200.

Lillie subsequently had an affair with Bertie's nephew Prince Louis of Battenberg, by whom she had a daughter, Jeanne-Marie. Edward refused to give her a divorce, so that Louis could marry her. As her financial straits worsened, she accepted an offer to try her hand as an actress at the age of twenty-eight. She also modelled for Pears soap advertisements. Bertie moved on to a new mistress, Daisy, Countess of Warwick. Edward died insane and destitute in 1897. Lillie then married Hugo de Bathe and died in 1929.

Soon after marrying his first wife Alys, the philosopher Bertrand Russell realized he no longer loved her . . .

When I arrived [at Philip and Ottoline Morrell's house at 44 Bedford Square] on March 19th [1911], on my way to Paris, I found that Philip had unexpectedly had to go to Burnley, so that I was left *tête-à-tête* with Ottoline. During dinner we made conversation about Burnley, and politics, and the sins of the Government. After dinner the conversation gradually became more intimate. Making timid approaches, I found them to my surprise not repulsed. It had not, until this moment, occurred to me that Ottoline was a woman who would allow me to make love to her, but gradually, as the evening progressed, the desire to make love to her became more and more insistent. At last it conquered, and I found to my amazement that I loved her deeply, and that she returned my feeling. Until this moment I had never had complete relations with any woman except Alys. For external and accidental reasons, I did not have full relations with Ottoline that evening, but we agreed to become lovers as soon as possible. My feeling was overwhelmingly strong, and I did not care what might be involved. I wanted to leave Alys, and to have her leave Philip.

What Philip might think or feel was a matter of indifference to me. If I had known that he would murder us both (as Mrs Whitehead assured me he would) I should have been willing to pay that price for one night. The nine years of tense self-denial had come to an end, and for the time being I was done with self-denial. However, there was no time to settle future plans during that one evening . . .

Ottoline was going to Studland . . . and we arranged that I should join her there for three days. Before going, I spent the weekend with Alys at Fernhurst . . . I then told Alys about Ottoline. She flew into a rage, and said that she would insist upon a divorce, bringing in Ottoline's name. Ottoline, on account of her child, and also on account of a very genuine affection for Philip, did not wish for a divorce from him. I therefore had to keep her name out of it. I told Alys that she could have the divorce whenever she liked, but that she must not bring Ottoline's name into it. She nevertheless persisted that she would bring Ottoline's name in. Thereupon I told her quietly but firmly that she would find that impossible, since if she ever took steps to that end, I should commit suicide in order to circumvent her. I meant this, and she saw that I did. Thereupon her rage became unbearable. After she had stormed for some hours, I gave a lesson in Locke's philosophy to her niece, Karin Costelloe, who was about to take her Tripos. I then rode away on my bicycle, and with that my first marriage came to an end. I did not see Alys again till 1950, when we met as friendly acquaintances.

Bertrand Russell, *Autobiography*, Allen & Unwin, 1967, Vol. 1, pp. 274–5.

Ottoline Morrell gave her own account of the affair:

Bertie's [Russell] almost abstract passion was shattering and overwhelming, for he seemed almost a stranger. He was consumed with desire to possess me, and to cast off the unhappiness of his own life, and to make me the excuse for leaving his wife, and liberating himself from the intense suppression in which he had lived for many years. It was as if he had suddenly risen from the grave and had broken the bonds that held him. What was I to do? For many years I had thought of him as the greatest intellect living, and a very important and wonderful man. No woman is dead to the flattering influence of a great man's passion.

Letters from him poured upon me; interviews were asked for, which had to be arranged in the midst of the usual life of London. I was indeed partly overcome, carried away and elated by this new experience; but underneath there lay a cold, horrible feeling of discomfort that I was not being true, and that the intoxication of his own feelings blinded him from seeing that I was not equally in love with him; to tell him this was more than I had courage to do. Whenever I tried it, he was so filled with despair that I was afraid he might kill himself, as he threatened to do. How could I allow him to return to the dreary life that he had risen from? It seemed that I could not refuse to take upon me the burden of this fine and valuable life . . .

In August I went off alone to Marienbad, leaving Philip at Peppard with Julian [their daughter]. Bertie came out there for a short time. I was in a hotel by myself, and he stayed near by, but came to see me every day. Unfortunately the manager of the hotel, a typical Prussian, who obviously disliked me for being English, did his best to make himself disagreeable by forbidding Bertie to visit me at the hotel. I hoped that my acquaintance with Rufus Isaacs, who was then Solicitor-General and was also staying at Marienbad, would have vouched for my respectability, but perhaps his Jewish origin told against him. Bertie left before very long, which was rather a relief to me, as I felt sensitive about being looked on as an abandoned woman . . .

[March 7, 1913] Bertie thinks he loves me, but what he really loves is a woman to listen to him and to rely on him; but he does not love enough to forget himself ever. I must love him and give to him, it is my work: and not expect anything back, for he cannot deviate a hair's breadth from what he is, or from his self-absorption. I don't believe he is much aware of me, nor does he ever want to follow me in my thoughts and wanderings. He says he does, but I find I cannot talk to him. But, after all, it *is* a good work, and he is noble. It is helping a good cause, and worth any amount of effort, and so *corraggio!* . . .

June 1913. I do *not* regret my advance in the Bertie affair. It was the courageous thing to do, and it was taking a *great risk*, and that is always the best course. I hate the *safe* and coward way.

Ottoline Morrell, *Ottoline at Garsington*, Faber, 1975, pp. 268, 279, 283.

Alma Mahler preferred to confer her favours on the celebrated cultural icons of her time, beginning with Gustav Mahler and continuing with Oskar Kokoschka and Walter Gropius, and concluding, from 1918 onwards, with the Austrian writer Franz Werfel, who describes the beginnings of this long-lived affair in his diary:

July 29, 1918: Day before yesterday I went to Semmering to visit Alma. Planned to stay the weekend, until late Monday; was happy and excited the two days before my departure . . .

I was looking forward, too, to Alma's love. Now I recall a remark that Blei dropped a few nights ago . . .: with a pregnant woman, he said, only a knave would ignore the dictate of conscience that pleasure cannot be an end in itself. Was that an unconscious dig at me? If it was not, not even unconsciously, it was surely a portent for me. I felt it at once and instantly vowed to keep Blei's words in mind and curb myself, for Alma's sake above all . . .

I arrived at Breitenstein on Semmering Saturday noon and was welcomed with joy, drawn in by the good, warmth-giving hand that opened the door. There was company, due to stay a week: Frau R. and her eighteen-year-old daughter. My presence created space problems, but Alma and Gucki [Alma's daughter] (who is getting more and more wonderful!) were happy to have me – if only to enliven the atmosphere, slightly depressed by Frau R.

I got the room next to Alma's bedroom and was thrilled by this happy turn. While I unpacked we were alone for half an hour, both looking forward gladly to the night.

Blei's words and my good, considerate intentions were forgotten. Alma, seven months pregnant, had been overtaxing herself all day, besides playing almost the whole second part of Mahler's Eighth Symphony on the harmonium with Gucki.

At bedtime it took nearly two hours to get Frau R. out of Alma's room. Stirred by the music, she could not stop philosophizing . . . Finally, after many half hours of waiting for everyone to fall asleep, Alma and I were alone.

She is the only person of genius I know here.

I think I love her more and more, as far as I can love – more, in some ways, than I know I can love.

Previously I had always only imagined women, months before. My enthusiasm created them; in reality they did not mean much to me.

Alma is real to me. In the first days after we kept looking at each other at the concert (Mengelberg and Schreker), she left me no time for imaginings.

After the concert she invited me to come with her. We declared ourselves, but although everything happened soon, my feelings for her did not ripen for some time. When I left for Switzerland (on January 18), and while I was there, I loved her with nostalgia – a feeling of which my love for her is never free.

This is not the time to discuss these developments. Today she is more real to me than a mere human being!

I had forgotten the sign and failed to control myself.

There is something suicidal in her climactic surrender. I know that now – having always been too irresponsible to admit it. This self-destructive urge at the climax is the living image of her Wagnerianism, justified by an erotic-musical nature that seems to me more encompassing, more *breathing*, more productive than the musical nature of the composers I have seen around her. Schönberg's, for instance . . .

We made love.

I did not spare her.

At dawn I went back to my room.

Quoted by Alma Mahler in her autobiographical *And the Bridge is Love*, Hutchinson, 1959, pp. 98–100.

The Bloomsbury circle were accomplished at philandering and infidelity and had a tendency to make a meal of it, rich in humbug. . . Gerald Brenan was acquainted with the newly wed Dora Carrington and Ralph Partridge, a curious match since the painter Carrington was besotted with the homosexual Lytton Strachey . . .

I got a letter from Carrington asking me to join her on a picnic at White Horse Hill above Uffington on July 7th [1921]. She would be alone, she said, as Ralph had to go up to London. Although I had some doubts in my mind about the advisability of accepting, I went. We met on our bicycles at the inn and, after climbing to the earth-works, sat down to eat our sandwiches behind a little copse on the forward slope. Then – I do not remember exactly how it came about – we kissed. She returned my kisses warmly and I held her hand, but it was getting late and we set off for the station to catch our separate trains. As I rode along watching the rich green country slide by I thought about what had happened. To me the kisses had meant very little, but I felt that I had acted irresponsibly and made up my mind that I would not do so again.

A fortnight passed and I went over to Tidmarsh for a couple of nights. Most of this visit is a blank in my mind, but one immense thing stands out. I was sitting in an armchair in the sitting room when Carrington passed across in front of the window, outlined against the setting sun. She just passed across and all at once something overturned inside me and I felt that I was deeply, irretrievably in love.

An avalanche of feelings followed, unlike anything I had ever experienced before. In that quarter of a minute the whole orientation of my life, all the thoughts in my head had been changed . . .

What private meetings followed this I do not know. They have gone out of my mind. All I remember is that we discussed whether or not we should tell Ralph. I was in favour of telling him, but Carrington was not, saying that since he would never understand the innocence of our feelings for one another, he would be deeply disturbed and hurt. Some day she would be able to tell him and then he would realize that this love that had suddenly broken out between us had really brought both of us closer to him. But I can see now that, quite apart from her fear that his jealousy would restrict our meetings or even put an end to them altogether, she felt that if our new feelings for one another were known to him and subjected to his interrogations, they would be spoiled and vulgarized. She liked to keep the essential part of her intimate attachments to herself and did not consider that anyone had the right to probe into them.

Our love letters to one another begin from this moment. I had to reply more cautiously unless I knew that Ralph was away from home because he always asked to read what I had written. But, present or absent, he was very much on our minds. As a concession to his feelings both of us denied being in love because that would suggest that we were either having or wishing to have an affair. The word Carrington used was 'fondness'. She insisted once again that she could not tell him what we felt for one another because 'he is such a dear creature that it would be wicked blackness to hurt him'. Besides her feelings for me were 'so pure and full of deeper affection that if he could see into her head he would not mind but would be pleased'. Although, she said, she lived with Ralph 'for friendship and not for passions', she believed his existence in our life to be essential . . .

[Ralph] was indeed very much in love with her and, since he wanted me to share his happiness, he treated me with great affection and pressed Carrington to do the same. I did not therefore feel jealous of him. I could say with perfect honesty that I loved him as I had never loved any man before, wanted nothing for myself that I had not already got and wished well to his marriage.

Only the strength of my feelings was something new, for up to this time I had not felt more than ordinary friendship for him . . . I only regretted that I was not allowed to tell him about this love, since it was so clear to me that there was nothing in my feelings to injure him, but I could not go against her wishes. Yet were they not coming to be my wishes too? Naive though my consciousness of my own innocence made me, I could hardly fail to see that if I told him he might say that I must stop seeing her.

What must seem strange and indeed almost incredible is that I felt no sexual attraction for Carrington, using that word in its narrower sense. I seemed to have been carried to heights where I was above all physical desires. Even when, one wet afternoon, we lay tossing in a little shed heaped with dry bracken, I made no sexual advances to her and felt no inclination to do so. When I try to explain this to myself today I see three reasons for it. The first is the terrible guilt I should have felt if I had tried to seduce my friend's wife. I could only justify my conduct to myself – and that imperfectly – by the knowledge that all my thoughts and desires were pure. Then I had come to associate sexual feelings with girls, usually of the working classes, for whom I felt merely a crude physical attraction. Such dallyings often left a nasty taste behind them and in my present elevated frame of mind I regarded the lustful images that had accompanied them as base and disgusting. Finally, Carrington's body was flat and boyish and offered nothing to the sensual imagination. No one would wish to sleep with her unless he loved her.

To complicate matters, the following year Ralph began an affair with Valentine Dobrée, a friend of Carrington's. She appears in Brenan's memoir under the name of Clare Bollard . . .

On May 11th I went to Tidmarsh and remained there till June 1st. Clare arrived in England and Ralph went up to London to see her. They were having an affair and he, far from being more considerate to Carrington on that account, treated her *de haut en bas* as though he were paying her out for something. It was as if he were saying to her that, whereas she had never responded to his love-making as he had wished, he had now found a beautiful and fascinating woman who did respond to it and who was in every way his sexual equal. As was to be expected, his behaviour led to a change in my way of thinking. If he could display his physical passion for Clare so ostentatiously and arrogantly, I saw no reason why I should not be allowed to make love quietly to Carrington, and at that thought all my guilt feelings and with them my sexual inhibitions melted away. She felt as I did and when he went up to London to see his mistress she came to my room when I was in bed and got in beside me. Yet she was uneasy. She insisted that she was not jealous, that she was a person who did not have possessive feelings, but said that she mistrusted Clare because she could see that Clare was trying to prejudice Ralph against her. This impression was confirmed when she went up to London and lunched with her, for Clare did not trouble to conceal her delight in her triumph.

Gerald Brenan, *Personal Record*, Cape, 1975, pp. 26–8, 30–31, 47.

Inevitably Ralph discovered his wife's infidelity with Brenan, who shortly thereafter returned to Spain.

A more important artist than Carrington also had difficulties accommodating affairs:

30 May 1930. Paris. Aristide Maillol came to lunch. Since our last meeting, he said, *il s'était passé des histoires tragiques chez lui*. His wife, who listens at doors and peeps through keyholes, caught him and [his model] Mlle Passavant in his studio amidst tenderness of one sort or another. She rushed in like a fury and '*a déchiré tous mes dessins*', meaning the large nude studies of Mlle Passavant which had hung on the walls and including a large red crayon drawing I had admired. She then became very dark red in the face, '*comme si elle était congestionnée*', and fell in a faint. For four hours Maillol and his seventy-year-old sister, Mme d'Espie, had to sprinkle her with

water and chafe her hands until she came to. '*Mais ce qu'il y a de plus étonnant, c'est que depuis ce temps, elle est douce comme un agneau. Depuis trente ans elle n'a jamais été aussi douce.*' Maillol seemed enchanted by the fact. I find this sudden meekness rather suspicious. He added *qu'elle n'avait pas à se plaindre.* He continues to love her despite everything. '*Je fais l'amour avec elle comme un jeune homme.*'

We then discussed the details of his 'flight' to Weimar. He is having difficulties about Mlle Passavant's visa because she is not yet twenty-one and neither her mother nor her father 'acknowledges' her. Rudier, Maillol's caster, has friends in the Ministry and is doing his best. They have even, Maillol related, had to concoct '*une pièce fausse*'. We have therefore postponed our departure until Tuesday evening. Mlle Passavant is to travel ahead and join the train at Reims. This '*départ pour Cythère*' is having a somewhat stormy and difficult start and, with a sixty-seven-year-old lover involved, does not lack a certain comicality . . .

11 June 1930. Weimar. Spent the day at the Press. I had arranged to meet Maillol and Mlle Passavant at five o'clock at the Schwanensee bathing pool. They were sitting in the café. It was immediately obvious that yesterday's upset between the two has deepened. She was quite pale, with red-rimmed eyes, and deliberately spoke not a word to him, replying to his questions either monosyllabically or not at all. To me she said that she has a sore throat, but nothing serious and nobody is to worry about her. We sat together for an hour in embarrassing frigidity until I suggested that we go home and send for a doctor. She emphatically declined. '*Ce n'est rien, je vous assure.*'

Maillol appeared at table without her. She had gone to bed, he explained. I commented that she probably does have a cold, but some sort of worry or disappointment seems to me to be a contributory factor. Yes, he answered, she has hinted something of the kind.

In short, we have here the old tragicomedy of the ageing man and a hot-blooded girl, the very stuff of the most ancient comedy. Mme Maillol is avenged! In this instance I am sorrier for Maillol than for Mlle Passavant, who must have known what to expect after having an affair with him for a year. Oddly enough, Goertz told me on Thursday already, straight after seeing her for the first time, that she is a sweet, delightful creature but belongs to the category of women who cannot hold a man for long because they are too sensual and demand too much of him.

Harry Kessler, *Diaries of a Cosmopolitan*, Weidenfeld & Nicolson, 1971, pp. 389, 391–2 (translated by Charles Kessler).

Dorothy Macmillan, daughter of the Duke of Devonshire and wife of the future Conservative Prime Minister, embarked on a lifelong affair with Robert Boothby:

Six years younger than Harold, one of his closest friends and vital political allies, Boothby possessed a strikingly attractive personality: he was moreover considered *the* coming man. Brilliant, a remarkable speaker, eccentric, ahead of his time, many saw him as a potential prime minister. The antithesis of his friend, Harold Macmillan, he affected total self-assurance; quoting a journalist who had praised him as being 'always ahead of his time, and always right', Boothby declared, 'From this conclusion I cannot dissent.' Extremely good-looking, he dressed with careful raffishness, in complete contrast to Macmillan with his unstylish clothes, gold-rimmed glasses, unappealing bushy moustache and toothily diffident half-smile . . . Boothby on the other hand dashed about in an open, two-seater Bentley and was socially at ease wherever he went, be it to Hatfield, Chartwell or Chatsworth . . .

It is not hard to imagine the appeal to Dorothy of Boothby, in comparison with Macmillan. One was a dashingly handsome bounder, the other worthy and almost dowdily prosaic. Boothby appeared destined for stardom – not so Macmillan; and the Cavendishes were traditionally drawn to success, in whatever field. Cavendish women also had a reputation for being highly sexed, and it seems that Macmillan – like Churchill – attached little

importance to the physical aspects of love. There may well have
been something cloying in Harold's love; from the letters of those
early days there emerges occasionally a sense of devotion bordering
on the dutiful, suggesting that he may have at times treated
Dorothy as a surrogate mother-figure. And there was of course the
added marital hazard of cohabiting with a formidably strong-willed
mother-in-law ... Bob Boothby took her away from all that,
amused her and probably made her feel truly herself for the first
time ... The attraction that Dorothy Macmillan held for Boothby,
apart from her obvious charm, is perhaps partly that she gave him
self-confidence; ostensibly full of bounce, Boothby was insecure in
his social origins ...

The relationship, in one form or another, was to continue until
Dorothy's death in 1966, and its impact on Boothby's life was
total. 'Even now, when the telephone rings,' he admitted in old
age, 'I still expect to hear her voice saying "It's me" – that was
how she always spoke on the telephone ...' In old age, telling all,
he claimed on the one hand that 'it wasn't an affair in the modern
sense. It was a romantic friendship in the true Victorian tradition'
... To him Dorothy was 'a very powerful woman': ... 'Several
times I got engaged, once in Venice, but Dorothy came all the way
from Chatsworth to pursue me there ... she was absolutely
unafraid of anything ... She broke off my engagement, and
stopped me twice more from getting married ... she was relentless,
there was a streak of cruelty in her, I have to admit, and very
selfish. But we were absolutely fixed upon each other.'

At an early stage in the affair [Macmillan] seriously considered
starting divorce proceedings; on the other hand, he seems to have
lived in dread of Dorothy's leaving him for Boothby, and there
was a moment when that seemed a distinct possibility. In the
strictest conjugal sense, the marriage was finished, with Dorothy
Macmillan recorded as declaring on more than one occasion, 'I am
faithful to Bob.' When Sarah was born in 1930, it was generally
accepted that Boothby, not Macmillan, was the father.

Somehow, Dorothy Macmillan managed a double life, being in

daily contact with Boothby, travelling at home and abroad with him whenever possible, yet at the same time running a household for her husband and – most important – never once letting him down when needed at Stockton or at the hustings. In return, Macmillan always treated Boothby in public with the utmost civility. Indeed, it was he who as Prime Minister bestowed a peerage on Boothby.

Alistair Horne, *Macmillan: 1894–1956*, Macmillan, 1988, pp. 85–9.

The tangled lives of Hollywood stars would fill a volume of its own, but the discreet and elegant love affair between Spencer Tracy, who was more or less living apart from his wife Louise, and Katharine Hepburn stands out.

The love story of Spencer Tracy and Katharine Hepburn was Hollywood's big secret. Although Hollywood fed on scandal, for almost twenty years nothing was said about the romance. In a town where nothing was sacred, this story seemed to be in a special category.

Even their close friends did not try to discuss the situation with either one of them, and certainly not with the press . . . Metro-Goldwyn-Mayer's policy was to ignore the romance. Its publicity releases stated that Tracy was married and living at home. The fact that he was living apart from his family was never announced by the press . . .

What Hollywood thought really made no difference. They were not 'Hollywood people'. Tracy, of course, had been more interested in living it up in the years before they met, but Miss Hepburn never tried to be a part of the Hollywood scene. Their life together was their own, whether they were walking in the Hollywood hills, relaxing in New England, or touring Europe.

As years passed and more people became aware of their deep feeling for each other, there was some speculation as to why they never married . . . Perhaps Katharine Hepburn liked it the way it was . . .

Miss Hepburn said, 'I don't believe in marriage. It isn't a natural institution – if it were, why sign a contract for it? One of the few happy marriages, perhaps the only truly happy marriage I've known, was my parents'. They never argued about "things", for my mother never wanted "things" the way most women do. They only argued about ideas.' . . .

Tracy was steady and calm, whereas Miss Hepburn would take off on giddy intellectual flights or be seized by sudden enthusiasms. They were very different, but complementary: together savoring nature, enjoying the arts and each other's company.

Larry Swindwell, *Spencer Tracy*, W.H. Allen, 1970, pp. 243, 244, 245.

Other Hollywood figures fleshed out the story:

I interviewed [George] Cukor for the *New York Times* in 1978, and . . . much of our conversation drifted off to his recollection of the Hepburn–Tracy relationship.

'There was something exceptionally sweet about it,' said Cukor. 'Though they were both extremely sophisticated people, he was like a little boy with her and she was like a little girl with him. He could be extremely gruff with her, that was the little roughneck boy from Milwaukee filtering through, but he had enormous respect for her and he *listened* to her.

'In the terrible matter of his drinking, I believe she *did* extend his life. She made sure he went to the finest doctors when the inevitable complications of his drinking set in, and she even went so far as to tie him to his bed in the little house when she sensed the symptoms indicating that one of his major disappearance-binges was coming on. Mostly she helped him by distracting him from his drinking with love, and with finding fascinating things they could do together in the entire new world of culture she had opened up to him.

'They went to museums together, they made several trips to

Europe together, she introduced him to great music and literature. It was fun watching them wandering around my property hand in hand, looking at the flowers, and then sitting down in the sun to read, or to listen to a Brahms concerto or a symphony on their portable record-player. Some of the rough edges had worn off Tracy with his interest in art and his own painting, and he already had some distinguished friends. For example, somehow he had got to know Supreme Court Justice William O. Douglas, who adored him. But with Kate, he soon was able to discuss Shakespeare and D.H. Lawrence in my salon, and he moved into the Hollywood intellectual set, which included Noël Coward, David Niven and Laurence Olivier. Strange, because he also still kept seeing his old buddies, like Pat O'Brien and Jimmy Cagney, which was a new experience for Kate . . .

'What I remember most is that they could bicker and argue and say dreadful things to one another, but always come out of it laughing and hugging, like teenagers. As far as benefits are concerned, it was not a one-sided affair. I've known Kate since 1933 . . . There was an enormous change in her after she worked with Spencer in *Woman of the Year* and fell in love with him. She's a strong, dominant woman, who was considered cold, with no sex appeal. Little by little, she could have become a typical old maid. However, her relationship with extrovert, down-to-earth Tracy and the sexual attraction she admits to, was good for her.' . . .

Gene Kelly has a slightly different perspective of the Tracy–Hepburn relationship in the 1950s.

'I always had a lot of people dropping by my house in those days,' says Kelly. 'There were no invitations. People would just come and we'd talk politics and we'd play a lot of word games, charades, twenty questions, Jotto, and such. The funny thing about Spence is that he'd just sit there quietly and sip a coke. I never saw him take a drink . . . We were all of the liberal bent, big admirers of Franklin D. Roosevelt, the New Deal, the Fair Deal. Politically, we all were the opposite of Spence. Katie joined in the political discussions, but everybody had too much respect for

Spence's feelings and nobody talked politics to him. Also, we knew he didn't like the word games, so we didn't play them when he was there.'

[Tracy denied that he and Hepburn never married because of his Catholicism. He is quoted as saying:] 'When we first started going together, Katie wanted to get married but my [deaf] son, John, was still living at home and I felt that until he grew up and could take care of himself, I couldn't do it. Later, when all that cleared up, *I* wanted to marry Katie, but by that time she didn't want to marry *me*.'

Bill Davidson, *Spencer Tracy*, Sidgwick & Jackson, 1987, pp. 107–8, 109–10, 165.

Politicians must conduct their infidelities in a clandestine fashion, which lays them open to blackmail, humiliation and ridicule, as Lord Lambton, among others, discovered:

Antony Claud Frederick Lambton, Viscount Lambton, was the second son and heir of the fifth Earl of Durham, his elder brother having died in 1941. Aged fifty ... Lord Lambton had been MP for Berwick-on-Tweed since 1951 and was now Parliamentary Under-Secretary of State for Defence for the Royal Air Force, in effect Air Minister, which he had been for the past three years. When his father died in 1970, he disclaimed the Durham peerage since he wished to remain in the House of Commons, but he continued with the Speaker Selwyn Lloyd's assent to use the courtesy title by which he had previously been known. Tony Lambton is an able man, a wealthy landowner, a good speaker and writer, and a brilliant marksman in the shooting field. He habitually wears dark glasses, with a studied languid air which women have found attractive. He has five daughters and one son by his wife Belinda (Bindy) ...

At some date in the late spring or early summer of 1972 Lambton was given the telephone number of a 'Madam' who controlled a ring of highly priced prostitutes ... One of its call girls went under the name of Norma Russell. In November 1972 she suddenly married Colin Levy, a man with a criminal record for offences of dishonesty. Lord Lambton made use of her services and those of other sexual partners whom she procured for him at her flat in Maida Vale. This was close by his London residence. His identity became known to her and he sometimes paid her by cheques signed in his own name.

In April 1973, in consequence of a domestic dispute with her husband, Norma Levy informed the police of her association with Lord Lambton, and this information was immediately passed on to MI5 to investigate whether any risk to security was involved. Although she did not intend to blackmail him, her husband, who had always been a consenting party to his wife's conduct, thought he could make money not by blackmail but by selling the story to a newspaper. For this purpose he and an associate, who was also involved with Norma Levy and also had a criminal record, attempted to take compromising ciné-pictures of Lord Lambton in bed in the flat to supplement the evidence provided by the cheques which Lambton had signed. However, they lacked the necessary technical material and skill to take recognisable photographs under these conditions. On 5 May 1973, armed with the under-developed films and one of the cheques, they approached the *News of the World* and offered to sell that newspaper their story for £30,000. In the ensuing days, members of the staff of the *News of the World* installed a tape recorder and photographic equipment for taking clandestine photographs through a hole in the wall of Norma Levy's bedroom. On 9 May Colin Levy used the recorder to tape a conversation between his wife and Lord Lambton about drugs, and on the following day a staff member of the *News of the World* took a series of compromising photographs. Eventually the *News of the World* decided not to buy the story, returning the tape recording and also handing Levy the negatives and prints of the compromising photographs that they had taken. On 17 May Levy and his associate took all this evidence to the *Sunday People* and offered to sell the story for £45,000. This paper took charge of all the evidence, paying Levy and his associate £750 and undertaking to pay a further £5,250 if it published a report confirming their allegations. In the event the *Sunday People* retained the material and produced it to the police, so that security was not actually endangered. But there was a risk to security by reason of the *News of the World* letting Levy and his associate have it in the first place, since potential buyers might have included undercover agents of a potentially hostile power or powers.

Norma Levy sometimes worked as a hostess in a London night-club and she told the owner's wife as well as the police that she thought the government ought to be informed of Lord Lambton's bedroom activities. This lady agreed and asked one of the club's regular customers to help. He did so by contacting James Prior, then leader of the House of Commons and close to Edward Heath. Recalling how the Profumo case had affected Macmillan, the Prime Minister was shocked by the news which Prior gave him. It was agreed that Prior should see the night-club owner's wife in his Whitehall office in the presence of a senior civil servant. This was duly done, and the lady imparted the information which ended shortly afterwards in Lambton's public exposure, disgrace and resignation both of his government office and his parliamentary seat.

H. Montgomery Hyde, *A Tangled Web*, Constable, 1986, pp. 274–6.

On 5 October 1983, Cecil Parkinson, M.P., a senior Cabinet minister in the Conservative government, acknowledged that he had had a 'relationship' with his former secretary Sara Keays, who was now pregnant with his child.

He went on to state that he would be 'making financial provision for both mother and child'. (£100,000 was the rumoured figure.) He admitted that it had been his intention to marry Miss Keays, that he had told her of his 'wish to marry her', but that he had later changed his mind. He added: 'My wife, who has been a source of great strength, and I decided to stay together and to keep our family together.' The contents of this statement, made, he said, with Miss Keays's consent, were confirmed by her London solicitors. At the same time officials at No. 10 Downing Street stated that Mrs Thatcher was aware of Mr Parkinson's statement but viewed it as a private matter, adding that the question of his resignation 'does not and will not arise'.

It emerged the following day that the Prime Minister had known about the 'relationship' and about Sara Keays's pregnancy at least three months earlier. Because of it apparently she had removed Mr Parkinson from the Party Chairmanship and installed the political fledgling John Selwyn Gummer in his place on the previous 14 September. Indeed she may have known about the 'relationship' for much longer, possibly as far back as April 1982, at the time of Cecil Parkinson's inclusion in the inner cabinet concerned with the Falklands war, when she may well have learned of it through the Home Secretary or the head of MI5 when Parkinson was presumably vetted for security. But there was no official confirmation or denial of this. However, Parkinson let it be known through parliamentary lobby correspondents and the like (contrary, it seems, to his agreement with his ex-mistress) that he had disclosed 'the full facts' to Mrs Thatcher after the polls had closed on 9 June in the General Election which he was credited with having so brilliantly and successfully masterminded . . .

On 10 October 1983, the day before the opening of the Conservative Party Conference in Blackpool, Cecil Parkinson said in a television interview on BBC's Panorama that 'if ever I ceased to be an asset and became a liability, and the Prime Minister felt so, then of course I would leave immediately.' His words were to come true sooner than he thought. He was not present at the opening day of the Conference and so did not hear the backbencher Mr Ivor Stanbrook, MP for Orpington, denounce him as a 'self-confessed adulterer and a damned fool', who should have insisted on resigning. At the same time Mr Stanbrook condemned the party establishment's 'evident determination to pretend that nothing is wrong' . . .

It was not until two days later, on the Thursday, that Parkinson made his first appearance at the Conference where he wound up the debate on free enterprise and industry. He was accompanied by his wife Ann and there was an outburst of rapturous applause when they mounted the platform along with Mrs Thatcher, although it was not exactly clear whom the applause was intended for, possibly all three. But there was no doubt about the recipient of the applause in Mr Parkinson's speech when, in an oblique reference to his adultery, he thanked the first woman he had betrayed, while making no reference to the second . . .

During the night of 13/14 October Miss Keays issued a statement to *The Times* which was also immediately transmitted to the Prime Minister as well as to her former lover in Blackpool. In this statement Miss Keays said *inter alia* that her baby had been conceived in a 'long-standing, loving relationship which I had allowed to continue because I believed in our eventual marriage'; that Mr Parkinson had first asked her to marry him in 1979; and that in May 1983, when she knew of her pregnancy, he changed his mind and decided that he no longer wished to marry her. At the same time she had told him that she could not deny her baby the right to the identity of its father. She went on to state that she had implored him during May and early June to inform the Prime Minister, because 'his name and mine were sufficiently linked in political circles for speculation to be inevitable,' but that he would not agree to this. However on polling day (9 June), according to Miss Keays, he changed his mind again and sought a reconciliation, asking her to marry him, a request which she had 'gladly accepted'; and on the same evening he told her that he had informed Mrs Thatcher of their relationship and that he would be obtaining a divorce in order to marry her. On 5 August, Miss Keays continued, Mr Parkinson had gone abroad on holiday with his wife and family, 'having reassured me of his intention to marry me', but on 1 September when Mr Parkinson met her he told her that he had once more changed his mind and that while he was abroad he had decided not to marry her after all. Meanwhile she had been asked by press reporters, on 23 August, whether it was true that she was pregnant by Mr Parkinson. Press comment, government pronouncements and 'the continued speculation about this matter' had put her in 'an impossible situation', she concluded, and she therefore felt she had 'both a public duty and a duty to my family to put the record straight'.

Cecil Parkinson saw Margaret Thatcher at 2 a.m. and told her that in his opinion Miss Keays's statement made it impossible for him to remain a member of the Government, besides which the Prime Minister and his own family would be seriously if not irretrievably damaged if he stayed. Mrs Thatcher asked him to give the matter further consideration and after several sleepless hours he returned to the Prime Minister's suite in the Imperial Hotel and offered his resignation which she accepted. Their brief talk, according to *The Times*, was said to have been distressing for both, and one of Parkinson's friends said he was 'quite broken'. He and his wife left Blackpool without more ado.

H. Montgomery Hyde, *A Tangled Web*, Constable, 1986, pp. 335–6, 336–7, 337, 337–8.

PART TWO

Cravings

Patty-cake, patty-cake
Marcus Antonius
What do you think of the
African Queen?

Gubernatorial
Duties require my
Presence in Egypt. Ya
Know what I mean?

Paul Pascal, 'Tact'

Desire is the precursor of infidelity. Illicit cravings must be reciprocated, but first they must be acknowledged. In societies where the pressure to conform is intense, such acknowledgement can be a painful process, as it undoubtedly is for Anna and Vronsky in *Anna Karenina*:

She had assured herself more than once during those last few days, and again a moment ago, that Vronsky in relation to her was only one of the hundreds of everlastingly identical young men she met everywhere, and that she would never allow herself to give him a thought; yet now, at the first moment of seeing him again, she was seized by a feeling of joyful pride. There was no need for her to ask him why he was there. She knew as well as if he had told her, that he was there in order to be where she was.

'I did not know that you were going too. Why are you going?' she asked, dropping the hand with which she was about to take hold of the handrail. Her face beamed with a joy and animation she could not repress.

'Why am I going?' he repeated, looking straight into her eyes. 'You know that I am going in order to be where you are,' said he. 'I cannot do otherwise.'

At this moment the wind, as if it had mastered all obstacles, scattered the snow from the carriage roofs, and set a loose sheet of iron clattering; and in front the deep whistle of the engine howled mournfully and dismally. The awfulness of the storm appeared still more beautiful to her now. He had said just what her soul desired but her reason dreaded. She did not reply, and he saw a struggle in her face.

'Forgive me if my words displease you,' he said humbly.

He spoke courteously and respectfully, but so firmly and stubbornly that she was long unable to reply.

'What you are saying is wrong, and if you are a good man, I beg you to forget it, as I will forget it,' she said at last.

'Not a word, not a movement of yours will I ever forget, nor can I . . .'

'Enough, enough!' she cried, vainly trying to give a severe expression to her face, into which he was gazing eagerly. She took hold of the cold handrail, ascended the steps, and quickly entered the little lobby leading into the carriage. But in that little lobby she stopped, going over in her imagination what had just taken place. Although she could remember neither his nor her own words, she instinctively felt that that momentary conversation had drawn them terribly near to one another, and this both frightened her and made her happy. After standing still for a few seconds she went into the carriage and sat down. The overwrought condition which tormented her before not only returned again, but grew worse and reached such a degree that she feared every moment that something within her would give way under the intolerable strain. She did not sleep at all that night, but the strain and the visions which filled her imagination had nothing unpleasant or dismal about them; on the contrary they seemed joyful, glowing, and stimulating . . .

When he got out of the train at Petersburg he felt, despite his sleepless night, as fresh and animated as after a cold bath. He stopped outside the carriage, waiting till she appeared. 'I shall see her again,' he thought and smiled involuntarily. 'I shall see her walk, her face . . . she will say something, turn her head, look at me, perhaps even smile.' But before seeing her he saw her husband, whom the station-master was respectfully conducting through the crowd. 'Dear me! the husband!' Only now did Vronsky for the first time clearly realize that the husband was connected with her. He knew she had a husband, but had not believed in his existence, and only fully believed in him when he saw him there: his head and shoulders, and the black trousers containing his legs, and especially when he saw that husband with an air of ownership quietly take her hand.

When he saw Karenin, with his fresh Petersburg face, his sternly self-confident figure, his round hat and his slightly rounded back, Vronsky believed in his existence, and had such a disagreeable sensation as a man tortured by thirst might feel on reaching a spring and finding a dog, sheep, or pig in it, drinking the water and making it muddy. Karenin's gait, the swinging of his thighs, and his wide short feet, particularly offended Vronsky, who acknowledged only his own unquestionable right to love Anna. But she was still the same, and the sight of her still affected him physically, exhilarating and stimulating him and filling him with joy. He ordered his German valet, who had run up from a second-class carriage, to get his luggage and take it home, and he himself went up to her. He saw the husband and wife meet, and with the penetration of a lover he noticed the signs of slight embarrassment when she spoke to her husband.

'No, she doesn't and can't love him,' he decided mentally.

Leo Tolstoy, *Anna Karenina*, OUP, 1918, Vol. I: XXX, XXXI, pp. 116–17, 119–20 (translated by Louise and Aylmer Maude).

A century later men and women would still stumble hesitatingly towards adultery, as in this vignette from *Couples*. Frank is married to Janet, and Marcia is married to Harold:

They had lunch, and lunch often again, meeting at the corners of new glass buildings or in the doorways of flower shops, a toothy ruddy man with a soft air of having done well at school and a small dark efficient woman looking a little breathless, hunting hand in hand through the marine stenches of the waterfront and the jostling glare of Washington Street for the perfect obscure restaurant, with the corner table, and the fatherly bartender, and the absence of business acquaintances and college friends. They talked, touching toes, quickly brushing hands in admonishment or pity, talked about themselves, about their childhoods spent behind trimmed hedges, about Shakespeare and psychiatry, which Marcia's lovely father had practiced, about Harold and Janet who, as they obligingly continued to be deceived, were ever more tenderly considered, so that they became almost sacred in their ignorance, wonderful in their fallibility, so richly forgiven for their frigidity, demandingness, obtuseness, and vanity that the liaison between their spouses seemed a conspiracy to praise the absent.

John Updike, *Couples*, Knopf, 1968, Ch. 2, p. 113.

In the liberal 1960s social disapproval was only a minor problem facing adulterers. Earlier generations in America had a harder time of it. In *The Age of Innocence*, Newland Archer, although married to May Welland, experiences a growing mutual attraction to her cousin Ellen Olenska, who is unhappily married to a rich Polish nobleman and seeking a divorce from him. Their discussion of the options available to them place the private nature of infidelity within a social web from which it seemed almost impossible to escape in nineteenth-century New York. He meets her on her return to New York from Washington:

'. . . You must see that this can't last.'

'What can't?'

'Our being together – and not together.'

'No. You ought not to have come today,' she said in an altered voice; and suddenly she turned, flung her arms about him and pressed her lips to his. At the same moment the carriage began to move, and a gas-lamp at the head of the slip flashed its light into the window. She drew away, and they sat silent and motionless while the brougham struggled through the congestion of carriages about the ferry-landing. As they gained the street Archer began to speak hurriedly.

'Don't be afraid of me: you needn't squeeze yourself back into your corner like that. A stolen kiss isn't what I want. Look: I'm not even trying to touch the sleeve of your jacket. Don't suppose that I don't understand your reasons for not wanting to let this feeling between us dwindle into an ordinary hole-and-corner love affair. I couldn't have spoken like this yesterday, because when we've been apart, and I'm looking forward to seeing you, every thought is burnt up in a great flame. But then you come; and you're so much more than I remembered, and what I want of you is so much more than an hour or two every now and then, with wastes of thirsty waiting between, that I can sit perfectly still beside you, like this, with that other vision in my mind, just quietly trusting to it to come true.'

For a moment she made no reply; then she asked, hardly above a whisper: 'What do you mean by trusting to it to come true?'

'Why – you know it will, don't you?'

'Your vision of you and me together?' She burst into a sudden hard laugh. 'You choose your place well to put it to me!'

'Do you mean because we're in my wife's brougham? Shall we get out and walk, then? I don't suppose you mind a little snow?'

She laughed again, more gently. 'No; I shan't get out and walk, because my business is to get to Granny's as quickly as I can. And you'll sit beside me, and we'll look, not at visions, but at realities.'

'I don't know what you mean by realities. The only reality to me is this.'

She met the words with a long silence, during which the carriage rolled down an obscure side-street and then turned into the searching illumination of Fifth Avenue.

'Is it your idea, then, that I should live with you as your mistress – since I can't be your wife?' she asked.

The crudeness of the question startled him: the word was one that women of his class fought shy of, even when their talk flitted closest about the topic. He noticed that Madame Olenska pronounced it as if it had a recognized place in her vocabulary, and he wondered if it had been used familiarly in her presence in the horrible life she had fled from. Her question pulled him up with a jerk, and he floundered.

'I want – I want somehow to get away with you into a world where words like that – categories like that – won't exist. Where we shall be simply two human beings who love each other, who are the whole of life to each other; and nothing else on earth will matter.'

She drew a deep sigh that ended in another laugh. 'Oh, my dear – where is that country? Have you ever been there?' she asked; and as he remained sullenly dumb she went on: 'I know so many who've tried to find it; and, believe me, they all got out by mistake at wayside stations: at places like Boulogne, or Pisa, or Monte Carlo – and it wasn't at all different from the old world they'd left, but only rather smaller and dingier and more promiscuous.' . . .

The carriage had crossed Forty-second Street: May's sturdy brougham-horse was carrying them northward as if he had been a Kentucky trotter. Archer choked with the sense of wasted minutes and vain words.

'Then what, exactly, is your plan for us?' he asked.

'For *us*? But there's no *us* in that sense! We're near each other only if we stay far from each other. Then we can be ourselves. Otherwise we're only Newland Archer, the husband of Ellen Olenska's cousin, and Ellen Olenska, the cousin of Newland Archer's wife, trying to be happy behind the backs of the people who trust them.'

'Ah, I'm beyond that,' he groaned.

'No, you're not! You've never been beyond. And *I* have,' she said, in a strange voice, 'and I know what it looks like there.'

He sat silent, dazed with inarticulate pain. Then he groped in the darkness of the carriage for the little bell that signaled orders to the coachman. He remembered that May rang twice when she wished to stop. He pressed the bell, and the carriage drew up beside the curbstone.

'Why are we stopping? This is not Granny's,' Madame Olenska exclaimed.

'No: I shall get out here,' he stammered, opening the door and jumping to the pavement. By the light of a street-lamp he saw her startled face, and the instinctive motion she made to detain him . . . She bent forward, and seemed about to speak; but he had already called out the order to drive on, and the carriage rolled away while he stood on the corner . . .

Some days later Archer calls on Ellen at her Granny's:

She murmured: 'I promised Granny to stay with her because it seemed to me that here I should be safer.'

'From me?'

She bent her head slightly, without looking at him.

'Safer from loving me?'

Her profile did not stir, but he saw a tear overflow on her lashes and hang in a mesh of her veil.

'Safer from doing irreparable harm. Don't let us be like all the others!' she protested.

'What others? I don't profess to be different from my kind. I'm consumed by the same wants and the same longings.'

She glanced at him with a kind of terror, and he saw a faint color steal into her cheeks.

'Shall I – once come to you; and then go home?' she suddenly hazarded in a low clear voice.

The blood rushed to the young man's forehead. 'Dearest!' he said, without moving. It seemed as if he held his heart in his hands, like a full cup that the least motion might overbrim.

Then her last phrase struck his ear and his face clouded. 'Go home? What do you mean by going home?'

'Home to my husband.'

'And you expect me to say yes to that?'

She raised her troubled eyes to his. 'What else is there? I can't stay here and lie to the people who've been good to me.'

'But that's the very reason why I ask you to come away!'

'And destroy their lives, when they've helped me to remake mine?'

Archer sprang to his feet and stood looking down on her in inarticulate despair. It would have been easy to say: 'Yes, come; come once.' He knew the power she would put in his hands if she consented; there would be no difficulty then in persuading her not to go back to her husband.

But something silenced the word on his lips. A sort of passionate honesty in her made it inconceivable that he should try to draw her into that familiar trap. 'If I were to let her come,' he said to himself, 'I should have to let her go again.' And that was not to be imagined.

But he saw the shadow of the lashes on her wet cheek, and wavered.

'After all,' he began again, 'we have lives of our own ... There's no use attempting the impossible. You're so unprejudiced about some things, so used, as you say, to looking at the Gorgon, that I don't know why you're afraid to face our case, and see it as it really is – unless you think the sacrifice is not worth making.'

She stood up also, her lips tightening under a rapid frown.

'Call it that, then – I must go,' she said, drawing her little watch from her bosom.

She turned away, and he followed and caught her by the wrist. 'Well, then, come to me once,' he said, his head turning suddenly at the thought of losing her; and for a second or two they looked at each other almost like enemies.

'When?' he insisted. 'Tomorrow?'

She hesitated. 'The day after.'

'Dearest –!' he said again.

She had disengaged her wrist; but for a moment they continued to hold each other's eyes, and he saw that her face, which had grown very pale, was flooded with a deep inner radiance. His heart beat with awe: he felt that he had never before beheld love visible.

'Oh, I shall be late – good-bye. No, don't come any farther than this,' she cried, walking hurriedly away down the long room, as if the reflected radiance in his eyes had frightened her. When she reached the door she turned for a moment to wave a quick farewell.

Edith Wharton, *The Age of Innocence*, Chs. 29, 31.

Edith Wharton experienced similar soul-searching in her own life, as she realized that she was sorely tempted to betray her husband Teddy for another man, Morton Fullerton. She clearly wrote to Henry James for advice – and he gave it:

I am deeply distressed at the situation you describe and as to which my power to suggest or enlighten now quite miserably fails me. I move in darkness; I rack my brain; I gnash my teeth; I don't pretend to understand or to imagine . . . Only sit tight yourself *and go through the movements of life.* That keeps up our connection with life – I mean of the immediate and apparent life; behind which, all the while, the deeper and darker and unapparent, in which things *really* happen to us, learns, under that hygiene, to stay in its place. Let it get out of its place and it swamps the scene; besides which its place, God knows, is enough for it! Live it all through, every inch of it – out of it something valuable will come – but live it ever so quietly; and – *je maintiens mon dire* – waitingly! . . . What I am really hoping is that you'll be on your voyage when this reaches the Mount. If you're not you'll be so very soon afterwards, won't you? – and you'll come down and see me here and we'll talk *à perte de vue*, and there will be something in that for both of us . . . Believe meanwhile and always in the aboundingly tender friendship – the understanding, the participation, the *princely* (though I say it who shouldn't) hospitality of spirit and soul of yours more than ever,
Henry James.

Henry James, *Letters*, October 1908, Braziller, 1965.

Desire in its extreme form has gripped Emma Bovary, whose love for
Léon is inextricably meshed with her dismay at her own dull life and dull
marriage:

Emma grew thinner, her cheeks pale and her face lengthened.
With her black braided hair, large eyes, straight nose, and bird-
light step, always noiseless now, it seemed as if she went through
life touching it scarcely at all, bearing on her brow the mysterious
mark of some sublime destiny. She was so sad and so quiet, so
sweet yet so withdrawn, that you felt in her presence a kind of icy
charm, as you may shiver in church at the scent of the flowers
mingling with the chill of the marble . . .

But within, she was all desire and rage and hatred. That
straight-pleated dress hid a heart in turmoil, those demure lips told
nothing of its suffering. She was in love with Léon; and she
sought a solitude that she might revel in his image undisturbed. It
marred the pleasure of her daydreams to see him in the flesh. The
sound of his step set her trembling. But in his presence her
agitation subsided, leaving nothing but an immense astonishment
that worked itself out in sadness.

Léon never knew, when he went away from her in despair, that
she would immediately get up and watch him through the window.
She started nervously studying his movements, covertly observing
his face, and she concocted a whole rigmarole to give herself a
pretext for visiting his room. She thought the chemist's wife a
lucky woman indeed to be sleeping under the same roof with him,
and her thoughts were for ever alighting on that house, like the
pigeons from the Golden Lion who went to bathe their pink feet
and white wings in the gutters there. But the more Emma became
conscious of her love, the harder she strove to conceal and to
suppress it. She would have been glad if he had guessed; she
envisaged various happenings and catastrophes that might give
him the hint. It was doubtless indolence, or fear, that held her
back. Modesty, too. She wondered whether she had been too
distant with him – and now the moment had gone by, and all was

lost! But her pride, her joy in saying 'I am a virtuous woman', and in contemplating her own attitudes of resignation in the mirror, brought her some solace for the sacrifice she believed herself to be making.

Then the appetites of the flesh, the craving for money, the melancholy of passion, all blended together in one general misery. Instead of turning her thoughts away, she riveted them to it the more firmly; she worked up her grief, and sought out its occasions. She was irritated by a meal badly served or a door left ajar; she moped to herself about the velvet she did not possess, the happiness that was passing her by, the loftiness of her dreams and the littleness of her house.

To make it harder, Charles had apparently no notion of what she suffered. His unquestioning belief that he made her happy seemed to her a stupid insult; his complacency on the point, ingratitude. For whose sake, then, this goodness of hers? Was not he the very obstacle to all felicity, the cause of all her wretchedness, the pointed buckle, as it were, on the complicated strap that bound her?

And so on him became centred the abundant hatred which resulted from her frustrations, and which every attempt to moderate served only to augment, her vain efforts giving her an added reason for despair, and contributing further to their estrangement. She rebelled against her own meekness. Her drab surroundings drove her to dreams of luxury; marital tenderness prompted the desire for a lover. She would have liked Charles to hit her, that she might have just cause for hatred and revenge. She was surprised sometimes at the hideous ideas that occurred to her. And all the while she must go on smiling, hearing herself insist that she was very happy, pretending to be so, acting the part.

Gustave Flaubert, *Madame Bovary*, Penguin, 1950, Part II, Ch. 5, pp. 120–22 (translated by Alan Russell).

Edward Ashburnham, the Good Soldier of Ford Madox Ford's novel of that title (1915), is also a victim of his emotions. Like Emma Bovary, he must first fall passionately in love before he can justify his adultery. He has just gone with his wife Leonora to Monte Carlo, when he falls in love with another woman:

Such was his honourable nature, that for him to enjoy a woman's favours made him feel that she had a bond on him for life. That was the way it worked out in practice. Psychologically it meant that he could not have a mistress without falling violently in love with her. He was a serious person – and in this particular case it was very expensive. The mistress of the Grand Duke – a Spanish dancer of passionate appearance – singled out Edward for her glances at a ball that was held in their common hotel. Edward was tall, handsome, blond, and very wealthy as she understood – and Leonora went up to bed early. She did not care for public dances, but she was relieved to see that Edward appeared to be having a good time with several amiable girls. And that was the end of Edward – for the Spanish dancer of passionate appearance wanted one night of him for his beaux yeux. He took her into the dark gardens and . . . he kissed her passionately, violently, with a sudden explosion of the passion that had been bridled all his life – for Leonora was cold, or at any rate, well behaved. La Dolciquita liked this reversion, and he passed the night in her bed.

When the palpitating creature was at last asleep in his arms he discovered that he was madly, was passionately, was overwhelmingly in love with her. It was a passion that had arisen like fire in dry corn. He could think of nothing else; he could live for nothing else. But La Dolciquita was a reasonable creature without an ounce of passion in her. She wanted a certain satisfaction of her appetites and Edward had appealed to her the night before. Now that was done with, and, quite coldly, she said that she wanted money if he was to have any more of her. It was a perfectly reasonable commercial transaction. She did not care two buttons for Edward or for any man and he was asking her to risk a very good situation with the Grand Duke. If Edward could put up sufficient money to serve as a kind of insurance against accident she was ready to like

Edward for a time that would be covered, as it were, by the policy. She was getting fifty thousand dollars a year from the Grand Duke; Edward would have to pay a premium of two years' hire for a month of her society. There would not be much risk of the Grand Duke's finding it out and it was not certain that he would give her the keys of the street if he did find out. But there was the risk — a twenty per cent risk, as she figured it out. She talked to Edward as if she had been a solicitor with an estate to sell — perfectly quietly and perfectly coldly without any inflections in her voice. She did not want to be unkind to him; but she could see no reason for being kind to him. She was a virtuous business woman with a mother and two sisters and her own old age to be provided comfortably for. She did not expect more than a five years' further run. She was twenty-four and, as she said: 'We Spanish women are horrors at thirty.' Edward swore that he would provide for her for life if she would come to him and leave off talking so horribly; but she only shrugged one shoulder slowly and contemptuously. He tried to convince this woman, who, as he saw it, had surrendered to him her virtue, that he regarded it as in any case his duty to provide for her, and to cherish her and even to love her — for life. In return for her sacrifice he would do that. In return, again, for his honourable love she would listen for ever to the accounts of his estate. That was how he figured it out.

She shrugged the same shoulder with the same gesture and held out her left hand with the elbow at her side:

'Enfin, mon ami,' she said, 'put in this hand the price of that tiara at Forli's or . . .' And she turned her back on him.

Edward went mad; his world stood on his head; the palms in front of the blue sea danced grotesque dances. You see, he believed in the virtue, tenderness, and moral support of women. He wanted more than anything to argue with La Dolciquita; to retire with her to an island and point out to her the damnation of her point of view and how salvation can only be found in true love and the feudal system. She had once been his mistress, he reflected, and by all the moral laws she ought to have gone on being his mistress or at the very least his sympathetic confidante. But her rooms were closed to him; she did not appear in the hotel. Nothing: blank silence. To break that down he had to have twenty thousand pounds. You have heard what happened.

He spent a week of madness; he hungered; his eyes sank in; he shuddered at Leonora's touch. I dare say that nine-tenths of what he took to be his passion for La Dolciquita was really discomfort at the thought that he had been unfaithful to Leonora. He felt uncommonly bad, that is to say – oh, unbearably bad, and he took it all to be love. Poor devil, he was incredibly naive. He drank like a fish after Leonora was in bed and he spread himself over the tables, and this went on for about a fortnight. Heaven knows what would have happened; he would have thrown away every penny that he possessed.

On the night after he had lost about forty thousand pounds and whilst the whole hotel was whispering about it, La Dolciquita walked composedly into his bedroom. He was too drunk to recognize her, and she sat in his armchair, knitting and holding smelling salts to her nose – for he was pretty far gone with alcoholic poisoning – and, as soon as he was able to understand her, she said:

'Look here, mon ami, do not go to the tables again. Take a good sleep now and come and see me this afternoon.'

He slept till the lunch-hour. By that time Leonora had heard the news. A Mrs Colonel Whelen had told her ... and she advised Leonora to go straight off to town – which might have the effect of bringing Edward to his senses – and to consult her solicitor and her spiritual adviser. She had better go that very morning; it was no good arguing with a man in Edward's condition.

Edward, indeed, did not know that she had gone. As soon as he woke he went straight to La Dolciquita's room and she stood him his lunch in her own apartments. He fell on her neck and wept, and she put up with it for a time. She was quite a good-natured woman. And, when she had calmed him down with Eau de Mélisse, she said:

'Look here, my friend, how much money have you left? Five thousand dollars? Ten?' For the rumour went that Edward had lost two kings' ransoms a night for fourteen nights and she imagined that he must be near the end of his resources.

The Eau de Mélisse had calmed Edward to such an extent that, for the moment, he really had a head on his shoulders. He did nothing more than grunt:

'And then?'

'Why,' she answered, 'I may just as well have the ten thousand dollars as the tables. I will go with you to Antibes for a week for that sum.'

Edward grunted: 'Five.' She tried to get seven thousand five hundred; but he stuck to his five thousand and the hotel expenses at Antibes. The sedative carried him just as far as that and then he collapsed again. He had to leave for Antibes at three; he could not do without it. He left a note for Leonora saying that he had gone off for a week with the Clinton Morleys, yachting.

He did not enjoy himself very much at Antibes. La Dolciquita could talk of nothing with any enthusiasm except money, and she tired him unceasingly, during every waking hour, for presents of the most expensive description. And, at the end of a week, she just quietly kicked him out. He hung about in Antibes for three days. He was cured of the idea that he had any duties towards La Dolciquita – feudal or otherwise. But his sentimentalism required of him an attitude of Byronic gloom – as if his court had gone into half-mourning. Then his appetite suddenly returned, and he remembered Leonora. He found at his hotel at Monte Carlo a telegram from Leonora, dispatched from London, saying: 'Please return as soon as convenient.' He could not understand why Leonora should have abandoned him so precipitately, why she only thought that he had gone yachting with the Clinton Morleys. Then he discovered that she had left the hotel before he had written the note. He had a pretty rocky journey back to town; he was frightened out of his life – and Leonora had never seemed so desirable to him.

Ford Madox Ford, *The Good Soldier*, III:IV.

No such passion troubles the cool connoisseurship of Keith Talent as he roams the housing estates of North Kensington:

In his bachelor days Keith had been a regular romeo. He had been a real ladykiller. In truth, he had been quite a one. Even Keith's dog Clive, in his dog heyday, had been no keener or less choosy or more incapable of letting a female scent go by without streaking after it with his nose on the ground and his tongue thrown over his shoulder like a scarf. Then came change, and responsibilities: Kath, his wife, and their baby girl, little Kim. And now it was all different. These days Keith kept a leash on his restless nature, restricting himself to the kind of evanescent romance that might come the way of any modern young businessman on his travels (the wife or sister or daughter or mother of some *cheat* in the East End, perhaps, where Keith went to get the perfume), plus the occasional indiscretion rather closer to home (Iqbala, the single parent in the next flat along), plus the odd chance encounter made possible when fortune smiles on young lovers (closing time, pub toilet), plus three regular and longstanding girlfriends, Trish Shirt, Debbee Kensit, who was special, and Analiese Furnish. And that was it . . .

. . . Debbee was *special*. Dark, rounded, pouting, everything circular, ovoid, Debbee was 'special'. Debbee was special because Keith had been sleeping with her since she was twelve years old. On the other hand, so had several other people. All completely kosher and Bristol-fashion because she'd had her tubes done and you just gave cash gifts of seventy-five quid to her mum, who wasn't bad either . . . Last autumn, Debbee had celebrated her fifteenth birthday. In the past Keith had gone round there as often as he could afford (or more often: he had sometimes knowingly bounced cheques on Mrs K.). Since November, though, he was less frequently to be seen there. But Debbee would always be special to Keith. She would always be special. At least until she was eighteen. Or sixteen.

And finally, invariably finally, there was Trish Shirt, blonde and pale and getting on a bit now, thinnish Trish (but sturdy-legged), who couldn't remember how old she was or what kind of blonde her hair had been when she started out, so many years ago. She lived under a supermarket on Ladbroke Grove, which was convenient, and even necessary, because she hated going out. Trish needed several tumblers of vodka before she could face the strip lighting and the caged goods. Keith brought Trish her dole, sparing her the fortnightly mortification, with money subtracted for her drink, thus sparing her a much more frequent ordeal. This figured strongly in the steady increase of his powers. Keith was like a god to Trish. 'I'd do anything for you, Keith. Anything,' she said. And Keith took her up on it. But every time he strode out of CostCheck clutching the keys to the heavy Cavalier, or silently got dressed (or rezipped himself) while staring at her pale body, Keith vowed that this visit would be his last. Every time he pushed open the plywood door, every time Trish came to welcome him on her knees, Keith was that little bit angrier. For this he would give Trish payment. God save us, what was he *doing* to himself? Why was he here, with her, with that, when he had funloving little Debbee, and sinuous Analiese (and Peggy and Iqbala and Petronella and Fran)? Well, it was true that Trish had something to be said for her. Trish had a certain quality. She was nearest.

How to account for Keith's way with women, such as it was? How to account for Keith's talent? He had a knack. Keith could tell women what they were thinking. No doubt this has never been easy. But it's quite an accomplishment, with these women, in these days.

On the other hand, how much of a way with women did Keith really need? One was drunk, one was nuts, and one was fifteen. The ladykiller. These, then, were Keith's birds.

Martin Amis, *London Fields*, Cape, 1989, pp. 48, 51, 51–2.

For Bob Slocum in *Something Happened*, every adulterous craving is a source of anxiety, every action to fulfil such cravings will have its consequences:

I have stopped flirting with Jane (what *would* I do with her afterward?) and started flirting platonically with Laura, Arthur Baron's secretary (which makes a much better impression). Laura is older and unhappily married. She is highly regarded by everyone but her husband, who is three years younger than she and perhaps homosexual, and my attentions are clearly friendly and humanitarian (although she does have a thick ass I think now and then I might like to toss over onto my lap and paddle bare with stinging, tingling noises. It's good I don't try, for I forget how heavy she'd be, and I would risk a hernia or slipped spinal disk. If I did that once to someone, I might want to do it always – and then I would be a pervert. Girls would talk about me unfavorably to their friends. I think I feel that way too about stuttering. I think I may *want* to stutter. What a liberating release it might be from the lifelong, rigorous discipline of speaking correctly. I'd feel tongue-tied and free. I might spank and stutter at the same time. I feel I might never want to stop once I started and would let my tongue wobble as it wanted to for the rest of my life and never have to say anything intelligible to anyone again. I would lose my job. I would lose my wife and friends. I don't have close friends anymore. I have friends, but I don't feel close to them. Some feel close to me. Red Parker is my friend, and I don't feel close to him). I really don't know *how* I would have disposed of Jane after taking her to bed with me in Red Parker's apartment early one evening probably after cocktails. She's only twenty-four. I can't imagine what in the world I would want to talk to her about once we no longer had to talk about going to bed. She's probably too young to understand there'd be nothing personal in the enmity and disgust I'd feel toward her afterward and in my never wanting to see or speak to her again. That's happened to me before. She'd probably conclude it had something to do with her. I'd have her lovely blue eyes fastened upon me in wondering, repentant apology. I could not say to her outright – I like her too much for:

'Nothing – nothing – nothing, dammit. You didn't do *anything* wrong. It has nothing at all to do with you. You aren't important enough to affect me. Don't you see?'

That might hurt her feelings too.

I would have to overcompensate with pleasantries and consideration: I might even have to lay her again, just because I'm a real nice guy. That's happened before too. (Or I might tell her my wife is undergoing tests for cancer and win some pity for myself that way. I've done that before also.) It's why I don't like to get involved with girls in the same office anymore. They're there. (If only she worked somewhere else. I could use her often these days. But then I might not have her.)

Joseph Heller, *Something Happened*, Knopf, 1974, pp. 437–8.

Deception

The one charm of marriage is that it makes a life of deception absolutely necessary for both parties.

Oscar Wilde, *The Picture of Dorian Gray*

Infidelity and deception walk arm in arm. In strict societies, deception is a precondition for adultery. In Mme d'Epinay's *Memoirs*, her sister-in-law Mme de Jully confides that she has a lover. The purpose of the confession is to enlist Mme d'Epinay's support in pulling the wool over her M. de Jully's eyes:

'. . . I am also in love: I must be free to discuss my love-affair with you, and to communicate with my lover, through you, and meet him at your house . . .'

'Your lover? . . .'

'Well? . . . So that takes your breath away! Because you married the eldest you think you are the only privileged member of the family.'

'Sister, truly – I can't help . . .'

'Laughing – for you wanted to, and it's what we had better do. Drop your prudery – we are by ourselves, we can trust one another, so why be reserved?'

'I thought you were in love with your husband. He is so very fond of you. I never thought he gave you cause for complaint. That is why I am so surprised.'

'That does require some explanation. I have not the slightest complaint to make of Jully. I have great respect and liking for him – but have never had more than that.'

'I thought you married him for love and that you loved him passionately.'

'So he has chosen to believe, but that was never the case. These are the facts. De B— was head-over-ears in love with me, and wanted to marry me. I should have consented for I liked him well enough, but I discovered that he had such a violent temper and was so jealous and so unfair, for – mark you – jealousy in a man always takes the form of unfairness and tyranny, that at last I really got frightened. Jully presented himself – I preferred him – and that is all.'

'But what about all those suitors that he has told me twenty times you refused for him?'

'He is quite right: I refused many offers, but they weren't worth considering. The more I know of M. de Jully the more I congratulate myself on my choice. He is a good fellow, kindly, easy-going, weak, no spirit, but no vice, just right for playing his part decently, and I am very grateful to him, for it's a great thing – that! But when he thought himself in love with me I can tell he made a mistake.'

'Whatever are you saying, sister, he adores you as much as he did the first day.'

'Is that what he says? Oh, well – he is mistaken again. There's a girl at the Comédie that he is giving presents to all day long. He would have her, if he had not paraded his passion for me, but in reality he is the one man I see least of and the one who least consults my wishes.'

'Sister, sister, you are unjust. Can you deny that your husband's one thought is what he can do to please you?'

'What! Because he is for ever giving me jewellery that I don't care about, and dresses which are nearly always exactly what I should not choose myself: because he takes boxes at the theatre for me on a day when I would rather stay at home. Ah! don't you see that it's his whims not mine that he indulges? But beg him to yield one of his whims and fancies to mine, and you will see this pearl of husbands turn – oh, so gently – into the most despotic of sultans.'

Mme de Jully reveals the name of her lover:

'He's Jelyotte.'

'Jelyotte! You don't mean it, sister! An operatic singer! a man for all the world to stare at, and whom you cannot decently have as a friend!'

'Gently! if you please: I have told you that I love him, and you reply as though I had asked your opinion as to whether I ought to love him.'

'True, but you also said that you wanted me to do you a service, and I tell you that I do not care to be M. Jelyotte's confidante or go-between.'

'You are deciding a little hastily, my dear sister, and I should not care to hear you use the same language twice: no need to drag in my lover's name – it is I who ask the favour – will you or won't you oblige me?'

'Oh, to you, sister, I could never refuse anything – but I must . . .'

'Very well – now, tell me, is not Jelyotte an estimable man? Does not everyone consider him above his station?'

'Yes, and that very statement condemns you. Society will never condone it.'

'Ah, my child, Society's a fool and he who attends to what people say, at the expense of his own happiness, is a bigger fool. Look here, Jelyotte is coming here to-night. You must put him in the blue room next to mine. During dinner I will complain of the noise my husband makes when he goes out hunting in the morning: then you must suggest to me that he should have the little room at the back of mine: I will agree, and all will be well.'

'Ah,' I told her, 'if that is all you ask of me, yes, most certainly.'

Mme d'Epinay, *Memoirs* (1751–2), Routledge, 1930, pp. 120–3.

Mme de Jully simply requires a little subterfuge. Horner, in Wycherley's *The Country Wife*, goes to much greater lengths, by putting it about, with the aid of a Quack, that he is impotent and thus no threat to the ladies:

Quack: What all alone, not so much as one of your Cuckolds here, nor one of their Wives! they use to take their turns with you, as if they were to watch you.

Horner: Yes it often happens, that a Cuckold is but his Wifes spye, and is more upon family duty, when he is with her gallant abroad hindring his pleasure, than when he is at home with her playing the Gallant, but the hardest duty a married woman imposed upon a lover, is keeping her Husband company always.

Quack: And his fondness wearies you almost as soon as hers.

Horner: A Pox, keeping a Cuckold company after you have had his Wife, is as tiresome as the company of a Country Squire to a witty Fellow of the Town, when he has got all his Mony.

Quack: And as at first a man makes a friend of the Husband to get the Wife, so at last you are faine to fall out with the Wife to be rid of the Husband.

Horner: Ay, most Cuckold-makers and true Courtiers, when once a poor man has crack'd his credit for 'em, they can't abide to come near him.

None the less the jealous Pinchwife is worried by the interest Horner is showing in his naïve new wife, a country girl. He discovers his wife returning that interest:

Mrs Pin: Well 'tis e'ne so, I have got the London Disease, they call Love, I am sick of my Husband, and for my Gallant; I have heard this distemper, call'd a Feaver, but methinks 'tis liker an Ague, for when I think of my Husband, I tremble, and am in a cold sweat, and have inclinations to vomit, but when I think of my Gallant, dear Mr Horner, my hot fit comes, and I am all in a Feaver, indeed, & as in other Feavers, my own Chamber is tedious to me, and I would fain be remov'd to his, and then methinks I shoul'd be well; ah poor Mr Horner, well I cannot, will not stay here, therefore I'le make an end of my Letter to him, which shall be a finer Letter than my last, because I have studied it like any thing; O Sick, Sick!

[*Takes the Pen and writes.*]

[*Enter Mr Pinchwife, who seeing her writing, steales softly behind her, and looking over her shoulder, snatches the Paper from her.*]

Mr Pin: What, writing more Letters?

Mrs Pin: O Lord, Budd, why d'ye fright me so?

[*She offers to run out: he stops her, and reads.*]

Mr Pin: How's this! nay you shall not stir Madam.

Deare, deare, deare, Mr Horner – very well – I have taught you to write Letters to good purpose – but let's see't.

First I am to beg your pardon for my boldness in writing to you, which I'de have you to know, I would not have done, had not you said first you lov'd me so extreamly, which if you do, you will never suffer me to lye in the arms of another man, whom I loath, nauseate, and detest – [Now you can write these filthy words] but what follows – Therefore, I hope you will speedily find some way to free me from this unfortunate match, which was never, I assure you, of my choice, but I'm afraid 'tis already too far gone; however, if you love me, as I do you, you will try what you can do, but you must help me away before to-morrow, or else alas I shall be for ever out of your reach, for I can defer no longer our – our – what is to follow – speak what? our Journey into the Country I suppose –

Oh Woman, damn'd Woman, and Love, damn'd Love, their old Tempter, for this is one of his miracles, in a moment he can make those blind that cou'd see, and those see that were blind, those dumb that could speak, and those prattle who were dumb before, nay, what is more than all, make these dow-bak'd, sensless, indocile animals, Women, too hard for us their Politick Lords and Rulers in a moment; But make an end of your Letter, and then I'le make an end of you thus, and all my plagues together.

[*Draws his Sword.*]

Mrs Pin: O Lord, O Lord you are such a Passionate Man, Budd.

Fortunately Mr Pinchwife is even more stupid than his wife, and is persuaded that she is writing this letter on behalf of her sister.

William Wycherley, *The Country Wife*, V:i, IV:i.

Madame de Barbezieux practises a different pretence in order to get back at her philandering husband:

M. de Barbezieux [a minister for war under Louis XIV] ended the year with a scandal which he might very well have avoided. He had recently married Mlle d'Alègre. He treated her like a child, and in no way restrained his love-affairs or changed his accustomed way of life. M. d'Elbeuf pretended to be her lover so as to insult him. The young woman, much offended by her husband's conduct, listened to bad advice and made him jealous. He yielded to that passion; lost all sense of proportion, saw things as they were not, and did what none but he has ever done, namely, declared himself publicly a cuckold; tried to prove it; failed, and was believed by no one. You cannot imagine anyone so furious at being unable to make himself thought a cuckold. All that he discovered was the indiscretions, the thoughtless actions of an innocent but ill-advised young girl, endeavouring to bring back her husband by pretending to give tit for tat. But Barbezieux was too angry to see reason. He sent a courier summoning her father to return at once from his estates in Auvergne, couched in such language that d'Alègre, who was not the cleverest of men, believed that he was being sent for to receive promotion. He was thus very unpleasantly surprised when he learned the facts. Separation was the only course, the affair having become so desperate. Mme de Barbezieux was a prisoner in her husband's house and ill in bed. Her husband vowed that she was pretending and wanted to put her in a convent there and then; her father and mother wished to keep her with them. At last, after an appalling rumpus on a very slight pretext, the King was asked by both gentlemen to intervene and decreed that she was to return to her parents until fully recovered, and that they were then to take her to a convent in Auvergne. Regarding the dowry, Barbezieux repaid it in full, but demanded from d'Alègre all the necessary to bring up and support his two little daughters. People greatly pitied d'Alègre and still more so his daughter, and Barbezieux was strongly criticized. What was still worse, he ever afterwards did d'Alègre every conceivable bad turn, and used all his power and influence to that end.

Duc de Saint-Simon, *Memoirs*, Hamish Hamilton, 1967, Vol. I, pp. 116–17 (translated by Lucy Norton).

Saint-Simon also recounts how Louis XIV agreed to appoint the Marquis de Puyguilhem as grandmaster of artillery, but on condition that the appointment be kept secret. The minister of war, Louvois, was strongly opposed to the appointment and on learning about it, voiced his concerns to the king:

The King was greatly vexed to learn that his secret had become known to the very man from whom he had most wished to hide it. He turned to Louvois saying with extreme gravity that nothing as yet was settled, dismissed him, and returned to his seat at the council. The meeting soon afterwards ended and the King went to mass; he noted Puyguilhem, but passed by without a word. That gentleman, completely mystified, waited all the rest of that day; but when the time came for the King's *petit coucher* and there was still no announcement, he brought the matter up. King Louis replied that it was not yet time, but that he would see. That ambiguous answer and the curt manner of its utterance put fear into Puyguilhem's soul. He was a great stealer of hearts and had a way with the ladies; he therefore went to Mme de Montespan and, confiding his trouble, implored her to act. She promised miracles, and with that hope kept him happy for some days longer.

At last, tired of waiting and wholly unaware of the reason for his disappointment, he took a course so rash that it would be unbelievable had it not been vouched for by the entire Court of that day. It so happened that Puyguilhem was sleeping with one of Mme de Montespan's favourite maids – for he baulked at nothing that would serve him for warnings and protection. He now resolved upon the most hazardous enterprise ever conceived. In all his various love-affairs, the King never failed to spend the night with the Queen. He was sometimes late in joining her, but he never missed, and thus, for convenience, he went to bed with his mistresses in the afternoon. Puyguilhem persuaded the above mentioned waiting-maid to hide him beneath the bed on which the King would lie with Mme de Montespan. She did so, and by their talk he learned of how Louvois had prevented his appointment; of the King's extreme anger at the telling of his secret; of his decision to refuse Puyguilhem on that account, and more especially in order to avoid having to mediate between him and Louvois in their quarrels. Puyguilhem heard all that was said by the King and his mistress, and perceived that she who had promised him marvels was doing him every imaginable disservice. One cough, the smallest movement, the faintest noise would have revealed the presence of that daredevil; and then what would have become of him? It is the kind of thing that makes one laugh and shudder all at the same moment.

He was luckier than he deserved, for they did not notice him. At length the King and his mistress rose; the King put on his clothes and returned to his apartments; Mme de Montespan attired herself for the rehearsal of a ballet, at which the King, the Queen, and the entire Court were to be present. The maid extracted Puyguilhem, who apparently felt no need to adjust his dress, for instead of returning to his room, he posted himself outside Mme de Montespan's door. When she emerged he offered her his wrist, asking in soft, respectful tones whether he might dare to hope that she had remembered him. She assured him that indeed she had spoken and, in the most gratifying manner possible, enumerated the various services she had rendered him. Now and again he stopped her, plying her with eager questions designed to lead her to still higher flights. After which, putting his mouth to her ear, he told her she was a liar, a trollop, a whore, a piece of dog-filth, repeating to her, word for word, the whole of her conversation

with the King. Mme de Montespan was so flabbergasted she had
no strength left for utterance, and only just managed to continue
walking without displaying the fact that her legs and entire body
were all a-tremble. When they arrived at the rehearsal room where
the Court was assembled she fainted quite away. The King flew to
her side in high alarm, and they had great difficulty in reviving
her. She told him what had happened that same evening, vowing
that only the devil himself could have informed Puyguilhem. King
Louis was furious because of the injuries she had suffered, but
remained completely at a loss to discover how Puyguilhem could
have known.

As for Puyguilhem himself, so much incensed was he at losing
the artillery that relations between him and the King became
uncomfortably strained. It was a situation that could not have
endured. At the end of a few days he . . . boldly reminded the
King of his promise. The answer came that this no longer applied.
The promise had been given on condition of secrecy, and
Puyguilhem had blabbed. At those words Puyguilhem drew his
sword and broke it across his foot, furiously exclaiming that he
would not serve a prince who so basely failed to keep his word.
Thereupon the King, transported with rage, took what may well
have been the finest action of his life. He turned away, opened the
window, and flung out his cane, saying that it would grieve him to
be obliged to strike a gentleman. Then immediately he left the room.

Next morning, Puyguilhem, who had not dared to show himself
in the meanwhile, was arrested in his bedroom and taken thence to
the Bastille.

Duc de Saint-Simon, *Memoirs*, Hamish Hamilton, 1972, Vol. III,
pp. 461–2 (translated by Lucy Norton).

In the previous century Robert Burton, in his incomparable *Anatomy
of Melancholy*, had come to the aid of the perplexed, by citing the various
ways in which adulterers could be identified by their jealous spouses:

To what passion may we ascribe those severe laws against jealousy, adulterers, as amongst the Hebrews, amongst the Egyptians (read Bohemus of the Carthaginians, of Turks), amongst the Athenians of old, Italians at this day, wherein they are to be severely punished, cut in pieces, burned, buried alive, with several expurgations (or trials of virtue), &c., are they not as so many symptoms of incredible jealousy? we may say the same of those vestal Virgins that fetched water in a sieve, as Tatia did in Rome, in the year 800 from the founding of the city, before the Senators; and Aemilia, innocent virgin, that ran over hot irons, as Emma, Edward the Confessor's mother, did, the King himself being a spectator, with the like. We read in Nicephorus that Cunegunda, the wife of Henricus Bavarus, Emperor, suspected of adultery, trod upon red hot coulters, and had no harm: such another story we find in Regino; in Aventinus and Sigonius, of Charles the Third, and his wife Richarda, in the year 887, that was so purged with hot irons. Pausanias saith that he was once an eye-witness of such a miracle at Diana's Temple, a maid without any harm at all walked upon burning coals. Pius the Second, in his description of Europe, relates as much, that it was commonly practised at Diana's Temple, for women to go barefoot over hot coals, to try their honesties. Plinius, Solinus, and many writers, make mention of Feronia's Temple, and Dionysius Halicarnassus of Memnon's statue, which were used to this purpose; Tatius of Pan his Cave (much like old S. Wilfrid's needle in Yorkshire), wherein they did use to try maids, whether they were honest: when Leucippe went in, a sweet sound was heard. Austin relates many such examples, all which Lavater contends to be done by the illusion of Devils; though Thomas ascribes it to good Angels. Some, saith Austin, compel their wives to swear they be honest, as if perjury were a lesser sin than adultery; some consult Oracles, as Pheron that blind King of Egypt. Others reward, as those old Romans use to do; if a woman were contented with one man, she had a crown of Chastity bestowed on her. When all this will not serve, saith Alexander Gaguinus, the Muscovites, if they suspect their wives, will beat them till they confess; and if that will not avail, like those wild Irish, be divorced at their pleasures, or else knock them on the heads, as the old Gauls have done in former ages.

Robert Burton, *Anatomy of Melancholy*, Part 3, Section 3, Member 2.

In modern England, the arrangements of deception are easy to make, but in Kingsley Amis's poem the price is more elemental than mere discovery:

> All fixed: early arrival at the flat
> Lent by a friend, whose note says *Lucky sod*;
> Drinks on the tray; the cover-story pat
> And quite uncheckable; her husband off
> Somewhere with all the kids till six o'clock
> (Which ought to be quite long enough);
> And all worth while: face really beautiful,
> Good legs and hips, and as for breasts – my God.
> What about guilt, compunction and such stuff?
> I've had my fill of all that cock;
> It'll wear off, as usual.
>
> Yes, all fixed. Then why this slight trembling,
> Dry mouth, quick pulse-rate, sweaty hands,
> As though she were the first? No, not impatience,
> Nor fear of failure, thank you, Jack.
> Beauty, they tell me, is a dangerous thing,
> Whose touch will burn, but I'm asbestos, see?
> All worth while – it's a dead coincidence
> That sitting here, a bag of glands
> Tuned up to concert pitch, I seem to sense
> A different style of caller at my back,
> As cold as ice, but just as set on me.

Kingsley Amis, 'Nothing to Fear',
Collected Poems 1944–1979, Hutchinson, 1979.

The diarist William Hickey recalls his friend Fanny Temple, later known as Fanny Hartford, whose lover practised deception on an epic scale:

A finer woman in every respect could not be. With her I became so great a favourite that she never was happy unless I was with her. Unlike the generality of women in that line of life, her manners were perfectly correct, nor did I ever once hear a vulgarism or coarse expression pass her lips. She was mistress of music, had an enchanting voice, which she managed with the utmost skill, danced elegantly and spoke French, *assez bien*. She inhabited an excellent house in Queen Ann Street, and had besides neat lodgings in the country, pleasantly situated near the water side just above Hammersmith, and kept her own chariot, with suitable establishment of servants, the whole being paid for, as well as her domestic expenses, which were liberally allowed for, by a gentleman of rank and fashion, possessed of a splendid fortune, whom she told me my family was well acquainted with. Yet notwithstanding I frequently entreated her to tell me his name, she never would, observing that she had made a solemn promise never to divulge it to any body whatsoever, and being a most liberal and worthy man, she considered herself bound in honour and conscience never to betray him. This being a line of conduct every man of sentiment must approve, I ceased to importune her on the subject. In a few weeks however I discovered the person without the smallest blame attaching to her. Thus, she and I had been one evening to Ranelagh, from whence I had accompanied her to Queen Ann Street, there to pass the night. Having supped, we were just stepping into bed, when we heard some one running quickly up stairs, and a great bustle in the passage, whereupon she exclaimed, 'My God! I am undone, there is Mr. ——.' I darted into a closet, the door of which was scarce closed, when in he walked, and to my inexpressible astonishment I recognized the voice of a gentleman I was perfectly well acquainted with, whom I knew was married to an amiable and accomplished woman, who had borne him eight children, all then living, with which wife he was upon the best terms, and they were by the world considered as a rare instance of conjugal fidelity in high life. He was too at this time considerably above sixty years old. Fanny, with a readiness that seldom fails the sex, called the maid to take out and air clean sheets, leading her friend by the hand into the dining room. The servant instantly locked the door, and gathering up my clothes, carried them down to the parlour, to which I softly descended, there dressed myself, and made good my retreat.

William Hickey, *Memoirs*, Hurst & Blackett, 1919, Vol. 1 (1749–1775), pp. 90–91.

As did the father of J.R. Ackerley:

The full tale of my father's deception was made known to me in two letters, sealed in a single envelope addressed to me and marked 'Only in the case of my death', which I found in his office . . .

'My dear lad,

'Seeing you this morning a grown man, with every sign of a great intelligence and a kindly nature towards human frailties, I think I ought to leave you a line to explain one or two things in my past which it is inevitable you will have to consider in case anything happens to me in the near future. I shan't leave much money behind me, not being built that way, but I don't think there will be any debts worth mentioning. Since I came to man's estate I have provided for my sisters and I wish them to have one thousand pounds clear. My will leaves everything to Mother . . . Now for the "secret orchard" part of my story. For many years I had a mistress and she presented me with twin girls ten years ago and another girl eight years ago. The children are alive and are very sweet things and very dear to me. They know me only as Uncle Bodger, but I want them to have the proceeds of my Life Insurance of £2000 . . . I would also like £500 paid to their mother . . . I am not going to make any excuses, old man. I have done my duty towards everybody as far as my nature would allow and I hope people generally will be kind to my memory.

All my men pals know of my second family and of their mother, so you won't find it difficult to get on their track.

'Your old Dad.'

. . . Only we, his family, remained in the dark, and my mother died seventeen years later, in 1946, in ignorance of his deception.

J.R. Ackerley, *My Father and Myself*, Coward-McCann, 1969, pp. 154–5, 160.

Sometimes the deception is a self-deception, as in the case of the dashing Marquis de Saint-Loup in Proust's *The Guermantes Way*:

Robert [de Saint-Loup] was ignorant of almost all the infidelities of his mistress, and tormented himself over what were mere nothings compared with the real life of Rachel, a life which began every day only after he had left her. He was ignorant of almost all these infidelities. One could have told him of them without shaking his confidence in Rachel. For it is a charming law of nature, which manifests itself in the heart of the most complex social organisms, that we live in perfect ignorance of those we love. On the one hand the lover says to himself: 'She is an angel, she will never give herself to me, I may as well die – and yet she loves me; she loves me so much that perhaps . . . but no, it can never possibly happen.' And in the exaltation of his desire, in the anguish of his expectation, what jewels he flings at the feet of this woman, how he runs to borrow money to save her from financial worries! Meanwhile, on the other side of the glass screen, through which these conversations will no more carry than those which visitors exchange in front of an aquarium in a zoo, the public are saying: 'You don't know her? You can count yourself lucky – she has robbed, in fact ruined, I don't know how many men, as girls go there's nothing worse. She's a swindler pure and simple. And crafty!' And perhaps this last epithet is not absolutely wrong, for even the sceptical man who is not really in love with the woman, who merely gets pleasure from her, says to his friends: 'No, no, my dear fellow, she's not at all a whore. I don't say she hasn't had an adventure or two in her time, but she's not a woman one pays, she'd be a damned sight too expensive if she was. With her it's fifty thousand francs or nothing.' The fact of the matter is that he himself has spent fifty thousand francs for the privilege of having her once, but she (finding a willing accomplice in the man himself, in the person of his self-esteem) has managed to persuade him that he is one of those who have had her for nothing. Such is society, where every being is double, and where the most thoroughly exposed, the most notorious, will be known to a certain other only as protected by a shell, by a sweet cocoon, as a charming natural curiosity. There were in Paris two thoroughly decent men whom Saint-Loup no longer greeted when he saw them and to whom he could not refer without a tremor in his voice, calling them exploiters of women: this was because they had both been ruined by Rachel.

Marcel Proust, *The Guermantes Way*, Chatto & Windus, 1992, pp. 323–4 (translated by C.K. Scott Moncrieff, Terence Kilmartin and D.J. Enright).

Most dispiriting of all is the mutual deception not of adulterers within a marriage, but of those who suppress the truth and thereby suppress all that is richest within their lives:

In a marriage there are all sorts of lies whose malignancy slowly kills everything, and that day I was running the gamut from the outright lie of adultery to the careful selectivity which comes when there are things that two people can no longer talk about. It is hard to say which kills faster but I would guess selectivity, because it is a surrender: you avoid touching wounds and therefore avoid touching the heart.

Andre Dubus, 'We Don't Live Here Anymore', *Separate Flights*, Godine (Boston), 1975, p. 31.

Shadowed by shades and spied upon by glass
Their search for privacy conducts them here,

With an irony that neither notices,
To a public house; the wrong time of the year
For outdoor games; where, over gin and tonic,
Best bitter and potato crisps, they talk
Without much zest, almost laconic,
Flipping an occasional remark.
Would you guess that they were lovers, this dull pair?
The answer, I suppose, is yes, you would.
Despite her spectacles and faded hair
And his worn look of being someone's Dad
You know that they are having an affair
And neither finds it doing them much good.
Presumably, in one another's eyes,
They must look different from what we see,
Desirable in some way, otherwise
They'd hardly choose to come here, furtively,
And mutter their bleak needs above the mess
Of fag-ends, crumpled cellophane and crumbs,
Their love-feast's litter. Though they might profess
To find great joy together, all that comes
Across to us is tiredness, melancholy.
When they are silent each seems listening;
There must be many voices in the air:
Reproaches, accusations, suffering
That no amount of passion keeps elsewhere.
Imperatives that brought them to this room,
Stiff from the car's back seat, lose urgency;
They start to wonder who's betraying whom,
How it will end, and how did it begin –
The woman taken in adultery
And the man who feels he, too, was taken in.

Vernon Scannell, 'Taken in Adultery', *Walking Wounded*, Eyre &
Spottiswoode, 1965.

Seduction

This curse pursues female Adultery,
They'll swim through blood for sin's variety:
Their pleasure like a sea groundless and wide,
A woman's lust was never satisfied.

John Marston, *The Insatiate Countess*

Ovid, in his *Amores*, gives instruction:

Your husband will be with us at the treat;
May that be the last supper he shall eat.
And am poor I, a guest invited there,
Only to see, while he may touch the fair?
To see you kiss and hug your nauseous lord,
While his lewd hand descends below the board?
Now wonder not that Hippodamia's charms,
At such a sight, the centaurs urged to arms:
That in a rage, they threw their cups aside,
Assailed the bridegroom, and would force the bride.
I am not half a horse, (I wish I were):
Yet hardly can from you my hands forbear.
Take, then, my counsel; which, observed, may be
Of some importance both to you and me.
Be sure to come before your man be there,
There's nothing can be done, but come howe're.
Sit next him, (that belongs to decency);
But tread upon my foot in passing by.

Read in my looks what silently they speak,
And slyly, with your eyes, your answer make.
My lifted eyebrow shall declare my pain,
My right hand to his fellow shall complain:
And on the back a letter shall design;
Besides a note that shall be writ in wine.
When e're you think upon our last embrace,
With your forefinger gently touch your face.
If any word of mine offend my dear,
Pull, with your hand, the velvet of your ear.
If you are pleased with what I do or say,
Handle your rings, or with your fingers play.
As suppliants use at altars, use the board
When e're you wish the devil may take your lord.
When he fills for you, never touch the cup;
But bid th'officious cuckold drink it up.
The waiter on those services employ;
Drink you, and I will snatch it from the boy:
Watching the part where your sweet mouth hath been,
And thence, with eager lips, will suck it in.
If he, with clownish manners, thinks it fit
To taste, and offers you the nasty bit,
Reject his greasy kindness, and restore
Th'unsavoury morsel he had chewed before.
Nor let his arms embrace your neck, nor rest
Your tender cheek upon his hairy breast.
Let not his hand within your bosom stray,
And rudely with your pretty bubbies play.
But, above all, let him no kiss receive;
That's an offence I never can forgive.
Do not, O do not that sweet mouth resign,
Lest I rise up in arms; and cry 'tis mine.
I shall thrust in betwixt, and void of fear
The manifest adulterer will appear.
These things are plain to sight, but more I doubt

What you conceal beneath your petticoat.
Take not his leg between your tender thighs,
Nor, with your hand, provoke my foe to rise.
How many love-inventions I deplore,
Which I, myself, have practised all before! . . .
Encourage him to tope, but kiss him not,
Nor mix one drop of water in his pot.
If he be fuddled well, and snores apace,
Then we may take advice from time and place.
When all depart, while compliments are loud,
Be sure to mix among the thickest crowd:
There I will be, and there we cannot miss,
Perhaps to grubble, or at least to kiss.
Alas, what length of labour I employ,
Just to secure a short and transient joy!
For night must part us; and when night is come,
Tucked underneath his arms he leads you home.
He locks you in, I follow to the door,
His fortune envy, and my own deplore.
He kisses you, he more than kisses too;
Th'outrageous cuckold thinks it all his due.
But, add not to his joy, by your consent;
And let it not be given, but only lent:
Return no kiss, nor move in any sort;
Make it a dull, and a malignant sport.
Had I my wish, he should no pleasure take,
But slubber o're your business for my sake.
And what e're fortune shall this night befall,
Coax me tomorrow, by foreswearing all.

Ovid, *Amores*, I.iv (translated by John Dryden).

The poet Matthew Prior (1664–1721) puts in a simple but eloquent plea:

Since we your Husband daily see
    So jealous out of Season;
Phillis, let you and I agree,
    To make him so with reason.

I'm vext to think, that ev'ry Night,
    A Sot within thy Arms,
Tasting the most Divine delight,
    Should sully all your Charms.

While fretting I must lye alone,
    Cursing the Pow'rs Divine;
That undeservedly have thrown
    A Pearl unto a Swine.

Then, Phillis, heal my wounded heart,
    My burning Passion cool;
Let me at least in thee have part,
    With thy insipid Fool.

Let him, by night, his joys pursue,
    And blunder in the dark;
While I, by day, enjoying you,
    Can see to hit the mark.

from *Literary Works* (eds. Wright and Spears),
Clarendon Press, 1971.

In Choderlos de Laclos's brilliant, malevolent *Dangerous Acquaintances*, Valmont recounts how, after a lengthy and mostly epistolary courtship, he succeeded in seducing the virtuous Madame de Tourvel . . .

It was six o'clock in the evening when I arrived at the fair recluse's house . . . I carefully examined the locality; and there and then I noted with my eyes the theatre of my victory. I might have chosen a more convenient one, for there was an ottoman in the same room. But I noticed that opposite it there was a portrait of the husband; and I confess I was afraid that with such a singular woman one glance accidentally directed that way might destroy in a moment the work of so many exertions. At last we were left alone and I began.

After having pointed out in a few words that Father Anselme must have informed her of the reasons for my visit, I complained of the rigorous treatment I had received from her; and I particularly dwelt upon the 'contempt' which had been shown me. She defended herself, as I expected; and as you would have expected too, I found the proofs of it on the suspicion and fear I had inspired, on the scandalous flight which had followed upon them, the refusal to answer my letters, and even the refusal to receive them, etc., etc. As she was beginning a justification (which would have been very easy) I thought I had better interrupt; and to obtain forgiveness for this brusque manner I covered it immediately by a flattery: 'If so many charms have made an impression on my heart,' I went on, 'so many virtues have made no less a mark upon my soul. Seduced no doubt by the idea of approaching them I dared to think myself worthy of doing so. I do not reproach you for having thought otherwise; but I am punished for my error.' As she remained in an embarrassed silence, I continued: 'I desired, Madame, either to justify myself in your eyes or to obtain from you forgiveness for the wrongs you think I have committed, so that at least I can end in some peace the days to which I no longer attach any value since you have refused to embellish them.'

Here she tried to reply, however: 'My duty did not permit me.' And the difficulty of finishing the lie which duty exacted did not permit her to finish the phrase. I therefore went on in the most tender tones: 'It is true then that it was from me you fled?' 'My departure was necessary.' 'And what took you away from me?' 'It was necessary.' 'And for ever?' 'It must be so.' I do not need to tell you that during this short dialogue the tender prude was in a state of oppression and her eyes were not raised to me.

I felt I ought to animate this languishing scene a little ... So, throwing myself at her feet, I exclaimed in that dramatic tone of mine you know: 'Ah! cruel woman, can there exist any happiness

for me which you do not share? Ah! Never! Never!' I confess that
at this point I had greatly been relying on the aid of tears; but
either from a wrong disposition or perhaps only from the painful
and continual attention I was giving to everything, it was impossible for me to weep.

Fortunately I remembered that any method is equally good in
subjugating a woman, and that it sufficed to astonish her with a
great emotion for the impression to remain both deep and favourable. I made up therefore by terror for the sensibility I found
lacking; and with that purpose, only changing the inflection of my
voice and remaining in the same position, I continued: 'Yes, I
make an oath at your feet, to possess you or die.' As I spoke the
last words our eyes met. I do not know what the timid person saw
or thought she saw in mine, but she rose with a terrified air, and
escaped from my arms, which I had thrown round her. It is true I
did nothing to detain her; for I have several times noticed that
scenes of despair carried out too vividly become ridiculous as soon
as they become long, or leave nothing but really tragic resources
which I was very far from desiring to adopt. However, as she
escaped from me, I added in a low and sinister tone, but loud
enough for her to hear: 'Well, then! Death!'

I then got up ... Since in love nothing is concluded except at
very close quarters, and we were rather far apart, it was above all
things necessary to get closer together. To achieve this, I passed as
quickly as possible to an apparent tranquillity, likely to calm the
effects of this violent state, without weakening its impression ...
'I came, did I not, to return you your letters? I beg you, deign to
receive them back. This painful sacrifice remained for me to
accomplish; leave me nothing that can weaken my courage.' And
taking the precious collection from my pocket, I said: 'There it is,
that deceitful collection of assurances of your friendship! It attached
me to life,' I went on. 'So give the signal yourself which must
separate me from you for ever.'

Here the frightened Mistress yielded entirely to her tender
anxiety. 'But, M. de Valmont, what is the matter, and what do you

mean? Is not the step you are taking today a voluntary one? Is it not the fruit of your own reflections? And are they not those which have made you yourself approve the necessary course I adopted from a sense of duty?' 'Well,' I replied, 'that course decided mine.' 'And what is that?' 'The only one which, in separating me from you, can put an end to my own.' 'But tell me, what is it?' Then I clasped her in my arms, without her defending herself in the least; and, judging from this forgetfulness of conventions, how strong and powerful her emotion was, I said, risking a tone of enthusiasm: 'Adorable woman, you have no idea of the love you inspire; you will never know to what extent you were adored, and how much this sentiment is dearer to me than my existence! May all your days be fortunate and tranquil; may they be embellished by all the happiness of which you have deprived me! At least reward this sincere wish with a regret, with a tear; and believe that the last of my sacrifices will not be the most difficult for my heart. Farewell.'

While I was speaking, I felt her heart beating violently; I observed the change in her face; I saw above all that she was suffocated by tears but that only a few painful ones flowed. It was at that moment only that I feigned to go away; but, detaining me by force, she said quickly: 'No, listen to me.' 'Let me go,' I answered. 'You will listen to me, I wish it.' 'I must fly from you, I must.' 'No,' she cried. At this last word she rushed or rather fell into my arms in a swoon. As I still doubted of so lucky a success, I feigned a great terror; but with all my terror I guided, or rather, carried her towards the place designed beforehand as the field of my glory; and indeed she only came to her senses submissive and already yielded to her happy conqueror.

Hitherto, my fair friend, I think you will find I adopted a purity of method which will please you . . .

I expected so great an event would not take place without the usual tears and despair; and if I noticed at first a little more confusion, and a kind of interior meditation, I attributed both to her prudishness; so, without troubling about these slight differences which I thought were purely local, I simply followed the high-road of consolations ... But I found a really frightening resistance, less from its excess than from the manner in which it showed itself.

Imagine a woman seated, immovably still and with an unchanging face, appearing neither to think, hear, nor listen; a woman whose fixed eyes flowed with quite continual tears which came without effort. Such was Madame de Tourvel while I was speaking; but if I tried to recall her attention to me by a caress, even by the most innocent gesture, immediately there succeeded to this apparent apathy, terror, suffocation, convulsions, sobs, and at intervals a cry, but all without one word articulated.

These crises returned several times and always with more strength; the last was so violent that I was entirely discouraged and for a moment feared I had gained a useless victory. I fell back on the usual commonplaces, and among them was this: 'Are you in despair because you have made me happy?' At these words the adorable woman turned towards me; and her face, although still a little distraught, had yet regained its heavenly expression. 'Your happiness!' said she. You can guess my reply. 'You are happy then?' I redoubled my protestations. 'And happy through me?' I added praises and tender words. While she was speaking, all her limbs relaxed; she fell back limply, resting on her armchair; and abandoning to me a hand which I had dared to take, she said: 'I feel that idea console and relieve me.'

You may suppose that having found my path thus, I did not leave it again; it was really the right, and perhaps the only, one. So when I wished to attempt a second victory I found some resistance at first, and what had passed before made me circumspect; but having called to my aid that same idea of happiness I soon found its results favourable. 'You are right,' said the tender creature, 'I cannot endure my existence except as it may serve to make you happy. I give myself wholly up to it; from this moment I give myself to you, and you will experience neither refusals nor regrets from me.'

It was with this naive or sublime candour that she surrendered to me her person and her charms, and that she increased my happiness by sharing it. The ecstasy was complete and mutual; and, for the first time, my own outlasted the pleasure.

Choderlos de Laclos, *Dangerous Acquaintances*, Routledge, 1924, pp. 337–42 (translated by Richard Aldington).

Julien Sorel, the ambitious hero of Stendhal's *Scarlet and Black*, shows similar persistence and guile when he decides to seduce Madame de Rênal, whose children he is tutoring . . .

M. de Rênal was angrily talking politics . . . Julien, irritated by the conversation, brought his chair closer up to Madame de Rênal's, all his movements concealed by the darkness. He ventured to put his hand down very close to the lovely arm that her dress left uncovered. He was agitated, he could no longer control his thoughts; he put his cheek close to this lovely arm and ventured to touch it with his lips.

Madame de Rênal shuddered. Her husband was only four feet away. She hurriedly gave Julien her hand and at the same time pushed him a little away from her. While M. de Rênal continued his abuse of people of no account and of Jacobins who grow rich, Julien was covering the hand left in his with passionate kisses, or which seemed such to Madame de Rênal. Yet the poor woman had had proof on that fatal day that the man she adored, though without admitting it to herself, was in love with someone else! All the time Julien had been away she had been a prey to intense unhappiness, and this had made her think.

What! she said to herself, Can I love him, feel love for him? Can I, a married woman, have fallen in love? Yet, she thought, I've never felt for my husband such a dark, secret passion as this which makes it impossible for me to put Julien out of my mind. After all, he's really only a boy who looks on me with respect. This is merely a passing folly. What does it matter to my husband what feelings I have for this young man? M. de Rênal would merely be bored by my conversations with Julien on things of the imagination. He himself thinks only of his business. I take nothing away from him to give to Julien.

There was no hypocrisy here to sully the purity of an innocent mind led astray by a passion never experienced before. She deceived herself, but all unknowingly, and yet some instinct of virtue in her took alarm. Such were the inner conflicts troubling her when Julien appeared in the garden. She heard him speak and almost at the same time saw him sit down beside her. Her heart was as it were carried away by this enchanting happiness that for a fortnight past had more amazed than charmed her. Everything came as a surprise to her. All the same, after a moment or two she said to herself: Is Julien's mere presence enough to blot out all his faults? She felt afraid – that was the moment at which she withdrew her hand.

His passionate kisses, unlike any she had ever received before, made her forget on the spot that he might be in love with another woman. Soon he was no longer guilty in her eyes. Relief from the stinging pain born of suspicion, and the presence of a happiness of which she had not even dreamed, aroused an ecstasy of love in her, a wild, unreasoning joy . . .

Madame de Rênal could not get a wink of sleep. Unable to keep her mind from dwelling on her feeling of happiness when Julien had covered her hand with burning kisses, it seemed to her she had not lived until that moment.

Suddenly the dreadful word – *adultery* – confronted her. All the most disgusting associations lent by debauchery of the lowest kind to the idea of love on its physical side rose up in her imagination, filling it with thoughts that strove to sully the heavenly pure and tender image she had made of Julien, and of the bliss of loving him. The future took on terrible colours. She saw herself a thing of scorn.

It was a fearful moment; her soul had penetrated into unknown regions. The previous evening she had enjoyed a happiness such as she had never experienced before, now she was suddenly plunged in agonizing grief. She had had no idea anyone could suffer so cruelly, it drove her frantic. For a minute she thought of confessing to her husband her fear of being in love with Julien. She would at least have had his name on her lips. Luckily she remembered a piece of advice her aunt had given her long ago, on the eve of her wedding, concerning the danger of confiding in a husband who is, after all, one's lord and master. She wrung her hands in excess of grief . . .

Julien continues with his seduction . . .

He went and listened at M. de Rênal's door. He could hear him snoring. The sound distressed him, for now he had no longer any pretext for not going to her room. But, what, good heavens! would he do when he got there? He had no plans, and even if he had had any, he felt so agitated that he would have been incapable of keeping to them.

In the end, suffering a thousand times more than if he had been going to his death, he turned into the little corridor leading to Madame de Rênal's room. With trembling hand he opened the door, making a frightful noise as he did so.

It was light in there; a lamp was burning just below the mantelpiece. He had not expected this fresh mishap. Seeing him enter, Madame de Rênal jumped out of bed. 'Wretch!' she exclaimed. For a moment all was confusion. Julien forgot his useless plans and became his natural self once more; failure to please so charming a woman seemed to him the greatest misfortune that could happen. All the reply he gave to her reproaches was to fling himself at her feet, his arms clasped round her knees. As she went on speaking to him with the utmost harshness, he burst into tears.

When Julien left Madame de Rênal's room a few hours later, it might be said, to adopt the language of novels, that he had nothing further left to wish for. He was, in truth, indebted to the love he had inspired and to the unexpected impression produced on him by her seductive charms for a victory to which all his unskilful cunning would never have led him.

Yet, even at the most sweetly blissful moments a victim of his own queer pride, he still aspired to play the part of a man accustomed to subduing women to his will, and made incredibly determined efforts to spoil what was lovable in himself. When he might have been attentive to the transports he aroused, and the remorse that only served to heighten their eager ecstasy, he kept the idea of a *duty to himself* unceasingly before his eyes. He was afraid of feeling terrible regret and of making himself for ever ridiculous if he departed from the model of perfection he had resolved to follow. In a word, what made Julien a superior being was the very thing that prevented him from enjoying this happiness right in front of his eyes. He was like a sixteen-year-old girl with charming colouring who is silly enough to put on rouge when going to a ball.

Frightened to death by Julien's sudden appearance, Madame de Rênal soon fell a victim to the cruellest apprehensions. Julien's tears and his despair disturbed her acutely; so much so, that, even when she had nothing left to refuse him, she pushed him away from her in a fit of genuine indignation, and a moment after flung herself into his arms. There was no apparent design in all this line of conduct. She believed herself lost beyond hope of redemption and sought, by loading Julien with the most eager caresses, to shut her eyes to the vision of hell. Nothing, in short, would have been lacking to our hero's happiness, not even the ardent response of the woman he had just seduced, had he but been able to enjoy it. The transports that, in spite of herself, excited her were not brought to an end by Julien's departure, nor were her struggles with the remorse that tore her in two.

Good heavens! Is being happy, is being loved no more than that? were Julien's first thoughts when he got back to his room. He was in that state of amazement and tumultuous agitation into which man's spirit sinks on obtaining what it has so long desired.

The heart, grown used to desiring, finds nothing more to desire, but has as yet no memories. Like a soldier returning from parade Julien was busily absorbed in reviewing every detail of his conduct. Have I been wanting in anything I owe to myself? Have I played my part well?

And what a part! That of a man accustomed to success in his dealings with women . . .

A very few days later, Julien, having recovered all the fiery enthusiasm natural at his age, was desperately in love . . . When Madame de Rênal felt sufficiently self-composed to think the matter over, she could not recover from her surprise to find such happiness existed – or that she should ever have doubted its existence.

Ah! she said to herself, if I'd only known Julien ten years ago, when I still could pass for a pretty woman!

Such thoughts were very far from Julien's mind. His love was still another name for ambition. It meant for him the joy of possessing so beautiful a woman, when he himself was a poor, unhappy creature whom men despised. His acts of adoration, and his rapture at the sight of his mistress's charms, ended by reassuring Madame de Rênal on the question of the difference in their ages. Had she possessed a little of that practical knowledge of the world which in the most civilized countries a woman of thirty has had at her disposal for a number of years already, she might have trembled for the duration of a love which apparently only existed on surprise and the transports of gratified self-esteem.

Stendhal, *Scarlet and Black* (1830), Penguin, 1953, Ch. 11, pp. 83–4, 84–5; Ch. 15, pp. 102–4; Ch. 16, pp. 107–8 (translated by Margaret Shaw).

In Byron's *Don Juan*, the lovely but guileless Donna Julia is taken by the innocent sixteen-year-old Don Juan. She, however, is married to Don Alfonso:

Wedded she was some years, and to a man
    Of fifty, and such husbands are in plenty;
And yet, I think, instead of such a ONE
    'Twere better to have TWO of five and twenty,
Especially in countries near the sun:
    And now I think o't, 'mi vien in mente,'[1]
Ladies even of the most uneasy virtue
Prefer a spouse whose age is short of thirty.

'Tis a sad thing, I cannot choose but say,
    And all the fault of that indecent sun,
Who cannot leave alone our helpless clay,
    But will keep baking, broiling, burning on,
That howsoever people fast and pray
    The flesh is frail, and so the soul undone:
What men call gallantry, and gods adultery,
Is much more common where the climate's sultry.

Happy the nations of the moral north!
    Where all is virtue, and the winter season
Sends sin, without a rag on, shivering forth;
    ('Twas snow that brought St Francis back to reason);
Where juries cast up what a wife is worth
    By laying whate'er sum, in mulct, they please on
The lover, who must pay a handsome price,
Because it is a marketable vice . . .

Juan she saw, and, as a pretty child,
    Caress'd him often, such a thing might be
Quite innocently done, and harmless styled,
    When she had twenty years, and thirteen he;
But I am not so sure I should have smiled
    When he was sixteen, Julia twenty-three,
These few short years make wondrous alterations,
Particularly amongst sun-burnt nations.

---

1. 'it comes to mind'.

Whate'er the cause might be, they had become
    Chang'd; for the dame grew distant, the youth shy,
Their looks cast down, their greetings almost dumb,
    And much embarrassment in either eye;
There surely will be little doubt with some
    That Donna Julia knew the reason why,
But as for Juan, he had no more notion
Than he who never saw the sea of ocean.

Yet Julia's very coldness still was kind,
    And tremulously gentle her small hand
Withdrew itself from his, but left behind
    A little pressure, thrilling, and so bland
And slight, so very slight, that to the mind
    'Twas but a doubt; but ne'er magician's wand
Wrought change with all Armida's fairy art
Like what this light touch left on Juan's heart.

And if she met him, though she smiled no more,
    She look'd a sadness sweeter than her smile,
As if her heart had deeper thoughts in store
    She must not own, but cherish'd more the while,
For that compression in its burning core;
    Even innocence itself has many a wile,
And will not dare to trust itself with truth,
And love is taught hypocrisy from youth.

But passion most dissembles yet betrays
    Even by its darkness; as the blackest sky
Foretells the heaviest tempest, it displays
    Its workings through the vainly guarded eye,
And in whatever aspect it arrays
    Itself, 'tis still the same hypocrisy;
Coldness or anger, even disdain or hate,
Are masks it often wears, and still too late.

Then there were sighs, the deeper for suppression,
    And stolen glances, sweeter for the theft,
And burning blushes, though for no transgression,
    Tremblings when met, and restlessness when left;
All these are little preludes to possession,
    Of which young Passion cannot be bereft,
And merely tend to show how greatly Love is
Embarrass'd at first starting with a novice . . .

'Twas on the sixth of June, about the hour
    Of half-past six – perhaps still nearer seven,
When Julia sate within as pretty a bower
    As e'er held houri in that heathenish heaven
Described by Mahomet, and Anacreon Moore,
    To whom the lyre and laurels have been given,
With all the trophies of triumphant song –
He won them well, and may he wear them long!

She sate, but not alone; I know not well
    How this same interview had taken place,
And even if I knew, I should not tell –
    People should hold their tongues in any case;
No matter how or why the thing befell,
    But there were she and Juan, face to face –
When two such faces are so, 'twould be wise,
But very difficult, to shut their eyes.

How beautiful she look'd! her conscious heart
    Glow'd in her cheek, and yet she felt no wrong.
Oh Love! how perfect is thy mystic art,
    Strengthening the weak, and trampling on the strong,
How self-deceitful is the sagest part
    Of mortals whom thy lure hath led along –
The precipice she stood on was immense,
So was her creed in her own innocence . . .

Julia had honour, virtue, truth, and love,
    For Don Alfonso; and she inly swore,
By all the vows below to powers above,
    She never would disgrace the ring she wore,
Nor leave a wish which wisdom might reprove;
    And while she ponder'd this, besides much more,
One hand on Juan's carelessly was thrown,
Quite by mistake – she thought it was her own;

Unconsciously she lean'd upon the other,
    Which play'd within the tangles of her hair;
And to contend with thoughts she could not smother,
    She seem'd by the distraction of her air.
'Twas surely very wrong in Juan's mother
    To leave together this imprudent pair,
She who for many years had watch'd her son so –
I'm very certain *mine* would not have done so.

The hand which still held Juan's by degrees
    Gently, but palpably confirm'd its grasp,
As if it said, 'detain me, if you please;'
    Yet there's no doubt she only meant to clasp
His fingers with a pure Platonic squeeze;
    She would have shrunk as from a toad, or asp,
Had she imagined such a thing could rouse
A feeling dangerous to a prudent spouse.

I cannot know what Juan thought of this,
    But what he did, is much what you would do;
His young lip thank'd it with a grateful kiss,
    And then, abash'd at its own joy, withdrew
In deep despair, lest he had done amiss,
    Love is so very timid when 'tis new:
She blush'd, and frown'd not, but she strove to speak,
And held her tongue, her voice was grown so weak.

The sun set, and up rose the yellow moon:
    The devil's in the moon for mischief; they
Who call'd her CHASTE, methinks, began too soon
    Their nomenclature; there is not a day,
The longest, not the twenty-first of June,
    Sees half the business in a wicked way
On which three single hours of moonshine smile –
And then she looks so modest all the while.

There is a dangerous silence in that hour,
    A stillness, which leaves room for the full soul
To open all itself, without the power
    Of calling wholly back its self-control;
The silver light which, hallowing tree and tower,
    Sheds beauty and deep softness o'er the whole,
Breathes also to the heart, and o'er it throws
A loving languor, which is not repose.

And Julia sate with Juan, half embraced
    And half retiring from the glowing arm,
Which trembled like the bosom where 'twas placed;
    Yet still she must have thought there was no harm,
Or else 'twere easy to withdraw her waist;
    But then the situation had its charm,
And then – God knows what next – I can't go on;
I'm almost sorry that I e'er begun.

Oh Plato! Plato! you have paved the way,
    With your confounded fantasies, to more
Immoral conduct by the fancied sway
    Your system feigns o'er the controllest core
Of human hearts, than all the long array
    Of poets and romancers: – You're a bore,
A charlatan, a coxcomb – and have been,
At best, no better than a go-between.

And Julia's voice was lost, except in sighs,
  Until too late for useful conversation;
The tears were gushing from her gentle eyes,
  I wish indeed, they had not had occasion,
But who, alas! can love, and then be wise?
  Not that remorse did not oppose temptation,
A little still she strove, and much repented,
And whispering 'I will ne'er consent' – consented.

Lord Byron, *Don Juan*, Canto I, stanzas 62–4, 69–74,
104–6, 109–117.

'Amongst sun-burnt nations', if Byron is to be believed, seduction and infidelity are as easy and irresistible as falling off a log. Not so in the West Country of England in the late nineteenth century. Sue Brideshead, a schoolteacher, has married an elderly teacher called Phillotson. She confides in her cousin Jude, who is in love with her, that her marriage is an unhappy one:

'I – I think I must be equally honest with you as you have been with me. Perhaps you have seen what it is I want to say? – that though I like Mr. Phillotson as a friend, I don't like him – it is a torture to me to – live with him as a husband! – There, now I have let it out – I couldn't help it, although I have been – pretending I am happy. – Now you'll have a contempt for me for ever, I suppose!' She bent down her face upon her hands as they lay upon the cloth, and silently sobbed in little jerks that made the fragile three-legged table quiver.

'I have only been married a month or two!' she went on, still remaining bent upon the table, and sobbing into her hands. 'And it is said that what a woman shrinks from – in the early days of her marriage – she shakes down to with comfortable indifference in half-a-dozen years. But that is much like saying that the amputation of a limb is no affliction, since a person gets comfortably accustomed to the use of a wooden leg or arm in the course of time!'

Jude could hardly speak, but he said, 'I thought there was something wrong, Sue! O, I thought there was!'

'But it is not as you think! – there is nothing wrong except my own wickedness, I suppose you'd call it – a repugnance on my part, for a reason I cannot disclose, and what would not be admitted as one by the world in general! . . . What tortures me so much is the necessity of being responsive to this man whenever he wishes, good as he is morally! – the dreadful contract to feel in a particular way in a matter whose essence is its voluntariness! . . . I wish he would beat me, or be faithless to me, or do some open thing that I could talk about as a justification for feeling as I do! But he does nothing, except that he has grown a little cold since he has found out how I feel . . . O, I am very miserable – I don't know what to do! . . . Don't come near me, Jude, because you mustn't. Don't – don't!'

But he had jumped up and put his face against hers – or rather against her ear, her face being inaccessible.

'I told you not to, Jude!'

'I know you did – I only wish to – console you! It all arose through my being married before we met, didn't it? You would have been my wife, Sue, wouldn't you, if it hadn't been for that?'

Instead of replying she rose quickly, and saying she was going to walk to her aunt's grave in the churchyard to recover herself, went out of the house. Jude did not follow her . . .

The morning after, when it was time for her to go, the neighbours saw her companion and herself disappearing on foot down the hill path which led into the lonely road to Alfredston. An hour passed before he returned along the same route, and in his face there was a look of exaltation not unmixed with recklessness. An incident had occurred.

They had stood parting in the silent highway, and their tense and passionate moods had led to bewildered inquiries of each other on how far their intimacy ought to go; till they had almost quarrelled, and she had said tearfully that it was hardly proper of him as a parson in embryo to think of such a thing as kissing her even in farewell, as he now wished to do. Then she had conceded that the fact of the kiss would be nothing: all would depend upon the spirit of it. If given in the spirit of a cousin and a friend she saw no objection: if in the spirit of a lover she could not permit it. 'Will you swear that it will not be in that spirit?' she had said.

No: he would not. And then they had turned from each other in estrangement, and gone their several ways, till at a distance of twenty or thirty yards both had looked round simultaneously. That look behind was fatal to the reserve hitherto more or less maintained. They had quickly run back, and met, and embracing most unpremeditatedly, kissed close and long. When they parted for good it was with flushed cheeks on her side, and a beating heart on his.

The kiss was a turning-point in Jude's career. Back again in the cottage, and left to reflection, he saw one thing: that though his kiss of that aerial being had seemed the purest moment of his faultful life, as long as he nourished this unlicensed tenderness it was glaringly inconsistent for him to pursue the idea of becoming the soldier and servant of a religion in which sexual love was regarded as at its best a frailty, and at its worst damnation.

Sue leaves her husband and joins Jude.

Thomas Hardy, *Jude the Obscure*, IV:ii, iii.

In Hardy, a kiss is all it takes. When, however, in Ford Madox Ford's *The Good Soldier*, Edward Ashburnham strolls into a dark park with the young Nancy, it is not at all clear what then occurs. Inference is all:

You will remember I said that Edward Ashburnham and the girl [Nancy Rufford] had gone off, that night, to a concert at the Casino and that Leonora had asked Florence, almost immediately after their departure, to follow them and to perform the office of chaperone. Florence, you may also remember, was all in black, being the mourning that she wore for a deceased cousin, Jean Hurlbird. It was a very black night and the girl was dressed in cream-coloured muslin, that must have glimmered under the tall trees of the dark park like a phosphorescent fish in a cupboard. You couldn't have had a better beacon.

And it appears that Edward Ashburnham led the girl not up the straight allée that leads to the Casino, but in under the dark trees of the park ... It appears that, not very far from the Casino, he and the girl sat down in the darkness upon a public bench. The lights from that place of entertainment must have reached them through the tree-trunks, since, Edward said, he could quite plainly see the girl's face – that beloved face with the high forehead, the queer mouth, the tortured eyebrows, and the direct eyes. And to Florence, creeping up behind them, they must have presented the appearance of silhouettes. For I take it that Florence came creeping up behind them over the short grass to a tree that, I quite well remember, was immediately behind that public seat. It was a not very difficult feat for a woman instinct with jealousy. The Casino orchestra was, as Edward remembered to tell me, playing the Rakocsy march, and although it was not loud enough, at that distance, to drown the voice of Edward Ashburnham it was certainly sufficiently audible to efface, amongst the noises of the night, the slight brushings and rustlings that might have been made by the feet of Florence or by her gown in coming over the short grass. And that miserable woman must have got it in the face, good and strong. It must have been horrible for her. Horrible! Well, I suppose she deserved all that she got.

Anyhow, there you have the picture, the immensely tall trees, elms most of them, towering and feathering away up into the black mistiness that trees seem to gather about them at night; the silhouettes of those two upon the seat; the beams of light coming from the Casino, the woman all in black peeping with fear behind the tree-trunk. It is melodrama; but I can't help it.

And then, it appears, something happened to Edward Ashburnham. He assured me – and I see no reason for disbelieving him – that until that moment he had had no idea whatever of caring for the girl. He said that he had regarded her exactly as he would have regarded a daughter. He certainly loved her, but with a very deep, very tender and very tranquil love. He had missed her when she went away to her convent-school; he had been glad when she had returned. But of more than that he had been totally unconscious. Had he been conscious of it, he assured me, he would have fled from it as from a thing accursed. He realized that it was the last outrage upon Leonora. But the real point was his entire unconsciousness. He had gone with her into that dark park with no quickening of the pulse, with no desire for the intimacy of solitude. He had gone, intending to talk about polo-ponies and tennis-racquets; about the temperament of the reverend Mother at the convent she had left and about whether her frock for a party when they got home should be white or blue. It hadn't come into his head that they would talk about a single thing that they hadn't always talked about; it had not even come into his head that the tabu which extended around her was not inviolable. And then, suddenly, that —

He was very careful to assure me that at that time there was no physical motive about his declaration. It did not appear to him to be a matter of a dark night and a propinquity and so on. No, it was simply of her effect on the moral side of his life that he appears to have talked. He said that he never had the slightest notion to enfold her in his arms or so much as to touch her hand. He swore that he did not touch her hand. He said that they sat, she at one end of the bench, he at the other; he leaning slightly towards her and she looking straight towards the light of the Casino, her face illuminated by the lamps. The expression upon her face he could only describe as 'queer'.

At another time, indeed, he made it appear that he thought she was glad. It is easy to imagine that she was glad, since at that time she could have had no idea of what was really happening. Frankly, she adored Edward Ashburnham. He was for her, in everything that she said at that time, the model of humanity, the hero, the athlete, the father of his country, the law-giver. So that for her, to be suddenly, intimately and overwhelmingly praised must have been a matter for mere gladness, however overwhelming it were. It must have been as if a god had approved her handiwork or a king her loyalty. She just sat still and listened, smiling.

And it seemed to her that all the bitterness of her childhood, the terrors of her tempestuous father, the bewailings of her cruel-tongued mother were suddenly atoned for. She had recompense at last. Because, of course, if you come to figure it out, a sudden pouring forth of passion by a man whom you regard as a cross between a pastor and a father might, to a woman, have the aspect of mere praise for good conduct. It wouldn't, I mean, appear at all in the light of an attempt to gain possession. The girl, at least, regarded him as firmly anchored to his Leonora. She had not the slightest inkling of any infidelities. He had always spoken to her of his wife in terms of reverence and deep affection. He had given her the idea that he regarded Leonora as absolutely impeccable and as absolutely satisfying. Their union had appeared to her to be one of those blessed things that are spoken of and contemplated with reverence by her church.

So that, when he spoke of her as being the person he cared for most in the world, she naturally thought that he meant to except Leonora and she was just glad. It was like a father saying that he approved of a marriageable daughter ... And Edward, when he realized what he was doing, curbed his tongue at once. She was just glad and she went on being just glad ...

It is, I have no doubt, a most monstrous thing to attempt to corrupt a young girl just out of a convent. But I think Edward had no idea at all of corrupting her. I believe that he simply loved her. He said that that was the way of it and I, at least, believe him and I believe too that she was the only woman he ever really loved. He said that that was so; and he did enough to prove it. And Leonora said that it was so and Leonora knew him to the bottom of his heart.

Ford Madox Ford, *The Good Soldier*, III:I.

Not all seduction scenes are highly successful, as Stanley Waltz learns when he tries to put some old-fashioned romance into his adulterous passion for Lena:

Lena seemed slow and more than usually deliberate as she went to the kitchen, from which she returned with a whiskey and water for me. Nothing for herself. I didn't like her mood. She looked like something was eating her. I noticed it the minute I came in. I was now sitting on the sofa, and she set the drink in front of me and took a nearby chair – the one I'd been sitting in last time – and watched me while I drank.

I took a generous swig. 'I'm married to a woman who never heard of Mencken.'

'Did you when you first married her?'

'No, that's right. I didn't. Or lots of things that you've taught me, Lena. Oh Lena –' I reached to take her hand across the table again, but this time she pulled away. 'What's the matter?'

'Matter?' She reached for her cigarette holder and in a twinkling was walking the room again snorting smoke. 'You come in here to what's supposed to be a rendezvous going fifteen to the dozen with complaints about your lot. Did you give any evidence that this was a love trist, carefully prepared for and long looked forward to? Did you even greet me? Did you even notice what I'm wearing?' She had worked around behind me and now clapped a hand over my eyes. 'What have I got on, you who so notices what a woman wears that you can give me blow by blow details about your married life. What have I put on for you?'

'I don't know, Lena. I'm sorry. I was just too upset.'

She restored my sight, allowing me to take in the green and red silk lounging pajamas, the golden slippers and the crimson band around her hair. She was really gift-wrapped. I whistled. 'Lena, you're gorgeous.'

'It's a little late for gorgeous. The whistles are quite tardy, you had your opportunity several minutes ago. No, you don't want me – you just don't want somebody else. You just come in here to complain about what your wife gives you for your birthday and what she wears, not to see me. How does your wife expect to hold you, you say. How do you expect to hold me if you don't notice what I'm wearing, who went to all the trouble to pretty up for her gentleman caller. How do you think that makes a woman feel? What am I, a woman or an emotional dumping ground?'

'You're a woman, Lena,' I said with a catch in my throat, 'and what a woman.'

'Do you realize what it is for a woman to give herself to a man? What's at stake?'

'I'm not asking you to give yourself to me, only lend yourself.'

'Oh my God! You're getting to be a born fool.'

'Over you, Lena, over you.'

I tried to take her again but she backed off once more, and once more circled the room, breathing fire and letting me have it. Suddenly I drained my glass and set it down. 'I'm going out and get drunk.'

I started for the door, but her next outburst stopped me cold.

'Go ahead! You're all alike. Prove conclusively what I'm trying to say and what you're leading me right up to, go ahead, save me the trouble. Spoiled children! Punks with infantile motivations, not masterful lovers having poetic affairs. You don't want to add a little poetry to your life, you just want to subtract a little of the prose. You just want a shoulder to cry on. "My wife doesn't understand me." Why don't you be a man for once. Admit you behaved poorly and apologize. Then I might relent and admit I was probably a little hard on you, but you deserved it. In that way clear the air – for the triumphant gesture. Instead of running off like some high school kid that didn't get his way, why don't you begin over? We might have what you came for, we might yet touch the stars, if you'd behave for once like a lover. Go on, why don't you sweep me off my feet and carry me to bed in triumph?'

'All right, I will!'

But that was easier said than done, as I saw when it was too late.

I strode briskly toward her, but began to slow down thought-fully as I got close to her. I have given a rough idea of her size, from which her weight can be imagined. I slung one arm around her shoulder and the other under her knees, in the traditional manner, but the instant I picked her up my own knees buckled under me and I gave an involuntary grunt that didn't set very well either . . .

My legs sagging, I staggered toward the bedroom. It was a good thirty feet away, and it seemed like thirty miles. It was very embarrassing, but we were both stuck with it. 'You're a magnificent hunk of woman, Lena,' I puffed, but it was little use. Halfway there I had to ease her down and readjust my grip. I let her feet down to the floor but kept her weight on my knee, so that she was sort of sitting on my lap for a moment. Then I heaved her up again with another grunt and plodded forward some more.

The rest of the journey I managed better, but when we reached the bedroom door a fresh embarrassment greeted us, the worst of all. I couldn't go through it. I had to maneuver us through sideways, and that extra effort disorganized my grip completely, so that this time I had to let her slide all the way to the floor. Since there was no room in the doorway to pick her up again, I stepped around behind and dragged her across the threshold by the armpits. 'I'll never forgive you for this,' she said.

Peter De Vries, *Let Me Count the Ways*, Gollancz, 1965, pp. 65–9.

Robert Coover provides a reconstruction of a scene never shown in the film *Casablanca*, a scene where Ilsa comes to Rick Blaine's home to plead on behalf of her husband Victor Laszlo:

Ilsa is staring off into space, a space that a moment ago Rick filled. She seems to be thinking something out. The negotiations are going badly; perhaps it is this she is worried about. He has just refused her offer of 'any price,' ignored her ultimatum ('You *must* giff me those letters!'), sneered at her husband's heroism, and scoffed at the very cause that first brought them together in Paris. How could he do that? And now he has abruptly turned his back on her (does he think it was just sex? what has happened to him since then?) and walked away toward the balcony door, meaning, apparently, to turn her out. She takes a deep breath, presses her lips together, and, clutching her tiny purse with both hands, wheels about to pursue him: 'Richard!' This has worked before, it works again: he turns to face her new approach: 'We luffed each other once . . . If those days meant . . . anything at all to you . . .'

'I wouldn't bring up Paris if I were you,' he says stonily. 'It's poor salesmanship.' . . .

She wipes the tears from her cheek, and calls once again on her husband, that great and courageous man whom they both admire, whom the whole world admires: '– you're our last hope! If you don't help us, Victor Laszlo will die in Casablanca!'

'What of it?' he says. He has been waiting for this opportunity. He plays with it now, stretching it out. He turns, reaches for a cigarette, his head haloed in the light from an arched doorway. 'I'm gonna die in Casablanca. It's a good spot for it.' This line is meant to be amusing, but Ilsa reacts with horror. Her eyes widen. She catches her breath, turns away. He lights up, pleased with himself, takes a practiced drag, blows smoke. 'Now,' he says, turning toward her, 'if you'll –'

He pulls up short, squints: she has drawn a revolver on him. So much for toothbrushes and hotel keys. 'All right. I tried to reason with you. I tried effrything. Now I want those letters.' Distantly, a melodic line suggests a fight for love and glory, an ironic case of do or die. 'Get them for me.'

'I don't have to.' He touches his jacket. 'I got 'em right here.'

'Put them on the table.'

He smiles and shakes his head. 'No.' Smoke curls up from the cigarette he is holding at his side like the steam that enveloped the five o'clock train to Marseilles. Her eyes fill with tears. Even as she presses on ('For the last time . . .!'), she knows that 'no' is final. There is, behind his ironic smile, a profound sadness, the fatalistic survivor's wistful acknowledgment that, in the end, the fundamental things apply. Time, going by, leaves nothing behind, not even moments like this. 'If Laszlo and the cause mean so much,' he says, taunting her with her own uncertainties, 'you won't stop at anything . . .'

He seems almost to recede. The cigarette disappears, the smoke. His sorrow gives way to something not unlike eagerness. 'All right, I'll make it easier for you,' he says, and walks toward her. 'Go ahead and shoot. You'll be doing me a favor.'

She seems taken aback, her eyes damp, her lips swollen and parted. Light licks at her face. He gazes steadily at her from his superior moral position, smoke drifting up from his hand once more, his white tuxedo pressed against the revolver barrel. Her eyes close as the gun lowers, and she gasps his name: 'Richard!' It is like an invocation. Or a profession of faith. 'I tried to stay away,' she sighs. She opens her eyes, peers up at him in abject surrender. A tear moves slowly down her cheek toward the corner of her mouth like secret writing. 'I thought I would neffer see you again . . . that you were out off my life . . .' She blinks, cries out faintly – 'Oh!' – and (he seems moved at last, his mask of disdain falling away like perspiration) turns away, her head wrenched to one side as though in pain.

Stricken with sudden concern, or what looks like concern, he steps up behind her, clasping her breasts with both hands, nuzzling in her hair. 'The day you left Paris . . .!' she sobs, though she seems unsure of herself. One of his hands is already down between her legs, the other inside her blouse, pulling a breast out of its brassière cup. 'If you only knew . . . what I . . .' He is moaning, licking at one ear, the hand between her legs nearly lifting her off the floor, his pelvis bumping at her buttocks. 'Is this . . . right?' she gasps.

'I – I don't know!' he groans, massaging her breast, the nipple between two fingers. 'I can't think!'

'But . . . you *must* think!' she cries, squirming her hips. Tears are streaming down her cheeks now. 'For . . . for . . .'

'What?' he gasps, tearing her blouse open, pulling on her breast as though to drag it over her shoulder where he might kiss it. Or eat it: he seems ravenous suddenly.

'I . . . I can't remember!' she sobs. She reaches behind to jerk at his fly (what else is she to do, for the love of Jesus?), she rips away her sash, unfastens her skirt, her fingers trembling.

'Holy shit!' he wheezes, pushing his hand inside her girdle as her skirt falls. His cheeks too are wet with tears. *'Ilsa!'*

'Richard!'

Robert Coover, 'You Must Remember This', *A Night at the Movies*, Heinemann, 1987, pp. 158, 159–61.

The Spouse's Shadow

The French are jealous of their mistresses, but never
of their wives.

Jacques Casanova, *Memoirs*

More often than not, the spouse intrudes, either by seeming to be about
to uncover the affair, or by inducing a weight of guilt. Julien Sorel, as
we saw on pp. 166–70, took considerable pains to seduce Madame de
Rênal. Now he is in a position to enjoy his spoils, but the husband
threatens: Mme de Rênal hides Julien, who has invaded her room by
climbing a ladder from the garden . . .

While Julien was eating his supper with a keen appetite and his
mistress was joking with him about the frugality of his meal, the
door of the room was all at once violently shaken. It was M. de
Rênal.

'Why have you locked yourself in?' he called out to her loudly.
Julien had only just time to slip under the sofa.

'What! you're completely dressed,' said M. de Rênal as he
entered, 'you're having supper and you've locked the door!'

On any ordinary day, such a question, addressed to her with
all his usual conjugal curtness, would have made Madame de
Rênal feel upset, but now she was conscious that her husband
had only to stoop down a little to catch sight of Julien. M. de
Rênal had flung himself into the chair on which Julien had been
sitting a moment before and which was directly facing the sofa.

Her headache served as an excuse for everything. While M. de
Rênal was giving her in his turn a long and detailed account of

how he had won the pool at billiards in the Casino – 'A pool of nineteen francs, by Jove,' he added – she noticed Julien's hat on a chair three feet away. With formidable presence of mind, she began to undress and at a given moment, passing rapidly behind her husband, she flung a dress over the chair with the hat on it.

At last M. de Rênal went away. She begged Julien to repeat the story of his life at the seminary. 'Yesterday, I wasn't listening while you were talking to me – I was only thinking of persuading myself to send you away.'

She was rashness itself. They were talking very loudly – it might have been about two o'clock in the morning – when they were interrupted by a violent knock on the door. It was M. de Rênal again.

'Open the door very quickly, and let me in,' he said, 'there are burglars in the house. Saint-Jean discovered their ladder this morning.'

'This is the end of everything,' cried Madame de Rênal, flinging herself into Julien's arms. 'He's coming to kill us both, he doesn't believe there are burglars. I shall die in your arms, happier in my death than I ever was in my life.' She made no reply to her husband, who was getting angry; she was clasping Julien in a passionate embrace.

'Save Stanislas's mother,' he said to her with a look of command. 'I'm going to jump down into the courtyard from the dressing-room window and escape into the garden, the dogs know me. Make my clothes into a bundle and throw it down into the garden as soon as you can. Meanwhile, let him break the door in. And mind particularly to make no admissions, I forbid it. It's better for them to suspect than be certain.'

'You'll be killed if you jump,' was her only answer, her only anxiety.

She accompanied him to the dressing-room; then gave herself time to hide his clothes. Finally she opened the door to discover her husband in a boiling rage. Without saying a word, he looked round her room, then went into the dressing-room and disap-peared. Julien's clothes were thrown out to him, he caught them and then ran rapidly down to the lower end of the garden in the direction of the Doubs. As he was running he heard the whistle of a bullet, and simultaneously the sound of a gun being fired.

It isn't M. de Rênal, he thought, he's too bad a shot for that. The dogs were running noiselessly at his side; a second shot apparently broke one dog's paw, for it began to utter piteous cries. Julien leapt over one of the terrace walls, ran about fifty paces under cover, and then started to run off in another direction. He heard voices calling to each other, and distinctly saw his enemy, the valet, firing off his gun. A farmer came up as well and began firing blindly on the other side of the garden, but Julien had already reached the banks of the Doubs, where he put on his clothes.

An hour later, he was three miles out of Verrières on the road to Geneva. If they suspect anything, thought Julien, they'll look for me along the Paris road.

Stendhal, *Scarlet and Black* (1830), Penguin, 1953, Ch. 30, pp. 238–40 (translated by Margaret Shaw).

At the end of the nineteenth century, in the Paris of the Belle Epoque, wives can occasionally be complicit in the adulteries of their husbands. Proust discourses on the mistresses of the Duc de Guermantes:

No doubt the love which M. de Guermantes had borne each of them in succession would begin one day to make itself felt anew: in the first place, this love, in dying, bequeathed them to the household like beautiful marble statues – beautiful to the Duke, become thus in part an artist, because he had loved them and was appreciative now of lines which he would not have appreciated without love – which brought into juxtaposition in the Duchess's drawing-room their forms that had long been inimical, devoured by jealousies and quarrels, and finally reconciled in the peace of friendship; and then this friendship itself was an effect of the love which had made M. de Guermantes observe in those who had been his mistresses virtues which exist in every human being but are perceptible only to the carnal eye, so much so that the ex-mistress who has become a 'good friend' who would do anything in the world for one has become a cliché, like the doctor or father who is not a doctor or a father but a friend. But during a period of transition, the woman whom M. de Guermantes was preparing to abandon bewailed her lot, made scenes, showed herself exacting, appeared indiscreet, became a nuisance. The Duke would begin to take a dislike to her. Then Mme de Guermantes had a chance to bring to light the real or imagined defects of a person who annoyed her. Known to be kind, she would receive the constant telephone calls, the confidences, the tears of the abandoned mistress and make no complaint. She would laugh at them, first with her husband, then with a few chosen friends. And imagining that the pity which she showed for the unfortunate woman gave her the right to make fun of her, even to her face, whatever the lady might say, provided it could be included among the attributes of the ridiculous character which the Duke and Duchess had recently fabricated for her, Mme de Guermantes had no hesitation in exchanging glances of ironical connivance with her husband.

Marcel Proust, *The Guermantes Way*, Chatto & Windus, 1992, pp. 557–8 (translated by C.K. Scott Moncrieff, Terence Kilmartin and D.J. Enright).

Bob Slocum in *Something Happened* goes to the length of sometimes wishing his wife would also commit adultery, so as to give her the same goal he has been enjoying throughout their marriage:

My wife is at that stage now where she probably *should* commit adultery – and would, if she had more character. It might do her much good. I remember the first time I committed adultery. (It wasn't much good.)

'Now I am committing adultery,' I thought.

It was not much different from the first time I laid my wife after we were married.

'Now I am laying my wife,' I thought.

It would mean much more to her (I think), for I went into my marriage knowing I would commit adultery the earliest chance I had (it was a goal; committing adultery, in fact, was one of the reasons *for* getting married), while she did not (and probably has not really thought of it yet. It may be that I do all of the thinking about it for her). I did not even give up banging the other girl I'd been sleeping with fairly regularly until some months afterward. I got four or five other girls up at least once those first two years also just to see for myself that I really could.

I think I might really feel like killing my wife, though, if she did it with someone I know in the company. My wife has red lines around her waist and chest when she takes her clothes off and baggy pouches around the sides and bottom of her behind, and I would not want anyone I deal with in the company to find that out. (I would want them to see her only at her best. Without those red marks.)

Joseph Heller, *Something Happened*, Knopf, 1974, pp. 508–9.

For the unnamed protagonist of one of John Updike's stories, the wife has not become a secondary figure, but is finely balanced against and contrasted with the mistress:

His wife was fair, with pale eyelashes and hair containing, when freshly shampooed, reddish lights. His mistress was as black-and-white as a drawing in ink: her breasts always shocked him with their electric silken pallor, and the contrast with the dark nipples and aureoles. In the summer, she tanned; his wife freckled. His wife had the more delicate mind, but his mistress, having suffered more, knew more that he didn't know. Their opposition was not simple. His wife's handwriting, developed out of the printing she had been taught at a progressive school, looked regular but was often illegible; the other's, with its hurried stenographic slant, was always clear, even when phrasing panic. His wife, carnally entered, opened under him as an intimidating moist void; his mistress in contrast felt dry and tight, so tight the first thrusts quite hurt. His wife, now that she saw herself on the edge of an abyss, clung to him with an ardor that his mistress would have found immodest. He had come to feel a furtive relief when a day passed without love-making being thrust upon him; pinned between whirlpools, he was sated with the sound and sight of women crying. His mistress cried big: with thrilling swiftness her face dissolved and, her mouth smeared out of all shape, she lurched against him with an awkward bump and soaked his throat in abusive sobs. Whereas his wife wept like a miraculous icon, her face immobile while the tears ran, and so silently that as they lay together in bed at night he would have to ask her, 'Are you crying?' Back and forth, back and forth like a sore fist his heart oscillated between them, and the oscillations grew in intensity as the two poles drew together and demanded that he choose one. He had allowed them to draw together, had allowed his wife to know, and allowed his mistress to know that she knew, in the hope that they would merge – would turn out to be, in fact, one woman, with no choice needed, or the decision settled between them. He had miscalculated. Though he had drawn them so close that one settling into his embrace could smell the other's perfume, each woman became more furiously herself.

. . . How could he balance their claims and rights? The list was entirely one-sided. Prudence, decency, pity – not light things – all belonged to the guardian of his children and home; and these he would lose. He would lose the half-run-down neighborhood that he loved, the summer evenings spent scratching in his little garden of lettuce, the gritty adhesion of his elder daughter's hand to his as they walked to the popsicle store, the decade of books and prints and records and furniture that had accumulated, the cellar full of carpentry tools, the attic full of old magazines. And he would as well lose his own conception of himself, for to abandon his children and a woman who with scarcely a complaint or a quarrel had given him her youth was simply not what he would do. He was the son of parents who had stayed together for his sake. That straight line, once snapped, could not be set straight again.

While on the other side there was nothing, or next to nothing – merely a cry, a cry for him that he had never heard before. No doubt it was momentary; but so was life. She had nothing to give him but bereavement and a doubtless perishable sense of his existing purely as a man. Her presence made him happy and her near presence made him very happy. Yet even when they were so close together their very skins felt wished away, strange glass obstacles came between them, transparent elbows and icy hard surfaces that constituted, he supposed, the structure of what is called morality.

John Updike, 'Solitaire', in *Museums and Women*, Knopf, 1972, pp. 81–3.

Another balance is struck in a cool poem by Pound:

Nine adulteries, 12 liaisons, 64 fornications and something approaching a rape
Rest nightly upon the soul of our delicate friend Florialis,
And yet the man is so quiet and reserved in demeanour
That he passes for both bloodless and sexless.
Bastidides, on the contrary, who both talks and writes of nothing save copulation,
Has become the father of twins,
But he accomplished this feat at some cost;
He had to be four times cuckold.

Ezra Pound, 'The Temperaments', *Selected Poems*, Faber, 1928.

Guilt afflicts Joe Sandwich, when he lunches with a woman not his wife. They are both ex-Catholics, with easy access to abject feelings of guilt:

After a good lunch and a bottle of wine we rose and embraced. I kissed her several times. She caressed me feverishly, opening my coat and then beginning to fumble with the buttons of my shirt. I shook my head and said, 'No,' and hurried back to the office.

We think we can escape guilt. I know better now! That remorseless auditor will seek us out wherever we go. Even as I stumbled out of Mrs de Shamble's house the memory of her hurt face began to haunt me. All that night I saw her wounded expression. In addition to spurning the gift she had offered me – the gift of herself – I had abandoned her to the shame of censorship, no less keen because implied rather than stated. 'It's not worth the taking, and you're a tramp for offering it to me,' I had in effect said. Very subtly, I had compromised her. I had behaved, in fact, like a cad.

That was one thing. Another was the contrition experienced on one's wife's behalf. I had kissed another woman – that was all. For such a bauble I had betrayed the woman I was married to? Far, far better to have done so for something more equal to the jewel bartered away. One hears of a wife's saying, quite rightly, after a glimpse of the other woman, 'You mean you'd leave me for *that?*' Such outrage would be equally valid if the 'that' referred to the degree of pleasure rather than to the extent of the rival's charms. I felt all this acutely every time I looked at Naughty [his wife] now. That bit of slap and tickle with Mrs de Shamble became more tawdry by the hour. The only way to redeem us all would be to raise it from that shabby level to something more like adult romantic enterprise.

When Mrs de Shamble's honor had been restored by being taken to bed, it was she who arose from it with the bitterest remorse. A characteristic need for expiation seized her – and here her present religious bent came into full play. The suggestion was made that we do some good work in a quarter, and under circumstances, for which no corrupting credit would accrue to us.

'Mrs Ditwielder, who lives behind me there,' she said, wringing her hands as she paced her living room floor, 'is in very bad shape. Her husband died and she has no money – she can't even buy oil for her furnace. She depends for heat on firewood, and we neighbors take turns chopping it for her. Fortunately she has a good woodlot. But she keeps running short. Why don't we go chop some for her?'

'She'd find out,' I protested. 'Then we'd get credit.'

'She doesn't know you. So even if she saw you, it would be the same as not being seen.'

Peter De Vries, *The Vale of Laughter*, Little Brown, 1967, Ch. 5, pp. 104–6.

In another novel by Peter De Vries, the vexing question of guilt is resolved:

'I can only put it this way. It's Cornelia Bly who's put me back on the straight and narrow . . . You see, even if my wife might stand for a certain amount of nonsense I have a mistress who won't. Cornelia Bly is – how shall I put it? – a Puritan of the intellect. She doesn't care that much for conventions, but imposes her own rules on human relations outside of them, like your true radical. No promiscuity for her! So while my wife wouldn't mind my sleeping with Cornelia, Cornelia wouldn't stand for a minute for my sleeping with someone else.'

'You mean you feel morally accountable to the woman who's led you astray?' I asked.

'Exactly,' he said, gratified by my grasp. He shifted forward in his chair and went on eagerly, 'You see, I wouldn't dare two-time her.'

'Is she a battle-ax?'

Augie laughed, but gently, as if the walls had ears. 'There's this, that most men do want a certain amount of domination. It's what I've always missed in my home life. I never got it from Isolde. Can you understand all this?'

'I may in time. I could understand it better now if it was the other way around – that you were married to your mistress and sleeping with your wife.'

'That's exactly the way it feels! That Cornelia is my wife and Isolde's the Other Woman.' Augie smiled. 'We have a little domestic joke, Cornelia and I. I call her C.B. Like a vice-president?'

'What about your guilt feeling?' I asked. 'Whatever became of that?'

'That's been transferred to my marriage.'

'You mean it's when you're with your wife that you feel pangs of conscience?'

'That I'm cheating on Cornelia,' he said, nodding.

'But won't this undermine your marriage?'

'Undermine it?' he said, with a tolerant smile for my opacity. 'Just the contrary. Don't you see, it gives my home life the quality of an affair, and what takes longer to wither than that? Isolde's even suited to the role physically – sitting around the house in those velvet slacks and subversive necklines, greeting me with cocktails and roses in her hair. It's for her I buy the jewels and the expensive perfumes, believe you me!'

'I believe you,' I said.

'So now I think I've answered all your questions. I've settled down into a reasonable groove, and my marriage is in no danger as every hour I spend with my wife has this tincture of cheating on another woman.'

Peter De Vries, *The Tunnel of Love*, Grosset & Dunlap, 1954, pp. 95–7.

Sex: Real and Imagined

I pardon that man's life. What was thy cause?
Adultery?
Thou shalt not die: die for adultery! No
The wren goes to't, and the small gilded fly
Does lecher in my sight.
Let copulation thrive.

William Shakespeare, *King Lear*

During the pilgrimage to Canterbury, the Reeve entertains his fellows with his tale about how a miller has cheated two students, Aleyn and John, whose corn he has ground. They stay the night with the miller and his family – his wife, their twenty-year-old daughter, and their baby, whose cradle stands at the foot of the parents' bed. When they are in their beds, Aleyn whispers to John:

> . . . 'This lange nyght ther tydes me na reste;
> But yet, nafors, al sal be for the beste.
> For, John,' seyde he, 'als evere moot I thryve,
> If that I may, yon wenche wil I swyve.
> Some esement has lawe yshapen us;
> For, John, ther is a lawe that says thus,
> That gif a man in a point be agreved,
> That in another he sal be releved.
> Oure corn is stoln, sothly, it is na nay,
> And we han had an il fit al this day;
> And syn I sal have neen amendement
> Agayn my los, I will have esement.
> By Goddes sale, it sal neen other bee!'
> This John answerde, 'Aleyn, avyse thee!

The millere is a perilous man,' he seyde,
'And gif that he out of his sleep abreyde,
He myghte doon us bathe a vileynye.'
    Aleyn answerde, 'I counte hym nat a flye.'
And up he rist, and by the wenche he crepte.
This wenche lay uprighte,[1] and faste slepte,
Til he so ny was, er she myghte espie,
That it had been to late for to crie,
And shortly for to seyn, they were aton.
Now pley, Aleyn, for I wol speke of John.
    This John lith stille a furlong wey or two,
And to hymself he maketh routhe and wo.
'Allas!' quod he, 'this is a wikked jape;
Now may I seyn that I is but an ape.
Yet has my felawe somwhat for his harm;
He has the milleris doghter in his arm.
He auntred[2] hym, and has his nedes sped,
And I lye as a draf-sak in my bed;
And when this jape is tald another day,
I sal been halde a daf, a cokenay!
I wil arise and auntre it, by my fayth!
"Unhardy is unseely," thus men sayth.'
And up he roos, and softely he wente
Unto the cradel, and in his hand it hente,
And baar it softe unto his beddes feet.
    Soone after this the wyf hir rowtyng[3] leet,
And gan awake, and wente hire out to pisse,
And cam agayn, and gan hir cradel mysse,
And groped heer and ther, but she foond noon.
'Allas!' quod she, 'I hadde almoost mysgoon;
I hadde almoost goon to the clerkes bed.
Ey, benedicite! thanne hadde I foule ysped.'

---

1. supine.   2. took a risk.   3. snoring.

And forth she gooth til she the cradel fond.
She gropeth alwey forther with hir hond,
And foond the bed, and thoghte noght but good,
By cause that the cradel by it stood,
And nyste wher she was, for it was derk;
But faire and wel she creep in to the clerk,
And lith ful stille, and wolde han caught a sleep.
Withinne a while this John the clerk up leep,
And on this goode wyf he leith on soore.
So myrie a fit ne hadde she nat ful yoore;
He priketh harde and depe as he were mad.
This joly lyf han thise two clerkes lad
Til that the thridde cok bigan to synge.

Geoffrey Chaucer, 'The Reeve's Tale'.

In another tale, the Miller tells of Nicholas, a student lodging with a carpenter and his beautiful young wife Alison, and how he devises a plan to spend a night alone with her. He persuades the carpenter that a new flood is imminent, and that they can save themselves only by hauling three tubs on to the roof, far apart from each other, and remaining silent until the rain has ended:

Lo, which a greet thyng is affeccioun!
Men may dyen of ymaginacioun,
So depe may impressioun be take.
This sely carpenter bigynneth quake;
Hym thynketh verraily that he may see
Noees flood come walwynge as the see
To drenchen Alisoun, his hony deere.
He wepeth, weyleth, maketh sory cheere;
He siketh with ful many a sory swogh;
He gooth and geteth hym a knedyng trogh,
And after that a tubbe and a kymelyn,[4]

4. shallow tub.

And pryvely he sente hem to his in,
And heng hem in the roof in pryvetee.
His owene hand he made laddres thre,
To clymben by the ronges and the stalkes
Unto the tubbes hangynge in the balkes,
And hem vitailled, bothe trogh and tubbe,
With breed and chese, and good ale in a jubbe,
Suffisynge right ynogh as for a day.
But er that he hadde maad al this array,
He sent his knave, and eek his wenche also,
Upon his nede to London for to go.
And on the Monday, whan it drow to nyght,
He shette his dore withoute candel-lyght,
And dressed alle thyng as it sholde be.
And shortly, up they clomben alle thre;
They seten stille wel a furlong way.

   'Now, Pater-noster, clom!' seyde Nicholay,
And 'clom,' quod John, and 'clom,' seyde Alisoun.
This carpenter seyde his devocioun,
And stille he sit, and biddeth his preyere,
Awaitynge on the reyn, if he it heere.

   The dede sleep, for wery bisynesse,
Fil on this carpenter right, as I gesse,
Aboute corfew-tyme, or litel moore;
For travaille of his goost he groneth soore,
And eft he routeth,[5] for his heed myslay.
Doun of the laddre stalketh Nicholay,
And Alisoun ful softe adoun she spedde;
Withouten wordes mo they goon to bedde,
Ther as the carpenter is wont to lye.
Ther was the revel and the melodye;
And thus lith Alisoun and Nicholas,
In bisynesse of myrthe and of solas,

5. snored.

Til that the belle of laudes gan to rynge,
And freres[6] in the chauncel gonne synge.

Geoffrey Chaucer, 'The Miller's Tale'.

Simon Forman (1552–1607) was an Elizabethan astrologer and physician with a substantial sexual appetite for other men's wives, which he chronicled in his diaries. The word 'halek' signifies sexual intercourse . . .

The 12th day June [1595], at 11 in the morning [Avis Allen] was with me, and Mr Allen came in the while. The 13 June, p.m. at 52 min. past 1, Friday, Avis Allen sent me her first letter, saying she would come no more at me. The 13th day, at 1 of the clock p.m., Friday, going down the stairs, I read John Ward's articles at stair-foot and, as I stood, a cat mewed twice. But I could not see her, which prophesied ill, and some hour after, the letter came. The 14th day of June, Saturday, in the morning at 12, I went to Mrs Allen to see her distilling, and came in a good time. We were reconciled, and made friends again between ourselves. And at 4 of the clock p.m., she came to me, and 30 minutes past 4 halekekeros harescum tauro. And at that instant time we renewed our friendship, and made a new league of friendship for ever to endure . . .

The 1st March [1596], strife with Pepper, about words. The 2nd March, halek Joan West. The 5th of March, Friday, I put on my new furred gown, a.m. 6. . . . The 12th of March, Friday p.m. 30 past 5, I went to garden, where I found Avis Allen; we became friends again and I did halek, etc., cum illa [with her]. The 29th of March, Avis Allen hit me in the mouth with her hand. The 5th of April, Monday, Avis Allen scratched me by the face that I bled . . . The 26th of June, Avis Allen delivered of a man-child, named Alexander, that died shortly after . . . .

1597. Avis Allen died 13th of June.

Marriage – Forman's code name for his wife was 'tronco' – did not curb his sexual energies . . .

6. friars.

9 July [1607], halek 8 a.m. Hester Sharp, et halek at 3 p.m. Anne Wiseman, and 9 p.m. halek tronco ... 9 August, Anne Condwell came to lie at my house to be cured of her disease and leg ... 11 August, 2.30 p.m. halek Anne Condwell.

A.L. Rowse, *Simon Forman*, Weidenfeld & Nicolson, 1974, pp. 291–5; 250–51.

Casanova, despite the prodigious number of women he seduced, does, if his memoirs are to be trusted, seem to have had some affection for his mistresses. In this scene he strikes up acquaintance with M. Baret, a shopkeeper, and, more to the point, his wife:

'My dowry of six thousand francs has served, most of it, to stock the shop and to pay our debts. We have goods which would pay our debts three times over; but in bad times capital sunk is capital dead.'

'I am sorry to hear all this, as if peace is not made your situation will become worse, for as you go on your needs will become greater.'

'Yes, for when my husband is better we may have children.'

'What! Do you mean to say his health prevents him from making you a mother? I can't believe it.'

'I don't see how I can be a mother who am still a maid; not that I care much about the matter.'

'I shouldn't have believed it! How can a man not in the agony of death feel ill beside you? He must be dead.'

'Well, he is not exactly dead, but he doesn't show many signs of life.'

This piece of wit made me laugh, and under cover of my applause I embraced her without experiencing much resistance. The first kiss was like an electric spark; it fired my imagination and I increased my attentions till she became as submissive as a lamb.

'I will help you, dearest, to meet the bill on Saturday;' and so saying I drew her gently into a closet where a soft divan formed a suitable altar for the completion of an amorous sacrifice.

I was enchanted to find her submissive to my caresses and my inquisitiveness, but she surprised me greatly when, as I placed myself in readiness for the consummation of the act, and was already in the proper posture between the two columns, she moved in such a way as to hinder my advance. I thought at first that it was only one of those devices intended to make the final victory more sweet by putting difficulties in the way; but, finding that her resistance was genuine, I exclaimed, –

'How was I to expect a refusal like this at a moment when I thought I saw my ardours reflected in your eyes?'

'Your eyes did not deceive you; but what would my husband say if he found me otherwise than as God has made me?'

'He can't have left you untouched!'

'He really has done so. You can see for yourself if you like. Can I, then, give to you what appertains to the genius of the marriage-bed?'

'You are right, my angel; this fruit must be kept for a mouth unworthy to taste it. I pity and adore you. Come to my arms, abandon yourself to my love, and fear nothing. The fruit shall not be damaged; I will but taste the outer surface and leave no trace behind.'

We passed three hours in trifling together in a manner calculated to inflame our passions despite the libations which we now and again poured forth. I was consoled by her swearing to be mine as soon as Baret had good grounds for thinking that she was his, and, after taking her on the Boulevards, I left her at her door, with a present of twenty-five louis . . .

Some days later Mme Baret makes good on her undertaking:

'My jewel, Baret thinks, or pretends to think, that he has done his duty as a husband; but he is no hand at the business, and I am disposed to put myself in your hands, and then there will be no doubt of my condition.'

'We shall thus, my sweet, be doing him a service, and the service shall be well done.'

As I said these words I was on the threshold of the temple, and I opened the door in a manner that overthrew all obstacles. A little scream and then several sighs announced the completion of the sacrifice, and, to tell the truth, the altar of love was covered with the blood of the victim. After the necessary ablutions the priest once more began his pious work, while the victim growing bolder so provoked his rage that it was not till the fourth mactation that we rested and put off our joust to another season. We swore a thousand times to love each other and to remain constant, and we may possibly have been sincere, as we were in our ecstasy of pleasure.

We only separated to dress; then after taking a turn in the garden we dined together, sure that in a sumptuous repast, washed down by the choicest wines, we should find strength to reanimate our desires and to lull them to sleep in bliss.

Jacques Casanova, *Memoirs*, Elek, 1959, III, pp. 262–4, 268–9.

At the height of the Victorian period, a model marriage went astray. The alliance of George Cavendish, a cousin of the Duke of Devonshire, and Emily Rumbold, the adopted daughter of Baron Delmar, runs into difficulties:

George Cavendish and Emily Rumbold's marriage was a quiet affair, owing to Baron Delmar's poor health. The wedding ceremony was performed in October 1848 ... But the marriage was not a happy one and Emily and her husband eventually became estranged. About 1859 she took a lover, Count Gaston de la Rochefoucauld, who was ten years younger and whom she apparently seduced. At this time the Count was an attaché at the French Embassy in Rome.

The cause of the divorce was Captain Cavendish's discovery in his wife's cabinet of a number of incriminating letters from Count de la Rochefoucauld. They were written in French, a language which Emily Cavendish spoke fluently from her upbringing in Paris, and they left no doubt that Mrs Cavendish and the Count had committed adultery ... George Cavendish filed a petition for divorce in 1866, naming the Count as co-respondent, and the letters were put in evidence by the petitioner but as the petition was uncontested, Cavendish was granted a decree on 16 June 1866 by the divorce judge, Sir James Wilde, later Lord Penzance, who also gave the petitioner custody of his infant child . . .

Here are translations of two extracts from the letters of the younger Count, who confessed that his mistress had 'picked the flower of his virginity': 'I have never kissed another woman, and whatever fortune may befall it will always be an indescribable happiness for me to remember that I lost my innocence through your enchanting caresses. This is perhaps the greatest happiness and the one consolation in my life and such as cannot again be found on earth. I do not believe that he who took your innocence was as pure as I was, and if there is greater joy than that which I know, I promise you never to seek or experience it, though I do not ask the same of you. I do not wish to hear other women spoken of: even to look at them disgusts me. You know it, and you know too that nothing in you disgusts me, but that everything that is you enchants me; and I love and worship it all. It is a kind of madness and you know it; for when you are kind you give me, at least in writing, the idea of what you would not do, if you harboured the least doubt about it.'

There follow fervent descriptions of various intimate sexual activities with his beloved, such as *cunnilingus, urinam bibendi, faeces devorandi,* and *delicias omnium corporis partium.* The letter continues: 'As much as the odour of women is repugnant to me in general, the more do I like it in you. I beg of you to preserve that intoxicating perfume; but you are too clean, you wash yourself too much. I have often told you so in vain. When you will be quite my own, I shall forbid you to do it too often, at most once a day; my tongue and my saliva shall do the rest.' . . .

So far as English society went, Emily Cavendish was ruined. But this did not worry her since she had come into the Delmars' money on the Baroness's death, and she could afford to live comfortably abroad where she chose. Her choice was the fashionable spa of Baden-Baden at the entrance to the Black Forest where she had previously spent some time with the Delmars to whose barony she succeeded by the order of the King of Prussia in 1869. Here in due course she was joined by la Rochefoucauld, who married her in 1870 after he had given up his diplomatic career in which he had risen to the rank of Minister Plenipotentiary.

H. Montgomery Hyde, *A Tangled Web*, Constable, 1986, pp. 79, 80–81, 81–2.

Verlaine peers through the keyhole as a classic act of adultery takes place:

The apprentice – fifteen, ugly, not too thin,
Nice in a softish uncouth way, dull skin,
Bright deep-set eyes – blue overalls – pulls out
His springy, stiff, well-tuned, quite man-sized spout
And rams the boss's wife – big but still good,
Flopped on the bed's edge – what an attitude! –
Legs up, breasts out, one hand parting her placket.
To see him crush her arse under his jacket
And quickstep forward more than back, it's clear
He's not afraid how deep he plants his gear
Or if the lady fruits – she doesn't care –
Isn't her trusty cuckold always there? –
So when she reaches, as he shoots his goal,
That rapture of the body as a whole,
She cries, 'You've made a child, I feel it, love,
And love you more,' and after his last shove
Adds, 'Look, the christening sweets', and squats and tries
To heft and kiss his bollocks through his flies.

Paul Verlaine, 'Low Scene' (translated by Alistair Elliot).

After Emma Bovary has been jilted by Rodolphe, she resumes her affair with Léon. Their reunion is one of the great erotic scenes of European fiction:

'Go and get me a cab!'

The youngster shot off down the Rue des Quatre Vents, and they were left for a minute face to face, in some embarrassment.

'Oh, Léon! Really – I don't know – whether I ought . . .', she simpered affectedly. Then she looked serious. 'You know it's not the thing!'

'Why not?' retorted the clerk. 'It's done in Paris!'

And that word, with its unassailable logic, decided her.

The cab hadn't arrived yet, though; Léon was afraid she might retreat inside the Cathedral again. At last it came in sight . . .

'Where to, sir?' said the cabby.

'Where you like!' said Léon, pushing Emma into the carriage; and the lumbering machine set off.

It went down the Rue Grand-Pont, across the Place des Arts, along the Quai Napoléon, over the Pont Neuf, and pulled up sharply before the statue of Pierre Corneille.

'Keep on!' came a voice from inside.

The cab started off again, and gathering speed down the hill beyond the Carrefour La Fayette, drove into the station yard at full gallop.

'No! Straight on!' cried the voice again.

It passed out through the iron gates, and presently striking the Drive, trotted gently along between the tall elms. The cabby mopped his brow, stuck his leather hat between his legs and turned beyond the side-avenues towards the green by the waterside.

All along the river, on the pebble-paved towing-path, went the fiacre, past the islands and a good way towards Oyssel.

Then suddenly it switched off through Quatre Mares, Sotteville, the Grande Chaussée, the Rue d'Elbeuf, and halted for the third time outside the Botanical Gardens.

'Go on, will you!' cried the voice yet more furiously.

Immediately it moved off again, past St Sever, the Quai des Curandiers, the Quai aux Meules, back over the bridge, across the Drill Square and behind the workhouse gardens, where old men in black jackets are to be seen strolling in the sunshine along the ivy-mantled terrace. It drove along the Boulevard Bouvreuil, down the Boulevard Cauchoise, then all the way up Mont Riboudet as far as the Côte de Deville.

There it turned and came back again, then went roaming at random, without aim or course ... Every now and then the driver, perched up on his box, would cast despairing glances at the public houses. He couldn't conceive what mania for locomotion possessed these individuals that they should want to drive on for ever. Once or twice he did slow up, and angry exclamations immediately broke out behind him; whereupon he whipped up his sweating hacks still harder, jolting the cab recklessly, banging into things right and left and not caring, demoralized, almost weeping with thirst, fatigue and despondency.

And by the harbour, in the midst of the wagons and barrels, in the streets, at every corner, the citizens opened their eyes wide in amazement at the spectacle, so extraordinary in a provincial town, of a carriage with drawn blinds, continually reappearing, sealed tighter than a tomb and being buffeted about like a ship at sea.

Once, in the middle of the day, when they were right out in the country and the sun was beating down at its fiercest on the old silver-plated carriage-lamps, an ungloved hand stole out beneath the little yellow canvas blinds and tossed away some scraps of paper, which were carried off on the wind and landed like white butterflies in a field of red clover in full bloom.

At about six o'clock the cab drew up in a side street in the Beauvoisine quarter, and a woman got out; she walked away with her veil lowered, and without a backward glance.

Gustave Flaubert, *Madame Bovary*, Penguin, 1950, Part III, Ch. 1, pp. 255–7 (translated by Alan Russell).

When Anna Karenina and Vronsky finally become lovers, the act is replete with guilt and despair:

That which for nearly a year had been Vronsky's sole and exclusive desire, supplanting all his former desires: that which for Anna had been an impossible, dreadful, but all the more bewitching dream of happiness, had come to pass. Pale, with trembling lower jaw, he stood over her, entreating her to be calm, himself not knowing why or how.

'Anna, Anna,' he said in a trembling voice, 'Anna, for God's sake! . . .'

But the louder he spoke the lower she drooped her once proud, bright, but now shame-stricken head, and she writhed, slipping down from the sofa on which she sat to the floor at his feet. She would have fallen on the carpet if he had not held her.

'My God! Forgive me!' she said, sobbing and pressing Vronsky's hand to her breast.

She felt so guilty, so much to blame, that it only remained for her to humble herself and ask to be forgiven; but she had no one in the world now except him, so that even her prayer for forgiveness was addressed to him. Looking at him, she felt her humiliation physically, and could say nothing more. He felt what a murderer must feel when looking at the body he has deprived of life. The body he had deprived of life was their love, the first period of their love. There was something frightful and revolting in the recollection of what had been paid for with this terrible price of shame. The shame she felt at her spiritual nakedness communicated itself to him. But in spite of the murderer's horror of the body of his victim, that body must be cut in pieces and hidden away, and he must make use of what he has obtained by the murder.

Then, as the murderer desperately throws himself on the body, as though with passion, and drags it and hacks it, so Vronsky covered her face and shoulders with kisses.

She held his hand and did not move. Yes! These kisses were what had been bought by that shame! 'Yes, and this hand, which will always be mine, is the hand of my accomplice.' She lifted his hand and kissed it. He knelt down and tried to see her face, but she hid it and did not speak. At last, as though mastering herself, she sat up and pushed him away. Her face was as beautiful as ever, but all the more piteous.

'It's all over,' she said. 'I have nothing but you left. Remember that.'

'I cannot help remembering what is life itself to me! For one moment of that bliss . . .'

'What bliss?' she said with disgust and horror, and the horror was involuntarily communicated to him. 'For heaven's sake, not another word!'

She rose quickly and moved away from him.

'Not another word!' she repeated, and with a look of cold despair, strange to him, she left him. She felt that at that moment she could not express in words her feeling of shame, joy, and horror at this entrance on a new life, and she did not wish to vulgarize that feeling by inadequate words. Later on, the next day and the next, she still could not find words to describe all the complexity of those feelings, and could not even find thoughts with which to reflect on all that was in her soul.

She said to herself: 'No, I can't think about it now; later, when I am calmer.' But that calm, necessary for reflection, never came. Every time the thought of what she had done, and of what was to become of her and of what she should do, came to her mind, she was seized with horror and drove these thoughts away.

'Not now; later, when I am calmer!' she said to herself.

But in her dreams, when she had no control over her thoughts, her position appeared to her in all its shocking nakedness. One dream she had almost every night. She dreamt that both at once were her husbands, and lavished their caresses on her. Alexey Alexandrovich [Karenin] wept, kissing her hands, saying: 'How beautiful it is now!' and Alexey Vronsky was there too, and he also was her husband. And she was surprised that formerly this had seemed impossible to her, and laughingly explained to them how much simpler it really was, and that they were both now contented and happy. But this dream weighed on her like a nightmare, and she woke from it filled with horror.

Leo Tolstoy, *Anna Karenina*, OUP, 1918, Vol. II: XI, pp. 168–9 (translated by Louise and Aylmer Maude).

No such traumas upset the affairs of Colette's heroines. Minne, married to her cousin Antoine, has a fling with twenty-two-year-old Baron Couderc. But the reality doesn't fully match her expectations:

Today, he was alone with Minne, this Minne who had arrived, completely calm, at the first rendezvous – ahead of time!

He kissed her hands, surreptitiously observing her. She bent her head and smiled her arrogant, equivocal smile. Then he flung himself greedily on Minne's mouth and, half-kneeling, fastened his lips long and thirstily on it, without a word, suddenly so ardent that one of his knees trembled uncontrollably in an involuntary St Vitus's dance.

With her head thrown back, she was choking a little. Her pile of fair hair was pulling away from the pins and on the point of tumbling down in a smooth cascade.

'Wait!' she whispered.

He unlocked his arms and stood up. The lamp lit his face up from below; a changed face with blanched nostrils, vivid bitten lips and a trembling chin, all its still childish features suddenly aged by desire which at once ravaged and ennobled them.

Minne remained seated, staring up at him with a docile, anxious expression. While she was securing her chignon, her lover seized her wrists.

'Oh Minne, don't put your hair up again!'

It was the first time he had used the intimate 'tu' in addressing her. She flushed a little, half offended, half pleased and lowered her lashes that were darker than her hair.

'Perhaps I love him?' she wondered secretly.

He knelt down, stretching out his hands towards Minne's blouse with its evidently complicated hooks and eyes and the double buttonholes of its starched collar. She saw Jacques' half-open mouth on the level of her lips, a child's panting mouth parched with the thirst to kiss her. Putting her arms round his neck, she spontaneously kissed that mouth like an over-fond sister or an innocently bold fiancée. He groaned and pushed her away with feverish, clumsy hands.

'Wait!' she reiterated.

Standing up, she calmly began to undo her white collar and her silk blouse, then her pleated skirt which dropped off at once to the floor. Half turning towards Jacques, she said, with a smile:

'You've no idea how heavy these pleated skirts are!'

He rushed forward to pick it up.

'No, leave it. I take my petticoat and skirt off together, one inside the other. It's easier to put them on again, you see.'

He nodded to show that he did, indeed, see. He saw Minne, in her drawers, calmly continuing to undress. Not enough hips or bosom to give her any resemblance to the curvaceous female popularly considered desirable. She still looked a young girl, because of the simplicity of her gestures and her elegant angularity and also because of the long, tight-fitting drawers which disdained fashion and came below the knee, emphasising its delicate, clear-cut outline.

'Marvellous legs! Like a page's!' he exclaimed aloud. The pounding of his heart made his tonsils feel swollen and painful.

Minne made a little grimace, then smiled. She seemed to be overcome by a sudden modesty when she had to undo her four suspenders but, once she was in her chemise, she recovered her calm and methodically arranged her two rings and the ruby stud which fastened her collar to her blouse on the velvet-draped mantelpiece.

She saw herself in the glass; pale, young and naked under the fine chemise. As her silvery-gold helmet of hair was toppling over one ear she undid it and laid her tortoise-shell hairpins out in a row. One puff of hair remained pulled down over her forehead and she said:

'When I was little, Mamma used to do my hair like that.'

Overcome by seeing Minne almost naked, Jacques hardly heard her. He was overwhelmed by a huge, bitter wave of love, of genuine love, furious and jealous and vindictive.

'Minne!'

Struck by the new note in his voice, she came nearer to him, veiled in her fair hair, holding her hands like shells over her tiny breasts.

'Whatever's the matter?'

She was close against him now, warm from the heavy dress she had taken off. Her sharp scent of lemon verbena made him think of summer, of thirst, of cool shade.

'Oh, Minne!' he sobbed. 'Swear to me you've never done this for anyone else.'

'For anyone else?'

'For anyone else, in front of anyone else. Never arranged your rings and your hairpins like that, never said that your mother used to do your hair like that . . . that you've never, in fact, that you've never . . .'

He was gripping her so hard in his arms that she bent backwards like a too tightly bound sheaf of corn and her hair brushed the carpet.

'Swear to you that I've never . . . Oh, how silly you are!'

He kept her tight against him, enchanted by her telling him he was being silly. He contemplated her from close to, as she lay bent back almost double over his arm, curiously observing the texture of her skin, the veins on her temple, green as rivers, the dark eyes in which the light danced. He remembered having gloated with the same passion over the pearly blue scales, the feathery antennae, all the marvels of a beautiful live butterfly he had caught one day in the holidays. But Minne allowed herself to be scrutinised without beating her wings.

A clock struck and they both started.

'Five o'clock,' sighed Minne. 'We must hurry up.'

Jacques' two arms slid down, stroking Minne's slender hips. The conceited egotism of his age nearly completely betrayed itself in a boast:

'Oh, *I've* . . .'

He was going to say, like a bragging young cock: '*I've* still plenty of time – it never takes *me* long!' But he checked himself, shamed before this child who had taught him so many things all at once. In a few minutes he had become aware of jealousy, of self-mistrust, of a little spasm of the heart he had never known before, and of that delicate fatherliness a man of twenty can suddenly feel for a frail, naked creature who trusts him and who might perhaps cry out with pain in the act of love.

. . . Minne, crushed down on the bed, endured her lover like an eager martyr, exalting in his tortures, and tried to induce the climax of passion by rhythmically writhing her body. But she did not cry out, either with pain or pleasure, and when he collapsed on top of her, with his eyes closed, his nostrils pale and pinched and his breath coming in sobs, she merely twisted her head, so that her silvery fair hair fell in a flood outside the bed, to have a better look at him.

They had to part while Jacques was still caressing her with the frenzy of a lover about to die and endlessly kissing that slender body which she made no attempt to defend. Now he would carefully trace its contours with its forefinger as if he were drawing it, now he would grip Minne's knees between his own so hard that he hurt her or, cruel in his infatuation, try to crush the faint rise of her breasts flat under his palms . . .

'One more!' thought Minne crudely.

She leant an angry shoulder against the faded upholstery of the cab and threw back her head, not from fear of being seen but from horror of everything that was going on outside.

'Well, that's over . . . One more! The third, and with no success. It's enough to make one give up. If my first lover, the house surgeon at the hospital, hadn't assured me that I'm "perfectly formed for love" I'd go and consult a great specialist.'

She went over all the details of her brief rendezvous and clenched her fists inside her muff.

'After all, that boy is as nice as anything! He was dying of pleasure in my arms and there was I waiting and saying to myself: "Obviously, it's not unpleasant . . . but show me something better!"'

'It's like it was with my second, that Italian Antoine met at Pleyel's . . . what was his name? . . . the one who had teeth right up to his eyes . . . Diligenti! When I asked him for what they call in books "infamous practices", he laughed and then he started all over again doing exactly what he'd just been doing! That's my luck, that's my life and I'm getting fed up with it.'

She did not think of Antoine at that moment except vaguely to shift the responsibility on to him. 'I bet it's his fault that I feel about as much pleasure as . . . as this seat. He must have wrenched something delicate inside me.

'Poor Minne!' she sighed. The cab was nearing the Place de L'Etoile. In a few minutes she would be at home, in the Avenue de Villiers, just by the Place Péreire. She would cross the icy pavement, climb the overheated staircase that smelt of fresh cement and putty – and then there would be Antoine's great arms and his joyous dog-like welcome. She lowered her head in resignation. There was no more hope for today.

Colette, *The Innocent Libertine*, Secker & Warburg, 1968, pp. 99–105 (translated by Antonia White).

Sex for D.H. Lawrence was a cosmic event, imbued with unfathomable mystery. In a scene from *Lady Chatterley's Lover* poised between the tender and the ludicrous, Connie, unhappy with her crippled and impotent husband, is drawn to the gamekeeper Mellors, whom she visits at the estate's chicken coops . . .

The keeper, squatting beside her, was also watching with an

amused face the bold little bird in her hands. Suddenly he saw a tear fall on to her wrist.

And he stood up, and stood away, moving to the other coop. For suddenly he was aware of the old flame shooting and leaping up in his loins, that he had hoped was quiescent for ever. He fought against it, turning his back to her. But it leapt, and leapt downwards, circling in his knees.

He turned again to look at her. She was kneeling and holding her two hands slowly forward, blindly, so that the chicken should run to the mother-hen again. And there was something so mute and forlorn in her, compassion flamed in his bowels for her.

Without knowing, he came quickly towards her and crouched beside her again, taking the chick from her hands, because she was afraid of the hen, and putting it back in the coop. At the back of his loins the fire suddenly darted stronger.

He glanced apprehensively at her. Her face was averted, and she was crying blindly, in all the anguish of her generation's forlornness. His heart melted suddenly, like a drop of fire, and he put out his hand and laid his fingers on her knee.

'You shouldn't cry,' he said softly.

But then she put her hands over her face and felt that really her heart was broken and nothing mattered any more.

He laid his hand on her shoulder, and softly, gently, it began to travel down the curve of her back, blindly, with a blind stroking motion, to the curve of her crouching loins. And there his hand softly, softly, stroked the curve of her flank, in the blind instinctive caress.

She had found her scrap of handkerchief and was blindly trying to dry her face.

'Shall you come to the hut?' he said, in a quiet, neutral voice.

And closing his hand softly on her upper arm, he drew her up and led her slowly to the hut, not letting go of her till she was inside. Then he cleared aside the chair and table, and took a brown, soldier's blanket from the tool chest, spreading it slowly. She glanced at his face, as she stood motionless.

His face was pale and without expression, like that of a man submitting to fate.

'You lie there,' he said softly, and he shut the door, so that it was dark, quite dark.

With a queer obedience, she lay down on the blanket. Then she felt the soft, groping, helplessly desirous hand touching her body, feeling for her face. The hand stroked her face softly, softly, with infinite soothing and assurance, and at last there was the soft touch of a kiss on her cheek.

She lay quite still, in a sort of sleep, in a sort of dream. Then she quivered as she felt his hand groping softly, yet with queer thwarted clumsiness, among her clothing. Yet the hand knew, too, how to unclothe her where it wanted. He drew down the thin silk sheath, slowly, carefully, right down and over her feet. Then with a quiver of exquisite pleasure he touched her warm soft body, and touched her navel for a moment in a kiss. And he had to come in to her at once, to enter the peace on earth of her soft, quiescent body. It was the moment of pure peace for him, the entry into the body of the woman.

She lay still, in a kind of sleep, always in a kind of sleep. The activity, the orgasm, was his, all his; she could strive for herself no more. Even the tightness of his arms round her, even the intense movement of his body, and the springing of his seed in her, was a kind of sleep, from which she did not begin to rouse till he had finished and lay softly panting against her breast.

Then she wondered, just dimly wondered, why? Why was this necessary? Why had it lifted a great cloud from her and given her peace? Was it real? Was it real?

Her tormented modern-woman's brain still had no rest. Was it real? And she knew, if she gave herself to the man, it was real. But if she kept herself for herself, it was nothing. She was old; millions of years old, she felt. And at last, she could bear the burden of herself no more. She was to be had for the taking. To be had for the taking.

The man lay in a mysterious stillness. What was he feeling? What was he thinking? She did not know. He was a strange man to her, she did not know him. She must only wait, for she did not dare to break his mysterious stillness. He lay there with his arms round her, his body on hers, his wet body touching hers, so close. And completely unknown. Yet not unpeaceful. His very stillness was peaceful.

She knew that, when at last he roused and drew away from her. It was like an abandonment. He drew her dress in the darkness down over her knees and stood a few moments apparently adjusting his own clothing. Then he quietly opened the door and went out.

D.H. Lawrence, *Lady Chatterley's Lover*, Heinemann, 1928, Ch. 10, pp. 163–5.

e.e.cummings is more succinct:

> may i feel said he
> (i'll squeal said she
> just once said he)
> it's fun said she
>
> (may i touch said he
> how much said she
> a lot said he)
> why not said she
>
> (let's go said he
> not too far said she
> what's too far said he
> where you are said she)
>
> may i stay said he
> (which way said she
> like this said he
> if you kiss said she

may i move said he
is it love said she)
if you're willing said he
(but you're killing said she

but it's life said he
but your wife said she
now said he)
ow said she

(tiptop said he
don't stop said she
oh no said he)
go slow said she

(cccome?said he
ummm said she)
you're divine!said he
(you are Mine said she)

Complete Poems (1935), Granada, 1981.

Ernest Hemingway confesses, in a letter to the art historian Bernard Berenson of 14 October 1952, how he nearly got caught:

I started *The Sun Also Rises* in Valencia on my birthday because I had never completed a novel and everyone else my age had and I felt ashamed. So I wrote it in 6 weeks. I wrote it in Valencia, Madrid, St Sebastian, Hendaye and Paris. Toward the last it was like a fever. Toward the last I was sprinting, like in a bicycle race, and I did not want to lose my speed making love or anything else and so had my wife go on a trip with two friends of hers down to the Loire. Then I finished and was hollow and lonely and needed a girl very badly. So I was in bed with a no good girl when my wife came home and had to get the girl out onto the roof of the sawmill (to cut lumber for picture frames) and change the sheets and come down to open the door of the court. Everybody happy at the surprise return except the girl on the roof of the sawmill. All small tactical problems you have to work out.

Ernest Hemingway, *Selected Letters*, Granada, 1981, p. 792.

In the New England village of Tarbox, a network of adulterous relationships flourishes in the easygoing 1960s. Piet, married to Angela, shares the bed of, among others, Georgene:

[Georgene] possessed, this conscientious clubwoman and firm mother, a lovely unexpected gift. Her sexuality was guileless. As formed by the first years of her marriage with Freddy, it had the directness of eating, the ease of running. Her insides were innocent. She had never had an affair before and, though Piet did not understand the virtue she felt in him, he doubted that she would ever take another lover. She had no love of guilt. In the beginning, deciding upon adultery with her, Piet had prepared himself for terrible sensations of remorse, as a diver in midair anticipates the underwater rush and roar. Instead, the first time – it was September: apples in the kitchen, children off at school, except for Judy, who was asleep – Georgene led him lightly by one finger upstairs to her bed. They deftly undressed, she him, he her. When he worried about contraception, she laughed. Didn't Angela use Enovid yet? *Welcome*, she said, *to the post-pill paradise*, a lighthearted blasphemy that immensely relieved him. With Angela the act of love had become overlaid with memories of his clumsiness and her failure to tolerate clumsiness, with the need for tact and her irritation with the pleadingness implicit in tact, her equal disdain of his pajama-clad courting and his naked rage, his helpless transparence and her opaque disenchantment. Georgene in twenty minutes stripped away these laminations of cross-purpose and showed him something primal. Now she kneeled under the sun and Piet rose to be with her and with extreme care, as if setting the wafery last cogwheels of a watch into place, kissed the glossy point of her left shoulder bone, and then of her right. She was double everywhere but in her mouths.

John Updike, *Couples*, Knopf, 1968, Ch. 1, p. 52.

In another New England village, Reverend Tom Marshfield embarks on an affair with Alicia, the church organist:

Alicia in bed was a revelation. At last I confronted as in an ecstatic mirror my own sexual demon. In such a hurry we did not always take time to remove socks and necklaces and underthings that clung to us then like shards or epaulettes, we would tumble upon her low square bed, whose headboard was a rectangle of teak and whose bedspread a quiltwork sunburst, and she would push me down and, her right hand splayed on her belly, tugging upward the tarnished gift of her pubic fur so as to make an unwispy fit, would seat herself upon my upraised phallus, whose mettle she had firmed with fingers and lips, and whimper; and come, and squirm, and come again, her vaginal secretions so copious my once-too-sensitive glans slid through its element calm as a fish, and politely declined to ejaculate, so that she came once more, and her naked joy, witnessed, forced a laugh from my chest. Such laughing was unprecedented for me; under my good wife's administration sex had been a solemn, once-a-week business, ritualized and worrisomely hushed . . .

Play, and pain. Her moans, her cries, at first frightened me, at the very first because I naively imagined I was in my newfound might hurting her ('You're wombing me!' she once cried, astraddle) and next because I feared such depth of pleasure was not enough my creation, was too much hers, and could too easily be shifted to the agency of another. There is this to be said for cold women; they stick. So beneath our raptures I heard the tearing silk of infidelity, and she heard the ticking clock that would lift me, from whatever height of self-forgetfulness, on to the next appointment, and home, to check the patch of invisible mending on my absence. Alicia found it hard to let me go, I know. For I was a rare man, in this latter world of over-experienced men. Her bestowals had not for some years, I judged, won such gratitude and ardor. So my swift resumption of my suit of black, even to rubber overshoes in the post-Paschal season of slush, caused all of her skin, bare on our bed, to stare amazed.

John Updike, *A Month of Sundays*, Knopf, 1975, Ch. 5, pp. 33–4, 35–6.

Sex sometimes approximates clock chess. In Martin Amis's lecherous early novel, Charles, involved with the youthful Rachel, receives a visit from an old flame, the pet-food salesgirl Gloria. Unfortunately Rachel, with whom he had slept that afternoon, is due to visit at nine o'clock . . .

Gloria had taken off her shoes and was lying on the bed. I sat on the edge of it.

'You're so nice to talk to, Charles. You always cheer me up.'

It was eight three precisely.

Eight five. Intricate tangle of bodies. Gloria's fingers were jogging my belt-buckle. Mine trembled between suede and moist cotton. Swampy kisses.

Eight fifteen. Gloria moved clear and pulled at her T-shirt. Blankly I started undoing buttons. Then I stopped undoing them. But Gloria freed her dear little shorts; they fell to the floor and she stepped out of them. Those wonderfully unsubtle, unliterary big breasts. Gloria smiled.

'I'm not on the pill, Charles.'

'Not you too – I mean, not to worry, I've . . .'

I hesitated again, and felt a shudder of sobriety. Gloria looped her thumbs in the band of her panties. And her panties bulged extraordinarily – as if housing a whole cock, if not two.

'I have some contraceptives,' I said.

Eight twenty-five. After some neck-ricking soixante-neuf and a short period inside her unsheathed, I clawed at the little pink holder and took its final trojan. – Not to worry, because this is my equivalent of a flash cigarette-case; the real supply is elsewhere.

Eight thirty-five. 'Yes, it was great for me as well,' I said, truthfully. 'No thanks, I'm trying to give them up. Gloria, the thing is that my sister and her husband are coming back soon. You've never spoken to Norman, have you? No. Well, you see, he's a very puritanical type – stiff-upper-lip, and all that. Very strict upbringing. Anyway, he might –' 'Oh, about five, ten to nine.' 'Oh, that's fine. No panic, really. But he might get in a sweat. You know these posh types. Can't relax about anything. And also I've got my interview tomorrow. At Leeds Polytechnic.'

'I've got to get back, too. I'm glad I could see you for this long.'

'So was I.'

The contraceptive joined its (slightly) heavier twin.

Eight forty-five. Gloria giggled as she worked the T-shirt over her smudged breasts. And I giggled, too, to stop myself crapping all over the floor with anxiety.

Eight fifty-five. 'Goodbye, my sweet. I'll ring you tomorrow.'

'Thanks for being so nice.'

I hurried her out of the front door.

'*Me?* You were the one who was so nice,' I said.

She giggled a second time, and ran down the path.

Draped flaccid over the banisters I treated myself to ten seconds of uninterrupted heavy breathing. Then I was downstairs like a whippet, talc-ing sheets and genitals, checking the pillow for make-up and the dog-ends for lipstick, roping tissues into the wastepaper basket two-handed and sending Gloria's glass beneath the bed with the side of my foot. I thanked the Lord I had slept with Rachel that afternoon: hence oyster smell and churned blankets. Gargling Dettol in the bathroom I looked for post-coital spots. My face was a raspberry purée. I immersed it in a basinful of cold water. If Rachel said anything I'd just have to stutter that I had been terribly worried about everything.

Martin Amis, *The Rachel Papers*, Cape, 1973, pp. 201–3.

One of the joys of academic life, at least until the Political Correctness posse butted in, was sleeping with your students. Howard Jacobson commemorates this now dangerous undertaking:

'That's eet, that's eet! Yo'm found eet, yo' bugger! Yis, that's eet!'

Lynne Shorthall, mature and by all accounts responsive student from Cradley Heath, on her way to collect the degree her husband never wanted her to study for, calls in at the Polytechnic in order to show off her ceremonial finery and say a last goodbye and thank you to her lecturers and tutors, and stays a little longer than expected in Sefton Goldberg's room.

Sefton Goldberg, on all fours above her, his knees and elbows glued with the perspiration of effort and anxiety to the polytechnic linoleum, as naked as Noah but for the academic gown and hood which Mrs Shorthall insists he wears, it being degree day, hopes to God he has remembered to lock his door. While Lynne Shorthall wrinkles up her nose and bites the air and gargles Black Country familiarities, Sefton Goldberg can think of nothing but the position of the little metal nipple on his Yale lock. Is it up or is it down? He thinks he can recall depressing it, but what if some fault in the mechanism, a loose fitting or some over-zealous spring is at this very moment urging and encouraging it up again? Is he imagining things or can he actually hear his door unlocking itself? What he would like is to get up and check, but such alarmism is inconsistent with his idea of manliness; and he is not well placed even to take the rudimentary precaution of stealing a glance. Now that his gown has ridden up his back and hangs over his face, he is as blind as a school photographer, and it is his other end, anyway − hence the degree of his anxiety and vulnerability − which confronts the door. Simultaneously recalling what he has read of the Japanese girl who has the gift of sight in her nose and the joke about the patient who swallows a glass eye, Sefton wonders if by sheer effort of will he can make himself see through that part of himself which he has never seen − achieve, quite literally, tunnel vision.

He does not, on this occasion at least, make medical history, but the amount of muscular flexing and stiffening required merely to *imagine* an anal squint makes Lynne Shorthall noisily, nasally happy, and causes her to prolong her last goodbye and thank you.

Howard Jacobson, *Coming from Behind*, Chatto & Windus, 1983, p. 7.

Milan Kundera's character Jan finds his sense of the absurd encroaches on his lovemaking:

Ten years earlier Jan had received irregular visits from a married woman. They had known each other for years, but hardly ever saw each other because the woman had a job, and even when she took time off to be with him, they had to be quick about it. First they would sit and talk a while, but only a very short while. Soon Jan would get up, walk over to her, give her a kiss, and take her in his arms.

When he released her, they would separate and begin to undress quickly. He threw his jacket on the chair. She took off her sweater and put it over the back of the chair. She bent down and began sliding off her pantyhose. He undid his trousers and let them drop. They were in a hurry. They stood opposite each other, leaning forward, he lifting first one, then the other leg out of his trousers (he would raise them high in the air like a soldier on parade), she bending to gather up the pantyhose at her ankles and pull her feet out of them, raising her legs as high in the air as he did.

Each time it was the same. And then one day something happened. He would never forget it: she looked up at him and smiled. It was a smile that was almost tender, a smile full of sympathy and understanding, a bashful smile that seemed to apologize for itself, but nonetheless a smile clearly brought on by a sudden insight into the absurdity of the situation as a whole. It was all he could do not to return it. For if the absurdity of the situation emerged from the semi-obscurity of habit – the absurdity of two people standing face to face, kicking their legs in the air in a mad rush – it was bound to have an effect on him as well. In fact, he was only a hair's breadth away from bursting out laughing. But he knew that if he did, they would not be able to make love. Laughter was like an enormous trap waiting patiently in the room with them, but hidden behind a thin wall. There was only a fraction of an inch separating intercourse from laughter, and he was terrified of overstepping it; there was only a fraction of an inch separating him from the border, and across the border things no longer had any meaning.

He controlled himself. He held back the smile. He threw off his trousers, went right up to her, and touched her body, hoping to drive away the demon of laughter.

Milan Kundera, *The Book of Laughter and Forgetting*, Faber, 1982, VII: 9, pp. 213–14.

Even adulterers grow old. Bob Druff, City Commissioner of Streets, aged fifty-eight, begins an affair with Margaret Glorio:

It turned out to be her place after all. They were in bed now, over their brandy snifters, over Meg Glorio's astonishing – to Druff astonishing, who'd never seen anything like it – clinging, red – silk? satin? – nightgown . . . Just looking at her now he almost fainted. And the thought that they'd just made love near killed him. She had finished him, he was a goner, some polished-off shell of his former self. She would blackmail him? She wanted streets named after her? He would give her esplanades, parades, entire arrondissements! He'd been a politician more than thirty years. He'd call in his markers, see to it they changed the name of the city.

'Margaret Town,' the commissioner said. 'Gloriville. Meg Glorio City.'

And he wasn't entirely kidding. At least a part of him serious, at least in his inclinations, in his good will serious. If not in his baggy boxer shorts. Oh, but they were mismatched (he'd be the first to admit it), he in his big boxers, she in her red silk or satin, flesh-transcended, lovematter nightgown.

And even if the actual lovemaking, though fine, and even several steps up from his usual performances, hadn't been anywhere near the standard of your normal, average blockbuster, history-making, place-namer fucks, face it, it was plenty good enough and, for Druff, better than good enough, something which at fifty-eight, or even at forty-eight, or at thirty-eight even, he would never have expected to have happen to him again . . .

The next day he calls on her again:

She was rubbing the commissioner's temples, massaging his neck, touching his hair. She was drawing her nails down his cheek. Her hand was in his lap. He had an erection.

'We should both lie down,' she said.

'Where?' he said. 'How? Does this sofa make up? You think we ought to do it on the sofa? I don't know, I don't have a rubber,' he said. 'I could stain the brocade. You think that stuff comes out of silk? Maybe you have rubbers. Could you lend me one? I'll pay you back.'

'I don't have soup bowls, why would I have rubbers?' . . .

He felt foolish undressing in front of her, just as foolish remov-ing his suit coat, shirt and tie as he did taking off his pants. He was no beauty, Druff. He looked even worse in his scarred body and toneless, troubled flesh than he did in clothes. He tried to place himself onto the low, distant futon, only two inches or so from the bare floor. He bowed from the waist, recovered. Feinting, he made as if to lean into a kneeling position, then straightened up again. Seeking various body leverages, this lone, unopposed wrestler.

'I've got you,' Margaret Glorio, sitting up, pronounced from the futon. One arm was wrapped about his leg, the other held him around the hip. She was in her underwear, her flesh tones bright as perfectly adjusted color on television. 'Go on, don't be afraid to put your weight on me. Lean on my shoulder. I won't let you fall.'

Using her back and shoulders for handholds, he carefully rappeled down the side of her body. 'Whew!' he said, beside her at last. But his hard-on was almost gone. And he couldn't properly maneuver on the futon, on its sheet like a picnic cloth set down on hard, stony ground. He thrashed away, but the floor, which he could feel through the scant, paltry mat, hurt his knees and dug into his elbows. He at last abandoned her and fell uselessly away. How, he wondered, did Japan manage to repopulate itself? 'Well,' Druff said, out of breath, 'that was pretty humiliating for me. How was it for you?' . . .

Effortlessly, she raised herself to a standing position. She was a big woman, tall as the diminished Druff, and not, he imagined, all that much lighter. He could only guess at the source of her agreeable strength. Maybe it came from the luxuriant hair that grew at her luxuriant pudendum. From his spectacular worm's-eye view as she moved away from him, he stared up at her stirring, eloquent ass, at her sparkling snatch, glittering like facets off some hairy diamond as it vanished and appeared in league with her long strides. Nothing doing? he wondered. Nah, not much. Nothing at all, in fact. Still, he thought, he was privileged to see this . . .

'I shouldn't be here,' he said. But he meant something else . . . He talked about love now. About what was permissible. Love's dead-center telemetry, blind Cupid's locked-in coordinates. Propinquity was nothing, vaunted chemistry, all inexact dead reckoning's girl-next-dooriness. Likewise Fate, the Kismets. Statistically, Druff figured, the odds of Fate coming through in matters of the heart were up there with hitting the Lotto. So if chemistry counted for nothing, propinquity, fate, what did? However did people end up in bed together?

Druff spoke up from the Japanese pallet and made a speech, wooing her, wooing himself, chasing her vote, his own, laying a little of the old Lincoln-Douglas on them both. 'No,' he said, 'she doesn't exist. She's like Betty Crocker. Not even. She's a hairstyle, a skirt length, a size six or so shoe. When I say demographics I speak as a politician. Colored or white, combined household income, highest degree earned. Did your mother come from Ireland? Margin for error two points plus or minus. We're fixed, I mean. Set in cement, chiseled in stone. Everyone who isn't denied us is denied us. I mean it. It's the demographics that require a fellow to forsake and forswear. We live by a finding, nature's negative fiat. My Christ, think of the ways screwing is out of bounds – all God's and custom's disparate dasn'ts. The incests of family, the inside-out incests of class. All the sexual holdouts. When A declines B because B doesn't measure up. Hey, just fear of trespass or a failure of nerve. An act of adultery's a miracle when you stop to think. I don't care how in synch with the times a man thinks he is, you can't just knock 'em down and pull 'em into an alley. God fixed his canon 'gainst that sort of thing. Let alone the decorums – this one protecting her cellulite, that one a failure of sheer damned inches. Or holdouts of the head or heart when character's a consideration – all love's and sexuality's crossed fingers. I talk through my hat if I tell you it's natural. It ain't natural. It's the most unnatural thing in the world. The shortfall in opportunity, in the alignment of inclinations: "SWM, athletic, non-smoker, social drinker, interested in movies, music, dancing, dining, books and laughter, sitting around the house on rainy Sunday afternoons reading the *Times*, seeks relationship with attractive SWF with similar tastes." Oh? Yeah? You think? "SWM looking to get it on with MBF alligator wrestler. Must be able to make her own shoes and handbags" is more like it. C may screw D but he's dreaming of Jeannie with the light brown hair.

'I tell you, Miss Glorio, there are drifts and tendencies and pronenesses. There's kinks and fixations, bent and bias. There's yens and itches. And if the lion ever lies down with the lamb, or the goat with the otter, it's dollars to doughnuts they're dreaming of Jeannie with the light brown hair, too.

'Because love has to be exonerated, the extenuating circumstances taken into account, the forgives and forgets.'

'I love it when you talk gabardine. It fetches me, it really does. It's a shame you can't fuck,' Meg Glorio told him.

Stanley Elkin, *The MacGuffin*, Simon & Schuster, 1991, pp. 106–7, 213, 214–15, 217–18.

Love

Life is a masque that changes,
  A fig for constancy!
No love at all were better,
  Than love which is not free.

Ernest Dowson, 'To His Mistress'

We associate adultery with sex rather than with love, but there are occasions when the core of the experience is amorous rather than erotic. The novelist Reverend Laurence Sterne, although married, had by his own admission enjoyed no sexual contact since 1752. His letters to young women were flirtatious in the extreme, and while no adulterous liaison took place, the impulse strikes the reader as more than avuncular. Catherine Fourmantel was a young singer who clearly entranced Sterne in 1759:

My dear Kitty,

If this Billet catches you in Bed, You are a lazy, sleepy little Slut – and I am a giddy foolish unthinking fellow for keeping You so late up – but this Sabbath is a day of rest – at the same time that it is a day of Sorrow – for I shall not see my dear Creature today – unless you meet me at Taylor's half an hour after twelve – but in this do as You like – I have ordered Matthew to turn thief & steal you a quart of Honey –

What is Honey to the sweetness of thee, who art sweeter than all the flowers it comes from. – I love you to distraction Kitty – & will love on so to Eternity – so adieu . . .

In 1767 Sterne, when his wife and daughter were living in France, wrote a series of long letters to Eliza, the wife of Daniel Draper. Again, the affection was avuncular rather than lustful, but Sterne's flirtatiousness reaches strange boundaries:

. . . Talking of widows – pray, Eliza, if ever you are such, do not think of giving yourself to some wealthy nabob – because I design to marry you myself. – My wife cannot live long – she has sold all the provinces in France already – and I know not the woman I should like so well for her substitute as yourself. – 'Tis true, I am ninety-five in constitution, and you but twenty-five – rather too great a disparity this! – but what I want in youth, I will make up in wit and good humour. – Not Swift so loved his Stella, Scarron his Maintenon, or Waller his Sacharissa, as I will love, and sing thee, my wife elect! All those names, eminent as they were, shall give place to thine, Eliza. Tell me, in answer to this, that you approve and honour the proposal, and that you would (like the Spectator's mistress) have more joy in putting on an old man's slipper, than associating with the gay, the voluptuous, and the young.

Laurence Sterne, *Letters*, Clarendon Press, 1935, pp. 82–3, 318–19.

The memoirist William Hickey became involved with Charlotte Barry, who was already another man's mistress. But he fell in love with her and persevered in his efforts to free her from the clutches of her violent lover, Captain Mordaunt. One day Hickey is left alone with Charlotte when Mordaunt leaves his house at Drayton to go up to London for the day:

The time of dinner coming without Mordaunt's appearing, we sat down together and had a comfortable meal. In the evening we strolled about the grounds, which were very pretty. Agreeably disappointed at Mordaunt's continued absence, we took our coffee, tea and, at ten o'clock, supper. I then *good-naturedly* began to hope, either that he had broken his neck or that Grant had blown out his brains. At eleven we determined to go to bed. My room was the next to Charlotte's, and as all the servants were in my interest they were ready enough to do everything to accommodate and please me. Upon Charlotte's retiring, the butler, with great civility, begged my pardon for what he was going to say, but as he and his fellow-servants were sensible of my goodness to them upon all occasions, and the same respecting their worthy mistress, they had desired him to assure me that their master should not take me by surprise, for in case he arrived in the night they would take care to keep him long enough at the gate, and make sufficient noise to apprise me of his approach. Besides which, his lady's maid would sit up. Thus secured against accident, I with confidence usurped the tyrant's place.

The affair prospered:

Charlotte and I kept a man and horse in full exercise galloping backwards and forwards between Drayton and London, for whenever Mordaunt was likely to be absent six or eight hours she instantly dispatched the man with a line to give me notice, in consequence of which I was with her as speedily as four horses could convey me.

Soon after Charlotte resolved to leave Mordaunt for Hickey:

On Mordaunt's return from Brighton Charlotte sent for me to say she was resolved to leave Mordaunt, and requested I would take her under my protection. This I with pleasure acceded to . . . After supper Charlotte abruptly told him she intended leaving him the next morning and no longer to submit to his brutality. This made him outrageous. Seizing a knife from the table, he swore with the most horrible oaths that rather than permit her to quit his house he would bury it in her heart, and from his action and manner I really expected him to put his threat in execution. I therefore instantly placed myself between him and Charlotte, reminding him that even insanity would not prevent his being hanged should he commit murder. He abused me in the grossest terms, insisting upon my leaving his house. Having armed myself with a poker I set him at defiance, spoke my sentiments of him with great freedom, and told him I would not stir unless Mrs Barry accompanied me. The perspiration ran down his face in streams from rage, and I actually thought he must have died with passion.

Despite being repeatedly pestered by the violent Mordaunt, Hickey and Charlotte stayed together. She refused to marry him, but they lived as man and wife until her death in 1783.

William Hickey, *Memoirs*, Hurst & Blackett [n.d.], Vol. 2 (1775–82), pp. 338, 341, 352.

Emma Bovary has surrendered to Rodolphe:

At first she felt in a kind of daze. She could see the trees, the paths, the ditches, Rodolphe; could feel his arms about her still, among the shivering leaves and the whistling grasses.

Noticing her reflection in the mirror, she started in surprise. Never had her eyes looked so big, so dark, so deep; her whole person had undergone some subtle transfiguration.

'I've a lover, a lover,' she said to herself again and again, revelling in the thought as if she had attained a second puberty. At last she would know the delights of love, the feverish joys of which she had despaired. She was entering a marvellous world where all was passion, ecstasy, delirium. A misty-blue immensity lay about her; she saw the sparkling peaks of sentiment beneath her, and ordinary life was only a distant phenomenon down below in the shadowy places between those heights.

She remembered the heroines of the books she had read, and that lyrical legion of adulteresses began to sing in her memory with sisterly voices that enchanted her. She was becoming a part of her own imaginings, finding the long dream of her youth come true as she surveyed herself in that amorous role she had so coveted. Gratified revenge too was hers. Had she not suffered enough?

Now was her hour of triumph. Love, so long pent up within her, surged forth at last with a wild and joyous flow, and she savoured it without remorse, disquiet or distress.

The next day passed in a new delight. They exchanged vows. She told him her sorrows, Rodolphe interrupted her with kisses. Gazing at him with eyes half-closed, she bade him call her by her name once more and tell her again that he loved her.

And subsequently to Léon . . .

To avoid the main streets, where she might be seen, Emma plunged into dark alley-ways, and emerged, wet with perspiration, at the lower end of the Rue Nationale, close by the fountain . . .

She turned a corner, and recognized his crimped hair curling out beneath his hat.

Léon continued along the pavement. She followed him to the hotel. He climbed the stairs. He opened the door. He went in . . . What an embrace! And after kisses, such a flood of words, as they recounted the troubles of the week, their misgivings, their anxiety about the letters. But it was all over now, and they gazed at one another with voluptuous laughter and tender endearments on their lips.

The bed was a large mahogany bed in the form of a cradle, with red damask curtains sweeping down from the ceiling in a wide curve. And there was nothing in the world so beautiful as her brown head and white skin against that crimson background, when she folded her naked arms in a gesture of modesty and hid her face in her hands.

The warm room with its noiseless carpet, its gaudy decorations and soft light, seemed made for the intimacies of passion. The arrow-headed curtain-rods, the brass-work, the big knobs on the fender, all lit up at once when the sun shone in. Between the candlesticks on the mantelpiece lay two of those large pink shells in which you hear the sound of the sea when you hold them to your ear.

How they loved that friendly room, full of gaiety despite its somewhat faded splendour! They always found the furniture set out the same, and sometimes under the clockstand were hairpins that she had left behind the previous Thursday. They lunched by the fire at a little round table inlaid with rosewood. Emma carved and served, babbling the while all manner of coquettish badinage. She laughed a rich wanton laugh when the champagne frothed over the brim of her delicate glass and on to the rings on her fingers. They were so utterly engrossed in the possession of one another, they fancied they were in their own home, there to dwell for the rest of their lives, an eternal young-married-couple. They used to say 'our room', 'our carpet', 'our armchairs'. There were even 'my slippers' – a pair to which she had taken a fancy and which Léon had given her. They were of pink satin trimmed with swansdown. When she sat on his knees, her legs would dangle in the air, while the pretty heelless slippers swung on the toes of her bare feet.

He was savouring for the first time the inexpressible delight of feminine elegance. Never had he known such grace of language, such quiet taste in dress, such languid drowsy-dove postures. He marvelled at the elevation of her soul and the lace on her petticoat. Besides, was not she a lady of style, and a married woman! A real mistress, in fact?

Gustave Flaubert, *Madame Bovary*, Penguin, 1950, Part II, Ch. 9, pp. 175–6; Part III, Ch. 5, pp. 274–6 (translated by Alan Russell).

And now a parenthesis. Since *Madame Bovary* is one of the classic texts in the portrayal of adultery, it is not surprising that other writers have registered its influence on them. In a somewhat irreverent way, Woody Allen resuscitates her when Persky, a magician, promises Kugelmass that he can project him into the book of his choice. Kugelmass chooses *Madame Bovary*:

Persky rapped three times on the cabinet and then flung open the doors.

Kugelmass was gone. At the same moment, he appeared in the bedroom of Charles and Emma Bovary's house at Yonville. Before him was a beautiful woman, standing alone with her back turned to him as she folded some linen. I can't believe this, thought Kugelmass, staring at the doctor's ravishing wife. This is uncanny. I'm here. It's her.

Emma turned in surprise. 'Goodness, you startled me,' she said. 'Who are you?' She spoke in the same fine English translation as the paperback.

It's simply devastating, he thought. Then, realizing that it was he whom she had addressed, he said, 'Excuse me. I'm Sidney Kugelmass. I'm from City College. A professor of humanities. C.C.N.Y.? Uptown. I – oh, boy!'

Emma Bovary smiled flirtatiously and said, 'Would you like a drink? A glass of wine, perhaps?'

She is beautiful, Kugelmass thought. What a contrast with the troglodyte who shared his bed! He felt a sudden impulse to take this vision into his arms and tell her she was the kind of woman he had dreamed of all his life.

'Yes, some wine,' he said hoarsely. 'White. No, red. No, white. Make it white.'

'Charles is out for the day,' Emma said, her voice full of playful implication.

After the wine, they went for a stroll in the lovely French countryside. 'I've always dreamed that some mysterious stranger would appear and rescue me from the monotony of this crass rural existence,' Emma said, clasping his hand. They passed a small church. 'I love what you have on,' she murmured. 'I've never seen anything like it around here. It's so . . . so modern.'

'It's called a leisure suit,' he said romantically. 'It was marked down.' Suddenly he kissed her. For the next hour they reclined under a tree and whispered together and told each other deeply meaningful things with their eyes. Then Kugelmass sat up. He had just remembered he had to meet Daphne at Bloomingdale's. 'I must go,' he told her. 'But don't worry, I'll be back.'

'I hope so,' Emma said.

He embraced her passionately, and the two walked back to the house. He held Emma's face cupped in his palms, kissed her again, and yelled, 'O.K., Persky! I got to be at Bloomingdale's by three-thirty.'

There was an audible pop, and Kugelmass was back in Brooklyn.

'So? Did I lie?' Persky asked triumphantly.

'Look, Persky, I'm right now late to meet the ball and chain at Lexington Avenue, but when can I go again? Tomorrow?'

'My pleasure. Just bring a twenty. And don't mention this to anybody.'

'Yeah. I'm going to call Rupert Murdoch.'

Kugelmass hailed a cab and sped off to the city. His heart danced on point. I am in love, he thought, I am the possessor of a wonderful secret. What he didn't realize was that at this very moment students in various classrooms across the country were saying to their teachers, 'Who is this character on page 100? A bald Jew is kissing Madame Bovary? . . .'

Kugelmass visited Persky the next day, and in a few minutes was again passed magically to Yonville. Emma couldn't hide her excitement at seeing him. The two spent hours together, laughing and talking about their different backgrounds. Before Kugelmass left, they made love. 'My God, I'm doing it with Madame Bovary!' Kugelmass whispered to himself. 'Me, who failed freshman English.'

As the months passed, Kugelmass saw Persky many times and developed a close and passionate relationship with Emma Bovary. 'Make sure and always get me into the book before page 120,' Kugelmass said to the magician one day. 'I always have to meet her before she hooks up with this Rodolphe character.'

'Why?' Persky asked. 'You can't beat his time?'

'Beat his time. He's landed gentry. Those guys have nothing better to do than flirt and ride horses. To me, he's one of those faces you see in the pages of *Women's Wear Daily*. With the Helmut Berger hairdo. But to her he's hot stuff.'

'And her husband suspects nothing?'

'He's out of his depth. He's a lacklustre little paramedic who's thrown in his lot with a jitterbug. He's ready to go to sleep by ten, and she's putting on her dancing shoes. Oh, well . . . See you later.'

And once again Kugelmass entered the cabinet and passed instantly to the Bovary estate at Yonville. 'How you doing, cupcake?' he said to Emma.

'Oh, Kugelmass,' Emma sighed. 'What I have to put up with. Last night at dinner Mr. Personality dropped off to sleep in the middle of the dessert course. I'm pouring my heart out about Maxim's and the ballet, and out of the blue I hear snoring.'

'It's O.K., darling. I'm here now,' Kugelmass said, embracing her. I've earned this, he thought, smelling Emma's French perfume and burying his nose in her hair. I've suffered enough. I've paid enough analysts. I've searched till I'm weary. She's young and nubile, and I'm here a few pages after Léon and just before Rodolphe. By showing up during the correct chapters, I've got the situation knocked.

Woody Allen, 'The Kugelmass Episode', *Side Effects*, Random House, 1980, pp. 45–8.

Philip Roth takes a more sombre look at *Madame Bovary*, when two lovers, an American writer living in London and a married English-woman whose own husband is also committing adultery, transport Flaubert's fiction into their own lives:

'One of the unfair things about adultery, when you compare the lover to the spouse, the lover is never seen in those awful dreary circumstances, arguing about the vegetables, or burning toast, or forgetting to ring up for something, or putting upon someone or being put upon. All that stuff, I think, people deliberately keep out of affairs. I'm generalizing from tiny, tiny experience, almost none. But I think they do. Because if they didn't it would be so unrestful. Unless you like two sets of domestic conflict, and you could go from one to the other.'

'Yes, with the lover everyday life recedes. Emma Bovary disease. In the woman's first flush of passion, every lover is Rodolphe. The lover who makes her cry to herself, "I have a lover! I have a lover!" "A kind of permanent seduction," Flaubert calls it.'

'My handbook, that book.'

'What's your favorite part?'

'Oh, the brutal stuff, of course. When she runs to Rodolphe in the end for the money, when she pleads for three thousand francs to save her and he says, "I haven't got it, dear lady."'

'You should read a little aloud to your daughter each night at bedtime. Flaubert's a good girls' guide to men.'

'"I haven't got it, dear lady." Delicious.'

'I used to tell my students that you don't need three men to go through what she does. One will usually fill the bill, as Rodolphe, then Léon, then Charles Bovary. First the rapture and the passion. All the voluptuous sins of the flesh. In his bondage. Swept away. After the torrid scene up at his château, combing your hair with his comb – and so on. Unbearable love with the perfect man who does everything beautifully. Then, with time, the fantastical lover erodes into the workaday lover, the practical lover – becomes a Léon, a rube after all. The tyranny of the actual begins.'

'What's a rube?'

'A hick. A provincial. Sweet enough, attractive enough, but not exactly a man of valor, sublime in all things and knowing all. A little foolish, you know. A little flawed. A little stupid. Still ardent, sometimes charming, but, if the truth be known, in his soul a bit of a clerk. And then, with marriage or without – though marriage will always speed things along – he who was a Rodolphe and has become Léon is transformed into Bovary. He puts on weight. He cleans his teeth with his tongue. He makes gulping sounds when he swallows his soup. He's clumsy, he's ignorant, he's coarse, even his back is irritating to look at. This merely gets on your nerves at first; in the end it drives you nuts. The prince who saved you from your boring existence is now the slob at the core of the boring existence. Dull, dull, dull. And then the catastrophe. Somehow or other, whatever his work, he fucks up colossally on the job. Like poor Charles with Hippolyte. He sets out to do the equivalent of removing a bunion and gives somebody gangrene. The once perfect man is a despicable failure. You could kill him. Actuality has triumphed over the dream.'

'And which are you to me, do you think?'

'At this moment? I'd say somewhere between a Rodolphe and a Léon. And slipping. No? On the slide to Bovary.'

'Yes.' Laughing. 'That's just about right.'

'Yes, somewhere between desire and disillusionment on the long plummet to death.'

Philip Roth, *Deception*, Cape, 1990, pp. 136–8.

Sometimes infidelity, when sustained over a long period, takes on the mantle of loving marriage. Boris Pasternak's mistress and companion, often imprisoned by Stalin's underlings, takes leave of her famous lover, who had since died:

My Love! I now come to the end of the book you wanted me to write. Forgive me for writing it as I have. It was beyond me to do it in a manner worthy of you.

When we first met at *Novy Mir* I was only just thirty-four years old. Now, as I write these final lines, it is my sixtieth birthday . . . The greater part of my conscious life has been devoted to you – and what is left of it will also be devoted to you.

Life, as you know, has not been kind to me. But I have no complaint against it: it bestowed on me the great gift of your love, of our friendship and closeness. You always used to say to me that life treats us more gently, with more compassion, than we generally expect. This is a great truth, and I never cease to be mindful of your words to me: '. . . one must never, in any circumstances, despair. In misfortune it is our duty to hope and to act.'

Olga Ivinskaya, *A Captive of Time*, Collins, 1978, p. 397 (translated by Max Hayward).

In a famous lyric Auden treasures the joy of being with the loved one at night, despite the fact that their liaison breaches convention – probably sexual as well as of constancy:

> Lay your sleeping head, my love,
> Human on my faithless arm;
> Time and fevers burn away
> Individual beauty from
> Thoughtful children, and the grave
> Proves the child ephemeral:
> But in my arms till break of day
> Let the living creature lie,
> Mortal, guilty, but to me
> The entirely beautiful.
>
> Soul and body have no bounds:
> To lovers as they lie upon
> Her tolerant enchanted slope
> In their ordinary swoon,
> Grave the vision Venus sends
> Of supernatural sympathy,
> Universal love and hope;
> While an abstract insight wakes
> Among the glaciers and the rocks
> The hermit's carnal ecstasy.
>
> Certainty, fidelity
> On the stroke of midnight pass
> Like vibrations of a bell
> And fashionable madmen raise
> Their pedantic boring cry:
> Every farthing of the cost,
> All the dreaded cards foretell,
> Shall be paid, but from this night
> Not a whisper, not a thought,
> Not a kiss nor look be lost.

Beauty, midnight, vision dies:
Let the winds of dawn that blow
Softly round your dreaming head
Such a day of welcome show
Eye and knocking heart may bless,
Find our mortal world enough;
Noons of dryness find you fed
By the involuntary powers,
Nights of insult let you pass
Watched by every human love.

W.H. Auden, 'Lullaby' (1937),
Collected Poems, Faber, 1976.

Ben Flesh is a serial lover, whose life is entangled with a group of identical siblings . . .

He had loved all the girl twins, all the girl triplets. From the time he was twenty-four until now they had been his collective type. All that could happen to married men had happened to him. He had courted them, loved them well, had affairs, been unfaithful, kissed, made up, moved in, moved out. He had loved and won, loved and lost, pined, mooned, yearned. He had had understandings, stood up at their weddings, given the brides away, proposed the toasts. He had flown in for their operations, collared the surgeons in the corridor, spitting his tears in their faces, thrown down his distraught warnings, pleading always his passionate *sui generis* priorities. Over the years his love letters to them would have made thick volumes. And though they were identical physically, he had loved each in her turn – achronologically – and despite the monolith of their triplet and twin characters, for different but not quite definable reasons.

'I don't know,' Ethel had once said to him when he was falling in love with Mary, 'what you see in her.'

'What,' Mary had asked when he was beginning to see Helen, 'has she got that I haven't got?'

And he could not have told her. Could not have told any of them. It was as if love were the most solipsistic of energies, spitting and writhing, convulsing on the ground like a live wire, uncoiling, striking at random.

'It's – what? – a feeling, an emotion,' he told Kitty when he was starting to itch for balding Maxene, 'like anger, something furious in feeling that will not listen to reason.'

'All *us* cats are gray at night, surely,' Lotte said when she learned he was seeing Laverne. 'Don't you *know* that?'

And it was so. If he knew anything it was their replicate bodies, their assembly-line lives, their gynecological heads and hearts, informed about their insides as a mechanic. Which, for one, made him a great lover, the official cartographer of Finsberg feeling, expert as a pro at the free-throw line, precise as a placekicker. And lent something cumulative to love, some strontium ninetiness in his ardor, the deposits compounding, compounding, till the word got round, the sisters deferring after the third or fourth, hoping probably to be last, as heart patients, say, might want their surgeons to have performed an operation a thousand times before it was to be performed on them.

'Oh, *God*,' Gertrude screamed in orgasm, 'the last *shall* be first!'

And for him cumulative, too. But if the sex was better each time for his practice, that did not mean it had ever been fumbling. No. Never. The kiss he had given Lotte beside the bus all those years before had had in it all the implications of his most recent fuck. And some increment of the social in his relations with the girls, of the historical. Because he had seen them through not only their own puberty but the century's, had heavy-petted them in the fifties, taken them, stoned on liquor, in lovers' lanes in the back of immense finned Cadillacs, like screwing in a giant fish, worrying with them through their periods, sometimes using rubbers, sometimes caught without – who knew when one would fall in love? – driving them in the late fifties to gynecologists in different boroughs and waiting for them in the car while they were fitted for diaphragms. And in the sixties going with them to the gynecologists' offices while their coils were inserted. Discoursing about the naughty liberation of the Pill and, when, in the late sixties, the warnings and scares began to appear, going with them right up to the shelves in pharmacies where they picked out their foams. Something of the mores of the times associated with each act. Could he, then, have fallen in love with history, with modern times, the age's solutions to its anxieties? Have had with each girl what other men had never had – the possibility of a second chance, a third, of doing it all over again, only differently, only better? Sexually evolving with them during the sexual revolution.

But sentiment, too. That refractive as well as cumulative. Associating with each sister the song, the device, the clothing and underclothing peculiar to her incumbency. A living nostalgia, differentiated as height marks on a kitchen wall. An archaeology of sex, love, and memory.

Stanley Elkin, *The Franchiser*, Farrar, Straus & Giroux, 1976, pp. 178–80.

Learning the Truth

There is no infidelity when there has been no love.

Honoré de Balzac, Letter to Mme Hanska, August 1833

After the rapture comes the discovery. Usually the unmasking of infidelity comes as a terrible blow, and the response is anguished or even violent. Order itself can seem overthrown. Fixed elements such as home, parenthood, financial security, and a sense of the future can seem, at the very least, under threat. But in Goethe's novel *Elective Affinities* (1809), the resolution of a double infidelity is more civilized. Charlotte and Eduard, although married, are secretly attracted to other partners: in Charlotte's case the Captain, and in Eduard's, Charlotte's young niece Ottilie. One night Eduard comes to his wife's door . . .

He knocked again, and a third time, a little louder, so that Charlotte could hear it quite distinctly in the quiet of the night, and started in alarm. Her first thought was: It could be – it must be – the Captain! Her second: It could not be! She thought it was a delusion; but she had heard it; she hoped she had heard it; and she was afraid she had heard it. She returned to her bedroom and tiptoed to the locked door. She reproached herself for her fears . . . and she called in a composed voice; 'Is someone there?'

A hushed voice answered: 'It is I.'

'Who?' asked Charlotte, not recognizing the voice. For her the Captain was standing on the other side of the door. Now the voice was a little louder: 'Eduard.' She opened the door, and her husband stood before her. He greeted her with a humorous remark. She managed to answer in the same vein. Then he involved himself in mysterious explanations of his mysterious visit. 'Well, let me confess that the real reason for my coming is: I made a vow to kiss your slipper tonight.'

'It has been a long time since you thought of doing anything like that,' said Charlotte.

'So much the worse,' Eduard replied, 'and so much the better.' She sat down in a deep chair to conceal the lightness of her gown. He knelt down before her, and she could not prevent his kissing her slipper. When the slipper came off in his hand, he clasped her foot, and pressed it lovingly to his heart.

Charlotte was one of those temperate women, who even after marriage continue to behave in the modest manner of loving girls. She never sought to charm her husband; she scarcely encouraged desire; yet without coldness or austerity, she was always rather like an affectionate bride who feels a certain shyness even toward that which is sanctioned. Tonight Eduard found her doubly shy. She fervently wished that her husband would leave, for she kept envisioning the reproachful image of her friend. But her mood, rather than repelling Eduard, attracted him all the more strongly. Her expression betrayed her emotions. She had been crying, and tears, so unbecoming to weak persons, make those who are normally strong and composed so much the more attractive. Eduard was gentle, affectionate, insisting – he implored her to allow him to stay – he did not demand but, half-serious and half-laughing, tried to persuade her. At last, he simply blew out the candle.

And immediately, in the dim light of the night lamp, their passions and their imaginations asserted their rights over reality. It was Ottilie who was closed in Eduard's embrace; while the Captain's image – now clearly, now vaguely – hovered before Charlotte. The absent and the present, strangely interwoven, blended in their blissful ecstasy.

But the present will assert itself. They spent part of the night in playful small talk which was quite unrestrained as their hearts had no part in it. But when Eduard woke the next morning, at his wife's side, the day before him seemed ominous; and the sun seemed to illumine a crime. He stole away; and Charlotte found herself alone when she woke.

It is not long before Charlotte confronts Eduard with their dual infatuations . . .

Determined to speak her mind once and for all, she went on: 'You love Ottilie, and every day you become more attached to her. Her affections, too, are centering more and more on you. Why not speak frankly of something which is clear and obvious at every moment? Should we not have enough foresight to ask ourselves how it will all end?'

'A precise answer to that question, of course, is impossible, but if we cannot be sure how things will turn out, the best decision is always to wait and see what the future will bring,' Eduard said, trying to control himself.

'It takes no great wisdom to see the future clearly in our case,' said Charlotte. 'At least we know this much: both of us are too old to walk blindly into something we should not and must not do. There is no one to take care of us; we have to be our own friends and our own advisers. People expect us not to go to extremes; we can't afford to expose ourselves to criticism or ridicule.'

'Can you blame me for having Ottilie's happiness at heart? Can't you understand that?' said Eduard, embarrassed for an answer to his wife's straightforward words. 'And I do not mean her future happiness, which is quite beyond our calculation, but her present situation. Imagine for a moment, honestly and without deceiving yourself, Ottilie torn away from us and at the mercy of strangers; for my part I am not cruel enough to let her suffer such a change.'

Charlotte clearly recognized the firm determination behind her husband's dissembling. For the first time she realized how far apart they had grown. Almost trembling, she cried, 'Can Ottilie be happy if she comes between us, if she takes my husband from me, if she takes their father from his children?'

'I should think that our children are well taken care of,' Eduard said, with a killing smile; but he added in a kindlier tone, 'Why go to such extremes?'

'Extremes border on passion,' Charlotte said. 'While there is still time, do not reject my advice, but help me to help both of us. In uncertain situations, the person who sees most clearly ought to act and help. This time it is I! My dear, dearest Eduard, let me prevail! Can you expect me simply to give up my well-deserved happiness, my most precious rights – can you ask me to abandon *you*?'

'Who has asked you to?' Eduard answered, rather embarrassed.

'You have,' Charlotte replied. 'Is not your wish to keep Ottilie near you an acknowledgement of everything which must come of it? I do not wish to press the matter, but, if you cannot master yourself, you will at least not be able to deceive yourself much longer.'

Eduard knew how right she was. It is a shock to hear in plain words what our heart has cherished secretly for a long time. Simply to change the subject for the moment Eduard said, 'I do not even know what your plans exactly are.'

'I intended to talk over the two possibilities with you. Each has its good points. In Ottilie's present stage of development, the school would be better for her. But when I think of her future, I see that the other situation promises more opportunities and wider scope.' Charlotte went on to tell her husband all the details of the two proposals, and then she summed up: 'My own feeling is, that, for several reasons, the lady's household is preferable to the school, particularly because I should not like to encourage the affection, if not passion, which the young Tutor feels for Ottilie.'

Eduard seemed to agree, but he did this only to gain time. When Charlotte, who wanted to come to a final decision, met with no pronounced opposition, she seized the opportunity to fix the date of Ottilie's departure; she had already made quiet preparations for Ottilie to leave a few days later.

Eduard was horrified. He believed himself betrayed and suspected behind his wife's affectionate words subtle plans to separate him forever from his happiness. On the surface he seemed to leave the whole matter to her; but in his heart his decision was already made. Only to get a breathing spell, and to prevent the threatening and unimaginable disaster of Ottilie's being sent away, he decided to leave home. He told Charlotte that he was going, but he was able to deceive her by explaining that he did not wish to be present when Ottilie left; that he did not even want to see her again. Charlotte, believing that she had won, encouraged him warmly. He ordered his horses, gave his valet the necessary instructions about packing and following him, and then, at the last moment, he sat down and wrote:

Eduard to Charlotte

'The misfortune which has befallen us, my dear, may be curable or it may not – I am sure of only one thing – if I am not to be driven to despair – I must gain some time for myself, and for all of us. Since I am making a sacrifice, I am entitled to require something in return. I am leaving my home, and I shall return only when there are prospects happier and more peaceful. Meanwhile, you are to remain in possession, but together with Ottilie. I want to be sure that she lives with you and not with strangers. Take care of her; treat her as you always have and even more affectionately, more gently. I promise you that I shall not try to get in touch with her without your knowledge. At least for a short time, please do not let me know how you are getting on; I shall assume the best; do the same about me. One promise only I implore you most fervently, most urgently to give me – not to make any attempt to send Ottilie away, into new surroundings. Once she is out of your castle, your park, and entrusted to strangers, she belongs to me, and I shall take her.'

Johann Wolfgang von Goethe, *Elective Affinities*, Regnery (Chicago), 1963, pp. 95–7, 123–6 (translated by Elizabeth Mayer and Louise Bogan).

Sometimes an affair is exposed when a spouse accidentally stumbles across a letter from a lover. In *A Nest of Gentlefolk*, the rich landowner

Lavretsky, who has married Varvara Pavlovna, the daughter of a retired general, makes just such a discovery:

Going into Varvara Pavlovna's room one day in her absence,. Lavretsky saw on the floor a small piece of paper, carefully folded. He automatically picked it up, just as automatically unfolded it, and read the following note, written in French:

'My angel Betsy (I cannot bring myself to call you *Barbe* or Varvara). I waited for you in vain at the corner of the boulevard; come tomorrow to our little apartment at half-past-one. Your good, fat husband (*ton gros bonhomme de mari*) is usually buried in his books about then . . . I kiss your hands and feet a thousand times. Awaiting you.

ERNEST.

Lavretsky did not at once realize what he had read; he read it a second time – and his head began to whirl and the floor to sway under his feet like the deck of a rolling ship. He cried out, and gasped, and wept, all in one breath.

He was beside himself. He had trusted his wife so blindly; the idea of deceit or treachery had never been present to his thoughts. This Ernest, this lover of his wife's, was a fair-haired, pretty boy of about twenty-three, with a turned-up nose and a thin little moustache, almost the most insignificant of all her acquaintances. Several minutes passed, half an hour; Lavretsky still stood, clenching the fatal note in his hand and staring mindlessly at the floor; he saw pale faces glimmering through a swirling darkness; his heart faltered agonizingly; he seemed to be falling, falling, falling . . . endlessly falling. The familiar light rustle of silken clothes roused him from his stupor; Varvara Pavlovna, in hat and shawl, was hurrying back from her walk. Lavretsky trembled all over and flung himself from the room; he felt that at that moment he could rend her to pieces, beat her half to death, like a peasant, or strangle her with his own hands. Varvara Pavlovna, in consternation, tried to stop him; he could only whisper 'Betsy!' – and rush from the house.

Lavretsky took a carriage and ordered it to drive out of the city. All the rest of that day, and all through the night, he wandered about on foot, constantly stopping and throwing up his hands in despair: at times he was quite out of his mind, at others he seemed amused and almost cheerful. In the morning, chilled through and through, he went into a wretched little outlying inn, asked for a room, and sat down in a chair before the window. He experienced a fit of spasmodic yawning. He could hardly stand, his body was completely exhausted, but he did not even feel his weariness; fatigue, however, had its way: he sat staring before him, thinking of nothing; he did not understand what had happened to him, or why he found himself alone, with stiff limbs, a bitter taste in his mouth, and a heavy load on his heart, in an unfamiliar empty room; he did not understand what had made her, Varvara, give herself to that Frenchman or how, knowing herself to be unfaithful, she had been able to be as calm as ever, as affectionate and trustful as ever, with him. 'I don't understand it!' he whispered with dry lips. 'Who can assure me now that in St. Petersburg . . .?' He did not finish the question, but yawned again, shivering violently and shrinking into himself. Bright and dark memories alike tormented him; suddenly it came into his mind that some days earlier, when he and Ernest were both present, she had sat down at the piano and sung 'Old husband, stern husband!' He remembered the expression on her face, the strange glint in her eyes and the red flush on her cheeks – and he got up from the chair, seized with a desire to go and say to them: 'You should not have played with me; my great-grandfather used to hang up his peasants by the ribs, and my grandfather was a peasant himself' – and kill them both. Then all at once it seemed to him that everything that was happening to him was a dream, and not even a dream, but simply some kind of jest; that he had only to shake himself and look around . . . He looked around and, like a hawk driving its talons into its prey, anguish struck deeper and deeper into his heart. To crown all, Lavretsky had been hoping to be a father in a few months' time . . . The past, the future, his whole life, were poisoned. He returned at last to Paris, stopped at an hotel, and sent Varvara Pavlovna M. Ernest's note with the following letter:

'The enclosed paper will explain everything. I must say, by the way, that this was most unlike you: you, always so careful, to leave such an important paper lying about!' (Poor Lavretsky spent several hours composing and brooding over this sentence.) 'I cannot see you again; I assume that you also have no wish for an interview with me. I am assigning 15,000 francs a year to you; I cannot give you more. Send your address to the office on the estate. Do as you please; live where you please. I wish you happiness. No answer is necessary.'

Lavretsky had written that he did not require an answer . . . but he waited, he hungered, for an answer, an explanation of this incomprehensible, inconceivable thing. Varvara Pavlovna sent him a long letter in French that same day. It made his wretchedness complete; his last doubts vanished – and he was ashamed that he had had any doubts remaining. Varvara Pavlovna did not attempt to justify herself: she wished only to see him, and begged him not to condemn her irrevocably. The letter was strained and cold, although traces of tears were visible here and there. Lavretsky laughed bitterly and sent a verbal reply by the messenger that everything was all right. Three days later he was no longer in Paris.

Ivan Turgenev, *A Nest of Gentlefolk*, OUP, 1959, XVI, pp. 60–63 (translated by Jessie Coulson).

Joseph Roth's Anselm Eibenschütz, an inspector of weights and measures, receives an anonymous letter after he is posted to a remote corner of the Austro-Hungarian empire:

One day, among his many anonymous denunciatory letters, there was an unusual one that went as follows: 'Respected Inspector, although one of the victims of your harshness and in consequence involved in a court case, and that on account of a single ten kilo weight, I take the liberty of informing you that your wife is deceiving you in an underhand way and shamefully. And in fact with your master clerk, Herr Josef Nowak. Respectfully, your obedient X.Y.'

Anselm Eibenschütz was as slow as he was honest. Besides, he had discovered too often that many denunciations contained false assertions. He put the letter in his pocket and went home. His wife received him with affection, as she had done for some days past. She even clung a little longer with her arms around his neck. 'I have been waiting for you with a special longing today,' she said in a whisper. Arm in arm they went to the dining-table. During the meal he observed her closely and he noticed something that had obviously escaped him hitherto: on her little finger she was wearing a ring that was unfamiliar to him. He took her left hand and asked, 'Where did you get that ring?' 'From my father,' she said. 'I have never worn it before.' It was a cheap ring, a man's ring, with an artificial sapphire. He asked again: 'Why have you suddenly put it on?' 'So that it might bring us luck,' she said. 'Us?' 'Both of us!' she confirmed.

Suddenly, too, he saw how she had altered. A new, large, tortoise-shell comb held the knot of her thick, dark-blue-gleaming hair together. Large golden earrings which she had not worn for a long time, earrings on which dangled tiny delicate gold discs, trembled on her earlobes. Her dark-brown countenance had recovered quite a youthful, indeed a maidenly, ruddy hue. One might say that she looked again as she had looked in the past, as a young girl, when he had first met her in Sarajevo, where her uncle, the master-at-arms, had invited her for the summer.

In the midst of these reflections, which by now had begun to frighten him, she uttered some unintelligible words, words without sense or meaning, so to say. They went: 'I should like at last to have a child.' By whom? he wanted to ask, for he naturally thought at once of the letter. But he said only: 'Why now? You have never wished for one. You have always said that a daughter would have no dowry and a son would at best have to be an Inspector of Weights and Measures like myself.'

She lowered her eyes and said: 'I love you so much!'

He stood up and kissed her. Then he went to the office.

It was a fairly long way and on the way he suddenly remembered, or thought he remembered, having seen the ring with the artificial sapphire once before, a long time ago, on the hand of the clerk Josef Nowak. Deviousness and cunning were repugnant to the Inspector. Nevertheless, he now resolved to be devious and cunning.

The clerk got up as usual when the Inspector entered. With unwonted friendliness the Inspector said: 'Good day, my dear Nowak! Anything new happened?' 'Nothing new!' said Nowak, bowing. He remained standing until Eibenschütz had sat down.

Eibenschütz read his papers for a while and then said, with a glance at Nowak's hands: 'What's happened to your ring with the sapphire, then, Herr Nowak? It was a very fine ring!'

Nowak seemed not in the least embarrassed. 'I'm afraid I have had to pawn it!'

'Why, because of money problems?' asked the Inspector. Then the prudence of the fair and ambitious contracts clerk deserted him for the first time and he said: 'It's to do with a woman!'

'Yes, yes,' said the Inspector, 'when I was your age, I had affairs of the heart too.'

It was the first time that the clerk found his superior so friendly. But he did not suspect from this that he had been detected.

This time he deceived himself. For with the thoroughness which was basic to him, and which made him such an outstanding assessor of weights and measures, Eibenschütz resolved to investigate the matter carefully. It was not that his heart was involved any longer. He merely had a transient notion that his honour was injured – but even this notion derived only from his army days and from the recollection of the concepts of honour held by his superiors, the officers. It was, as stated, no more than a fleeting notion. Above all it behoved him, the man of honour, to search for the whole truth, one might say to establish and to check the weight and measure of events.

Joseph Roth, *Weights and Measures*, Peter Owen, 1982, pp. 27–30 (translated by David Le Vay).

A letter in Alison Lurie's *The War Between the Tates*, a study of marital warfare, had revealed the truth to Erica, whose husband Brian has been having an affair with his student Wendy:

It was nothing, it had meant nothing, it was not important, and anyhow it was finished. He was only sorry she had ever had to hear of it. (Were there, then, other things of which she had not had to hear? Brian declared there were not, but how could she trust him now?) He expressed regret, pain at having troubled her – but all as if he were apologizing for having come home with dirty clothes. He had walked into a bog by mistake, and got mud on his shoes and socks, even on his pants – a nuisance, but they could be sent to the cleaners; Brian himself was not muddy, in his opinion. He did not realize that he had betrayed not only Erica, but himself; that he had become permanently smaller and more ordinary.

And he had made her smaller. The wife who is betrayed for a grand passion retains some of her dignity. Pale-faced and silent, or even storming and wailing as in classical drama, she has a tragic authority. She too has been the victim of a natural disaster, an act of the gods. But if she was set aside merely for some trivial, carnal impulse, her value also must be trivial.

What is so awful, so unfair, is that identity is at the mercy of circumstances, of other people's actions. Brian, by committing casual adultery, had turned Erica into the typical wife of a casually unfaithful husband: jealous and shrewish and unforgiving – and also, since she had been so easily deceived, dumb and insensitive. Her children, by becoming ill-mannered adolescents, had turned her into an incompetent and unsympathetic mother . . .

It was like being on stage. The lights change from amber to blue; the scenery alters behind the actors: the drop curtain showing cottages and gardens is raised. The villagers have not moved, but now they appear awkward, small and overdressed against the new backdrop of mountains and ruins. And nothing can be done about it. That is the worst thing about being a middle-aged woman. You have already made your choices, taken the significant moral actions of your life long ago when you were inexperienced. Now you have more knowledge of yourself and the world; you are equipped to make choices, but there are none left to make.

Alison Lurie, *The War Between the Tates*, Heinemann, 1974, pp. 57–8.

The redoubtable etiquette expert Miss Manners takes a stern line on obtaining information from letters:

DEAR MISS MANNERS:

I am heartbroken because I discovered that my husband has been receiving love letters from another woman, but he keeps changing the subject by saying I have no right to read his mail. Who is right?

GENTLE READER:

You are quite right to seek advice from an etiquette column, rather than a psychologically oriented one. Miss Manners believes that the true value in people is not what is in their murky psyches, which many keep in as shocking a state as their bureau drawers, but in how they treat one another. You are wrong, however, in your dispute with your husband. To be deceived is the natural human condition; to read another person's mail is despicable.

Judith Martin, *Miss Manners' Guide to Excruciatingly Correct Behaviour*, Hamish Hamilton, 1983, p. 215.

In *Ulysses*, Leopold Bloom makes an awkward deduction after he returns home and prepares to go to bed:

Bloom's acts?
He deposited the articles of clothing on a chair, removed his

remaining articles of clothing, took from beneath the bolster at the head of the bed a folded long white nightshirt, inserted his head and arms into the proper apertures of the nightshirt, removed a pillow from the head to the foot of the bed, prepared the bedlinen accordingly and entered the bed.

How?

With circumspection, as invariably when entering an abode (his own or not his own): with solicitude, the snakespiral springs of the mattress being old, the brass quoits and pendent viper radii loose and tremulous under stress and strain: prudently, as entering a lair or ambush of lust or adder: lightly, the less to disturb: reverently, the bed of conception and of birth, of consummation of marriage and of breach of marriage, of sleep and of death.

What did his limbs, when gradually extended, encounter?

New clean bedlinen, additional odours, the presence of a human form, female, hers, the imprint of a human form, male, not his, some crumbs, some flakes of potted meat, recooked, which he removed.

If he had smiled why would he have smiled?

To reflect that each one who enters imagines himself to be the first to enter whereas he is always the last term of a preceding series even if the first term of a succeeding one, each imagining himself to be first, last, only and alone, whereas he is neither first nor last nor only nor alone in a series originating in and repeated to infinity.

What preceding series?

Assuming Mulvey to be the first term of his series, Penrose, Bartell d'Arcy, Professor Goodwin, Julius Mastiansky, John Henry Menton, Father Bernard Corrigan, a farmer at the Royal Dublin Society's Horse Show, Maggot O'Reilly, Matthew Dillon, Valentine Blake Dillon (Lord Mayor of Dublin), Christopher Callinan, Lenehan, an Italian organgrinder, an unknown gentleman in the Gaiety Theatre, Benjamin Dollard, Simon Dedalus, Andrew (Pisser) Burke, Joseph Cuffe, Wisdom Hely, Alderman John Hooper, Dr Francis Brady, Father Sebastian of Mount Argus, a bootblack at the General Post Office, Hugh E. (Blazes) Boylan and so each and so on to nolast term.

What were his reflections concerning the last member of this series and late occupant of the bed?

Reflections on his vigour (a bounder), corporal proportion (a billsticker), commercial ability (a bester), impressionability (a boaster).

Why for the observer impressionability in addition to vigour, corporal proportion and commercial ability?

Because he had observed with augmenting frequency in the preceding members of the same series the same concupiscence, inflammably transmitted first with alarm, then with understanding, then with desire, finally with fatigue, with alternating symptoms of epicene comprehension and apprehension.

With what antagonistic sentiments were his subsequent reflections affected?

Envy, jealousy, abnegation, equanimity.

James Joyce, *Ulysses*, Bodley Head, 1960, pp. 862–4.

Dolly Oblonskaya, married to a womanizing husband, discusses his latest infidelity with her sister-in-law Anna Karenina:

'Dolly,' she said, 'he has told me!'

Dolly looked coldly at Anna. She expected now to hear words of insincere sympathy; but Anna said nothing of the kind.

'Dolly dear!' she began, 'I do not wish to take his part or console you; that would be impossible, but, dearest, I am simply sorry for you, sorry from the bottom of my heart!'

Her bright eyes under their thick lashes suddenly filled with tears. She moved closer to her sister-in-law and with her energetic little hand took hold of Dolly's. The latter did not draw back from her but her face retained its rigid expression. She said:

'It is impossible to console me. Everything is lost after what has happened, everything destroyed!'

As soon as she had said it her face softened. Anna lifted Dolly's dry thin hand, kissed it, and said:

'But what is to be done, Dolly, what is to be done? What is the best way of acting in this dreadful position? That is what one has to consider.'

'Everything is at an end, and that's all,' said Dolly. 'And the worst of it is, you understand, that I can't leave him: there are the children, and I am bound. Yet I can't live with him; it is torture for me to see him.'

'Dolly, my darling, he has spoken to me, but I want to hear it from you. Tell me everything.'

Dolly looked at her inquiringly.

Sincere sympathy and affection were visible in Anna's face.

'If you like,' said Dolly suddenly, 'but I'll begin from the beginning. You know how I was married. With the education Mama gave me, I was not merely naive, but silly! I knew nothing. I know they say husbands tell their wives how they have lived, but Stiva . . .' She corrected herself. 'But Stephen Arkadyevich never told me anything. You will hardly believe it, but up to now I thought I was the only woman he had ever known. In this way I lived for eight years. Only think, that I not only did not suspect him of unfaithfulness, but thought it impossible. I then . . . just imagine, with such ideas suddenly to find out all the horrors, all the abomination . . . Try to understand me. To be fully convinced of one's happiness and suddenly . . .' continued Dolly, suppressing her sobs, 'to read a letter, his letter to his mistress, my children's governess. No, it is too horrible!' She hurriedly drew out her handkerchief and hid her face in it.

'I could perhaps understand a momentary slip,' she went on after a pause, 'but deliberately, cunningly to deceive me . . . and with whom? To go on living with me as my husband, and with her at the same time . . . it's awful; you cannot realize . . .'

'Oh yes, I do, I do understand, Dolly dear, I do understand,' said Anna, pressing her hand.

'And do you think he realizes the horror of my situation?' continued Dolly. 'Not at all! He is happy and contented.'

'Oh no,' Anna quickly interrupted. 'He is pitiable, he is overwhelmed with remorse . . .'

'Is he capable of remorse?' interrupted Dolly, looking searchingly into her sister-in-law's face.

'Oh yes, I know him. I could not look at him without pity. We both know him. He is kind-hearted, but he is proud too, and now he is so humiliated. What moved me most is . . . (and here Anna guessed what would touch Dolly most) that two things tormented him. He is ashamed of the children, and that, loving you . . . yes, yes, loving you more than anything else in the world,' she hurriedly went on, not listening to Dolly who was about to reply, 'he has hurt you, hit you so hard. He kept saying, "No, no, she will not forgive me!"'

Dolly, gazing beyond her sister-in-law, listened thoughtfully.

'Yes, I understand that his position is dreadful; it is worse for the guilty than for the innocent one,' she said, 'if he feels that the misfortune all comes from his fault. But how can I forgive him, how can I be a wife to him after her? . . . Life with him now will be a torture for me, just because I love my old love for him . . .' Sobs cut short her words.

But as if intentionally every time she softened, she again began to speak of the thing that irritated her.

'You know she is young, she is pretty,' she said. 'You see, Anna, my youth and my good looks have been sacrificed, and to whom? For him and his children. I have served his purpose and lost all I had in the service, and of course a fresh, good-for-nothing creature now pleases him better. They probably talked about me, or, worse still, avoided the subject . . . You understand?'

And hatred again burned in her eyes.

'And after that he will tell me . . . Am I to believe him? Never . . . No, it's all ended, all that served as a consolation, as a reward for my labours, my sufferings . . . It is terrible, my soul has so revolted that instead of love and tenderness for him I have nothing but anger left, yes, anger. I could kill him . . . What am I to do? Think it over, Anna, help me! I have turned over in my mind everything I could think of, and can find nothing.'

Anna could not think of anything, but her heart responded to every word and every look of Dolly's.

'All I can say is,' began Anna, 'I am his sister and I know his character, his capacity for forgetting everything,' she made a gesture with her hand in front of her forehead, 'that capacity for letting himself be completely carried away, but on the other hand for completely repenting. He can hardly believe now – can hardly understand – how he could do it.'

'No, he understands and understood,' Dolly interrupted. 'And I . . . you forget me . . . Does it make it easier for me?'

'Wait a bit. When he was speaking to me, I confess I did not quite realize the misery of your position. I saw only his side, and that the family was upset, and I was sorry for him, but now having spoken with you I as a woman see something else. I see your suffering and I cannot tell you how sorry I am for you. But, Dolly dearest, I fully understand your sufferings – yet there is one thing I do not know. I do not know . . . I do not know how much love there still is in your soul – you alone know that. Is there enough for forgiveness? If there is – then forgive him.'

'No,' Dolly began, but Anna stopped her and again kissed her hand.

'I know the world better than you do,' she said. 'I know men like Stiva and how they see these things. You think he spoke to her about you. That never happens. These men may be unfaithful, but their homes, their wives, are their holy places. They manage in some way to hold these women in contempt and don't let them interfere with the family. They seem to draw some kind of line between the family and those others. I do not understand it, but it is so.'

'Yes, but he kissed her . . .'

'Dolly, wait a bit. I have seen Stiva when he was in love with you. I remember his coming to me and weeping (what poetry and high ideals you were bound up with in his mind!), and I know that the longer he lived with you the higher you rose in his esteem. You know we used to laugh at him because his every third word was, "Dolly is a wonderful woman." You have been and still are his divinity, and this infatuation never reached his soul . . .'

'But suppose the infatuation is repeated?'

'It cannot be, as I understand . . .'

'And you, would you forgive?'

'I do not know, I cannot judge . . . Yes, I can,' said Anna, after a minute's consideration. Her mind had taken in and weighed the situation, and she added, 'Yes, I can, I can. Yes, I should forgive. I should not remain the same woman – no, but I should forgive, and forgive it as utterly as if it had never happened at all.'

'Well, of course . . .' Dolly put in quickly as if saying what she had often herself thought, 'or else it would not be forgiveness. If one is to forgive, it must be entire forgiveness. Well now, I will show you your room.' She rose, and on the way embraced Anna. 'My dear, how glad I am you came! I feel better now, much better.'

Tolstoy, *Anna Karenina*, OUP, 1918, Vol. I: XIX, pp. 76–80 (translated by Louise and Aylmer Maude).

Peter De Vries gives the moment of discovery a comic edge when Stew Smackenfelt is challenged by his wife Dolly as to whether he is having an affair with his mother-in-law Ginger.

'You've been seeing my mother.'

Smackenfelt had had the sense of being watched from behind, as he sat reading the Casting News in *Variety*, down in his cellar fastness. He had heard Dolly descend the stairs several minutes before, then forgotten her while she rummaged in a storage chest for something never made clear. Then been arrested, in a sudden stillness, by the certainty of being fixed by a gaze striking the back of his head, like a dart from an invisible blowgun.

'I see her all the time, Dolly. Here, there, everywhere.'

'You know what I mean. You've been taking her out. To dinner and so on.'

'Well, a woman doesn't like to be cooking all the time. She likes to dine out now and again, take in a movie. You know?'

'Is there something between you?'

He couldn't help laughing at this. 'Do you really think you're in a position to ask?'

'My God.' She subsided on a chair, the three-legged stool Ginger had hauled from the bin the day she had first joined him downcellar, here where he went to lick his wounds. She gazed around, her eye coming to rest at last on the wrestling mat. 'My God, all the while behind my back.'

'It's like they say, the wife is the last to know,' he then reassuringly chaffered.

'Oh, Stew, how could you!'

'Oh, for God's sake, can't you see I'm joking?'

'About a matter like this!' She threw her hands out and rolled her eyes upward, as though calling on unseen witnesses to judge her part.

He slapped the *Variety* down on the floor. 'There *is* no matter, that's what I mean. If what you mean is having an affair. What need would we have to go to a movie with the house full of beds – and wrestling mats!'

'How do I know I can believe that?' she said, eyeing him sidewise, having twisted about on the camp stool at an angle accommodating this dramatic expression. 'It all fits. Your never wanting her to leave – that's unnatural in a husband . . .'

'Is it? Lots of men like their mothers-in-law, I rather suspect.

It's the daughters who can't stand their mothers. I never thought the mother-in-law was an ogre at all. I think it's a myth.'

'I see.' She looked at him narrowly. 'I'm beginning to see what you mean. It's the wife who's the ogre.'

'Oh, Jesus H. Christ!' He threw up his hands.

'The violence of your reaction only proves that's the motive you're trying to hide. That's what you're trying to do to me. It's your vengeance. That's what you're saying to the world, with this affair. Or whatever it is. It's all aimed at me. Then that's the way it is.' She rose and took a step away. 'Then I'll take myself as freely left to my own devices.'

'Now wait a minute, baby. Let's get causes and effects straight here, shall we? The sequence of events. You call my interest in your mother a reaction to your own little caper, which you then justify as a retaliation for mine. You can't have it both ways. You can't seize on something that comes *after* Zap – if it does – as justification for taking up with him. That kind of reasoning is like the kid who shot his parents and then asked for mercy on the ground that he was an orphan.'

Stew marries Ginger. Dolly marries Zap.

Peter De Vries, *Forever Panting*, Little, Brown, 1973, pp. 143–5.

Such happy endings are rare. In *Rabbit Redux*, when Harry (Rabbit) Angstrom suspects his wife is having an affair with her colleague Charlie Stavros, the resolution is painful and difficult:

'Yes or no about you and Stavros.'

'No.' But lying she felt, as when a child watching the snow dams melt, that the truth must push through, it was too big, too constant: though she was terrified and would scream, it was something she must have, her confession like a baby. She felt so proud.

'You dumb bitch,' he says. He hits her not in the face but on the shoulder, like a man trying to knock open a stuck door.

She hits him back, clumsily, on the side of the neck, as high as she can reach. Harry feels a flash of pleasure: sunlight in a tunnel. He hits her three, four, five times, unable to stop, boring his way to that sunlight, not as hard as he can hit, but hard enough for her to whimper; she doubles over so that his last punches are thrown hammerwise down into her neck and back, an angle he doesn't see her from that much – the chalk-white parting, the candle-white nape, the bra strap showing through the fabric of the back of the blouse. Her sobbing arises muffled and, astonished by a beauty expressed by her abasement, by a face that shines through her reduction to this craven faceless posture, he pauses. Janice senses that he will not hit her any more. She abandons her huddle, flops over to her side, and lets herself cry out loud – high-pitched, a startled noise pinched between sieges of windy gasping. Her face is red, wrinkled, newborn; in curiosity he drops to his knees to examine her. Her black eyes flash at this and she spits up at his face, but misjudges; the saliva falls back into her own face. For him there is only the faintest kiss of spray. Flecked with her own spit Janice cries, 'I do, I *do* sleep with Charlie!'

'Ah, shit,' Rabbit says softly, 'of course you do,' and bows his head into her chest, to protect himself from her scratching, while he half-pummels her sides, half-tries to embrace her and lift her.

'I love him. Damn you, Harry. We make love all the time.'

'Good,' he moans, mourning the receding of that light, that ecstasy of his hitting her, of knocking her open. Now she will become another cripple he must take care of. 'Good for you.'

'It's been going on for *months*,' she insists, writhing and trying to get free to spit again, furious at his response. He pins her arms, which would claw, at her sides and squeezes her hard. She stares into his face. Her face is wild, still, frozen. She is seeking what will hurt him most. 'I do things for him,' she says, 'I never do for you.'

'Sure you do,' he murmurs, wanting to have a hand free to stroke her forehead, to re-enclose her. He sees the gloss of her forehead and the gloss of the kitchen linoleum. Her hair wriggles outward into the spilled wriggles of the marbled linoleum pattern, worn where she stands at the sink. A faint sweetish smell beneath them, of the sluggish sink tie-in. She abandons herself to crying and softness and relief, and he has no trouble lifting her and carrying her in to the living-room sofa. He has zombie-strength: his shins shiver, his palm sore from the clipper handles is a crescent of bronze.

She sinks lost into the sofa's breadth.

He prompts her, 'He makes better love than me,' to keep her confession flowing, as a physician moistens a boil.

She bites her tongue, trying to think, surveying her ruins with an eye towards salvage. Impure desires – to save her skin, to be kind, to be exact – pollute her primary fear and anger. 'He's different,' she says. 'I'm more exciting to him than to you. I'm sure it's just mostly our not being married.'

'Where do you do it?'

Worlds whirl past and cloud her eyes – car seats, rugs, tree undersides seen through windshields, the beigy-gray carpeting in the narrow space between the three green steel desks and the safe and the Toyota cut-out, motel rooms with their cardboard panelling and scratchy bedspreads, his dour bachelor's apartment stuffed with heavy furniture and tinted relatives in silver frames. 'Different places.'

'Do you want to marry him?'

'No. *No.*' Why does she say this? The possibility opens an abyss. She would not have known this. A gate she had always assumed gave onto a garden gave onto emptiness. She makes to move closer to Harry, to drag him down closer to her; she is lying on the sofa, one shoe off, her bruises just beginning to smart, while he kneels on the carpet, having carried her here. He remains stiff when she pulls at him, he is dead, she has killed him.

He asks, 'Was I so lousy to you?'

'Oh, sweetie, no. You were good to me. You came back. You work in that dirty place. I don't know what got into me, Harry, I honestly don't.'

'Whatever it was,' he tells her, 'it must be still there.' He looks like [their son] Nelson, saying this, a mulling discontented hurt look, puzzling to pry something open, to get something out. She sees she will have to make love to him. A conflicted tide moves within her, desire for this pale and hairless stranger, abhorrence of this desire, fascination with the levels of betrayal possible.

John Updike, *Rabbit Redux*, Knopf, 1971, pp. 64–6.

Even more raw is this scene from a novella by Andre Dubus. Jack is married to Terry, Hank to Edith. Jack and Edith have been secret lovers for some time; Hank and Terry have become lovers more recently. Terry is talking to Jack at some length about their marriage . . .

'. . . If you love me for what I do then you can't want me to be unfaithful because if I screw somebody else it's because I love him, so either you don't love me and so you don't care or you don't know me and you just love someone who looks like me, and what you like to do is add to my tricks. Screw Hank. Shake hands. Sit, roll over, play dead, fetch – loving me like a dog. Because I'm not like that . . . No fucking tricks! But not you!' She stood up and looked at me. 'Am I right? You don't love me, you love the tricks? Is that true? My stupid spaghetti sauce, the martini waiting in the freezer when you come home in the afternoons, the way I for Christ's sweet sake look and walk and screw?'

'I love Edith,' I said, and looked her full in the face; probably I didn't breathe. Her face jerked back, as if threatened by a blow; then she was shaking her head, slowly at first then faster back and forth, and I said: 'Terry. Terry, yes: I love her. I don't love you. I haven't for a long time. I don't know why. Maybe no one ever knows why. I'm sorry, Terry, but I can't help it, I –'

'Nooooo,' she wailed, and she was across the room, dropping her glass, tears now, shaking her head just below my face, pounding my chest, not rage but like a foiled child: she could have been striking a table or wall. 'No, *Jack*. No, *Jack* –' Then she shoved me hard against the wall and I bounced off and pushed her with both hands: she fell loudly on her back, her head thumped the floor, and I crouched with clenched fists, looking down at her frightened face and its sudden pain. She rolled on one side and slowly got up . . .

'That fucking bitch whore Edith. My fucking friend Edith. So up Terry. Alone then. I should have known. I did know. I knew all the time. I just wouldn't let myself know that I knew. How long have you been screwing her?'

'May. Late May.'

'Yes. I thought so. I thought so tonight going to meet Hank and I thought so while we high school screwed in the car, I saw you, the way you look at her like you haven't looked at me in years, and I saw you screwing her and when Hank finished I told him I wanted to be alone, just to take me back to DiBurro's where my car was. Did you love me until you fell in love with Edith?'

'No.' I shook my head. 'No. I guess that's why I lo—'

'Don't say it! I don't have to keep hearing that. I —' She lowered her head, the hair covering her eyes, then she went to her purse on the table and got a cigarette and lit it at the stove, holding her hair back behind her neck. When she turned to face me she looked down at the gold wedding ring on her finger, then she twisted it as though to pull it off, but she didn't; she just kept turning it on her finger and looking at it . . .

Jack agrees to leave, and goes to see Edith to explain what has occurred:

When I got back to the kitchen, Edith was waiting with the drink. I took it from her and put it on the table and held her.

'Hank said he'd guessed long ago,' she said. 'He said he was happy for us and now he's sad for us. Which means he was happy you were taking care of me and now he's sorry you can't.'

I reached down for the drink and, still holding her, drank it fast over her shoulder and then quietly we went to the guest room. In the dark she folded back the spread and sheet; still silent and standing near each other we slowly undressed, folding clothes over the back of chairs, and I felt my life was out of my hands, that I must now play at a ritual of mortality and goodbye, the goodbye not only to Edith but to love itself, for I would never again lie naked with a woman I loved, and in bed then I held her tightly and in the hard grip of her arms I began to shudder and almost wept but didn't, then I said: 'I can't make love, I'm just too sad, I –' She nodded against my cheek and for a long while we quietly held each other and then I got up and dressed and left her naked under the sheet and went home.

Andre Dubus, 'We Don't Live Here Anymore', *Separate Flights*, Godine (Boston), 1975, pp. 60–62, 71.

Worst of all, perhaps, is uncertainty. In *The Father*, Strindberg plays on one of the most misery-inducing anxieties of all, when Laura torments her husband the Captain with the thought that their daughter Bertha may not be his child . . .

Laura: It has recently been proved that no one can be sure who is a child's father.
   Captain: What has that to do with us?
   Laura: You can't be sure that you are Bertha's father.
   Captain: I – can't be sure –!
   Laura: No. No one can be sure, so you can't.
   Captain: Are you trying to be funny?
   Laura: I'm only repeating what you've said to me. Anyway, how do you know I haven't been unfaithful to you?
   Captain: I could believe almost anything of you, but not that. Besides, if it were true you wouldn't talk about it.
   Laura: Suppose I were prepared for anything – to be driven out, despised, anything – rather than lose my child? Suppose I am telling you the truth now, when I say to you: 'Bertha is my child, but not yours!' Suppose –!
   Captain: Stop!
   Laura: Just suppose. Your power over her would be ended.

Captain: If you could prove I was not the father.

Laura: That wouldn't be difficult. Would you like me to?

Captain: Stop it! At once!

Laura: I'd only need to name the true father, and tell you the time and place. When was Bertha born? Three years after our marriage –

Captain: Stop it, or –!

Laura: Or what? All right, I'll stop. But think carefully before you take any decision. And, above all, don't make yourself ridiculous.

Captain: God – I could almost weep –!

Laura: Then you *will* be ridiculous.

Captain: But not you!

Laura: No. Our relationship to our children is not in question.

Captain: That is why one cannot fight with you.

Laura: Why try to fight with an enemy who is so much stronger?

Captain: Stronger?

Laura: Yes. It's strange, but I've never been able to look at a man without feeling that I am stronger than him.

Captain: Well, for once you're going to meet your match. And I'll see you never forget it.

Laura: That'll be interesting.

The Captain's doubts grow . . .

Captain: By your behaviour you have succeeded in filling my mind with doubt, so that soon my judgment will be clouded and my thoughts begin to wander. This is the approaching dementia for which you have been waiting, and which may come at any time . . . Free me from my doubts, and I will abandon the battle.

Laura: What doubts?

Captain: About Bertha's parentage.

Laura: Are there any doubts about that?

Captain: In my mind there are. You have awoken them.

Laura: I?

Captain: Yes. You have dripped them into my ear like poison, and events have fostered their growth. Free me from my uncertainty, tell me straight out: 'It is so!' and already I forgive you.

Laura: How can I confess to a crime I have not committed?

Captain: What does it matter? You know I shan't reveal it. Do you think a man goes around trumpeting his shame?

Laura: If I say it isn't true you won't be sure; but if I say it is, you will be. So you would rather it was true.

Captain: Yes. It's strange, but I suppose it's because the one cannot be proved, whereas the other can.

Laura: Have you any grounds for your suspicions?

Captain: Yes and no.

Laura: I suppose you'd like me to be guilty so that you could throw me out and keep the child to yourself. But you won't catch me with a trick like that.

Captain: Do you think I'd want to keep some other man's child if I knew you were guilty?

Laura: I'm sure you wouldn't. And that's why I realise you were lying just now when you said you already forgave me.

Captain [*gets up*]: Laura, save me and my sanity. You don't understand what I'm saying. If the child is not mine, I have no rights over her, and want none – and that is all that *you* want. Isn't it? Or do you want something else too? Do you want to retain your power over the child, but to keep me here as the breadwinner?

Laura: Power? Yes. What has this life-and-death struggle been for if not for power?

August Strindberg, *The Father*, I:i, II (translated by Michael Meyer).

Careless lovers sometimes find their embraces interrupted by a surprised and usually very angry spouse. Samuel Pepys's embarrassment and shame on being caught groping his maid certainly has the ring of truth:

25.10.1668:. . . At night W. Batelier comes and sups with us; and after supper, to have my head combed by Deb, which occasioned the greatest sorrow to me that ever I knew in this world; for my wife, coming up suddenly, did find me imbracing the girl con my hand sub su coats; and endeed, I was with my main in her cunny. I was at a wonderful loss upon it, and the girl also; and I endeavoured to put it off, but my wife was struck mute and grew angry, and as her voice came to her, grew quite out of order; and I do say little, but to bed; and my wife said little also, but could not sleep all night; but about 2 in the morning waked me and cried, and fell to tell me as a great secret that she was a Roman Catholique and had received the Holy Sacrament; which troubled me but I took no notice of it, but she went on from one thing to another, till at last it appeared plainly her trouble was at what she saw; but yet I did not know how much she saw and therefore said nothing to her. But after her much crying and reproaching me with inconstancy and preferring a sorry girl before her, I did give her no provocations but did promise all fair usage to her, and love, and foreswore any hurt that I did with her – till at last she seemed to be at ease again; and so toward morning, a little sleep.

Samuel Pepys, *Diary*, Bell, 1976, Vol. 9, pp. 337–8.

With greater calmness the eighteenth-century diarist William Hickey looks back on an incident when he was a widower in India:

My friend, Bob Pott, now consigned to me from Moorshedabad a very pretty little native girl, whom he recommended for my own private use. Her name was Kiraun. After cohabiting with her a twelvemonth she produced me a young gentleman whom I certainly imagined to be of my own begetting, though somewhat surprized at the darkness of my son and heir's complexion; still, that surprize did not amount to any suspicion of the fidelity of my companion. Young Mahogany was therefore received and acknowledged as my offspring, until returning from the country one day quite unexpectedly, and entering Madam Kiraun's apartments by a private door of which I had a key, I found her closely locked in the arms of a handsome lad ... with the infant by her side, all three being in a deep sleep, from which I awakened the two elders. After a few questions I clearly ascertained that this young man had partaken of Kiraun's personal favours jointly with me from the first months of her residing in my house, and that my friend Mahogany was full entitled to the deep tinge of skin he came into the world with, being the produce of their continued amour. I consequently got rid of my lady, of her favourite, and the child, although she soon afterwards from falling into distress became a monthly pensioner of mine, and continued so during the many years I remained in Bengal.

William Hickey, *Memoirs*, Hurst & Blackett, 1925, Vol. 4, pp. 276–7.

Hickey also tells of the cuckolding of a soldier, who believed he was blissfully married:

In the Autumn young Horneck of the Guards married Miss Keppel, a natural daughter of Lord Albemarle's, then one of the most beautiful creatures I ever beheld and not more than fourteen years of age. A more lovely pair never were united, but their juvenile appearance made them look much more like brother and sister than husband and wife. The match was one of love and for some time they were as happy as the accomplishment of their utmost wish could render them. In outward appearance she was innocence personified, but in mind vicious beyond imagination and artful in the highest degree. In a few months after their marriage Horneck was ordered upon the Tower duty, and as he was not over burthened with cash, his friends advised him to part with his house, and put Mrs. Horneck into small, ready furnished lodgings, which prudent measure he resolved to adopt ...

After Horneck had been absent from his *Cara sposa*, he determined agreeably to surprize her with an unexpected visit, for which purpose he prevailed on his commanding officer not to notice his sleeping one night out of the Tower, and getting into a hackney coach at dusk drove to the West end of the town. Quitting the carriage in Piccadilly, he walked to Savile row, where meaning suddenly to take his lovely girl to his arms, he knocked a single knock, and upon a maid servant opening the door he whispered her not to announce his arrival and was proceeding up stairs, when the maid greatly agitated, entreated him not to go up until she had prepared her mistress; he however paid no attention to the woman's desire, went up, and entering the drawing room was struck dumb with horror and astonishment at seeing his lovely young bride sitting at a small round table with bottles and glasses upon it, she being beastly and stupidly drunk, her hair dishevelled and bosom quite bare. Opposite to her sat her own butler, nearly in the same state of intoxication, but upon Horneck's going into the room, he contrived to rise from his chair and stagger away until forced back by his master.

Horneck then looked into the sleeping apartment, and perceived the bed in a very rumpled state. Ringing the bell, he ordered all the servants up, when assembled asking them the meaning of the disgusting scene he beheld. The footman answered that the conduct of his mistress had been so publicly abandoned and shameless, they took it for granted it must have reached his ears; that since his absence she had scarcely ever been sober for six hours together; that the butler usually dined with her and both drank to the same degree of excess he then saw ... He had also the melancholy conviction of her having before she had been a week his wife prostituted her person to many of his immediate and particular friends.

Mrs Horneck went abroad with her lover.

William Hickey, *Memoirs*, Hurst & Blackett, 1919, Vol. I, pp. 303, 303–4.

Amazingly, such scenes also occurred in royal circles, as Lord Glenbervie recorded in his diary on 12 February 1804:

The following scandalous anecdote I have reason to believe to be perfectly correct. Mr Collen or Cullen Smith [Charles Culling Smith], who married Lady Anne Fitzroy (first Lady Anne Wellesley) has been long supposed to be, *au dernier point*, in the good graces of the Duchess of York. Lady Anne is one of the Duchess's Ladies of the Bedchamber. She and her husband are both very handsome and are fond of one another, but perhaps he does not think it consistent with modern gallantry, or courtly duty, to make the Duchess play the part of Potiphar's wife. The anecdote is, that the other day the Duke of York, having returned to Oatlands suddenly and unexpectedly, actually surprised the Duchess and Mr Smith in the very fact. Violent fury on his part, and threats of an immediate divorce and public ignominy and disgrace. He immediately hastened to the King and told him the whole affair. The King said, 'I am very sorry for it, Frederick. It is an infamous business, but it must be hushed up' – and it would seem that it is to be hushed up.

Sylvester Douglas, Lord Glenbervie, *Diaries*, Constable, 1928, p. 363.

Colette's heroine Claudine, immersed in a lesbian affair with Rézi, with the knowledge of her husband Renaud, turns up unexpectedly at their love nest and suspects it is occupied . . .

Ah! the curtain had stirred! . . . That tiny movement riveted me to the pavement, still as a doll. Whoever was up in 'our' flat? Maybe it was the wind blowing in from a window on the courtyard that had lifted that net . . . But while my logical self was reasoning, the beast in me, bitten by a suspicion, then suddenly enraged, had guessed before it had understood.

I raced across the street; I climbed the two flights, as in a nightmare, treading on steps of cotton-wool that sank and rebounded under my feet. I was going to drag with all my might on the brass bell-pull, ring till I brought the house down . . .

I pulled at the brass handle timidly, starting at the unfamiliar sound of that bell that had never rung for us . . . And for two long seconds, seized with a childish cowardice, I kept saying to myself: 'Oh! If only they wouldn't open it!'

The approaching step brought all my courage back on a wave of anger. Renaud's voice enquired irritably:

'Who's there?'

I had no breath left. I leant against the sham marble wall that chilled my arm. And the sound of the door he had opened a little way made me want to die . . .

. . . but not for long. I *had* to pull myself together! Hell, I was Claudine! I was Claudine! I flung off my fear like a coat. I said: 'Open the door, Renaud, or I'll scream.' I looked straight into the face of the man who opened it; he was completely dressed. He recoiled, in sheer astonishment. And he only let out one mild expletive, like a gambler annoyed by ill luck:

'The deuce!'

The impression of being the stronger stiffened my courage still more. I was Claudine! And I said:

'I saw someone at the window from down below. So I came up to say "Hullo" to you.'

'It was wicked of me to do it,' he muttered.

He made no move to try and stop me, but stood back to let me pass, then followed me.

In a flash, I crossed the little drawing-room and raised the flowered curtain in the doorway . . . Ah! Just as I thought! Rézi was there, of course she was there – and putting on her clothes again . . . In corset and knickers, her lace and linen petticoat over her arm, her hat on her head, just as for me . . . I shall always see that fair-skinned face decomposing, looking as if it were dying under my gaze. I almost envied her for being so frightened. She stared at my hands and I saw her thin lips go white and dry. Without taking her eyes off me, she stretched out a groping arm towards her dress. I took one step forward. She nearly fell, and threw up her arms to protect her face. That gesture, which revealed her downy armpits whose warmth I so often inhaled, unleashed a hurricane in me. I would snatch up that water-jug and

hurl it . . . or maybe that chair. The lines of the furniture quivered
before my eyes like hot air over the fields . . .

Renaud, who had followed me, lightly touched my shoulder. He
was hesitant, a trifle pale, but, above all, worried. I asked him,
speaking with difficulty:

'What are you . . . you two . . . doing here?'

He smiled nervously, in spite of himself.

'Why . . . we were waiting for you, as you see.'

I was dreaming . . . or he had gone out of his mind . . . I turned
again towards the woman there . . . The truth was I had not the
faintest idea what I ought to do. You don't learn the part of an
outraged wife in five minutes, just like that.

I was still barring the door. I thought Rézi was going to faint.
How odd that would be! *He*, at least, wasn't frightened. Like me,
he was following, with more interest than emotion, the succeeding
phases of terror on Rézi's face. He seemed finally to have grasped
that this hour was not going to bring the three of us together . . .

'Listen, Claudine . . . I meant to tell you . . .'

With a sweep of my arm, I cut short his sentence. In any case,
he seemed none too anxious to continue it, and he shrugged his
left shoulder with a rather fatalistic air of resignation.

It was Rézi who roused all my fury! I advanced on her slowly. I
could see myself advancing on her. This double consciousness
made me uncertain what I meant to do. Was I going to strike her,
or only increase her shameful fear to swooning point?

She drew back and moved round behind the little table on
which the tea stood. She had reached the wall! She was going to
escape me! Ah! I wasn't going to let her.

But already her hand was on the door-curtain, she was groping
at it, walking backwards, keeping her eyes fixed on me. Involuntarily, I stooped down to pick up a stone . . . There were no
stones . . . She had disappeared.

I let my arms drop; all my energy suddenly drained away.

There we were, the two of us, looking at each other. Renaud's
face was – almost – his kind, everyday face. He looked troubled.

His beautiful eyes were a little sad. Oh heavens, the next moment he was going to say: 'Claudine,' and if I voiced my anger, if I let the strength that still sustained me ebb away in reproaches and tears, I should leave the place on his arm, plaintive and forgiving . . . I *wouldn't*! I was . . . I was Claudine, hang it! And besides, I should be too furious with him for having made me forgive him.

I had waited too long. He stepped forward, he said: 'Claudine . . .'

I leapt back, and, instinctively, I started to flee, like Rézi. Only *I* was fleeing from myself.

I did well to make my escape. The street, the glance I threw up at the betraying curtain revived all my pride and resentment. Moreover, I knew now where I was going.

It took less than a quarter of an hour to rush home in a cab, grab my suitcase, and be downstairs again, having flung my key on a table. I had some money, not much, but enough.

'Gare de Lyon, driver.'

Before getting into the train, I sent a telegram to Papa, then another to Renaud: 'Send clothes and linen to Montigny for an indefinite stay.'

Once in Montigny, Claudine writes to Renaud:

'Dear Renaud, – I find it difficult to write to you because this is the first time. And I feel I shall never be able to say all I want to say to you before the evening post goes.

'I've got to ask your forgiveness for having gone away and to thank you for having let me go. It has taken me four days, all alone in my home with my misery, to understand something you could have convinced me of in a few minutes . . . All the same, I think these four days have not been wasted.

'You have written me all your loving tenderness, dear giant, without saying a word to me about Rézi, without telling me: "You did with her just what I did, with so little difference . . ." Yet that would have been very reasonable, almost flawless as a piece of logic. But you knew that *it was not the same thing* . . . and I'm grateful to you for not having said it.

'I don't want ever, ever again to make you unhappy, but you must help me over this, Renaud. Yes, I am your child . . . something more than your child, an over-petted daughter whom you ought sometimes to refuse what she asks for. I wanted Rézi and you gave her to me like a sweet . . . You've got to teach me that some kinds of sweets are harmful and that, if one eats them all, one must be on the look-out for bad brands . . . Don't, dear Renaud, be afraid of making your Claudine unhappy by scolding her. I like being dependent on you and being a little frightened of a friend I love so much.

'I wanted to tell you something else too; it's that I shan't come back to Paris. You have entrusted me to the country I love, so come and find me again here, keep me here, love me here. If you have to leave me sometimes, because you have to or because you want to, I will wait here faithfully and with no mistrust. There is enough beauty and sadness here in Fresnois for you to have no fear of boredom if I am with you all the time. For I am more beautiful here, more loving, more sincere.

'Whatever happens, come, because I can't go on any longer without you. I love you, I love you; it's the first time I've written it to you. Come! Remember that I have just been waiting four whole long days, my dear husband, for you not to be too young for me any more . . .'

Colette, *Claudine Married*, Secker & Warburg, 1960, pp. 166–70, 191–2 (translated by Antonia White).

Real life can be just as brutal as the roughest imaginings of the novelist. Horace Walpole records an especially violent incident:

Having no more public events to tell you, I am sorry I must leap to a private story, in which there is far from being either bravery or gallantry, but which is savage enough to have been transmitted from the barbarians on the Mosquito shore ... Well! but my story comes only 'cross the Irish Channel. Lord C., a recent peer of that kingdom, and married to a great heiress there, a very amiable woman, had, however, a more favourite mistress. The nymph, like My Lord, was no mirror of constancy, but preferred a younger, handsomer swain. The Peer, frantic with jealousy, discovered an assignation, and, hiring four bravoes, broke in upon the lovers; when, presenting a pistol to the head of his rival, he bade him make instant option of being shot, or reduced to the inability of giving any man jealousy. The poor young man was so ungallant as to prefer a chance for life on any terms. The brutal Lord ordered his four ruffians to seize the criminal, and with his own hand performed the bloody operation. The victim died the next day, the murderer escaped, but one of his accomplices is taken.

Horace Walpole (quoted in T.H. White, *The Age of Scandal*, Cape, 1950, p. 159).

The beautiful and famous courtesan Liane de Pougy had settled down with a husband fifteen years her junior. One morning Georges Ghika told his fifty-seven-year-old wife that he had something to tell her:

On July 4 [1926], curtains drawn on the appalling day that was about to start, I heard footsteps in my bedroom. I opened my eyes and could just make out my husband's silhouette in the duskiness, standing by my bed. Only half awake I said: 'Georges? Is that you?' – 'Yes, my darling. Have you slept well?' He got into bed with me, took me in his arms, covered me with kisses and said in a rather strangled voice: 'Listen, I've got a confession to make.' Accustomed as I was to him as the being from whom all sweetness came, I imagined some clumsiness; yes, the only thought to enter my head was that he had broken one of my ornaments, a piece of opaline perhaps. I smiled and said 'Confess!' Then he began mumbling that he couldn't do without me, that he adored me, that he would kill himself an hour after I died, but that he couldn't do without Tiny One [Marcelle Thiébaut]. I didn't want to understand. I stammered: 'But Tiny One is here, you have got her.' – 'No,' he said, 'but I shall have her. I've got to. I've never deceived you, I want to tell you everything. Yesterday evening we kissed for the first time, we told each other of our love. The child loves me as I love her. I'm a bit old for her, but she doesn't mind. If you agree, nothing need change. The three of us can live together. I can't be happy with you and without her, or with her and without you.' My whole body began to tremble. I said to him: 'But you are murdering me. It's appalling, get out of my bed.' He hugged me tighter. 'But I adore you. You'll see, you'll have two people to adore you instead of just one. We'll cherish you, we'll take care of you, we'll make you so happy. She's mad about you – she'll obey you, you will always be the mistress, the queen. She will take second place, she will submit to you. I have told her all that and she has accepted it. Everything will go on as it is now except that I will go to her at night. No one will know anything about it, not even the maids or Madame Garat.' I prayed to God, with open hands I said to Him: 'Let Your will be done, oh God! Make me say what You want me to say. Help me, Saint Anne! This is the worst blow fate could give me. Don't let me cry like a fool, don't let me faint, but I wouldn't mind dying. Protect me!' Georges went on: 'You'll see, we'll be gay and happy. In Paris she can sleep in my bedroom and I can have the little divan in the dressing-room. During the day it can go in your big cupboard.' – 'Get up,' I said, because I didn't want him to feel me trembling. 'I have got to think. I have got to go away and think without hate or anger or torment. I shall go away with Camille for a week, somewhere far away from here, from you two, and then I shall tell you what we are going to do.' – 'If you leave,' he said, getting up at last, 'if you leave I shall hate her. I'm going to bring her in. She is waiting. Neither of us has slept all night.'

Then Manon came in, pale and trembling, trying to look me in the face. She threw herself into my arms as though to kiss me. I pushed her away gently and said: 'Do you love my husband?' She cried out: 'I love you both! I'll do what you say. I'll kill myself if I must.' I replied: 'That's beside the point. I see now that you're both mad, I'm the only grown-up here. I am going to think this over, somewhere far away from you. I shall leave.' Then Georges began again: 'If you leave I shall hate her.' This annoyed the girl, who sat down opposite my bed and said, 'No, I'm the one who will leave.' I made up my mind: 'Yes, Mademoiselle, that in fact is the best thing you can do. It is better that I should be the one to stay in my own family house. Go, I accept that you go. Madame Garat will fetch your trunk down. Go to your room.' Georges, furious: 'If you drive her away, I will follow her.' Me, calmed by the decision made and the completeness of the renunciation: 'I am not driving her. Mademoiselle Thiébaut says herself that she would like to leave, I accept. As for you, YOU HAVE GONE ALREADY!'

July 5. [Georges] went away with Mademoiselle Thiébaut yesterday morning and here I am quite alone with the ocean and my disaster. I have not yet shed a single tear. Eighteen years of magnificent happiness have brought me to a quite atrocious resignation.

Liane de Pougy, *My Blue Notebooks*, Harper & Row, 1979, pp. 197–8 (translated by Diana Athill).

Maria Callas's husband was subjected to a slower torture. He looked on helplessly as his glamorous wife fell rapidly under the spell of Aristotle Onassis, who had invited the couple to join him on a cruise. Meneghini was slow to catch on . . .

Maria seemed more vivacious than I had ever seen her. She danced continuously, and always with Onassis. I was almost happy about it. 'Maria is still a young girl,' I thought while observing them. 'She's letting herself go. It'll do her good.' I had encouraged the voyage in the first place because of her health, and her vitality now was a sign that the sea air suited her.

August 8 and 9, things continued in the same fashion, with Maria always vibrant and dancing. The following day was Sunday, and we had arrived at Athens. We went to a party in the evening from which we returned at four in the morning. Onassis and Maria wanted to continue the festivities on the yacht. 'I'm going to bed,' I said.

I was more dead than alive, and I fell asleep immediately. I awoke at 9:30 the next morning and realized that Maria was not there. I was worried and I went around the yacht looking for her. I ran into Onassis, who was smiling and ebullient. He said that he had been to sleep and had already shaved. A horrible suspicion passed through my mind. If Onassis had been asleep, then where had Maria been? I felt faint. I went to my cabin and she was there, having just returned. 'You gave me a big fright,' I said. It seemed as if she didn't hear me. She was vague and preoccupied. She began to rhapsodize about the beauty of the night, and the magic of the dawn over the sea. Then, suddenly changing the tone and assuming a derisive, offensive attitude, she launched into an acrimonious tirade, telling me that I should stop being her shadow.

'You act like my jailer,' she said. 'You never leave me alone. You control me in everything. You're like some hateful guardian, and you've kept me hemmed in all these years. I'm suffocating!' Then she began to criticize my shape, my way of doing things. 'You're not adventuresome, you don't know languages, your hair is always uncombed, you can't manage to dress smartly.'

It was a terrible blow. I knew that something had happened to her. Onassis suddenly came to mind, the way they were together, dancing that night. I began to understand, but I couldn't bring myself to believe that something of that nature could have happened to Maria . . .

I remembered that a couple of days before, Maria and I had thought of asking Onassis's advice about a delicate question involving my wife's career. She had been asked to appear in a major film. I thought perhaps her long conversations with Onassis might have concerned that subject. 'Onassis,' I told myself, 'is a man of great experience, astute in business matters, and he would be able to give her sound advice.' I was thinking such things, perhaps only to keep at bay the awful reality that was forming before my eyes.

That same day I received the news that my mother had suffered another heart attack. I endured terrible hours that day. On other occasions Maria had always been attuned to my suffering, but that day she was not aware of anything.

By evening I was destroyed. Around midnight I said to Maria that I would be going to bed. 'Go then, I'm staying here,' she said simply. I stretched out on the bed, but was unable to sleep. Around 2 a.m. I heard the door open. I thought it was Maria. In that darkness I saw the figure of a woman almost completely naked. She entered the cabin and threw herself on the bed. 'Maria,' I said, embracing her. Immediately I realized it was not my wife. The woman was sobbing. 'What's going on?' I said, jumping up. It was Tina Onassis.

'Battista,' she said, 'we are both miserable. Your Maria is downstairs in the lounge in my husband's arms. Now there is nothing more that can be done. He has taken her away from you.'

I had developed a friendship with Tina. She was a very beautiful woman, good and kind. We often spoke together. She had revealed to me that her marital life with her husband had never been happy, and that Onassis was a brutal drunk.

At first I couldn't imagine why Tina was confiding all this to me. Later I realized she was probably doing it so I would pass it along to Maria and in turn open her eyes. Now Tina was there, on my bed, weeping. 'I'm especially sorry for you,' she said. 'I had already decided to leave him, and this will be my opportunity to initiate divorce proceedings. But you two were in love. When I met you, I envied the love and affection you two shared. Poor Battista, but also poor Maria. She'll learn soon enough what kind of man he is.'

Tina went back to her cabin, leaving me in a piteous state. I continued to toss about on the bed in anticipation of an overwhelming sorrow. Maria re-entered at 6.10 in the morning. I asked her how she could be so late, but she didn't answer.

I didn't see her the entire next day. In the evening I went to bed early and passed the night without closing my eyes. Maria came in shortly after five the next morning.

I pretended to wake up at that moment. She told me the sea was splendid, even though it was squally. Nothing else. I prayed to God that the accursed cruise would end soon. I was certain in my heart that, once we arrived back at our home, everything would return to normal.

I wanted to believe that everything that had transpired with Maria was only a flirtation, a passing infatuation, precipitated by the sea and the vacation. On August 13, at two in the afternoon, we arrived at Monte Carlo. Two hours later we were in Nice's airport. By five in the evening we were back in Milan. Between us, for the entire trip, there was a glacial silence.

Giovanni Battista Meneghini, *My Wife Maria Callas*, Bodley Head, 1983, pp. 292–5, (translated by Henry Wisneski).

The Sense of Betrayal

Cuckoldry is an essential appendage of wedlock; your
shadow does not follow you more closely or naturally.
When you hear the three words: 'He is married,' add:
'Therefore he is, has been, will or may be cuckolded.'
Do this, and no one will ever accuse you of faulty
logic.

François Rabelais, *Gargantua and Pantagruel*

After the discovery has been made, the cuckolded husband or betrayed
wife must come to terms with the situation. Responses vary from
bitterness to more drastic action. Catullus, obsessed with love, finds the
desertion of his girlfriend hard to stomach:

Roadhouse and members of that bawdy fraternity
that roars behind the ninth pillar
from the temple where those two brothers, Castor and Pollux,
wear their caps, signifying good fortune.
Are you the only
men on earth fit to mount girls and ride them, the rest of us
merely goats?
Come now, line up,
bent double in a circle, a hundred of you, or two hundred,
come, do you think I am not able to take on
two hundred of you in one grand bout of pederasty?
What's more, I'll cover the front doors of your fine house
with nimble sketches of the phallus.

. . . My girl has left me,
loved more than any woman born was she,
and I have fought, spilled blood for her,
but she has taken the house for a place to sleep and live.
O great and noble gentlemen, she's slept with all of you
to her dishonour, slept with pimps
that walk at night in darkest alley-ways,
and you particularly, dainty, long-haired Ignatius,
son of a homosexual Spanish rabbit,
made handsome by an ancient Spanish custom,
your beard and teeth daily and delicately
bathed in Spanish urine.

Catullus (translated by Horace Gregory).

Propertius responds with grief and self-pity:

Often I've dreaded the blows of your fickle heart,
But, Cynthia, never this present perfidy.
See, to what perils fortune drags me off,
And yet, in my hour of fear, how slow your coming!
You rearrange your coiffure of yesterday,
You search out in lengthy session the right complexion,
And with oriental jewels bedeck your breast –
Just like a beauty preparing to meet
A new admirer.

Calypso was not so unfeeling that time Ulysses
Set sail and left her to weep by the desolate waves:
Long she sat in sorrow with hair unkempt
And long complained to the unjust sea;
And though she never thought to see him again,
She kept him in memory still and grieved
For the joys long shared.

Hypsipyle, sick at heart in her empty room,
Stood and watched as the winds bore Jason away;

And having once loved and pined for her guest from Thessaly,
Was never touched by another love.
And when Alphesiboea avenged on her own two brothers
Her husband's death, love burst the bonds of blood;
While Evadne, who found on her husband's mournful pyre
Her own last rites, became a fable
Of Argive fidelity.

And yet no thought of these women could change your ways,
And make you, like them, a theme for a famous story.
No more false vows, then, Cynthia, to recall
Those broken already; don't rouse the forgetful Gods.
To my cost, my overbold one, as much as yours,
Will you have to bewail any retribution
That overtakes you.

Back from the ocean's vastness rivers will flow,
In inverse order the year spin out its seasons,
Before the love in my inmost heart shall change.
Be, then, whatever you like, but never
Belong to another.

And do not hold those eyes of yours so cheap,
Through which I have so often believed your falsehoods.
By them you would take your oath that, if you lied,
Might they tumble out on your outstretched hands!
And can you raise them up to the mighty sun
Without a tremor, knowing you're guilty
Of conduct so wanton?

Did you have to change colour so often, or squeeze the tears
From eyes that had no wish to weep? –
Those eyes for which I perish, a warning to others
Like me that it's never safe to trust
To your loved one's blandishments.

Propertius, 'Cynthia's Fickleness' (translated by Ronald Musker).

Standing at the head of a long tradition – especially strong in medieval times – of tales about how a gullible husband is cuckolded is this story by Apuleius (ca. AD 180):

This man depended for his livelihood on his small earnings as a jobbing smith, and his wife had no property either but was famous for her sexual appetite. One morning early, as soon as he had gone off to work, an impudent lover of his wife's slipped into the house and was soon tucked up in bed with her. The unsuspecting smith happened to return while they were still hard at work. Finding the door locked and barred, he nodded approval – how chaste his wife must be to take such careful precautions against any intrusions on her privacy! Then he whistled under the window, in his usual way, to announce his return. She was a resourceful woman and, disengaging her lover from a particularly tight embrace, hid him in a big tub that stood in a corner of the room. It was dirty and rotten, but quite empty. Then she opened the door and began scolding: 'You lazy fellow, strolling back as usual with folded arms and nothing in your pockets! When are you going to start working for your living and bring us home something to eat? What about me, eh? Here I sit every day from dawn to dusk at my spinning wheel, working my fingers to the bone and earning only just enough to keep oil in the lamp. What a miserable hole this is, too! I only wish I were my friend Daphne: she can eat and drink all day long and take as many lovers as she pleases.'

'Hey, what's all this?' cried the smith, his feelings injured. 'What fault of mine is it if the contractor has to spend the day in court and lays us off until tomorrow? And it isn't as though I hadn't thought about our dinner: you see that useless old tub cluttering up our little place? I have just sold it to a man for five drachmae. He'll be here soon to put down the money and carry it away. So lend me a hand, will you? I want to move it outside for him.'

She was not in the least disconcerted, and quickly thought of a plan for killing any suspicions he might have. She laughed rudely: 'What a wonderful husband I have, to be sure! And what a good nose he has for a bargain! He goes out and sells our tub for five drachmae. I'm only a woman, but I have already sold it for seven without even setting foot outside the house.'

He was delighted. 'Who on earth gave you such a good price?'

'Hush, you idiot,' she said. 'He's still down inside the thing, having a good look to see whether it's sound.'

The lover took his cue from her at once. He bobbed up and said: 'I'll tell you what, ma'am, your tub is very old and seems to be cracked in scores of places.' Then he turned to the smith: 'I don't know who you are, little man, but I should be much obliged for a candle. I must scrape the inside and see whether it's the sort of article I need. I haven't any money to throw away; it doesn't grow on apple-trees these days, does it?'

So the simple-minded smith lighted a candle without delay and said: 'No, no, mate, don't put yourself to so much trouble. You stand by while I give the tub a good clean-up for you.'

He peeled off his tunic, took the candle, lifted up the tub, turned it bottom upwards, then got inside and began working away busily.

The eager lover at once lifted up the smith's wife, laid her on the tub bottom upwards above her husband's head and followed his example. She greatly enjoyed the situation, like the whore she was. With her head hanging back over the side of the tub she directed the work by laying her finger on various spots in turn with: 'Here, darling, here! . . . Now there . . .' until both jobs were finished to her satisfaction. The smith was paid his seven drachmae, but had to carry the tub on his own back to the lover's lodgings.

Apuleius, *The Golden Ass*, Penguin, 1950, Ch. 12, pp. 207–9 (translated by Robert Graves).

In Chaucer's marvellous version of the story of Troilus and Criseyde, Troilus's beloved Cressida has been sent to the Greek camp, where she is to join her father Calchas as part of a prisoner exchange. The Greek Diomed immediately sets about wooing the beautiful Trojan girl . . .

... Whan that Criseyde unto hire bedde wente
Inwith hire fadres faire brighte tente,

Retornyng in hire soule ay up and down
The wordes of this sodeyn[1] Diomede,
His grete estat, and perel of the town,
And that she was allone and hadde nede
Of frendes help; and thus bygan to brede
The cause whi, the sothe for to telle,
That she took fully purpos for to dwelle.

The morwen com, and gostly[2] for to speke,
This Diomede is come unto Criseyde;
And shortly, lest that ye my tale breke,
So wel he for hymselven spak and seyde,
That alle hire sikes soore adown he leyde.
And finaly, the sothe for to seyne,
He refte hire of the grete of al hire peyne ...

But trewely, the storie telleth us,
Ther made never woman moore wo
Than she, whan that she falsed Troilus.
She seyde, 'Allas! for now is clene ago[3]
My name of trouthe in love, for everemo!
For I have falsed oon the gentileste
That evere was, and oon the worthieste!

'Allas! of me, unto the worldes ende,
Shal neyther ben ywriten nor ysonge
No good word, for thise bokes wol me shende.[4]
O, rolled shal I ben on many a tonge!
Throughout the world my belle shal be ronge!
And wommen moost wol haten me of alle.
Allas, that swich a cas me sholde falle!

1. swift.   2. truly.
3. gone.   4. ruin.

Thei wol seyn, in as muche as in me is,
I have hem don dishonour, weylaway!
Al be I nat the first that dide amys,
What helpeth that to don my blame awey?
But syn I se ther is no bettre way,
And that to late is now for me to rewe,
To Diomede algate[5] I wol be trewe . . .

Troilus remains convinced that Cressida will, as she has undertaken, return to Troy, but her uncle Pandarus, who has brought them together, knows this is increasingly unlikely:

. . . 'She comth to-nyght, my lif that dorste I leye!'

Pandare answerde, 'It may be, wel ynough,'
And held with hym of al that evere he seyde.
But in his herte he thoughte, and softe lough,
And to hymself ful sobreliche he seyde,
'From haselwode,[6] there joly Robyn pleyde,
Shal come al that that thow abidest heere.
Ye, fare wel al the snow of ferne yere!'

Troilus writes to Criseyde, pleading for news:

This lettre forth was sent unto Criseyde,
Of which hire answere in effect was this:
Ful pitously she wroot ayeyn, and seyde,
That also sone as that she myghte, ywys,
She wolde come, and mende al that was mys.
And fynaly she wroot and seyde hym thenne,
She wolde come, ye, but she nyste[7] whenne.

5. nevertheless.
6. a land from which no news ever comes.
7. did not know.

But in hire lettre made she swich festes
That wonder was, and swerth she loveth hym best;
Of which he fond but botmeles bihestes.
But Troilus, thow maist now, est or west,
Pipe in an ivy lef, if that the lest!
Thus goth the world. God shilde us fro meschaunce,
And every wight that meneth trouthe avaunce!

Encressen gan the wo fro day to nyght
Of Troilus, for tarying of Criseyde;
And lessen gan his hope and ek his myght,
For which al down he in his bed hym leyde.
He ne eet, ne dronk, ne slep, ne no word seyde,
Ymagynyng ay that she was unkynde;
For which wel neigh he wex out of his mynde . . .

Troilus finds her brooch in the captured armour of Diomed:

He goth hym hom, and gan ful soone sende
For Pandarus; and al this newe chaunce,
And of this broche, he tolde hym word and ende,
Compleynyng of hire hertes variaunce,
His longe love, his trouthe, and his penaunce.
And after deth, withouten wordes moore,
Ful faste he cride, his reste hym to restore.

Than spak he thus, 'O lady myn, Criseyde,
Where is youre feith, and where is youre biheste?
Where is youre love? where is youre trouthe?' he seyde.
'Of Diomede have ye now al this feeste!
Allas! I wolde han trowed atte leeste
That, syn ye nolde[8] in trouthe to me stonde,
That ye thus nolde han holden me in honde![9]

8. do not wish.
9. put off with promises.

'Who shal now trowe on any othes mo?
Allas! I nevere wolde han wend, er this,
That ye, Criseyde, koude han chaunged so;
Ne, but I hadde agilt and don amys,
So cruel wende I nought youre herte, ywis,
To sle me thus! Allas, youre name of trouthe
Is now fordon, and that is al my routhe.' . . .

This Pandarus, that al thise thynges herde,
And wiste wel he seyde a soth of this,
He nought a word ayeyn to hym answerde;
For sory of his frendes sorwe he is,
And shamed for his nece hath don amys,
And stant, astoned of thise causes tweye,
As stille as ston; a word ne kowde he seye.

But at the laste thus he spak, and seyde:
'My brother deer, I may do the namore.
What sholde I seyen? I hate, ywys, Cryseyde;
And, God woot, I wol hate hire evermore!
And that thow me bisoughtest don of yoore,
Havyng unto myn honour ne my reste
Right no reward, I dide al that the leste.

'If I dide aught that myghte liken the,
It is me lief; and of this tresoun now,
God woot that it a sorwe is unto me!
And dredeles, for hertes ese of yow,
Right fayn I wolde amende it, wiste I how.
And fro this world, almyghty God I preye
Delivere hire soon! I kan namore seye.'

Geoffrey Chaucer, *Troilus and Criseyde*,
V: 1021–71, 1169–76, 1422–42, 1667–87, 1723–43.

Shakespeare, in his version of the same episode, injects a bitter, angry note by having Diomed's seduction of Cressida surreptitiously observed by Troilus, Ulysses and the scurrilous cynic Thersites, who react in dramatic counterpoint.

Tro. Cressid comes forth to him.

Dio.   How now, my charge!

Cre. Now, my sweet guardian! Hark, a word with you. [*Whispers*]

Tro. Yea, so familiar!

Uly. She will sing any man at first sight.

The. And any man may sing her, if he can take her cliff; she's noted.

Dio. Will you remember?

Cre. Remember? Yes.

Dio. Nay, but do, then;
And let your mind be coupled with your words.

Tro. What shall she remember?

Uly. List!

Cre. Sweet honey Greek, tempt me no more to folly.

The. Roguery!

Dio. Nay, then –

Cre.   I'll tell you what –

Dio. Foh, foh! Come, tell a pin. You are forsworn.

Cre. In faith, I cannot. What would you have me do?

The. A juggling trick – to be secretly open.

Dio. What did you swear you would bestow on me?

Cre. I prithee, do not hold me to mine oath;
Bid me do anything but that, sweet Greek.

Dio. Good night.

Tro. Hold, patience!

Uly. How now, Troyan?

Cre. Diomed –

Dio. No, no, good night; I'll be your fool no more.

Tro. Thy better must.

Cre.   Hark, a word in your ear.

Tro. O plague and madness!

Uly. You are moved, prince; let us depart, I pray,
      Lest your displeasure should enlarge itself
      To wrathful terms. This place is dangerous;
      The time right deadly. I beseech you, go.
Tro. Behold, I pray you!
Uly.   Nay, good my lord, go off;
      You flow to great distraction. Come, my lord.
Tro. I prithee, stay.
Uly.   You have not patience; come.
Tro. I pray you, stay! By hell, and all hell's torments, I will not
      speak a word!
Dio.   And so, good night.
Cre. Nay, but you part in anger.
Tro.   Doth that grieve thee?
      O withered truth!
Uly.   How now, my lord?
Tro.   By Jove,
      I will be patient.
Cre.   Guardian! Why, Greek!
Dio. Foh, foh! Adieu; you palter.
Cre. In faith, I do not. Come hither once again.
Uly. You shake, my lord, at something. Will you go?
      You will break out.
Tro.   She strokes his cheek!
Uly.   Come, come.
Tro. Nay, stay; by Jove, I will not speak a word.
      There is between my will and all offences
      A guard of patience. Stay a little while.
The. How the devil Luxury, with his fat rump and potato finger,
      tickles these together. Fry, lechery, fry!
Dio. But will you, then?
Cre. In faith, I will, la; never trust me else.
Dio. Give me some token for the surety of it.
Cre. I'll fetch you one.   [*Exit.*]
Uly. You have sworn patience.

Tro.   Fear me not, my lord;
          I will not be myself, nor have cognition
          Of what I feel. I am all patience.
                              [*Enter Cressida.*]
The.   Now the pledge! Now, now, now!
Cre.   Here, Diomed, keep this sleeve.
Tro.   O beauty, where is thy faith?
Uly.   My lord –
Tro.   I will be patient; outwardly I will.
Cre.   You look upon that sleeve; behold it well.
          He loved me – O false wench! Give't me again.
Dio.   Whose was't?
Cre.   It is no matter, now I have't again.
          I will not meet with you tomorrow night.
          I prithee, Diomed, visit me no more.
The.   Now she sharpens. Well said, whetstone!
Dio.   I shall have it.
Cre.   What, this?
Dio.   Ay, that.
Cre.   O, all you gods! O pretty, pretty pledge!
          Thy master now lies thinking on his bed
          Of thee and me, and sighs, and takes my glove,
          And gives memorial dainty kisses to it,
          As I kiss thee. Nay, do not snatch it from me;
          He that takes that doth take my heart withal.
Dio.   I had your heart before; this follows it.
Tro.   I did swear patience.
Cre.   You shall not have it, Diomed; faith, you shall not;
          I'll give you something else.
Dio.   I will have this. Whose was it?
Cre.   It is no matter.
Dio.   Come, tell me whose it was.
Cre.   'Twas one's that loved me better than you will.
          But, now you have it, take it.
Dio.   Whose was it?

Cre. By all Diana's waiting-women yond,
      And by herself, I will not tell you whose.
Dio. Tomorrow will I wear it on my helm,
      And grieve his spirit that dares not challenge it.
Tro. Wert thou the devil, and wor'st it on thy horn,
      It should be challenged.
Cre. Well, well, 'tis done, 'tis past. And yet it is not;
      I will not keep my word.
Dio.   Why then, farewell;
      Thou never shalt mock Diomed again.
Cre. You shall not go. One cannot speak a word
      But it straight starts you.
Dio.   I do not like this fooling.
The. Nor I, by Pluto; but that that likes not you
      Pleases me best.
Dio. What, shall I come? The hour?
Cre.   Ay, come –
      O Jove! –
      Do come – I shall be plagued.
Dio.   Farewell till then.
Cre. Good night, I prithee, come.
                              [*Exit Diomedes.*]
      Troilus, farewell. One eye yet looks on thee,
      But with my heart the other eye doth see.
      Ah, poor our sex! This fault in us I find,
      The error of our eye directs our mind.
      What error leads must err. O, then conclude,
      Minds swayed by eyes are full of turpitude.   [*Exit.*]
The. A proof of strength she could not publish more,
      Unless she said, 'My mind is now turned whore.'
Uly. All's done, my lord.
Tro.   It is.
Uly.   Why stay we, then?
Tro. To make a recordation to my soul
      Of every syllable that here was spoke.

But if I tell how these two did coact,
Shall I not lie in publishing a truth?
Sith yet there is a credence in my heart,
An esperance so obstinately strong,
That doth invert th'attest of eyes and ears,
As if those organs had deceptious functions,
Created only to calumniate.
Was Cressid here?

Uly.   I cannot conjure, Troyan.

Tro. She was not, sure.

Uly.   Most sure she was.

Tro. Why, my negation hath no taste of madness.

Uly. Nor mine, my lord. Cressid was here but now.

Tro. Let it not be believed for womanhood!
Think we had mothers; do not give advantage
To stubborn critics apt, without a theme
For depravation, to square the general sex
By Cressid's rule. Rather think this not Cressid.

Uly. What hath she done, prince, that can soil our mothers?

Tro. Nothing at all, unless that this were she.

The. Will he swagger himself out on's own eyes?

Tro. This she? No, this is Diomed's Cressida.
If beauty have a soul, this is not she;
If souls guide vows, if vows be sanctimonies,
If sanctimony be the gods' delight,
If there be rule in unity itself,
This was not she. O madness of discourse,
That cause sets up with and against itself:
Bifold authority, where reason can revolt
Without perdition, and loss assume all reason
Without revolt. This is, and is not, Cressid.

William Shakespeare, *Troilus and Cressida*, V:ii.

The subject of this despairing poem by Thomas Wyatt (died 1542) is never made explicit, but the bitterness of the final lines strongly implies a sexual betrayal and desertion . . .

> They fle from me that sometyme did me seke
>> With naked fote stalking in my chambre.
> I have sene theim gentill tame and meke
>> That nowe are wyld and do not remembre
>> That sometyme they put theimself in daunger
> To take bred at my hand; and nowe they raunge
> Besely seking with a continuell chaunge.
>
> Thancked be fortune, it hath ben othrewise
>> Twenty tymes better; but ons in speciall,
> In thyn arraye after a pleasaunt gyse,
>> When her lose gowne from her shoulders did fall,
>> And she me caught in her armes long and small;
> Therewithall swetely did me kysse,
> And softely saide, *dere hert, howe like you this?*
>
> It was no dreme: I lay brode waking.
>> But all is torned thorough my gentilnes
> Into a straunge fasshion of forsaking;
>> And I have leve to goo of her goodenes,
>> And she also to use new fangilnes.
> But syns that I so kyndely ame served,
> I would fain knowe what she hath deserved.

from *Collected Poems*, Routledge, 1963.

In another poem, Wyatt bewails the faithlessness of his beloved in a heartfelt way that infuses a well-worn Renaissance formula with real passion:

Alas the greiff and dedly wofull smert!
The carefull chaunce shapen afore my shert;
    The sorrowfull tears, the sighes hote as fyer,
That cruell love hath long soked from myn hert;
    And, for reward of ouer greate desire,
    Disdaynfull dowblenes have I for my hiere.

O lost servis! O payn ill rewarded!
O pitifull hert, with payn enlarded!
    O faithfull mynde, too sodenly assented!
Retourn, Alas, sithens thou art not regarded;
    Too great a prouf of true faith presented
    Causeth by right suche faith to be repented.

O cruell causer of undeserved chaunge,
By great desire unconstantly to raunge,
    Is this your waye for prouf of stedfastenes?
Perdy you knowe – the thing was not so straunge
    By former prouff – to muche my faithfulnes.
    What nedeth then suche coloured dowblenes?

I have wailed thus, weping in nyghtly payn;
In sobbes and sighes, Alas! and all in vayn;
    In inward plaint and hertes wofull torment:
And yet, Alas, lo, crueltie and disdayn
    Have set at noght a faithful true intent,
    And price hath privilege trouth to prevent.

But though I sterve and to my deth still morne,
And pece mele in peces though I be torne,
    And though I dye yelding my weried gooste,
Shall never thing again make me retorne.
    I qwite th'entreprise of that that I have lost,
    To whome so ever lust for to proofer moost.

from *Collected Poems*, Routledge, 1963.

Robert Aytoun (1570–1638), in 'The Forsaken Mistress', berates a woman for being promiscuous with her favours and thus not worthy of his:

> I do confess thou'rt smooth and fair,
>   And I might have gone near to love thee;
> Had I not found the slightest pray'r
>   That lips could speak, had pow'r to move thee;
>   But I can let thee now alone
>   As worthy to be lov'd by none.
>
> I do confess thou'rt sweet, yet find
>   Thee such an unthrift of thy sweets,
> Thy favours are but like the wind
>   Which kisseth everything it meets!
>   And since thou canst love more than one
>   Thou'rt worthy to be lov'd by none.
>
> The morning rose that untouched stands,
>   Arm'd with her briars, how sweet she smells!
> But pluck'd, and strained through ruder hands,
>   Her sweet no longer with her dwells;
>   But scent and beauty both are gone,
>   And leaves fall from her one by one.
>
> Such fate, ere long, will thee betide,
>   When thou hast handled been awhile,
> Like fair flow'rs to be thrown aside.
>   And thou shalt sigh when I shall smile,
>   To see thy love to every one
>   Hath brought thee to be loved by none.

from *Poems*, London, 1871.

Shakespeare, in Sonnet 152, offers a more profound version of a similar theme:

> In loving thee thou know'st I am forsworn;
> But thou art twice forsworn to me love swearing, –
> In act thy bed-vow broke, and new faith torn
> In vowing new hate after new love bearing.
> But why of two oaths' breach do I accuse thee,
> When I break twenty? I am perjur'd most:
> For all my vows are oaths but to misuse thee,
> And all my honest faith in thee is lost.
> For I have sworn deep oaths of thy deep kindness –
> Oaths of thy love, thy truth, thy constancy;
> And to enlighten thee gave eyes to blindness,
> Or made them swear against the thing they see:
> > For I have sworn thee fair, – more perjur'd eye,
> > To swear against the truth so foul a lie!

In Shakespeare's *The Merry Wives of Windsor*, Ford, disguised as Master Broome, has little difficulty persuading Falstaff to attempt to woo his wife, Mistress Ford, on Broome's behalf:

Falstaff: As I am a gentleman, you shall, if you will, enjoy Ford's wife.

Ford: O good sir!

Falstaff: I say you shall.

Ford: Want no money, Sir John, you shall want none.

Falstaff: Want no Mistress Ford, Master Broome, you shall want none. I shall be with her, I may tell you, by her own appointment. Even as you came in to me, her assistant, or go-between, parted from me. I say I shall be with her between ten and eleven: for at that time the jealous rascally knave her husband will be forth. Come you to me at night, you shall know how I speed.

Ford: I am blest in your acquaintance. Do you know Ford, Sir?

Falstaff: Hang him, poor cuckoldy knave, I know him not. Yet I wrong him to call him poor. They say the jealous wittolly knave hath masses of money, for the which his wife seems to me well-favoured. I will use her as the key of the cuckoldy rogue's coffer, and there's my harvest home.

Ford: I would you knew Ford, sir, that you might avoid him, if you saw him.

Falstaff: Hang him, mechanical salt-butter rogue. I will stare him out of his wits: I will awe him with my cudgel. It shall hang like a meteor o'er the cuckold's horns. Master Broome, thou shalt know, I will predominate over the peasant, and thou shalt lie with his wife. Come to me soon at night: Ford's a knave, and I will aggravate his stile. Thou, Master Broome, shalt know him for knave and cuckold. Come to me soon at night.

[*Exit Falstaff*]

Ford: What a damn'd Epicurean rascall is this? My heart is ready to crack with impatience; who says this is improvident jealousy? My wife hath sent to him, the hour is fixed, the match is made. Would any man have thought this? See the hell of having a false woman! My bed shall be abus'd, my coffers ransack'd, my reputation gnawn at; and I shall not only receive this villainous wrong, but stand under the adoption of abominable terms, and by him that does me this wrong. Terms, names: Amaimon sounds well; Lucifer, well; Barbason, well: yet they are devils' additions, the names of fiends. But cuckold, wittoll, cuckold? The devil himself hath not such a name. Page is an ass, a secure ass; he will trust his wife, he will not be jealous. I will rather trust a Fleming with my butter, Parson Hugh the Welshman with my cheese, an Irishman with my acqua vitae bottle, or a thief to walk my ambling gelding, than my wife with herself. Then she plots, then she ruminates, then she devises: and what they think in their hearts they may effect. They will break their hearts but they will effect. Heaven be prais'd for my jealousy! Eleven o'clock the hour. I will prevent this, detect my wife, be reveng'd on Falstaff, and laugh at Page. I will about it, better three hours too soon, than a minute too late. Fie, fie, fie! Cuckold! cuckold! cuckold!

William Shakespeare, *The Merry Wives of Windsor*, II: ii.

Ford's rage, though in earnest, is set within a comic framework; no disaster will spring from his anxieties. But when Othello accuses his innocent wife of infidelity, it is clear from his language alone that he is dangerously out of control:

Des. I hope my noble lord esteems me honest.

Oth. O, ay, as summer's flies are in the shambles,
    That quicken even with blowing:
    O thou black weed, why art so lovely fair?
    Thou smell'st so sweet, that the sense aches at thee,
    Would thou hadst ne'er been born!

Des. Alas, what ignorant sin have I committed?

Oth. Was this fair paper, this most goodly book,
    Made to write 'whore' on? . . . What committed?
    Committed! O thou public commoner!
    I should make very forges of my cheeks,
    That would to cinders burn up modesty,
    Did I but speak thy deeds. What committed!
    Heaven stops the nose at it, and the moon winks,
    The bawdy wind, that kisses all it meets,
    Is hush'd within the hollow mine of earth,
    And will not hear't: . . . what committed, –
    Impudent strumpet!

Des.   By heaven, you do me wrong.

Oth. Are not you a strumpet?

Des.   No, as I am a Christian:
    If to preserve this vessel for my lord
    From any hated foul unlawful touch,
    Be not to be a strumpet, I am none.

Oth. What, not a whore?

Des.   No, as I shall be sav'd.

William Shakespeare, *Othello*, IV: ii, 66–88.

In *The Winter's Tale*, Leontes wrongly suspects his wife Hermione has taken Polixenes, king of Bohemia, as her lover:

> Inch-thick, knee-deep; o'er head and hearts a fork'd one.
> Go, play, boy, play: thy mother plays, and I
> Play too; but so disgrac'd a part, whose issue
> Will hiss me to my grave: contempt and clamour
> Will be my knell. Go, play, boy, play. There have been,
> (Or I am much deceiv'd) cuckolds ere now,
> And many a man there is (even at this present,
> Now, while I speak this) holds his wife by th'arm,
> That little thinks she has been sluic'd in's absence
> And his pond fish'd by his next neighbour, by
> Sir Smile, his neighbour: nay, there's comfort in't,
> Whiles other men have gates, and those gates open'd,
> As mine, against their will. Should all despair
> That have revolted wives, the tenth of mankind
> Would hang themselves. Physic for't there's none;
> It is a bawdy planet, that will strike
> Where 'tis predominant; and 'tis powerful, think it,
> From east, west, north, and south; be it concluded,
> No barricado for a belly. Know't,
> It will let in and out the enemy,
> With bag and baggage: many thousand on's
> Have the disease, and feel't not.

William Shakespeare, *The Winter's Tale*, I:ii, 1861–2071.

The amoral Vicomte de Valmont recalls a casual adventure, in which he went to elaborate lengths to secure a night of passion with a woman whose husband and lover were both near by:

The adventure of itself is a very small thing; it was only a revival with the Vicomtesse de M ... I found the Vicomtesse here, and when she added her requests to the entreaties of the others that I should spend the night in the Château: 'Well! I consent,' I said to her, 'on condition that I spend it with you.' 'Impossible,' she replied, 'Vressac is here.' Till that moment I had merely meant to say something polite; but that word 'impossible' roused me, as it always does. I felt humiliated at being sacrificed to Vressac and I resolved not to endure it; so I insisted.

The circumstances were not favourable. Vressac has been clumsy enough to arouse the Vicomte's suspicions; so that the Vicomtesse cannot receive him in her own house; and this visit to the good Comtesse had been arranged between them with the purpose of snatching a few nights. At first the Vicomte even showed his annoyance at meeting Vressac there; but since he is even more a sportsman than a jealous husband he stayed none the less; and the Comtesse, who is still the same as she was when you knew her, after putting the wife in the main corridor, lodged the husband on one side and the lover on the other and left them to arrange it between them. The evil genius of both of them caused me to be lodged opposite.

That very day (that is to say yesterday), Vressac who, as you may suppose, is flattering the Vicomte, went shooting with him in spite of his dislike for sport, and intended to console himself at night in the wife's arms for the boredom the husband caused him all day; but I considered he would need a rest and devoted my attention to the means of persuading his mistress to give him time for it.

I succeeded and made her agree to quarrel with him over this day's shooting, to which obviously he had only consented for her sake. A worse pretext could not have been found; but no woman possesses to a higher degree than the Vicomtesse that talent common to them all of putting caprice in the place of common sense and of being never so difficult to soothe as when she is in the wrong. Moreover it was not a convenient time for explanation; and, as I only wanted one night, I agreed that they should patch matters up the next day.

Vressac then was sulked with when he came back. He tried to ask the reason; she started a quarrel with him. He attempted to justify himself; the husband, who was present, served as a pretext for breaking off the conversation; finally he tried to profit by a moment when the husband was out of the room to request that he might be given a hearing at night. It was then that the Vicomtesse was sublime. She grew indignant with the audacity of men who, because they have received favours from a woman, think they have the right to abuse her even when she has reason to complain of them; and having changed the topic thus skilfully, she talked delicacy and sentiment so well that Vressac was rendered mute and confused and I myself was tempted to think she was right; for you must know that as a friend of them both I was present at the conversation.

She finally declared positively that she would not add the fatigues of love to those of shooting and that she would blame herself for disturbing such soft pleasures. The husband came back; the wretched Vressac, who thereby lost the opportunity of replying, addressed himself to me; and after he had told me his grievances at great length (which I knew as well as he did) he begged me to speak to the Vicomtesse and I promised him to do so. I did indeed speak to her; but it was to thank her and to arrange with her the hour and means of our meeting.

She told me that since she was lodged between her husband and her lover, she had thought it more prudent to go to Vressac than to receive him in her apartment; and that since I was opposite her she thought it safer also to come to me; that she would arrive as soon as her waiting-woman had left her alone; and that I had only to leave my door ajar and to wait for her.

Everything was carried out as we had agreed; she came to my room about one o'clock in the morning ... Since I am without vanity, I will not dwell upon the details of the night; but you know me, and I was satisfied with myself.

At dawn we had to separate. And here the interest begins. The scatter-brain thought she had left her door ajar; we found it closed with the key inside; you can have no idea of the expression of despair with which the Vicomtesse said to me at once: 'Ah! I am ruined.' It must be admitted that it would have been amusing to leave her in this situation, but could I allow a woman to be ruined *for* without being ruined *by* me? . . .

I soon found out that the door in question could be broken in by making a great deal of noise. I therefore persuaded the Vicomtesse, not without difficulty, to give piercing cries of terror, such as 'Thieves!' 'Murder!' etc., etc. And we agreed that at the first cry I should break down the door while she rushed into bed. You cannot think how much time was needed to bring her to the point even after she had agreed to do it. However it was the only thing to do and at the first kick the door gave way.

It was fortunate for the Vicomtesse that she did not waste any time. For at the same moment the Vicomte and Vressac were in the corridor and the waiting-woman rushed to her mistress's room.

I alone kept my head and I made use of it to extinguish a night-light which was still burning and to throw it on the ground; for you will realise how ridiculous it would have been to feign this panic terror with a light in the room. I then abused the husband and the lover for their heavy sleeping, assuring them that the cries, at which I had run out, and my efforts to break down the door had lasted at least five minutes.

The Vicomtesse, who had recovered her courage in her bed, seconded me well enough and vowed by all the gods that there was a thief in her apartment. She protested with more sincerity that she had never been so afraid in her life. We looked everywhere and found nothing, when I pointed out the overturned night-light and concluded that no doubt a rat had caused the damage and the terror; my opinion was accepted unanimously and after a few hackneyed pleasantries about rats the Vicomte was the first to return to his room and his bed, begging his wife to have quieter rats in future.

Vressac remained alone with us and went up to the Vicomtesse to tell her that this was a vengeance of Love; upon which she looked at me and replied: 'He must have been angry for he has avenged himself amply; but,' she added, 'I am quite exhausted, I must go to sleep.'

I was in an expansive mood; consequently, before we separated I pleaded Vressac's cause and brought about a reconciliation. The two lovers embraced and I in my turn was embraced by them both. I had no more interest in the Vicomtesse's kisses; but I admit that Vressac's gave me pleasure. We went out together, and after I had received his lengthy thanks we each went back to bed.

If you think this story amusing, I do not ask you to keep it secret. Now that I have had my amusement it is just that the public should have its turn.

Choderlos de Laclos, *Dangerous Acquaintances*, Routledge, 1924, pp. 192–6 (translated by Richard Aldington).

The Vicomtesse is a sideshow. The real focus of Valmont's attentions is Madame de Tourvel, whom, inevitably, he betrays:

Valmont loves me no more, he never loved me. Love does not disappear in this way. He deceives me, he betrays me, he outrages me. I endure all the misfortunes and humiliations which can be gathered together, and they come upon me from him . . .

It was yesterday; for the first time since my return I was to dine out. Valmont came to see me at five; never had he seemed so tender. He let me know that my plan of going out vexed him, and, as you may suppose, I soon decided to stay at home. However, suddenly two hours later his manner and tone changed perceptibly. I do not know if anything escaped me which could offend him; but in any case, a little later he pretended to recollect an engagement which forced him to leave me and he went away; yet it was not without expressing very keen regrets which seemed to me tender and which I then thought sincere.

Left to myself, I thought it more polite not to avoid my first engagement since I was free to carry it out. I completed my toilet and entered my carriage. Unhappily my coachman took me by the

Opera and I found myself in the confusion of the exit; a few steps in front of me in the next line I saw Valmont's carriage. My heart beat at once, but it was not from fear; and the one idea which filled me was the desire that my carriage would go forward. Instead of that, his was forced to retire, and stopped opposite mine. I leaned forward at once; what was my astonishment to see at his side a woman of ill-repute, well known as such! I leaned back, as you may suppose; this alone was enough to rend my heart; but, what you will scarcely believe, this same creature, apparently informed by an odious confidence, did not leave her carriage window, kept looking at me, and laughed so loudly it might have made a scene.

In the state of prostration I was in I allowed myself to be driven to the house where I was to sup, but it was impossible to remain there; every moment I felt ready to faint and I could not restrain my tears.

When I returned I wrote to M. de Valmont and sent him my letter immediately; he was not at home. Desirous, at any price, to emerge from this state of death or to have it confirmed for ever, I sent the man back with orders to wait, but my servant returned before midnight and told me that the coachman, who had come back, had said that his master would not be in that night. This morning I thought there was nothing to do but to ask for my letters once more and to request him never to come to my house again.

Spurned, Madame de Tourvel retires broken-hearted to a convent.

Choderlos de Laclos, *Dangerous Acquaintances*, Routledge, 1924, pp. 361–2 (translated by Richard Aldington).

Baron Charlus tells the narrator of Proust's *Remembrance of Things Past* about Odette Swann's lovers:

'I was with some club-mates, and each of us took a woman home with him, and, although all I wanted was to go to sleep, slanderous tongues alleged – it's terrible how malicious people are – that I went to bed with Odette. In any case she took advantage of the slanders to come and bother me, and I thought I might get rid of her by introducing her to Swann. From that moment on she never let me go. She couldn't spell the simplest word, it was I who wrote all her letters for her. And it was I who, later on, was responsible for taking her out. That, my boy, is what comes of having a good reputation, you see. Though I only half deserved it. She used to force me to get up the most dreadful orgies for her, with five or six men.'

And the lovers whom Odette had had in succession (she had been with this, that, and the other man, not one of whose names had ever been guessed by poor Swann, blinded by jealousy and by love, by turns weighing up the chances and believing in oaths, more affirmative than a contradiction which the guilty woman lets slip, a contradiction far more elusive and yet far more significant, of which the jealous lover might take advantage more logically than of the information which he falsely pretends to have received, in the hope of alarming his mistress), these lovers M. de Charlus began to enumerate with as absolute a certainty as if he had been reciting the list of the Kings of France. And indeed the jealous lover, like the contemporaries of a historical event, is too close, he knows nothing, and it is for strangers that the chronicle of adultery assumes the precision of history, and prolongs itself in lists which are a matter of indifference to them and become painful only to another jealous lover, such as I was, who cannot help comparing his own case with that which he hears spoken of and wonders whether the woman he suspects cannot boast an equally illustrious list. But he can never find out; it is a sort of universal conspiracy, a 'blind man's buff' in which everyone cruelly participates, and which consists, while his mistress flits from one to another, in holding over his eyes a bandage which he is perpetually trying to tear off without success, for everyone keeps him blindfold, poor wretch, the kind out of kindness, the cruel out of cruelty, the coarse-minded out of their love of coarse jokes, the well-bred out of politeness and good-breeding, and all alike respecting one of those conventions which are called principles.

Marcel Proust, *The Captive*, Chatto & Windus, 1992, Vol. 5, pp. 339–41 (translated by C.K. Scott Moncrieff, Terence Kilmartin and D.J. Enright).

In the same book the narrator finds that his jealousy of Albertine continues after her death . . .

If I had found it difficult to imagine that Albertine, so alive in me (wearing as I did the double harness of the present and the past), was dead, perhaps it was equally paradoxical in me that this suspicion of the misdeeds which Albertine, stripped now of the flesh that had enjoyed them, of the mind that had conceived the desire for them, was no longer either capable of or responsible for, should excite in me such suffering, which I should only have blessed could I have seen it as the token of the spiritual reality of a person materially non-existent, instead of the reflexion, destined itself to fade, of impressions that she had made on me in the past. A woman who could no longer experience pleasures with others ought no longer to have excited my jealousy, if only my tenderness had been able to come to the surface. But it was precisely this that was impossible, since it could not find its object, Albertine, except among memories in which she was still alive. Since, merely by thinking of her, I brought her back to life, her infidelities could never be those of a dead woman, the moment at which she had committed them becoming the present moment, not only for Albertine, but for that one of my various selves thus suddenly evoked who happened to be thinking of her. So that no anachronism could ever separate the indissoluble couple, in which each new culprit was immediately mated with a jealous lover, pitiable and always contemporaneous. I had, during the last months, kept her shut up in my own house. But in my imagination now, Albertine was free; she was abusing her freedom, was prostituting herself to this person or that. Formerly, I used constantly to think of the uncertainty of the future that stretched before us, and endeavour to read its message. And now, what lay ahead of me, like a counterpart of the future – as worrying as the future because it was equally uncertain, equally difficult to decipher, equally mysterious, and crueller still because I did not have, as with the future, the possibility, or the illusion, of influencing it, and also because it would go on unfolding throughout the whole length of my life without my companion's being present to soothe the anguish that it caused me – was no longer Albertine's future, it was her past. Her past? That is the wrong word, since for jealousy there can be neither past nor future, and what it imagines is invariably the present.

Marcel Proust, *The Fugitive*, Chatto & Windus, 1992, pp. 560–61 (translated by C. K. Scott Moncrieff, Terence Kilmartin and D. J. Enright).

Milan Kundera's Sabina ponders why betrayal attracts her more than fidelity:

He loved her from the time he was a child until the time he accompanied her to the cemetery; he loved her in his memories as well. That is what made him feel that fidelity deserved pride of place among the virtues: fidelity gave a unity to lives that would otherwise splinter into thousands of split-second impressions.

Franz often spoke about his mother to Sabina, perhaps even with a certain unconscious ulterior motive: he assumed that Sabina would be charmed by his ability to be faithful, that it would win her over.

What he did not know was that Sabina was charmed more by betrayal than by fidelity. The word 'fidelity' reminded her of her father, a small-town puritan, who spent his Sundays painting away at canvases of woodland sunsets and roses in vases. Thanks to him, she started drawing as a child. When she was fourteen, she fell in love with a boy her age. Her father was so frightened that he would not let her out of the house by herself for a year. One day, he showed her some Picasso reproductions and made fun of them. If she couldn't love her fourteen-year-old schoolboy, she could at least love cubism. After completing school she went off to Prague with the euphoric feeling that now at last she could betray her home.

Betrayal. From tender youth we are told by father and teacher that betrayal is the most heinous offense imaginable. But what is betrayal? Betrayal means breaking ranks. Betrayal means breaking ranks and going off into the unknown. Sabina knew of nothing more magnificent than going off into the unknown.

Though a student at the Academy of Fine Arts, she was not allowed to paint like Picasso. It was the period when so-called socialist realism was prescribed and the school manufactured portraits of Communist statesmen. Her longing to betray her father remained unsatisfied: Communism was merely another father, a father equally strict and limited, a father who forbade her love (the times were puritanical) and Picasso, too. And if she married a second-rate actor, it was only because he had a reputation for being eccentric and was unacceptable to both fathers.

Then her mother died. The day following her return to Prague from the funeral, she received a telegram saying that her father had taken his life out of grief.

Suddenly she felt pangs of conscience. Was it really so terrible that her father had painted vases filled with roses and hated Picasso? Was it really so reprehensible that he was afraid of his fourteen-year-old daughter's coming home pregnant? Was it really so laughable that he could not go on living without his wife?

And again she felt a longing to betray: betray her own betrayal. She announced to her husband (whom she now considered a difficult drunk rather than an eccentric) that she was leaving him.

But if we betray B., for whom we betrayed A., it does not

necessarily follow that we have placated A. The life of a divorcée-painter did not in the least resemble the life of the parents she had betrayed. The first betrayal is irreparable. It calls forth a chain reaction of further betrayals, each of which takes us farther and farther away from the point of our original betrayal.

Milan Kundera, *The Unbearable Lightness of Being*, Faber, 1984, pp. 90–92.

After the Affair

The adulterer is a more grievous offender than the thief.

St John Chrysostom, Homily X

Anna Karenina has, after much turbulence, left her husband, her son, and her home, and gone away to live with her lover Vronsky and their child. At first she is intensely happy, but her happiness is clouded by insecurity:

There was nothing she now feared more – though she had no reason to do so – than the loss of his love. But she could not help being grateful to him for his treatment of her, and showing him how much she valued it. He, who in her opinion had such a decided vocation for statesmanship, in which he ought to have played a conspicuous part, had sacrificed his ambitions for her and never showed the least regret. He was even more lovingly respectful to her than before, and the thought that she must never be allowed to feel the awkwardness of her situation never left his mind for a moment. He, so virile a man, not only never contradicted her, but where she was concerned seemed to have no will of his own and to be only occupied in anticipating her every wish. She could not help appreciating this, although his strained attentiveness, the atmosphere of solicitude with which he surrounded her, became burdensome at times.

Vronsky meanwhile, in spite of the complete fulfilment of what he had so long desired, was not completely happy. He soon felt that the realization of his longing gave him only one grain of the

mountain of bliss he had anticipated. That realization showed him
the eternal error men make by imagining that happiness consists in
the gratification of their wishes. When first he united his life with
hers and donned civilian clothes, he felt the delight of freedom in
general, such as he had not before known, and also the freedom of
love – he was contented then, but not for long. Soon he felt rising
in his soul a desire for desires – boredom. Involuntarily he began
to snatch at every passing caprice, mistaking it for a desire and a
purpose. Sixteen hours daily had to be filled somehow, living
abroad as they did completely at liberty, quite cut off from the
round of social life that had filled his time in Petersburg. The
pleasures of a bachelor's life, enjoyed by him on his previous
travels abroad, were not to be thought of now, for one attempt of
that kind had produced in Anna an unexpected fit of depression
quite disproportionate to the offence of a late supper with some
acquaintances. Intercourse with local Society or with the Russians
was, in consequence of the indefiniteness of their relation, likewise
impossible. Sight-seeing, apart from the fact that he had already
seen everything, had for him – a Russian and an intelligent man –
none of that inexplicable importance the English manage to attach
to it.

   After a while Anna and Vronsky experience growing discord:

The irritation which divided them had no tangible cause, and all
attempts at an explanation not only failed to clear it away but
increased it. It was an inner irritation, caused on her side by a
diminution of his love for her, and on his by regret that for her
sake he had placed himself in a distressing situation, which she,
instead of trying to alleviate, made still harder. Neither of them
spoke of the cause of their irritation, but each thought the other in
the wrong, and at every opportunity tried to prove that this was
so.
   For her he, with all his habits, thoughts, wishes, mental and
physical faculties – the whole of his nature – consisted of one thing

only: love for women, and this love she felt ought to be wholly concentrated on her alone. This love was diminishing; therefore, in her judgment, part of his love must have been transferred to other women, or to one other woman. She was jealous, not of any one woman, but of the diminution of his love. Not having as yet an object for her jealousy, she sought one. At the slightest hint she transferred her jealousy from one object to another. Now she was jealous of the coarse women with whom, through his bachelor connections, he might so easily have intercourse; now of the Society women whom he might meet; now, of some imaginary girl whom he might marry after repudiating her. This last jealousy tormented her more than anything else, especially since in an expansive moment he had carelessly told her that his mother understood him so little that she had tried to persuade him to marry the young Princess Sorokina.

And being jealous, Anna was indignant with him and constantly sought reasons to justify her indignation. She blamed him for everything that was hard in her situation. The torture of expectation, living betwixt heaven and earth, which she endured there in Moscow, Karenin's dilatoriness and indecision, her loneliness – she attributed all to him. If he loved her he would fully understand the difficulty of her situation, and would deliver her from it. That they were living in Moscow, instead of in the country, was also his fault. He could not live buried in the country as she desired. He needed society, and so he had placed her in this terrible position, the misery of which he would not understand. And it was likewise his fault that she was for ever parted from her son.

Even the rare moments of tenderness which occurred between them did not pacify her; in his tenderness she now saw a tinge of calm assurance which had not been there before and irritated her.

Leo Tolstoy, *Anna Karenina*, OUP, 1918, Vol. V: VIII, pp. 31–3; Vol. VII: XXIII, pp. 346–8, (translated by Louise and Aylmer Maude).

Dmitri Gurov, holidaying alone in Yalta, encounters Anna Sergeyevna. Both are unsatisfied within their marriages and their love rapidly develops although they have difficulty understanding each other:

'Let us go to your hotel,' he said softly. And both walked quickly.

The room was close and smelt of the scent she had bought at the Japanese shop. Gurov looked at her and thought: 'What different people one meets in the world!' From the past he preserved memories of careless, good-natured women, who loved cheerfully and were grateful to him for the happiness he gave them, however brief it might be; and of women like his wife who loved without any genuine feeling, with superfluous phrases, affectedly, hysterically, with an expression that suggested that it was not love nor passion, but something more significant; and of two or three others, very beautiful, cold women, on whose faces he had caught a glimpse of a rapacious expression – an obstinate desire to snatch from life more than it could give, and these were capricious, unreflecting, domineering, unintelligent women not in their first youth, and when Gurov grew cold to them their beauty excited his hatred, and the lace on their linen seemed to him like scales.

But in this case there was still the diffidence, the angularity of inexperienced youth, an awkward feeling; and there was a sense of consternation as though someone had suddenly knocked at the door. The attitude of Anna Sergeyevna – 'the lady with the dog' – to what had happened was somehow peculiar, very grave, as though it were her fall – so it seemed, and it was strange and inappropriate. Her face drooped and faded, and on both sides of it her long hair hung down mournfully; she mused in a dejected attitude like 'the woman who was a sinner' in an old-fashioned picture.

'It's wrong,' she said. 'You will be the first to despise me now.'

There was a water-melon on the table. Gurov cut himself a slice and began eating it without haste. There followed at least half an hour of silence.

Anna Sergeyevna was touching; there was about her the purity of a good, simple woman who had seen little of life. The solitary candle burning on the table threw a faint light on her face, yet it was clear that she was very unhappy.

'How could I despise you?' asked Gurov. 'You don't know what you are saying.'

'God forgive me,' she said, and her eyes filled with tears. 'It's awful.'

'You seem to feel you need to be forgiven.'

'Forgiven? No. I am a bad, low woman; I despise myself and don't attempt to justify myself. It's not my husband but myself I have deceived. And not only just now; I have been deceiving myself for a long time. My husband may be a good, honest man, but he is a flunkey! I don't know what he does there, what his work is, but I know he is a flunkey! I was twenty when I was married to him. I have been tormented by curiosity; I wanted something better. "There must be a different sort of life," I said to myself. I wanted to live! To live, to live! . . . I was fired by curiosity . . . you don't understand it, but, I swear to God, I could not control myself; something happened to me: I could not be restrained. I told my husband I was ill, and came here . . . And here I have been walking about as though I were dazed, like a mad creature; . . . and now I have become a vulgar, contemptible woman whom anyone may despise.'

Gurov felt bored already, listening to her. He was irritated by the naive tone, by this remorse, so unexpected and inopportune; but for the tears in her eyes, he might have thought she was jesting or playing a part.

'I don't understand,' he said softly. 'What is it you want?'

She hid her face on his breast and pressed close to him.

'Believe me, believe me, I beseech you . . .' she said. 'I love a pure, honest life, and sin is loathsome to me. I don't know what I am doing. Simple people say: "The Evil One has beguiled me." And I may say of myself now that the Evil One has beguiled me.'

'Hush, hush! . . .' he muttered.

He looked at her fixed, scared eyes, kissed her, talked softly and affectionately; and by degrees she was comforted, and her gaiety returned; they both began laughing.

Anton Chekhov, 'The Lady with the Dog', *Select Tales*, Vol. 1, Chatto & Windus, 1949 (translated by Constance Garnett).

In a single paragraph, the swift progress of an affair from passion to pretence and closure is charted:

It was the same that night, after the studio party where they drank enough to impassion their intent: in the motel she made love with a fury, but he knew it was forced, that her tightening arms, her bucking hips were turned against the fetters which clanked at her heart. The affair was short because that clanking never went away. It was in her voice: when she was pretending – and nearly always she pretended – her voice was low and flat, as if she had just waked from a deep sleep; but most of the time her voice was high and brittle with cheer, her laughter was forced and shrill, and he could hear in it the borders of hysteria. Like most unfaithful wives she was remorseless: she felt she deserved a lover. Yet it did her no good. Her heart was surrounded by obdurate concentric circles of disappointment and bitterness; she could not break through, so Peter couldn't either, and finally they broke it off and both pretended that aversion to the deceptions and stolen time of adultery was the reason.

Andre Dubus, 'Going Under', *Selected Stories*, Picador, 1990, pp. 131–2.

Chéri, after six years as the lover of Léa, who is twice his age, has married Edmée – but can't resist returning to Léa. They spend the night together, but the next morning Léa realizes they have no future:

She laughed sadly and quivered . . .'Quick, child, quick, go hunt your youth, it's only just caught on the bones of old women, you still have it and she has it, the girl who's waiting for you. You've tasted youth. You know it doesn't satisfy but that one always goes back for more . . . Oh it wasn't just last night that you started making comparisons. And what was I doing, giving good advice and showing off my noble soul? What do I know of you two? She loves you, now it's her turn to tremble, she'll suffer like a lover and not like a mother gone astray. You can talk to her as a master and not as a capricious gigolo . . . Go. Go quickly.'

She spoke in a voice of hasty supplication. He listened, standing, planted before her, his chest bare, his hair stormy, so tempting that she knotted her hands together to prevent them seizing him. He guessed it perhaps and did not undress. A hope, crazy as that which might come during their fall to people dropping off a tower, flashed between them and went out.

'Go,' she said in a low voice. 'I love you. It's too late. Go away. But go at once. Dress yourself.'

She rose and fetched him his shoes, spread out his socks and his crumpled shirt. He stood in place, moving his fingers awkwardly as if they were numb and she had to find his braces, his cravat; but she refrained from coming close to him and did not help him. While he dressed she glanced frequently into the court as if she were expecting something.

Dressed, he looked more pale with eyes which augmented their halo of fatigue.

'You don't feel ill?' she asked him. And she added timidly, her eyes lowered, 'You could . . . could rest a moment.' But at once she mastered herself and came back to him as if he were in great danger; 'No, no, you'll be better at home . . . Hurry, it's not yet noon, a good hot bath will refresh you and the open air . . . Here, your gloves . . . Oh yes and your hat on the floor . . . Put your coat on, you might catch cold . . . Au revoir, my Chéri, au revoir . . . Yes, that's it, give Charlotte my . . .' She closed the door behind him and silence put an end to her desperate, vain words. She heard Chéri stumble on the staircase and she ran to the window. He descended the steps and stopped in the middle of the court.

'He's coming back, he's coming back,' she cried, lifting her arms.

A gasping, old woman repeated her gestures in the long oblong mirror and Léa asked herself what she could have in common with this old lunatic.

Chéri continued his path toward the street, opened the gate and passed through. On the sidewalk he buttoned his topcoat to hide his evening clothes of the night before. Léa let the curtain fall. But she still had time to see that Chéri lifted his head toward the spring sky and the flowering chestnut trees and that in walking he filled his lungs with air like a man escaping from prison.

Colette, *Chéri*, Dial Press, 1929 (translated by Janet Flanner).

Seymour Levin, trying to revive his love for his mistress Pauline, is overcome by doubts:

He had, since their separation, harbored a secret belief that they had through love marked each other for future use; he hadn't expected the future to explode in his face, shattering all he had to think, decide, do. The responsibility was terrifying – taking away another man's wife, the miserable mess of divorce, having to fit himself to her, all her habituations and impedimenta, to suit to her clutter his quiet bachelor's life, needs, aspirations, plans, which though more than once destroyed and replaced, remained essentially what they had been, except that their fulfillment was farther in front of the nose with every step he took. He was distended by the fast thrust of events, of too many revived possibilities – where would he put them all? He feared his destiny had been decided apart from him, by chance, her, not him. She called the signals and he awoke running in the play. He had grave doubts, if he took her on again, that he could be master of his fate to any significant degree; he had already lost – the terrible thing – his freedom to feel free.

Levin beat himself into a concrete frenzy to resuscitate his love for her, but try breathing green, purple, rose. He tried every way he could, by every use of the imagination, to recapture love as it had been in fullest flower, as though the mind could recreate what it apparently rejected. Memory was a dark door leading through dark doors floating in space to Orpheus always descending. Levin a whirlwind of enraged impotence at what had become of him. In love he had unwillingly pulled the stopper, ug glug, no further feeling. This though he told himself he *must* still love her. Love for her was in him as experience, as valued idea, pleasure received, which he wanted to repeat. Except it wasn't where it had been, or should be. He had had and hadn't it. What in Christ's name had he done with the love he had only a month ago felt for her? Had he butchered it in the vize of will, sublimated it beyond repair, or recall, like a magician prestidigitating a girl into a tree, then forgetting the hocus pocus so that when he wanted a woman he embraced wood? Was such a thing even remotely possible? These thoughts drew others equally unhappy into their orbit. Was it love murdered or love imperfect, less than love to begin with? Had he loved her for the lay and not much else, giving it a tainted reciprocity of feeling? Was it a guilty response to experience he should have accepted as one accepts sunlight? Why must he forever insist on paying for being alive?

And with the lay as good as gone – he had believed – had he then, after a show of self-castigation to make himself look decent in the mirror, stopped loving the little he had loved? Or would this, in time, have happened anyway, out of boredom, without the necessity of a sudden decisive surrender of her? Or was his interest in Pauline basically that she belonged to someone else – life's initial tease – and once he had her as far as she went, when her thing broke down in various motels, best send her back to daddy, the lover's gut glutted? Who knows the answer? Not Levin.

Bernard Malamud, *A New Life*, Chatto & Windus, 1980, pp. 335–6.

While in Venice, Connie hears of the gamekeeper Mellors's marital problems, and for her disillusionment comes in the form of revulsion:

She had a letter from Mrs Bolton: . . .

'About Mr Mellors, I don't know how much Sir Clifford told you. It seems his wife came back all of a sudden one afternoon, and he found her sitting on the doorstep when he came in from the wood. She said she was come back to him and wanted to live with him again, as she was his legal wife, and he wasn't going to divorce her. But he wouldn't have anything to do with her, and wouldn't let her in the house, and did not go in himself; he went back into the wood without ever opening the door.

'But when he came back after dark, he found the house broken into, so he went upstairs to see what she'd done, and he found her in bed without a rag on her. He offered her money, but she said she was his wife and he must take her back. I don't know what sort of a scene they had. His mother told me about it, she's terribly upset. Well, he told her he'd die rather than ever live with her again, so he took his things and went straight to his mother's on Tevershall hill . . . And she kept going to old Mrs Mellors's house, to catch him, and she began swearing he'd got in bed with her in the cottage, and she went to a lawyer to make him pay her an allowance. She's grown heavy, and more common than ever, and as strong as a bull. And she goes about saying the most awful things about him, how he has women at the cottage, and how he behaved to her when they were married, the low, beastly things he did to her, and I don't know what all. I'm sure it's awful, the mischief a woman can do, once she starts talking. And no matter how low she may be, there'll be some as will believe her, and some of the dirt will stick. I'm sure the way she makes out that Mr Mellors was one of those low beastly men with women, is simply shocking. And people are only too ready to believe things against anybody, especially things like that. She declares she'll never leave him alone while he lives. Though what I say is, if he was so beastly to her, why is she so anxious to go back to him? But of course she's coming near her change of life, for she's years older than he is. And these common, violent women always go partly insane when the change of life comes upon them —'

This was a nasty blow to Connie. Here she was, sure as life, coming in for her share of the lowness and dirt. She felt angry with him for not having got clear of a Bertha Coutts: nay, for ever having married her. Perhaps he had a certain hankering after lowness. Connie remembered the last night she had spent with him, and shivered. He had known all that sensuality, even with a Bertha Coutts! It was really rather disgusting. It would be well to be rid of him, clear of him altogether. He was perhaps really common, really low.

She had a revulsion against the whole affair, and almost envied the Guthrie girls their gawky inexperience and crude maidenliness. And she now dreaded the thought that anybody would know about herself and the keeper. How unspeakably humiliating! She was weary, afraid, and felt a craving for utter respectability, even for the vulgar and deadening respectability of the Guthrie girls. If Clifford knew about her affair, how unspeakably humiliating! She was afraid, terrified of society and its unclean bite . . .

Connie had a revulsion in the opposite direction now. What had he done, after all? what had he done to herself, Connie, but give her an exquisite pleasure and a sense of freedom and life? He had released her warm, natural sexual flow. And for that they would hound him down.

D.H. Lawrence, *Lady Chatterley's Lover*, Heinemann, 1928, Ch. 17.

Litvinov and Irina fall in love in Moscow but Irina leaves the impoverished Litvinov in order to marry General Ratmirov. Years later, they meet each other again in Baden. Litvinov, although engaged to Tatyana, calls on Irina, and their relationship is renewed. Litvinov breaks with Tatyana, and Irina agrees to run away with Litvinov. When the arrangements are almost complete, Irina sends Litvinov a letter:

'My dear one, I have been thinking all night of your plan . . . I am

not going to shuffle with you. You have been open with me, and I
will be open with you; I *cannot* run away with you, I *have not the
strength* to do it. I feel how I am wronging you; my second sin is
greater than the first, I despise myself, my cowardice, I cover
myself with reproaches, but I cannot change myself. In vain I tell
myself that I have destroyed your happiness, that you have the
right now to regard me as a frivolous flirt, that I myself drew you
on, that I have given you solemn promises . . . I am full of horror,
of hatred for myself, but I can't do otherwise, I can't, I can't. I
don't want to justify myself, I won't tell you I was carried away
myself . . . all that's of no importance; but I want to tell you, and
to say it again and yet again, I am yours, yours for ever, do with
me as you will when you will, free from all obligation, from all
responsibility! I am yours . . . But run away, throw up everything
. . . no! no! no! I besought you to save me, I hoped to wipe out
everything, to burn up the past as in a fire . . . but I see there is no
salvation for me; I see the poison has gone too deeply into me; I
see one cannot breathe this atmosphere for years with impunity. I
have long hesitated whether to write you this letter, I dread to
think what decision you may come to, I trust only to your love for
me. But I felt it would be dishonest on my part to hide the truth
from you – especially as perhaps you have already begun to take
the first steps for carrying out our project. Ah! it was lovely but
impracticable. O my dear one, think me a weak, worthless woman,
despise, but don't abandon me, don't abandon your Irina! . . . To
leave this life I have not the courage, but live it without you I
cannot either. We soon go back to Petersburg, come there, live
there, we will find occupation for you, your labours in the past
shall not be thrown away, you shall find good use for them . . .
only live near me, only love me; such as I am, with all my
weaknesses and my vices, and believe me, no heart will ever be so
tenderly devoted to you as the heart of your Irina. Come soon to
me, I shall not have an instant's peace until I see you. – Yours,
yours, yours, I.'

The blood beat like a sledge-hammer in Litvinov's head, then slowly and painfully sank to his heart, and was chill as a stone in it. He read through Irina's letter, and just as on that day at Moscow he fell in exhaustion on the sofa, and stayed there motionless. A dark abyss seemed suddenly to have opened on all sides of him, and he stared into this darkness in senseless despair. And so again, again deceit, no, worse than deceit, lying and baseness . . . And life shattered, everything torn up by its roots utterly, and the sole thing which he could cling to – the last prop in fragments too! 'Come after us to Petersburg,' he repeated with a bitter inward laugh, 'we will find you occupation' . . . Find me a place as a head clerk, eh? and who are *we*? . . .

'Why not obey her?' flashed through his brain. 'She loves me, she is mine, and in our very yearning towards each other, in this passion, which after so many years has burst upon us, and forced its way out with such violence, is there not something inevitable, irresistible, like a law of nature? Live in Petersburg . . . and shall I be the first to be put in such a position? And how could we be in safety together? . . .'

And he fell to musing, and Irina's shape, in the guise in which it was imprinted for ever in his late memories, softly rose before him . . . But not for long . . . He mastered himself, and with a fresh outburst of indignation drove away from him both those memories and that seductive image.

'You give me to drink from that golden cup,' he cried, 'but there is poison in the draught, and your white wings are besmirched with mire . . . Away! Remain here with you after the way I . . . I drove away my betrothed . . . a deed of infamy, of infamy!' He wrung his hands with anguish, and another face with the stamp of suffering on its still features, with dumb reproach in its farewell eyes, rose from the depths . . .

And for a long time Litvinov was in this agony still; for a long time, his tortured thought, like a man fever-stricken, tossed from side to side . . . He grew calm at last; at last he came to a decision. From the very first instant he had a presentiment of this decision; . . . it had appeared to him at first like a distant, hardly perceptible point in the midst of the darkness and turmoil of his inward conflict; then it had begun to move nearer and nearer, till it ended by cutting with icy edge into his heart.

Litvinov once more dragged his box out of the corner, once more he packed all his things, without haste, even with a kind of stupid carefulness, rang for the waiter, paid his bill, and despatched to Irina a note in Russian to the following purport:

'I don't know whether you are doing me a greater wrong now than then; but I know this present blow is infinitely heavier . . . it is the end. You tell me, "I cannot"; and I repeat to you, "I cannot . . ." do what you want. I cannot and I don't want to. Don't answer me. You are not capable of giving me the only answer I would accept. I am going away to-morrow early by the first train. Good-bye, may you be happy! We shall in all probability not see each other again.'

Ivan Turgenev, *Smoke*, Heinemann, 1896, pp. 278–80, 283–4.

A change of heart destroys Litvinov's happiness, but often illicit love affairs have to be brought to a more decisive conclusion. In the case of the love between Launcelot and King Arthur's Queen Guinevere, only a duel can resolve the dishonour. After a great tournament, Launcelot and other wounded knights retire to the castle, where Guinevere is staying:

Sir Launcelot had grete chere with the quene. And than he made a promyse with the quene that the same nyght he sholde com to a wyndow outewarde towarde a gardyne, and that wyndow was barred with iron, and there sir Launcelot promysed to mete her whan all folkes were on slepe . . .

Than the knyghts that were hurt were serched, and soffte salves were layde to their woundis, and so hit passed on tyll souper-tyme. And all the chere that myght be made them there was done unto the quene and all her knyghtes. And whan season was they wente unto their chambirs, but in no wyse the quene wolde nat suffir her wounded knyghtes to be fro her, but that they were layde inwyth draughtes by hir chambir, uppon beddis and paylattes, that she myght herselff se unto them that they wanted nothynge.

So whan sir Launcelot was in hys chambir whych was assygned unto hym, he called unto hym sir Lavayne and tolde hym that nyght he must speke with hys lady, quene Gwenyver.

'Sir,' seyde sir Lavayne, 'let me go with you, and hyt please you, for I drede me sore of the treason of sir Mellyagaunte.'

'Nay,' seyde sir Launcelot, 'I thanke you, but I woll have nobody wyth me.'

Than sir Launcelot toke hys swerde in hys honde and prevaly wente to the place where he had spyed a ladder toforehande, and that he toke undir hys arme, and bare hit thorow the gardyne and sette hit up to the wyndow. And anone the quene was there redy to mete hym.

And than they made their complayntes to othir of many dyverce thyngis, and than sir Launcelot wysshed that he myght have comyn in to her.

'Wyte you well,' seyde the quene, 'I wolde as fayne as ye that ye myght com in to me.'

'Wolde ye so, madame,' seyde sir Launcelot, 'wyth youre harte that I were with you?'

'Ye, truly,' seyde the quene.

'Than shall I prove my myght,' seyde sir Launcelot, 'for youre love.'

And than he sette hys hondis uppon the barrys of iron and pulled at them with suche a myght that he braste hem clene out of the stone wallys. And therewithall one of the barres of iron kutte the brawne of hys hondys thorowoute to the bone. And than he lepe into the chambir to the quene.

'Make ye no noyse,' seyde the quene, 'for my wounded knyghtes lye here fast by me.'

So, to passe uppon thys tale, sir Launcelot wente to bedde with the quene and toke no force of hys hurte honde, and toke hys pleasaunce and hys lykynge untyll hit was the dawnyng of the day; for wyte you well he slept nat, but wacched. And whan he saw hys tyme that he myght tary no lenger, he toke hys leve and departed at the wyndowe, and put hit togydir as well as he myght agayne, and so departed untyll hys owne chambir. And there he tolde sir Lavayne how that he was hurte. Than sir Lavayne dressed hys honde . . .

Sir Mellyagaunte wente to the quenys chambir and founde her ladyes there redy clothed.

'A! Jesu mercy,' seyde sir Mellyagaunte, 'what ayles you, madame, that ye slepe thys longe?'

And therewithall he opened the curtayn for to beholde her. And than was he ware where she lay, and all the hede-sheete, pylow, and over-shyte was all bebled of the bloode of sir Launcelot and of hys hurte honde. Whan sir Mellyagaunte aspyed that blood, than he demed in her that she was false to the kynge and that som of the wounded knyghtes had lyene by her all that nyght.

'A ha, madame!' seyde sir Mellyagaunte, 'now I have founde you a false traytouras unto my lorde Arthur, for now I preve well hit was nat for nought that ye layde thes wounded knyghtis within the bondys of your chambir. Therefore I calle you of tresoun afore my lorde kynge Arthure. And now I have proved you, madame, wyth a shamefull dede; and that they bene all false, or som of them, I woll make hit good, for a wounded knyght thys nyght hath layne by you.'

'That ys false,' seyde the quene, 'that I woll report me unto them.'

But whan the ten knyghtes harde sir Mellyagaunteys wordys, than they spake all at onys and seyd,

'Sir Mellyagaunte, thou falsely belyest my lady, the quene, and that we woll make good uppon the, any of us. Now chose whych thou lyste of us, whan we ar hole of the woundes thou gavyst us.'

'Ye shall nat! Away with youre proude langayge! For here ye may all se that a wounded knyght thys nyght hath layne by the quene.'

Than they all loked and were sore ashamed whan they saw that bloode. And wyte you well sir Mellyagaunte was passyng glad that he had the quene at suche avauntayge, for he demed by that to hyde hys owne treson. And so in thys rumour com in sir Launcelot and fownde them at a grete affray.

Launcelot denies that he or any other knight has spent the night with the queen, and challenges Mellyagaunt to a duel. Mellyagaunt is slain. But Arthur inevitably finds out about his wife's adultery:

'My lorde,' seyde sir Aggravayne, 'I shall telle you, for I may kepe hit no lenger ... We know all that sir Launcelot holdith youre quene, and hath done longe, and we be your syster sunnes, we may suffir hit no lenger. And all we wote that ye shulde be above sir Launcelot, and ye are the kynge that made hym knyght, and therefore we woll preve hit that he is a traytoure to youre person.'

'Gyff hit be so,' seyde the kynge, 'wyte you well, he ys non othir. But I wolde be lothe to begyn such a thynge but I myght have prevys of hit, for sir Launcelot ys an hardy knyght, and all ye know that he ys the beste knyght amonge us all, and but if he be takyn with the dede he woll fyght with hym that bryngith up the noyse, and I know no knyght that ys able to macch hym. Therefore, and hit be sothe as ye say, I wolde that he were takyn with the dede.' ...

'My lorde,' seyde sir Aggravayne, 'ye shall ryde to-morne an-huntyng, and doute ye nat, sir Launcelot woll nat go wyth you. And so whan hit drawith towarde nyght ye may sende the quene worde that ye woll ly oute all that nyght, and so may ye sende for your cookis. And than, uppon payne of deth, that nyght we shall take hym wyth the quene, and we shall brynge hym unto you, quycke or dede.' ...

So on the morne kynge Arthure rode an-huntyng and sente worde to the quene that he wolde be oute all that nyght. Than sir Aggravayne and sir Mordred gate to them twelve knyghtes and hyd hemselff in a chambir in the castell of Carlyle ...

Whan the nyght cam sir Launcelot tolde sir Bors how he wolde go that nyght and speke wyth the quene.

'Sir,' seyde sir Bors, 'ye shall nat go thys nyght be my counceyle.'

'Why?' seyde sir Launcelot . . .

'I mystruste that the kynge ys oute thys nyght from the quene bycause peradventure he hath layne som wacche for you and the quene. Therefore I drede me sore of som treson.'

'Have ye no drede,' seyde sir Launcelot, 'for I shall go and com agayne and make no taryynge.' . . .

So sir Launcelot departed and toke hys swerde undir hys arme, and so he walked in hys mantell, that noble knyght, and put hymselff in grete jouparté. And so he past on tylle he cam to the quenys chambir, and so lyghtly he was had into the chambir . . .

But thus as they were togydir there cam sir Aggravayne and sir Mordred wyth twelve knyghtes with them of the Rounde Table, and they seyde with grete cryyng and scaryng voyce,

'Thou traytoure, sir Launcelot, now ar thou takyn! . . . Come oute of the quenys chambir! For wyte thou well thou arte besette so that thou shalt nat ascape.'

'A, Jesu mercy!' seyd sir Launcelot, 'thys shamefull cry and noyse I may nat suffir, for bette were deth at onys than thus to endure thys payne.'

Than he toke the quene in hys armys and kyssed her and seyde,

'Moste nobelest Crysten quene, I besech you, as ye have ben ever my speciall good lady, and I at all tymes your poure knyght and trew unto my power, and as I never fayled you in ryght nor in wronge sytthyn the firste day kynge Arthur made me knyght, that ye woll pray for my soule if that I be slayne. For well I am assured that sir Bors, my nevew, and all the remenaunte of my kynne, with sir Lavayne and sir Urré, that they woll nat fayle you to rescow you from the fyer. And therfore, myne owne lady, recomforte yourselff, whatsomever com of me, that ye go with sir Bors, my nevew, and they all woll do you all the plesure that they may, and ye shall lyve lyke a quene uppon my londis.'

'Nay, sir Launcelot, nay!' seyde the quene. 'Wyte thou well that I woll nat lyve longe aftir thy dayes. But and ye be slayne I woll

take my dethe as mekely as ever ded marter take hys dethe for Jesu
Crystes sake.'

'Well, madame,' seyde sir Launcelot, 'syth hit ys so that the day
ys com that oure love muste departe, wyte you well I shall selle my
lyff as dere as I may. And a thousandfolde,' seyde sir Launcelot, 'I
am more hevyar[1] for you than for myselff! And now I had levir
than to be lorde of all Crystendom that I had sure armour uppon
me, that men myght speke of my dedys or ever I were slayne.'

Guinevere is condemned to death but rescued by Launcelot. After
Arthur's death, the lovers retire, separately, to monasteries. The ultimate
consequence of the rift between Arthur and his queen is the dissolution
of his kingdom.

Thomas Malory, *Morte D'Arthur*, XIX, XX.

In the brittle and heartless world portrayed by Evelyn Waugh in the
1930s, honour doesn't come into it. When Brenda Last begins an affair
with John Beaver, she decides to leave her husband for good:

On Monday morning Tony found this letter on his breakfast tray.

Darling Tony,
I am not coming back to Hetton. Grimshawe can pack everything and
bring it to the flat. Then I shan't want her any more.
You must have realized for some time that things were going wrong.
I am in love with John Beaver and I want to have a divorce and marry
him. If John Andrew had not died things might not have happened like this.
I can't tell. As it is, I simply can't begin over again. Please do not mind too
much. I suppose we shan't be allowed to meet while the case is on but I hope
afterwards we shall be great friends. Anyway I shall always look on you as
one whatever you think of me.

Best love from
Brenda

When Tony read this his first thought was that Brenda had lost

1. sorrowful.

her reason. 'She's only seen Beaver twice to my knowledge,' he said.

But later he showed the letter to Jock, who said, 'I'm sorry it should have happened like this.'

'But it's not true, is it?'

'Yes, I'm afraid it is. Everyone has known for some time.'

But it was several days before Tony fully realised what it meant. He had got into a habit of loving and trusting Brenda.

'How's the old boy taking it?'

'Not so well. It makes me feel rather a beast,' said Brenda. 'I'm afraid he minds a lot.'

'Well, you wouldn't like it if he didn't,' said Polly to console her.

'No, I suppose not.'

'I shall stick by you whatever happens,' said Jenny Abdul Akbar.

'Oh, everything is going quite smoothly now,' said Brenda. 'There was a certain amount of *gêne* with relatives.'

Tony had been living with Jock for the last three weeks. Mrs. Rattery had gone to California and he was grateful for company. They dined together most evenings. They had given up going to Brat's; so had Beaver; they were afraid of meeting each other. Instead Tony and Jock went to Brown's, where Beaver was not a member. Beaver was continually with Brenda nowadays, at one of half a dozen houses . . .

In the first week Tony had had several distasteful interviews. Allan had attempted to act as peacemaker.

'You just wait a few weeks,' he had said. 'Brenda will come back. She'll soon get sick of Beaver.'

'But I don't want her back.'

'I know just how you feel, but it doesn't do to be medieval about it. If Brenda hadn't been upset at John's death this need never have come to a crisis. Why last year Marjorie was going everywhere with that ass Robin Beaseley. She was mad about him at the time, but I pretended not to notice and it all blew over. If I were you I should refuse to recognise that anything has happened.'

Marjorie had said, 'Of *course* Brenda doesn't love Beaver. How could she? . . . And if she thinks she does at the moment, I think it's your duty to prevent her making a fool of herself. You must refuse to be divorced – anyway until she has found someone more reasonable.'

Lady St. Cloud [Brenda's mother] had said, 'Brenda has been very, very foolish. She always was an excitable girl, but I am sure there was never anything *wrong*, quite sure. *That* wouldn't be like Brenda at all. I haven't met Mr. Beaver and I do not wish to. I understand he is unsuitable in every way. Brenda would never want to marry anyone like that. I will tell you exactly how it happened, Tony. Brenda must have felt a tiny bit neglected – people often do at that stage of marriage. I have known countless cases – and it was naturally flattering to find a young man to beg and carry for her. That's all it was, nothing *wrong*. And then the terrible shock of little John's accident unsettled her and she didn't know what she was saying or writing. You'll both laugh over this little fracas in years to come.'

Tony had not set eyes on Brenda since the afternoon of the funeral. Once he spoke to her over the telephone.

It was during the second week when he was feeling most lonely and bewildered by various counsels. Allan had been with him urging a reconciliation. 'I've been talking to Brenda,' he had said. 'She's sick of Beaver already. The one thing she wants is to go back to Hetton and settle down with you again.'

While Allan was there, Tony resolutely refused to listen, but later the words, and the picture they evoked, would not leave his mind. So he rang her up and she answered him calmly and gravely.

'Brenda, this is Tony.'

'Hullo, Tony, what is it?'

'I've been talking to Allan. He's just told me about your change of mind.'

'I'm not sure I know what you mean.'

'That you want to leave Beaver and come back to Hetton.'

'Did Allan say that?'

'Yes; isn't it true?'

'I'm afraid it's not. Allan is an interfering ass. I had him here this afternoon. He told me that you didn't want a divorce but that you were willing to let me stay on alone in London and do as I liked provided there was no public scandal. It seemed a good idea and I was going to ring you up about it. But I suppose that's just his diplomacy too. Anyway I'm afraid there's no prospect of my coming back to Hetton just at present.'

'Oh I see. I didn't think it was likely . . . I just rang you up.'

'That's all right. How are you, Tony?'

'All right, thanks.'

'Good, so am I. Goodbye.'

That was all he had heard of her. Both avoided places where there was a likelihood of their meeting.

Evelyn Waugh, *A Handful of Dust*, Chapman & Hall, 1948, Chs. 3, 4.

Tony drifts into the loss of a wife; Encolpius, however, is prepared to fight to save his male lover and servant Giton from the clutches of Ascyltus. The three of them have found their way to an inn after a drunken party:

The instant my drunken hands relaxed their grip on Giton, Ascyltus, that wizard of my destruction, ravished the boy away in the darkness to his own bed and took his pleasure of another man's love. Whether Giton felt nothing at all, or merely pretended not to notice, I do not know; but all night long, oblivious of every moral law, every human right, he lay with Ascyltus in adulterous embrace. Waking, I went groping with my hand for the boy's body in the bed and found, O gods, my treasure stolen! For one instant – if the word of a lover can be believed – I was tempted to run myself through with my sword and join, as poets say, *that sleep*

I slept to the endless sleep of death. But in the end prudence prevailed. I slapped Giton awake, and fixing Ascyltus with a look of terrible fury, I cried, 'Since, in your perversity, you have broken your promise and trampled upon our friendship, pack your belongings and leave. Go stain some other bed with your adulteries.'

He made no objection, and we divided our spoils with painstaking fairness. Then he said: 'Very well. Now we split the boy.'

I took this as merely some feeble parting joke, but the next thing I knew he had wrenched out his sword with fratricidal fury. 'No longer, miser,' he cried, 'shall you hunch over your treasure in lonely lust. Either give me my share, or I'll cut off my piece with my sword in revenge.'

I pulled out my sword, threw my cloak about my arm and prepared to give battle. Leaping between us as we raved, poor Giton took us by the knees in turn, and with the tears streaming down his face implored us not to let that humble tavern witness a new Thebaid, nor to soil with each other's blood the sanctity of a glorious friendship. 'If you must have murder,' he cried, 'behold, I offer you my throat, bared to your blow; plunge your swords home; kill me, for it was on my account that you broke your word as friends.'

Touched by this pitiful entreaty, we put our swords away. For his part, Ascyltus promptly proposed a solution to our problem. 'Let the boy,' he said, 'follow the one he prefers. Let him have a free choice of his own lover.' Convinced that a relationship as old as Giton's and mine was like a bond of blood, unbreakable, I accepted without fear. In fact, I fairly jumped at the proposal and the decision was referred to the judge without delay. With no hesitation, without even the pretense of hesitation, the boy rose and chose – Ascyltus! Thunderstruck by this bolt from the blue, I dropped my sword and collapsed on the bed. Had I not begrudged my enemy a total triumph, I would have done away with myself then and there. Ascyltus, flushed with success, swaggered out with his winnings, leaving me, once the dearest of his friends, the companion of his every joy and sorrow, alone with my anguish and despair, in a strange land, dejected.

Petronius, *Satiricon*, New English Library, 1960, sections 79–80, pp. 85–6 (translated by William Arrowsmith).

After the affair, the price to be paid is not only personal but social, and the disapproval of the community is used to compound the censure of illicit lovers. The dissolute actor Edmund Kean had a fight on his hands after his affair with an alderman's wife came to light. Although Alderman Robert Cox appeared to tolerate his wife Charlotte's infidelity, the discovery of Kean's letters to her brought matters to a head when the adultery became the subject of a court case.

The trial was held on 17th January, 1825, before the Lord Chief Justice. The Common serjeant appeared for the plaintiff. Mr Scarlett was leading counsel for the defence. The court was packed to suffocation. A few of Edmund's friends were present, and Elliston turned up to support him. But the leaders of fashion, the shorthand Press writers and the noisy idlers who made up the rest of the throng were there to laugh, jeer, gloat and get hysterical pleasure from the public exposure of a man whose conduct they had for years resented.

Mr Scarlett did not attempt to excuse his client's conduct. But he suggested first that Mrs Cox was a wanton and secondly that the Alderman had condoned her infidelity with Mr Kean. For these reasons he urged the jury to decide that the plaintiff far from being entitled to the £2000 he had claimed should not get more than a farthing's damages.

In his summing up the Lord Chief Justice ruled that ... the allegations that Mrs Cox had had two affairs previous to her meeting with Kean was unproved. He also said there was no reason to suppose that the plaintiff had actually been aware of his wife's infidelity.

At the same time, he pointed out that the Alderman's behaviour had been very far from that of a devoted husband ... The jury brought in a verdict for the plaintiff and awarded him £800.

The case of *Cox v. Kean* was over, but the sequel followed with such thoroughness and immediacy that it might almost have been rehearsed in advance. Verbatim reports of the trial appeared in all the newspapers. Indecent songs, ballads, playlets and caricatures dealing with Edmund and his mistress sold like hot cakes. A pamphlet entitled *Secrets Worth Knowing*, which was a pornographic forgery of Charlotte's 'suppressed' letters to her lover, was rushed through the Press by an enterprising publisher. And in spite of the growing plethora of information – real and concocted – a Sunday newspaper advertised widely in advance: '*Cox v. Kean* – Verbatim report of this trial *with all* the letters, tragical and comical, will be given gratis in a supplement . . .'

Though the Coxes won no sympathy, the *Times* led a ferocious campaign against Edmund. Its report of the trial next morning occupied most of its space . . . The report included all the spicier letters . . . The *Times* launched an editorial campaign to force Kean into temporary retirement. It described him as being 'advanced many steps in profligacy beyond the most profligate of his sisters and brethren of the stage', and continued: 'It is of little consequence whether the character of King Richard III or Othello be well or ill acted; but it is of importance that public feeling be not shocked, and public decency be not outraged.'

. . . Within a day or two the story of Kean's adultery became depicted as a major national scandal. Virtually every newspaper and periodical treated the issue raised by the *Times* as though it were the burning question of the hour. Most, though not quite all of them, tried to outdo each other in their protestations of moral outrage. Thus the *Sunday Monitor*, as soon as its chance came, said that the story of Kean's adultery was so vile that 'Happily no parallel' to it could be 'found in ancient or modern times.' . . .

[The *Times*] predicted that Drury Lane would be crowded 'with all the numerous class of morbidly curious idlers who flock to a play or an execution to see how a man looks when he is hanged or deserves to be hanged.'

The *Times* got what it asked for. The audience that jammed the vast auditorium of Drury Lane on the night of 24th January, 1825, included very few playgoers who had come to see a great actor in one of his greatest parts. For the most part, it was a mob of demonstrators, with a minority of counter-demonstrators recruited from Kean's tavern kingdom. It included bruisers, prostitutes, young bloods with hunting horns to blow, white-haired members of the Society for the Suppression of Vice with propaganda placards to raise on high, drunkards, thieves and an amorphous collection of sensation-seekers . . .

The demonstrators greeted Edmund on his entrance with a great prurient yell, like the cry of some barbarian army scenting rape. They pelted him with orange peel and rotten eggs; they jeered and hooted at him; screamed out obscenities; bellowed 'Heart-Strings', 'Little Breeches' and 'Go Back to Mother Cox' – roared with cruel laughter at their own cruel sallies. The counter-demonstrators fought back with shouts of 'Down with the *Times*' and 'Down with Cant', but they only succeeded in swelling the general clamour, which never for a moment subsided while Edmund was on the stage, so that his whole performance might as well have been given in dumb show. At the end, he stood before his persecutors, 'the proud representative of Shakespeare's heroes', as he liked to call himself, mutely appealing for a chance to speak, until a further shower of missiles drove him out of sight, though not into submission.

Giles Playfair, *The Flash of Lightning*, Kimber, 1983, pp. 113–17.

In Fontane's novel *Effi Briest*, set in nineteenth-century Prussia, Effi, unhappily married to Baron von Innstetten, has had an affair with Crampas which, when discovered seven years later, prompts Innstetten to challenge Crampas to a duel, in which Crampas is killed. An envelope arrives in Effi's mother's handwriting:

She took a pair of sewing scissors with mother-of-pearl handles and slowly cut along the envelope. And now a new surprise awaited her. The letter itself was, indeed, closely written in her mother's hand, but there was a bundle of bank notes fastened round with a wide paper band, on which was written, in red, the amount it contained, and this was in her father's hand. She pushed the bundle on one side and leaning back in her rocking-chair, she began to read. But before she had gone far, the letter fell from her hand and the blood drained from her face ... She stood up and went into the drawing-room, where she was clearly glad to find something to hold on to as she felt her way along the rosewood grand-piano. With this support, she arrived at her room, on the right-hand side. Groping to open the door, she made for her bed on the opposite side of the room and collapsed in a faint.

Minutes passed. When Effi had recovered, she sat down on a chair beside the window and looked out on to the quiet street. If only there could have been noise and conflict down there! But there was merely the sun shining on the roadway and the shadows cast by the railings and the trees. The feeling of being alone in the world came over her in all its gravity. Only an hour ago, she was a happy woman, the darling of everyone whom she knew, and now an outcast! She had read only the beginning of the letter but enough to have a clear view of her situation. Where should she go? She could find no reply to that question, yet she felt a deep longing to escape from her surroundings ...

The letter was lying on the table in front of her but she hadn't the heart to read on. Finally, she said: 'What am I afraid of now? What can anyone tell me that I haven't already told myself? The cause of it all is dead; it's impossible for me to return home, the divorce will be pronounced in a few weeks' time and the custody of the child will be given to the father. Of course, I'm the guilty party and a guilty woman can't bring up her child. And how could she find the means to do it anyway? I expect I'll be able to fend for myself all right. I must see what mama writes on the subject, what she thinks I ought to do.'

As she said this, she picked up the letter again to read the end as well:

'. . . And now as to your future, my dear Effi. You'll have to fend for yourself and as far as material resources are concerned, you may depend on our support. Berlin will be the best place for you to live (this sort of thing can be best concealed in a big town) and there you'll be one of the many who have been forced to do without fresh air and sunlight. You'll be living a lonely life and, if you don't want to do that, you'll probably have to move out of your social class. You'll be excluded from the society in which you've been moving up till now. And the saddest thing for us and for you (even for you if we understand you rightly) is that you will be excluded from our house, too. We can't offer you any asylum in Hohen-Cremmen, there can be no refuge for you in our house, because that would mean cutting ourselves off from everyone we know and this we are emphatically not inclined to do. Not because we are particularly worldly and would look upon it as completely unbearable to have to say good-bye to so-called "Society". No, that's not the reason, but simply because we want to make our position plain and show the whole world that we condemn – I'm afraid I must use this word – your actions – the actions of our only daughter, the daughter whom we loved so dearly . . .'

Effi could not read on. Her eyes filled with tears and after vainly struggling against them, she finally burst into a violent fit of sobbing and weeping which brought relief to her feelings.

Theodor Fontane, *Effi Briest*, Chs. 30–31 (translated by Douglas Parmée).

Prussian Protestantism could be stifling to a young woman such as Effi, but her fate would have been worse two centuries earlier in New England, where the ferocity of social and religious disapproval could be close to murderous. In *The Scarlet Letter*, Hester Prynne, sent ahead to the colony by her husband from the Old World, has borne an illegitimate child. She is condemned to stand for three hours on the pillory platform and to wear a mark of shame for the remainder of her life.

The door of the jail being flung open from within, there appeared, in the first place, like a black shadow emerging into the sunshine, the grim and grisly presence of the town-beadle, with a sword by his side and his staff of office in his hand. This personage prefigured and represented in his aspect the whole dismal severity of the Puritanic code of law, which it was his business to administer in its final and closest application to the offender. Stretching forth the official staff in his left hand, he laid his right upon the shoulder of a young woman, whom he thus drew forward; until, on the threshold of the prison-door, she repelled him, by an action marked with natural dignity and force of character, and stepped into the open air, as if by her own free-will. She bore in her arms a child, a baby of some three months old . . .

When the young woman – the mother of this child – stood fully revealed before the crowd, it seemed to be her first impulse to clasp the infant closely to her bosom; not so much by an impulse of motherly affection, as that she might thereby conceal a certain token, which was wrought or fastened into her dress. In a moment, however, wisely judging that one token of her shame would but poorly serve to hide another, she took the baby on her arm, and, with a burning blush, and yet a haughty smile, and a glance that would not be abashed, looked around at her townspeople and neighbors. On the breast of her gown, in fine red cloth, surrounded with an elaborate embroidery and fantastic flourishes of gold thread, appeared the letter A. It was so artistically done, and with so much fertility and gorgeous luxuriance of fancy, that it had all the effect of a last and fitting decoration to the apparel which she wore; and which was of a splendor in accordance with the taste of the age, but greatly beyond what was allowed by the sumptuary regulations of the colony.

The Reverend Mr Dimmesdale bent his head, in silent prayer, as it seemed, and then came forward.

'Hester Prynne,' said he, leaning over the balcony, and looking down steadfastly into her eyes, '. . . If thou feelest it to be for thy soul's peace, and that thy earthly punishment will thereby be made more effectual to salvation, I charge thee to speak out the name of thy fellow-sinner and fellow-sufferer! Be not silent from any mistaken pity and tenderness for him; for, believe me, Hester, though he were to step down from a high place, and stand there beside thee, on thy pedestal of shame, yet better were it so, than to hide a guilty heart through life. What can thy silence do for him, except it tempt him – yea, compel him, as it were – to add hypocrisy to sin? Heaven hath granted thee an open ignominy, that thereby thou mayest work out an open triumph over the evil within thee, and the sorrow without. Take heed how thou deniest to him – who, perchance, hath not the courage to grasp it for himself – the bitter, but wholesome, cup that is now presented to thy lips!'

The young pastor's voice was tremulously sweet, rich, deep, and broken. The feeling that it so evidently manifested, rather than the direct purport of the words, caused it to vibrate within all hearts, and brought the listeners into one accord of sympathy. Even the poor baby, at Hester's bosom, was affected by the same influence; for it directed its hitherto vacant gaze towards Mr Dimmesdale, and held up its little arms, with a half pleased, half plaintive murmur. So powerful seemed the minister's appeal, that the people could not believe but that Hester Prynne would speak out the guilty name; or else that the guilty one himself, in whatever high or lowly place he stood, would be drawn forth by an inward and inevitable necessity, and compelled to ascend the scaffold.

Hester shook her head.

'Woman, transgress not beyond the limits of Heaven's mercy!' cried the Reverend Mr Wilson, more harshly than before. 'That little babe hath been gifted with a voice, to second and confirm the counsel which thou hast heard. Speak out the name! That, and thy repentance, may avail to take the scarlet letter off thy breast.'

'Never!' replied Hester Prynne, looking, not at Mr Wilson, but into the deep and troubled eyes of the younger clergyman. 'It is too deeply branded. Ye cannot take it off. And would that I might endure his agony, as well as mine!' . . .

Discerning the impracticable state of the poor culprit's mind, the elder clergyman, who had carefully prepared himself for the occasion, addressed to the multitude a discourse on sin, in all its branches, but with continual reference to the ignominious letter. So forcibly did he dwell upon this symbol, for the hour or more during which his periods were rolling over the people's heads, that it assumed new terrors in their imagination, and seemed to derive its scarlet hue from the flames of the infernal pit. Hester Prynne, meanwhile, kept her place upon the pedestal of shame, with glazed eyes, and an air of weary indifference. She had borne, that morning, all that nature could endure; and as her temperament was not of the order that escapes from too intense suffering by a swoon, her spirit could only shelter itself beneath a stony crust of insensibility, while the faculties of animal life remained entire. In this state, the voice of the preacher thundered remorselessly, but unavailingly, upon her ears. The infant, during the latter portion of her ordeal, pierced the air with its wailings and screams; she strove to hush it, mechanically, but seemed scarcely to sympathize with its trouble. With the same hard demeanour, she was led back to prison, and vanished from the public gaze within its iron-clamped portal. It was whispered, by those who peered after her, that the scarlet letter threw a lurid gleam along the dark passage-way of the interior.

Nathaniel Hawthorne, *The Scarlet Letter*, Chs. 2, 3.

Although Helen's desertion of her husband Menelaus for the Trojan Paris has brought war to the walls of Troy, their self-absorption makes a sensuous mockery of the havoc and death their actions have caused. An attempt is made to resolve the dispute by single combat between Menelaus and Paris. Paris is defeated but saved from death by Aphrodite's intervention.

Then [Aphrodite] went herself to summon Helen. She found Helen on the high tower, surrounded by Trojan women. Aphrodite put out her hand, plucked at her sweet-scented robe, and spoke to her in the disguise of an old woman she was very fond of, a wool-worker who used to make beautiful wool for her when she lived in

Lacedaemon. 'Come!' said the goddess, mimicking this woman. 'Paris wants you to go home to him. There he is in his room, on the inlaid bed, radiant in his beauty and his lovely clothes. You would never believe that he had just come in from a duel. You would think he was going to a dance or had just stopped dancing and sat down to rest.'

Helen was perturbed and looked at the goddess. When she observed the beauty of her neck and her lovely breasts and sparkling eyes, she was struck with awe. But she made no pretence of being deceived. 'Lady of mysteries,' she said, 'what is the object of this mummery? Now that Menelaus has beaten Paris and is willing to take home his erring wife, you are plotting, I suppose, to carry me off to some still more distant city, in Phrygia or in lovely Maeonia, for some other favourite of yours who may be living in those parts? So you begin by coming here, and try to lure me back to Paris. No; go and sit with him yourself. Forget that you are a goddess. Never set foot in Olympus again, but devote yourself to Paris. Pamper him well, and one day you may be his wife – or else his slave. I refuse to go and share his bed again – I should never hear the end of it. There is not a woman in Troy who would not curse me if I did. I have enough to bear already.'

The Lady Aphrodite rounded on her in fury. 'Obstinate wretch!' she cried. 'Do not provoke me, or I might desert you in my anger, and hate you as heartily as I have loved you up till now, rousing the Trojans and Achaeans to such bitter enmity as would bring *you* to a miserable end.'

Helen was cowed, child of Zeus though she was. She wrapped herself up in her white and glossy robe, and went off without a sound. Not one of the Trojan women saw her go: she had a goddess to guide her.

When they reached the beautiful house of Paris, the maids in attendance betook themselves at once to their tasks, while Helen, the great lady, went to her lofty bedroom. There the goddess herself, laughter-loving Aphrodite, picked up a chair, carried it across the room and put it down for her in front of Paris. Helen, daughter of aegis-bearing Zeus, sat down on it, but turned her eyes aside and began by scolding her lover: 'So you are back from the battlefield – and I was hoping you had fallen there to the great soldier who was once my husband! You used to boast that you were a better man than the mighty Menelaus, a finer spearman, stronger in the arm. Then why not go at once and challenge him again? Or should I warn you to think twice before you offer single combat to the red-haired Menelaus? Do nothing rash – or you may end by falling to his spear!'

Paris had his answer ready. 'My dear,' he said, 'do not try to put me on my mettle by abusing me. Menelaus has just beaten me with Athene's help. But I too have gods to help me, and next time I shall win. Come, let us go to bed together and be happy in our love. Never has such desire overwhelmed me, not even in the beginning, when I carried you off from lovely Lacedaemon in my seagoing ships, and we spent the night on the isle of Cranae in each other's arms – never till now have I been so much in love with you or felt such sweet desire.'

As he spoke, he made a move towards the bed, leading her to it. His wife followed him; and the two lay down together on the well-made wooden bed.

Homer, *The Iliad*, Penguin, 1950, III, pp. 74–5 (translated by E.V. Rieu).

From a bed in Troy to a bed in Brighton, traditional destination for Britons seeking a dirty weekend. Tony and Brenda Last, previously encountered on pp. 337–40, have agreed to divorce, with Brenda acting as the plaintiff. This requires Tony to be detected in the throes of an adulterous relationship, a bogus one that will allow his wife to continue her authentic one.

There was a general rendezvous at the first-class booking office. The detectives were there earliest, ten minutes before their time. They had been pointed out to Tony at the solicitor's office so that he should not lose them. They were cheerful middle-aged men in soft hats and heavy overcoats. They were looking forward to their week-end, for most of their daily work consisted in standing about at street corners watching front doors and a job of this kind was eagerly competed for in the office. In more modest divorces the solicitors were content to rely on the evidence of the hotel servants. The detectives were a luxury and proposed to treat themselves as such.

There was a slight fog in London that day. The station lamps were alight prematurely.

Tony came next, with Jock at his side, loyally there to see him off. They bought the tickets and waited. The detectives, sticklers for professional etiquette, made an attempt at self-effacement, studying the posters on the walls and peering from behind a pillar.

'This is going to be hell,' said Tony.

It was ten minutes before Milly came. She emerged from the gloom with a porter in front carrying her suitcase and a child dragging back on her arm behind her . . . 'Sorry if I'm late,' she said. 'Winnie here couldn't find her shoes. I brought her along too. I knew you wouldn't mind really. She travels on a half ticket.'

Winnie was a plain child with large gold-rimmed spectacles. When she spoke she revealed that two of her front teeth were missing.

'I hope you don't imagine she's coming with us.'

'Yes, that's the idea,' said Milly. 'She won't be any trouble – she's got her puzzle.'

Tony bent down to speak to the little girl. 'Listen,' he said. 'You don't want to come to a nasty big hotel. You go with this kind gentleman here. He'll take you to a shop and let you choose the biggest doll you can find and then he'll drive you back in his motor to your home. You'll like that, won't you?'

'No,' said Winnie. 'I want to go to the seaside. I won't go with that man. I don't want a doll. I want to go to the seaside with my mummy.'

Several people besides the detectives were beginning to take notice of the oddly assorted group.

'Oh God!' said Tony. 'I suppose she's got to come.' . . .

Rooms at the hotel had been engaged for Tony by the solicitors. It was therefore a surprise to the reception clerk when Winnie arrived. 'We have reserved in your name double and single communicating rooms, bathroom and sitting-room,' he said. 'We did not understand you were bringing your daughter. Will you require a further room?'

'Oh, Winnie can come in with me,' said Milly.

The two detectives who were standing nearby at the counter exchanged glances of disapproval.

Tony wrote *Mr. and Mrs. Last* in the Visitors' Book.

'And daughter,' said the clerk with his finger on the place.

Tony hesitated. 'She is my niece,' he said, and inscribed her name on another line, as *Miss Smith* . . .

The next morning the detectives greet Tony at the hotel.

'Have you had your breakfast?'

'Yes, in the dining room with Winnie.'

'But Mr. Last, what are you thinking of? You've got to get evidence from the hotel servants.'

'Well, I didn't like to wake Milly.'

'She's paid for it, isn't she? Come, come, Mr. Last, this won't do at all. You'll never get your divorce if you don't give your mind to it more.'

'All right,' said Tony. 'I'll have breakfast again.'

'In bed, mind.'

'In bed.' And he went wearily upstairs to his rooms.

Winnie had drawn the curtains but her mother was still asleep. 'She woke up once and then turned over. Do get her to come out. I want to go on the pier.'

'Milly,' said Tony firmly. 'Milly.'

'Oh,' she said. 'What time is it?'

'We've got to have breakfast.'

'Don't want any breakfast. I think I'll sleep a little.'

'You've had breakfast,' said Winnie.

'Come on,' said Tony. 'Plenty of time to sleep afterwards. This is what we came for.'

Milly sat up in bed. 'O.K.,' she said. 'Winnie darling, give mother her jacket off the chair.' She was a conscientious girl ready to go through with her job, however unattractive it might seem. 'But it's early.'

Tony went into his room and took off his shoes, collar and tie, coat and waistcoat, and put on a dressing gown.

'You are greedy,' said Winnie, 'eating two breakfasts.'

'When you're a little older you'll understand these things. It's the Law. Now I want you to stay in the sitting-room for quarter of an hour very quietly. Promise? And afterwards you can do exactly what you like.'

'Can I bathe?'

'Yes, certainly, if you're quiet now.'

Tony got into bed beside Milly and pulled the dressing gown tight around his throat. 'Does that look all right?'

'Love's young dream,' said Milly.

'All right then. I'll ring the bell.'

When the tray had been brought Tony got out of bed and put on his things. 'So much for my infidelity,' he said. 'It is curious to reflect that this will be described in the papers as "intimacy".'

'Can I bathe now?'

'Certainly.'

Evelyn Waugh, *A Handful of Dust*, Chapman & Hall, 1948, Ch. 4.

Tony's fate – and there is worse to come – is part of a peculiarly British form of humiliation, neatly blended with hypocrisy. But revenge is an understandable response to betrayal, as the plots of innumerable Jacobean tragedies make clear. A more succinct expression of the desire for revenge comes from the poet Thomas Carew (ca. 1595–1640) in his 'To My Inconstant Mistris':

When thou, poore excommunicate
    From all the joyes of love, shalt see
The full reward, and glorious fate,
    Which my strong faith shall purchase me,
    Then curse thine owne inconstancie.

A fayrer hand than thine, shall cure
    That heart, which thy false oathes did wound;
And to my soule, a soule more pure
    Than thine, shall by Loves hand be bound,
    And both with equall glory crown'd.

Then shalt thou weepe, entreat, complaine
    To Love, as I did once to thee;
When all thy tears shall be as vaine
    As mine were then, for thou shalt bee
    Damn'd for thy false Apostasie.

A less conventional, more subtle version of the theme is offered by John Donne (1572–1631) in 'Woman's Constancy':

Now thou has lov'd me one whole day,
To morrow when thou leav'st, what wilt thou say?
Wilt thou then antedate some new made vow?
               Or say that now
We are not just those persons, which we were?
Or, that oathes made in reverentiall feare
Of Love, and his wrath, any may forsweare?
Or, as true deaths, true maryages untie,
So lovers' contracts, images of those,
Binde but till sleep, death's image, them unloose?
               Or, your owne end to Justifie,
For having purpos'd change, and falsehood; you
Can have no way but falsehood to be true?
Vaine lunatique, against these 'scapes I could
               Dispute, and conquer, if I would,

> Which I abstaine to doe,
> For by to morrow, I may thinke so too.

That's talk rather than action. In Roman times, as Edward Gibbon makes repeatedly clear, murderous revenge was a routine response to the barbarous violation of other men's wives:

The pleasures of [Valentinian the Third, the last Roman emperor of the family of Theodosius] were injurious to the peace and honour of noble families. The birth of the empress Eudoxia was equal to his own, and her charms and tender affection deserved those testimonies of love which her inconstant husband dissipated in vague and unlawful amours. Petronius Maximus, a wealthy senator of the Anician family, who had been twice consul, was possessed of a chaste and beautiful wife: her obstinate resistance served only to irritate the desires of Valentinian; and he resolved to accomplish them either by stratagem or force. Deep gaming was one of the vices of the court; the emperor, who, by chance or contrivance, had gained from Maximus a considerable sum, uncourteously exacted his ring as a security for the debt; and sent it by a trusty messenger to his wife, with an order in her husband's name that she should immediately attend the empress Eudoxia. The unsuspecting wife of Maximus was conveyed in her litter to the Imperial palace; the emissaries of her impatient lover conducted her to a remote and silent bed-chamber; and Valentinian violated, without remorse, the laws of hospitality. Her tears, when she returned home, her deep affliction, and her bitter reproaches against her husband, whom she considered as the accomplice of his own shame, excited Maximus to a just revenge; the desire of revenge was stimulated by ambition; and he might reasonably aspire, by the free suffrage of the Roman senate, to the throne of a detested and despicable rival. Valentinian, who supposed that every human breast was devoid, like his own, of friendship and gratitude, had imprudently admitted among his guard several domestics and followers of Aetius. Two of these, of Barbarian race, were persuaded to execute a sacred and honourable duty, by punishing with death the assassin of their patron; and their intrepid courage did not long expect a favourable moment. Whilst Valentinian amused himself in the field of Mars with the spectacle of some military sports, they suddenly rushed upon him with drawn weapons, dispatched the guilty Heraclius, and stabbed the emperor to the heart, without the least opposition from his numerous train, who seemed to rejoice in the tyrant's death.

Edward Gibbon, *The Decline and Fall of the Roman Empire*, Ch. XXXV.

In modern times we must adopt a more subtle approach in settling scores, and Miss Manners relishes dreaming up a few:

DEAR MISS MANNERS:

... My husband is having an affair with a longtime friend of mine. I know this for a fact, although they do not know I know, and I intend to keep it that way. Bringing it out into the open would irrevocably damage, if not end, our marriage. I believe if I let it alone, he will get over it, and we can go on as before. She has told me, in the past, about many such affairs she has had, and I'm sure she is not serious about this one.

OK – so how do I behave to him, and how do I behave to her? On the one hand, I don't want to let on that I know, for the reasons stated, but on the other hand, I am no saint, and if I could speed along the end of this by making both of them really miserable, I wouldn't be sorry. They see each other two nights a week and every other Saturday – he is 'working late' then, and she keeps her phone off the hook.

The only other person who knows about this is my sister, who has suggested that I openly have an affair myself, which would serve them right. However, even if I knew someone I wanted to do that with, I don't want to leave the children (three, seven, and ten); I know their father is devoted to them. Nor do I want to give him an 'excuse'. I just want to go on as always, acting natural, but the problem is I can't act natural. So what do I do?

GENTLE READER:

Miss Manners thinks you are quite right not to attempt to 'act natural'. Behaviour natural to this situation would be quite ugly, and thus go against your interests. Yet the agitation produced by your awareness of the situation produces an energy higher than you would have if the situation were normal. The idea is to use this heightened emotion for an effect that would serve your interests, rather than betray them.

What makes people truly uncomfortable is not so much having what others lack, but lacking what others have. Allow Miss Manners to suggest a more subtle way than your sister's of making them jealous of what you are doing two nights a week and every other Saturday. To him, you might let it be known that you and the children are immensely enjoying those free periods you have together. Plan pleasant family activities for that time – building, baking, putting on a play together, or, if you must, even going to the zoo where all the attractive divorced fathers are on Saturdays – which they will babble to him about afterwards, thus making him aware that the time he spends away is the most valuable and memorable part of their childhood.

To her, if you really want to be evil (and why not – it will make you feel better), you might make vague statements with a radiant face that make her believe, without your saying so, that you are spending that same time period with a man who makes you look more thrilled than your husband apparently did. This will pique her; but she will mention it to your husband to salve his conscience. He will know, from the children's testimony, that it is not true, so it will give him the idea that she has a dirty mind. It will also pique him. Two people in those states of mind are not going to enjoy themselves for very long.

Judith Martin, *Miss Manners' Guide to Excruciatingly Correct Behaviour*, Hamish Hamilton, 1983, pp. 220–21.

'Indelible Constancy'

You know, of course, that the Tasmanians, who never committed adultery, are now extinct.

W. Somerset Maugham, *The Bread Winner*

It may add a saccharine note to end with a few paeans to fidelity, but after an abundance of tears, humiliation, self-righteousness and gore, it won't hurt to strive for a more positive and uplifting conclusion. Ernest Dowson provides a double-edged link:

Last night, ah, yesternight, betwixt her lips and mine
There fell thy shadow, Cynara! thy breath was shed
Upon my soul between the kisses and the wine;
And I was desolate and sick of an old passion,
　　Yea, I was desolate and bowed my head:
I have been faithful to thee, Cynara! in my fashion.

All night upon mine heart I felt her warm heart beat,
Night-long within mine arms in love and sleep she lay;
Surely the kisses of her bought red mouth were sweet;
But I was desolate and sick of an old passion,
　　When I awoke and found the dawn was gray:
I have been faithful to thee, Cynara! in my fashion.

I have forgot much, Cynara! gone with the wind,
Flung roses, roses, riotously with the throng,
Dancing, to put thy pale, lost lilies out of mind;
But I was desolate and sick of an old passion,

Yea, all the time, because the dance was long:
I have been faithful to thee, Cynara! in my fashion.

I cried for madder music and for stronger wine,
But when the feast is finished and the lamps expire,
Then falls thy shadow, Cynara! the night is thine;
And I am desolate and sick of an old passion,
    Yea hungry for the lips of my desire:
I have been faithful to thee, Cynara! in my fashion.

Ernest Dowson, 'Non Sum Qualis Eram Bonae Sub Regno
Cynarae'.

Few poets have made such a career of promiscuity as Byron, so he can
scarcely conceal his incredulity on encountering an example of the
opposite. He wrote to Thomas Moore from Venice on 24 December
1816:

Six-and-twenty years ago, Col. [Fitzgerald], then an ensign, being
in Italy, fell in love with the Marchesa [Castiglione], and she with
him. The lady must be, at least, twenty years his senior. The war
broke out; he returned to England, to serve – not his country, for
that's Ireland – but England, which is a different thing; and *she* –
heaven knows what she did. In the year 1814, the first annunciation
of the Definitive Treaty of Peace (and tyranny) was developed to
the astonished Milanese by the arrival of Col. [Fitzgerald], who,
flinging himself full length at the feet of Mad. [Castiglione],
murmured forth, in half-forgotten Irish Italian, eternal vows of
indelible constancy. The lady screamed, and exclaimed, 'Who are
you?' The Colonel cried, 'What! don't you know me? I am so and
so,' &c., &c., &c.; till, at length, the Marchesa, mounting from
reminiscence to reminiscence through the lovers of the intermediate
twenty-five years, arrived at last at the recollection of her *povero*
sub-lieutenant. She then said, 'Was there ever such virtue?' (that
was her very word) and, being now a widow, gave him apartments
in her palace, reinstated him in all the rights of wrong, and held

him up to the admiring world as a miracle of incontinent fidelity, and the unshaken Abdiel of absence.

Lord Byron, *Letters & Journals*, Murray, 1976, Vol. 5, p. 147.

The urbane New England poet L.E. Sissman puts in an unselfrighteous plea for old-fashioned uxoriousness:

> Alfa is nice. Her Roman eye
> Is outlined in an O of dark
> Experience. She's thirty-nine.
> Would it not be kind of fine
> To take her quite aback, affront
> Her forward manner, take her up
> On it? Echo: of course it would.
>
> Betta is nice. Her Aquiline
> Nose prowly marches out between
> Two ravens' wings of black sateen
> Just touched, at thirty-five, with gray.
> What if I riled her quiet mien
> With an indecent, subterrene
> Proposal? She might like me to.
>
> Gemma is nice. Her Modenese
> Zagato body, sprung on knees
> As supple as steel coils, shocks
> Me into plotting to acquire
> The keys to her. She's twenty-nine.
> Might I aspire to such a fine
> Consort in middle age? Could be.
>
> Della is nice. Calabrian
> Suns engineered the sultry tan
> Over (I'm guessing) all of her long
> And filly frame. She's twenty-one.
> Should I consider that she might

Look kindly on my graying hairs
And my too-youthful suit? Why not?

O Megan, all-American
Wife waiting by the hearth at home,
As handsome still at forty-five
As any temptress now alive,
Must I confess my weariness
At facing stringent mistresses
And head for haven? Here I come.

L.E. Sissman, 'Safety at Forty',
Scattered Returns, Atlantic Monthly Press (Boston), 1969.

Colette, who wrote so often and so luxuriantly about the pains and pleasures of love, was especially tender on the subject of infidelity. Here, in contrast, is a scene of reconciliation, when Minne, previously encountered on pp. 212–216 makes up with her husband Antoine:

Minne put out a friendly little hand from the bed.

'But I love you very much too, I really do.'

'Do you?' he asked with a forced laugh. 'Then I wish you'd love me enough to ask me for anything that would give you pleasure, *anything*, you understand, even things one doesn't normally ask from a husband, and then that you should come to me afterwards and complain to me, as you did when you were little. "So-and-so's been horrid to me, Antoine: scold him or kill him" or whatever else it was you wanted.'

This time she had understood. She sat up in bed, not knowing how to release the sudden tenderness that wanted to dart out from herself to Antoine like a shining imprisoned snake. She turned very pale and stared at him, wide-eyed. Whatever kind of man was this cousin of hers?

Men had desired her, one to the point of wanting to kill her, the other to the point of delicately repulsing her. But not one of them had said to her: 'Be happy, I ask nothing for myself: I'll give you jewels, sweets, lovers . . .'

What recompense could she make to that martyr waiting there in his pyjamas? Let him at least take what she had to give him, her obedient body, her soft, insensible mouth, her silky, Circassian slave's hair.

'Come into my bed, Antoine.' . . .

'Come into my bed, Antoine.' She had said that to him last night, convinced that she owed it him in fairness, like a prostitute who can only repay a man's love with her body. And the unhappy man, maddened that the reward should be so nearly a punishment, had flung himself into Minne's outstretched arms.

At first he had only meant to hold her against him. He had embraced only her torso intoxicated almost to tears, to feel her so warm and scented, so small and supple, in his arms. But she nestled up to him with her whole body and clasped his feet with her smooth, cold ones. Weakening, he murmured 'No, no,' arching his back to get further away from her. But an audacious little hand touched his secretly and, with one bound, he was on her, pulling back the sheet.

She saw him looming above her as she had so often seen him before, faunlike and bearded, and smelt the familiar smell of amber and burnt wood that his tall brown body exhaled. But, tonight, Antoine had deserved more than she was able to give him. 'He must have me really properly tonight, he must be truly satisfied. To make his joy complete, I must imitate his own sighs and cries of pleasure . . . I'll moan "Ah! Ah!" like Irène Chaulieu and try to think of something else.'

She slipped out of her long nightdress, offered her soft breasts to Antoine's hands and kisses and lay back, passive, on the pillow with the pure smile of a saint defying demons and torturers.

He was considerate with her, nevertheless, hardly shaking her with a slow, gentle, deep rhythm. She half-opened her eyes: those of Antoine, still master of himself, seemed to be seeking a Minne beyond herself. She remembered Irène Chaulieu's lessons and sighed 'Ah! Ah!' like a fainting schoolgirl, then fell silent, ashamed.

Absorbed, his eyebrows knotted in a harsh, voluptuous mask of Pan, Antoine prolonged his silent joy. 'Ah! Ah!!' she said again, in spite of herself. For an increasing, almost unbearable anguish was tightening in her throat, like the choking back of sobs about to burst out.

A third time, she moaned, and Antoine stopped, troubled, for never before had Minne cried out. But his withdrawal did not cure Minne who was now trembling all over and turning her head from left to right, from right to left on the pillow like a child with meningitis. She clenched her fists, and Antoine could see the muscles of her delicate jaws standing out, tense.

He remained fearful, raised up on his wrists, not daring to take her again. She gave a low, angry groan, opened wild eyes and cried:

'Go on!'

For a paralysed moment he stayed fixed in the same position above her; then he invaded her with a controlled force, an acute curiosity, that was better than his own pleasure. His brain remained entirely lucid and in command of his body while she writhed like a mermaid, her eyes closed, her cheeks pale and her ears crimson. Now she clasped her hands and pressed them against her clenched mouth, as if seized with a childish despair. Now she panted, her mouth open, digging her nails fiercely into Antoine's arm. One of her feet, hanging out of the bed, suddenly jerked up and rested for a second on Antoine's brown thigh, making him shudder with delight.

At last she gazed up at him with a look he had never seen before and murmured 'Your Minne ... your Minne ... all yours ...' while at last he felt her happy body surge against him in waves.

Minne, sitting up in her crumpled bed, was overwhelmed with a tumultuous joy that burst up from the depths of herself. She no longer wanted anything, no longer regretted anything. Life presented itself before her, easy and sensual and commonplace as a beautiful girl. Antoine had worked this miracle. Minne listened for her husband's step, and yawned. She smiled, in the shadowy room, with a touch of contempt for the Minne of yesterday, that frigid child in quest of the impossible. There was no longer any impossible, there was no longer anything to search for, there was nothing to do but flower, to become rosy and happy, nourished only by the vanity of being a woman like other women. Antoine would soon be back. It was time to get up, to run towards the sun that pierced the shutters, order a cup of steaming, velvety chocolate. The day would pass lazily; Minne, hanging on Antoine's arm, would think of nothing – except of all the similar nights and days that lay ahead. Antoine was noble, Antoine was wonderful.

Colette, *The Innocent Libertine*, Secker & Warburg, 1968, pp. 208–9, 209–12 (translated by Antonia White).

One of Philip Larkin's most famous poems celebrates the handholding effigies in Arundel church. I include it here, and, to avoid any suggestion of sentimentality, add a footnote from L.E. Sissman:

> Side by side, their faces blurred,
> The earl and countess lie in stone,
> Their proper habits vaguely shown
> As jointed armour, stiffened pleat,
> And that faint hint of the absurd –
> The little dogs under their feet.
>
> Such plainness of the pre-baroque
> Hardly involves the eye, until
> It meets his left-hand gauntlet, still
> Clasped empty in the other; and
> One sees, with a sharp tender shock,
> His hand withdrawn, holding her hand.
>
> They would not think to lie so long.
> Such faithfulness in effigy
> Was just a detail friends would see:

A sculptor's sweet commissioned grace
Thrown off in helping to prolong
The Latin names around the base.

They would not guess how early in
Their supine stationary voyage
The air would change to soundless damage,
Turn the old tenantry away;
How soon succeeding eyes begin
To look, not read. Rigidly they

Persisted, linked, through lengths and breadths
Of time. Snow fell, undated. Light
Each summer thronged the glass. A bright
Litter of birdcalls strewed the same
Bone-riddled ground. And up the paths
The endless altered people came,

Washing at their identity.
Now, helpless in the hollow of
An unarmorial age, a trough
Of smoke in slow suspended skeins
Above their scrap of history,
Only an attitude remains:

Time has transfigured them into
Untruth. The stone fidelity
They hardly meant has come to be
Their final blazon, and to prove
Our almost-instinct almost true:
What will survive of us is love.

Philip Larkin, 'An Arundel Tomb',
The Whitsun Weddings, Faber, 1964.

'All that survives of us is love.' Maybe
Not even that, it seems. Rising above
The glass case housing shilling relics of
This agèd and advanced church – art postcards,
Piper's pied altar duly reproduced,
Wide-eyed and side-whiskered accounts of how
The great spire toppled in a storm of wind –
There stands a rack of cheap guides. One depicts
The earl and countess supine on their tomb
And holding hands in perpetuity.
Alas, the facing text gives them away:
'Though many visitors to Chichester,'
It says, 'are touched by this unique display
Of marital devotion, it is thought
That a Victorian mason rearranged
Their marble hands, once crossed upon each breast,
To meet and intertwine.' Good night, sweet Fitz-
Alan, trapped in the prettifying power
Of a hypocoristic century
By its unloved assigns. All that survives
Of us and of our petrifying wives
For certain is a lying effigy.

L.E. Sissman, 'An Arundel Footnote', *Pursuit of Honor*,
Atlantic Monthly Press (Boston), 1971.

Acknowledgements

The editor and publishers wish to thank the following for permission to use copyright material:

Aitken, Stone & Wylie on behalf of the author for material from Philip Roth, *Deception*, Jonathan Cape, 1990;

Anvil Press Poetry Ltd for Paul Verlaine, 'Low Scene' from *Femmes/ Hombres Women/Men*, trans. Alistair Elliot, 1979;

BasicBooks, a division of HarperCollins Publishers, Inc. for material from Annette Lawson, *Adultery*. Copyright © Aurispa Ltd, 1988;

George Braziller, Inc. Publishers for material from Millicent Bell, *The Friendship of Edith Wharton and Henry James*, 1965;

The Calder Educational Trust for material from Stendhal, *Rome, Naples and Florence*, trans. Richard Coe, John Calder (Publishers) Ltd. Translation copyright © John Calder (Publishers) Ltd, 1959;

Curtis Brown Group Ltd on behalf of the authors for material from H. Montgomery Hyde, *A Tangled Web: Sex Scandals in British Politics and Society*, Constable. Copyright © Harford Productions Ltd, 1986; George Ridley, *Bend'Or Duke of Westminster*, Robin Clarke. Copyright © G. K. Ridley, 1985; and on behalf of the Author's Estate for material from André Maurois, *Victor Hugo*, trans. Gerard Hopkins, Jonathan Cape, 1956;

Faber & Faber Ltd with HarperCollins Publishers, Inc. for material from Miles Kundera, 'Fidelity and Betrayal' in *The Unbearable Lightness of Being*, trans. Michael Henry Heim, 1984. Copyright © Harper & Row, Inc., 1984; W. H. Auden, 'Lullaby' from *Collected Poems*, 1976; with Farrar Straus & Giroux, Inc. for Philip Larkin , 'An Arundel Tomb' from *The Whitsun Weddings*; and with New Directions Publishing Company for Ezra Pound, 'The Temperaments' from *Collected Shorter Poems and Personae*. Copyright 1926 by Ezra Pound;

Farrar Straus & Giroux, Inc. for material from Stanley Elkin, *The Franchiser*. Copyright © Stanley Elkin, 1976; and Giovanni Battista Meneghini with Renzo Allegri, *My Wife Maria Callas*, trans. Henry Wisneski, 1982. Translation copyright © Farrar, Straus & Giroux, Inc., 1982;

Hodder & Stoughton Ltd and Kathryn E. Brough for material from James Brough, *The Prince and the Lily*, 1975;

HarperCollins Publishers, Inc. for material from Philip Zeigler, *Melbourne*, Collins, 1976; and with Doubleday for material from Olga Ivinskaya, *A Captive of Time*, trans. Max Hayward, Collins, 1978;

HarperCollins Publishers, Inc. for material from Liane de Pougy, *My Blue Notebooks*, trans. Diana Athill. Translation copyright © Diana Athill, 1979;

William Heinemann Ltd with Georges Borchardt, Inc. on behalf of the author for material from Robert Coover, *A Night at the Movies*. Copyright © Robert Coover, 1987; and with Random House, Inc. for material from Alison Lurie, *The War Between the Tates*. Copyright © Alison Lurie, 1974;

A. M. Heath & Company Ltd on behalf of the author for material from Howard Jacobson, *Coming from Behind*, Chatto & Windus, 1983;

David Higham Associates Ltd on behalf of the authors for material from T. H. White, *The Age of Scandal*, Oxford University Press; Christopher Hibbert, *George IV*, Allen Lane, 1973; J. R. Ackerley, *My Father and Myself*, The Bodley Head, 1968; A. J. P. Taylor, *An Old Man's Diary*, Hamish Hamilton, 1964; and August Strindberg, *The Father*, trans. Michael Meyer, Secker & Warburg, 1964;

Alfred A. Knopf, Inc. with Margaret Hanbury on behalf of the author for material from Gerald Brenan, *Personal Record 1920-1972*. Copyright © Lynda Jane Nicholson Price, 1974; with Faber & Faber Ltd for Milan Kundera, *The Book of Laughter and Forgetting,* trans. Michael Heim. English translation copyright © Alfred A. Knopf, Inc., 1980; with Donadio & Ashworth on behalf of the author for Joseph Heller, *Something Happened*. Copyright © Scapegoat Productions, Inc., 1966, 1974;

Little, Brown & Company and Watkins/Loomis Agency, Inc. on behalf of the author for material from Peter De Vries, *Let Me Count the Ways*. Copyright © Peter De Vries, 1965; Peter De Vries, *The Vale of Laughter*.

Deutsch. Copyright © John Updike, 1968; John Updike, 'Solitaire' from *Museums and Women*, Penguin Books, 1975, first published in the UK by André Deutsch. Copyright © John Updike, 1972; John Updike, *A Month of Sundays*, Penguin Books, 1976, first published in the UK by André Deutsch. Copyright © John Updike, 1975; John Updike, *Rabbit Redux*, Penguin Books, 1972, first published by André Deutsch. Copyright © John Updike, 1971;

Peters Fraser & Dunlop Group Ltd on behalf of the author for material from Evelyn Waugh, *A Handful of Dust*, 1934; and Alistair Horne, *Macmillan 1894-1956*, Macmillan, 1988;

Giles Playfair for material from *Kean*, Geoffrey Bles Ltd, 1939;

Laurence Pollinger Ltd on behalf of the author for material from Larry Swindell, *Spencer Tracy*, World Publishing Company, 1970; and on behalf of the Estate of Frieda Lawrence Ravagli for material from D. H. Lawrence, *Lady Chatterley's Lover*;

Murray Pollinger on behalf of the author for material from Ottoline Morrell, *Ottoline at Garsington: Memoirs of Lady Ottoline Morrell*, ed. Robert Gathorne-Hardy, Faber & Faber, 1975;

Random Century Group on behalf of the translators for material from Marcel Proust, *In Search of Lost Time*, trans. C. K. Scott Moncrieff, T. Kilmartin and D. J. Enright, Chatto & Windus, 1992, and Chekhov, 'The Lady with the Dog' from *Selected Tales*, Vol.I, trans. Constance Garnett, Chatto & Windus, 1944; with Farrar Straus & Giroux, Inc. for material from Bernard Malamud, *A New Life*, Chatto & Windus, 1980. Copyright © Bernard Malamud, 1961, renewed copyright © Ann Malamud, 1989; with Jonathan Clowes Ltd on behalf of the author for Kingsley Amis, 'Nothing to Fear' from *A Look Found the Estate*. Copyright © Kingsley Amis, 1967; with Peters Fraser & Dunlop Group Ltd for material from Martin Amis, *London Fields*, 1989, and *The Rachel Papers*, 1973, Jonathan Cape;

Random House, Inc. for material from François Rabelais, *Gargantua and Pantagruel*, Book III, trans. Jacques Le Clercq, 1934;

Routledge for material from Mme d'Epinay, *Memoirs*, trans. E. G. Allingham, Routledge & Kegan Paul, 1930; Choderlos de Laclos, *Dangerous Acquaintances*, ed. Richard Aldington, Routledge & Kegan

Index

Abels, Jules, 92–5
Ackerley, J.R., 154–5
Allen, Woody
  'The Kugelmass Episode', 237–40
Amis, Kingsley, 152
Amis, Martin
  London Fields, 138–9
  The Rachel Papers, 223–4
Apuleius
  The Golden Ass, 291–2
Arabian Nights, *xx*
Aretino Pietro, 53–6
Ashdown, Paddy, *xix*
Aubrey, John
  Brief Lives, 35–7
Auden, W.H., 243–4
Augustus, Emperor, 46–7
Aytoun, Robert, 304

Bakker, Jim, *xx*
Balzac, Honoré, 86–7, 247
Biard, Léonie, 89–90
Bible:
  John XVIII, 33–4
  Leviticus XX, *xi–xii*
  Matthew V, 84
Boccaccio
  Decameron, *xx*
Boothby, Robert, 109–11
Boswell, James
  Journals, 11–12, 17–18, 60–67
  Life of Samuel Johnson, 27–9
Branden, Lady (Elizabeth), 84–6
Brenan, Gerald, 104–7
Brough, James, 96–9
Burton, Robert
  Anatomy of Melancholy, 150–52

Byron, Lord
  Don Juan, *xvii*, 170–76
  Letters and Journals, 7–8, 10–11, 46,
    70–80, 360–61

Caligula, Emperor, 47–8
Callas, Maria, 284–7
Canning, George, 91
Carew, Thomas, 354–5
Caroline of Brunswick, Princess, 80–
  83, 91
Carrington, Dora, 104–7
Casanova, Jacques, *xvii*, 188, 203–5
Catullus, 288–9
Cavendish, Emily, 205–7
Charles II of England, King, *xviii*,
  57–8
Chaucer, Geoffrey
  The Canterbury Tales, *xx*, 198–202
  Troilus and Criseyde, 292–6
Chekhov, Anton
  'The Lady with the Dog', 322–4
Cleugh, James, 53–6
Clough, A.C., 3
Cogni, Margarita, 73–6
Colette, *xxi*
  Chéri, 324–6
  Claudine Married, 277–81
  The Innocent Libertine, 212–16, 362–
    5
Covver, Robert
  'You Must Remember This', 184–
    7
cummings, e.e., 219–20

Davidson, Bill, 112–14

De Vries, Peter
    Forever Panting, 264–6
    Let Me Count the Ways, 181–4
    The Tunnel of Love, 196–7
    The Vale of Laughter, 194–6
Disraeli, Benjamin, 91
Donne, John, 355–6
Dowson, Ernest, 232, 259–60
Drouet, Juliette, 88–9
Dryden, John, 158–60
Dubus, Andre
    'Going Under', 324
    'We Don't Live Here Anymore',
        19–21, 156, 269–71

Edward VII of England, King, 96–9
Elkin, Stanley
    The Franchiser, 244–6
    The MacGuffin, 227–31
Epinay, Madame d', *xv*, 18–19, 142–4
Epton, Nina, 35, 52–3, 58–9
Evelyn, John
    Diary, 42

Fisher, Helen, *xi*, *xvi*
Flaubert, Gustave
    Madame Bovary, *x*, *xx*, *xxi*, 132–3,
        207–9, 235–7, 240
Fontane, Theodor
    Effi Briest, 344–6
Ford, Ford Madox
    The Good Soldier, 133–8, 178–81
Forman, Simon, 202–3
François I of France, King, 52–3

George IV of England, King, 80, 83,
    91
Gibbon, Edward
    *The Decline and Fall of the Roman
        Empire*, 48–51, 356–7
Gladstone, William Ewart, 91
Glenbervie, Lord, 276–7
Goethe, Johann Wolfgang von
    Elective Affinities, 247–51

Goncourt, Edmond and Jules
    Journals, 44, 87, 91
Grammont, Count de, 7, 39–42
Green, J.R., 57–8
Grey, Earl, 91
Guiccioli, Countess Teresa, 76–80
Gwynn, Nell, *xviii*

Hamilton, Anthony, 7, 39–42
Hamilton, Lady (Emma), 69–70
Hanska, Evelina, 86–7, 247
Hardy, Thomas
    Jude the Obscure, 176–8
Hawthorne, Nathaniel
    The Scarlet Letter, *xiv*, 346–9
Heller, Joseph
    Something Happened, 15–16, 140–41,
        191–2
Hemingway, Ernest, 220–21
Henri III of France, King, *xiii*
Hepburn, Katharine, 111–14
Hibbert, Christopher, 80–83
Hickey, William
    Memoirs, 153–4, 233–5, 274–6
Homer
    Iliad, *xvii*, 349–51
Horne, Alistair, 109–11
Hugo, Victor, 87–90
Hyde, H. Montgomery, 95–6, 114–19,
    205–7

Ivinskaya, Olga, 242

Jacobson, Howard
    Coming from Behind, 225–6
James, Henry, 131
Jerome of Westphalia, King, 87
John Chrysostom, Saint, 319
Johnson, Samuel, *xv*, 27–9
Joyce, James
    Ulysses, 258–60

Kean, Edmund, 342–4
Keays, Sara, 116–19

Kennedy, Edward, *xix*
Kennedy, John F., *xviii*
Kessler, Harry, 107–9
Kundera, Milan
   The Book of Laughter and Forgetting,
    226–7
   The Unbearable Lightness of Being,
    316–18

Laclos, Choderlos de
   Dangerous Acquaintances, *xv*, *xx*, 21–
    2, 161–6, 308–13
Lamb, Lady Caroline, 70–72
Lambton, Viscount, 114–126
Langtry, Lillie, 96–9
Larkin, Philip, 365–6
Lawrence, D.H.
   A propos of Lady Chatterley, 26–7
   Lady Chatterley's Lover, 216–19,
    328–9
Lawson, Annette, *x*, *xii*, *xvi*, 21–2
Lewis, C.S., *xiii*
Lloyd George, David, *xviii*
Louis XIV of France, King, 58–9,
   148–50
Lurie, Alison
   The War Between the Tates, 12–14,
    257–8

Macmillan, Dorothy, 109–11
Macmillan, Harold, 109–11, 116
Mahabharata, *xii*
Mahler, Alma, 102–4
Maillol, Aristide, 107–9
Malamud, Bernard
   A New Life, 326–7
Malory, Thomas
   Morte d'Arthur, *xvii*, 332–7
Marcus Aurelius, Emperor, 49
Marguerite of Navarre, *xx*
Marston, John, 158
Martin, Judith, 258, 357–8
Maugham, W. Somerset, 359
Maurois, André, 90

Melbourne, Viscount (William
   Lamb), 84–6, 91
Mellor, David, *xviii–xix*
Meneghini, G.B., 284–7
Montagu, Lady Mary Wortley, 3–5,
   43
Montesquieu, Charles Louis de
   Persian Letters, 5–6
Morrell, Ottoline, 99–102

Napoleon III of France, Emperor,
   91–2
Nelson, Horatio, 69–70
Netanyahu, Binyamin, *xix*
Norris, Steven, *xix*

Onassis, Aristotle, 284–7
Orléans, Duc d' (nephew of Louis
   XIV), 59–60
O'Shea, Kitty, 92–5
Ovid
   Amores, *xii*, 158–60

Palmerston, Viscount, 91
Parkinson, Cecil, 116–19
Parnell, Charles Stewart, 92–5
Partridge, Ralph, 104–7
Pascal, Paul, 123
Pasternak, Boris, 242
Pearl, Cora, 91–2
Pepys, Samuel
   Diary, 38, 56–7, 273–4
Petronius
   Satyricon, 340–42
Playfair, Giles, 342–4
Pougy, Liane de, 282–4
Pound, Ezra, 194
Prescott, Orville, 51–2
Prior, Matthew, 160–61
Propertius, 289–90
Proust, Marcel
   Remembrance of Things Past, 155–6,
    190–91, 313–16

Rabelais, François, 288
Ridley, George, 44–5
Roberts, Nikkie, *xiii*
Rochefoucauld, Count Gaston de la,
    205–7
Rochester, Earl of, 15
Roth, Joseph
    Weights and Measures, 254–7
Roth, Philip
    Deception, 240–42
Rousseau, Jean-Jacques
    La Nouvelle Héloïse, 21–2
Rowse, A.L., 202–3
Russell, Bertrand, 99–102
Russell, Jack, 69–70

Saint-Simon, Duc de
    Memoirs, 42–3, 59–60, 147–50
Scannell, Vernon, 157
Shakespeare, William, 305
    King Lear, 198
    The Merry Wives of Windsor,
        305–6
    Othello, 32–3, 307
    Troilus and Cressida, *xxi*, 297–
        301
    The Winter's Tale, 308
Sissman, L.E., 361–2, 367
Stendhal
    Rome, Naples and Florence, 8–10
    Scarlet and Black, *xx*, 166–70, 188–
        90
Sterne, Laurence, 232–3
Stone, Lawrence, *xiv*, 68–9
Strindberg, August
    The Father, 271–3
Suetonius
    The Twelve Caesars, 46–8
Swaggart, Jimmy, *xx*
Swindwell, Larry, 111–12

Taylor, A. J. P., 91
Theroux, Alexander
    An Adultery, 29–32
Tolstoy, Leo
    Anna Karenina, *x*, *xxi*, 123–5, 209–
        12, 260–64, 319–21
Tracy, Spencer, 111–14
Turgenev, Ivan
    A Nest of Gentlefolk, 251–4
    Smoke, 329–32

Updike, John
    Couples, 125–6, 221–2
    A Month of Sundays, 23–6, 222–3
    Rabbit Redux, 266–9
    'Solitaire', 192–4

Verlaine, Paul, 207
Vivian, Florence, 95–6

Walpole, Horace, 43–4, 68, 281–2
Waterford, Marquess of, 95–6
Waugh, Evelyn
    A Handful of Dust, 337–40, 351–4
Wellington, Duke of, 91
Werfel, Franz, 102–4
Westminster, Duke of (Bend'Or), 44–
    5
Wharton, Edith
    The Age of Innocence, 126–31
White, T.H.
    The Age of Scandal, 67–8, 282
Wilde, Oscar, 35, 142
Wood, Anthony à
    Life and Times, 37
Wyatt, Thomas, 302–3
Wycherley, William
    The Country Wife, 144–7

Ziegler, Philip, 84–6